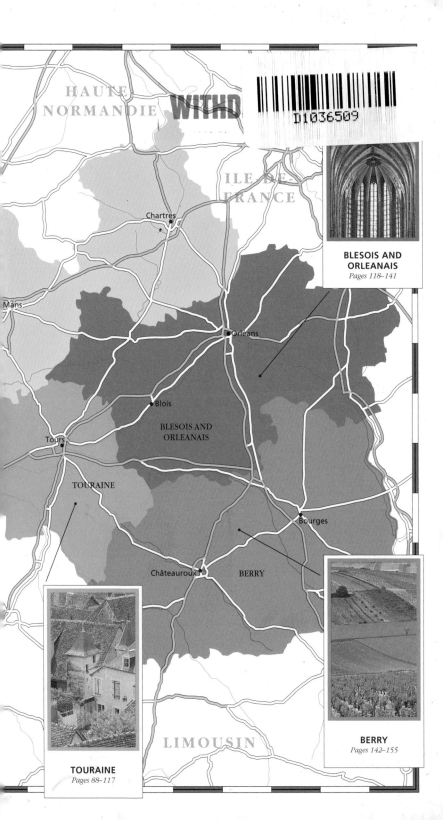

HAUTE
NORMANDIE

ILE-DE-
FRANCE

Chartres

Mans

Orleans

**BLESOIS AND
ORLEANAIS**
Pages 118–141

Blois

BLESOIS AND
ORLEANAIS

Tours

TOURAINE

Bourges

Châteauroux

BERRY

LIMOUSIN

TOURAINE
Pages 88–117

BERRY
Pages 142–155

EYEWITNESS TRAVEL

LOIRE VALLEY

EYEWITNESS TRAVEL

LOIRE
VALLEY

MAIN CONTRIBUTOR: JACK TRESIDDER

LONDON, NEW YORK,
MELBOURNE, MUNICH AND DELHI
www.dk.com

PRODUCED BY Duncan Baird Publishers
London, England

PROJECT EDITOR Stephanie Driver
EDITOR Slaney Begley
EDITORIAL ASSISTANT Joanne Levêque
DESIGNERS Paul Calver, Jill Mumford
DESIGN ASSISTANT Christine Keilty

PHOTOGRAPHERS
John Heseltine, Paul Kenward, Kim Sayer

ILLUSTRATORS
Joanna Cameron, Roger Hutchins, Robbie Polley,
Pat Thorne, John Woodcock

Printed and bound in China by Leo Paper Products Ltd

First American Edition, 1996
12 13 14 15 10 9 8 7 6 5 4 3 2 1
Published in the United States by DK Publishing,
375 Hudson Street, New York, New York 10014

**Reprinted with revisions 1997 (twice), 1999, 2000,
2001, 2003, 2004, 2007, 2010, 2013**

Copyright 1996, 2013 © Dorling Kindersley Limited, London
A Penguin Company

Published in Great Britain by Dorling Kindersley Limited.

A CATALOGUE RECORD FOR THIS BOOK IS AVAILABLE FROM
THE LIBRARY OF CONGRESS.

ISSN 1542-1554

ISBN 978-0-75669-497-5

FLOORS ARE REFERRED TO THROUGHOUT IN
ACCORDANCE WITH EUROPEAN USAGE; IE THE "FIRST FLOOR"
IS THE FLOOR ABOVE GROUND LEVEL.

FRONT COVER MAIN IMAGE: VILLANDRY AND THE LOVE GARDENS, INDRE ET LOIRE

MIX
Paper from
responsible sources
FSC™ C018179
www.fsc.org

**The information in this DK Eyewitness Travel Guide
is checked regularly.**
Every effort has been made to ensure that this book is as up-to-date
as possible at the time of going to press. Some details, however,
such as telephone numbers, opening hours, prices, gallery hanging
arrangements and travel information are liable to change. The
publishers cannot accept responsibility for any consequences arising
from the use of this book, nor for any material on third party
websites, and cannot guarantee that any website address in this
book will be a suitable source of travel information. We value the
views and suggestions of our readers very highly. Please write to:
Publisher, DK Eyewitness Travel Guides, Dorling Kindersley,
80 Strand, London, WC2R 0RL UK, or email: travelguides@dk.com.

CONTENTS

Joan of Arc

INTRODUCING THE LOIRE VALLEY

**Fifteenth century portrait of
King Charles VIII**

The town of Argenton-sur-Creuse

THE LOIRE VALLEY AREA BY AREA

Abbaye de la Trinité (Vendôme)

Stained-glass portrait of Agnès Sorel

TRAVELLERS' NEEDS

SURVIVAL GUIDE

Young boys fishing at Pornichet marina in Loire-Atlantique

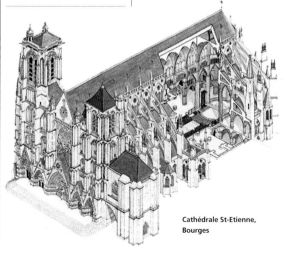
Cathédrale St-Etienne, Bourges

HOW TO USE THIS GUIDE

This guide will help you get the most from your stay in the Loire Valley. It provides both expert recommendations and detailed practical information. *Introducing the Loire Valley* maps the region and sets it in its historical and cultural context. *The Loire Valley Area by Area* describes the important sights, with maps, photographs and illustrations. Suggestions for food, drink, accommodation, shopping and activities are in *Travellers' Needs*, and the *Survival Guide* has tips on everything from the French telephone system to getting to the Loire and travelling around the region.

THE LOIRE VALLEY AREA BY AREA

In this guide, the Loire Valley has been divided into six regions, each of which has its own chapter. A map of these regions can be found inside the front cover of the book. The most interesting places to visit in each region have been numbered and plotted on a *Regional Map*.

Each area of the Loire Valley can be quickly identified by its colour coding.

1 Introduction
The landscape, history and character of each region is described here, showing how the area has developed over the centuries and what it has to offer the visitor today.

A locator map shows the region in relation to the whole of the Loire Valley.

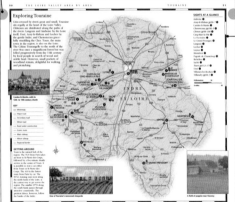

2 Regional Map
This gives an illustrated overview of the whole region. All the sights are numbered, and there are also useful tips on getting around by car and public transport.

Features and story boxes highlight special or unique aspects of a particular sight.

3 Detailed information on each sight
All the important towns and other places to visit are described individually. They are listed in order, following the numbering on the Regional Map. *Within each town or city, there is detailed information on important buildings and other major sights.*

4 Major Towns

An introduction covers the history, character and geography of the town. The main sights are described individually and plotted on a Town Map.

A Visitors' Checklist gives contact points for tourist and transport information, plus details of market days and local festival dates.

The town map shows all major through-roads as well as minor streets of interest to visitors. All the sights are plotted, along with the bus and train stations, parking, tourist offices and churches.

5 Street-by-Street Map

Towns or districts of special interest to visitors are shown in detailed 3D, with photographs of the most important sights, giving a bird's-eye view of the area.

A suggested route for a walk covers the most interesting streets in the area.

For all the top sights, a Visitors' Checklist provides the practical information you will need to plan your visit.

6 Top Sights

These are given two or more pages. Important buildings are dissected to reveal their interiors.

Stars indicate the works of art or features that no visitor should miss.

INTRODUCING
THE
LOIRE VALLEY

DISCOVERING THE LOIRE VALLEY

This fertile land was once the playground of kings and their courts, who left behind a trail of magnificent châteaux ranging in style from exuberant Renaissance to Classical grandeur. But the Loire Valley offers more than just castles. Ancient abbeys, majestic cathedrals such as those at Chartres and Bourges, and

Statue of Joan of Arc

prosperous modern cities like Angers, Tours and Nantes are all part of the area's rich heritage. Picturesque rural Loire, with its dense forests, misty marshes, windswept coastline and neat vineyards, also tempts visitors. These two pages give an at-a-glance flavour of each region, plus a quick guide to where to go and what to see and do.

Château d'Azay-le-Rideau on an island in the Indre River

ANJOU

- Tales of the riverbank
- Striking Saumur and the Abbaye de Fontevraud
- Regal Angers

The landscape of Anjou is threaded with sparkling tributary rivers creating ideal roaming and picnic territory. The **Corniche Angevine** *(see p68)* route curves dramatically around the south side of the Loire and is dotted with unspoiled villages, while many areas of southern Anjou are covered with vineyards. Fascinating tufa caves, once troglodyte dwellings, are now chic homes and restaurants.

Amid lush countryside to the east lie two must-see sights: **Saumur** *(see pp80–83)* with its hilltop château and the vast **Abbaye de Fontevraud** *(see pp86–7)*, France's most complete abbey complex.

Angers *(see pp72–7)*, straddling the River Maine, was once the capital of a

substantial empire. Its forbidding château contrasts with today's modern city which is bursting with culture and energy.

TOURAINE

- Renaissance châteaux
- Prosperous Tours
- Delicious ruby red wines

Breathtaking châteaux, gardens and vineyards characterize Touraine. Be a king for a day and check out the fairytale turrets of Renaissance pleasure-palaces such as **Azay-le-Rideau** *(see pp96–7)* and **Chenonceau** *(see pp106–9)*, with its striking arched gallery spanning the River Cher. Head to **Villandry** *(see pp94–5)* for the finest ornamental gardens.

Regional capital **Tours** *(see pp112–17)* is a great base for visiting the châteaux. Its lively old quarter is crammed with cafés and boutiques, yet still retains a medieval charm. In

contrast, the area's rolling pastoral terrain attracts lovers of outdoor persuits. Cycling among these fertile fields will work up a thirst for the fine Chinon and Bourgeuil wines.

BLESOIS AND ORLEANAIS

- **Chambord:** *folie de grandeur*
- Grand medieval towns
- Lush landscapes

Teeming with wild boar and deer, this area boasts some magnificent royal hunting lodges. **Château de Chambord** *(see pp132–5)*, the largest château in the Loire, is a truly staggering example.

Blois *(see pp124–7)* and **Orléans** *(see pp138–9)* were once powerful medieval strongholds. Now busy commercial towns, their charming old quarters are full of interest to the visitor. A casualty of war, Orléans

A quiet street of the medieval town of Blois

has been reconstructed, but retains some delightful historic buildings. Blois has many steep cobbled streets and half-timbered houses.

For a more bucolic experience, the scenery of the **Sologne** *(see p141)*, is scattered with pretty woods and lakes, while architecture fans will adore the water gates, stone buildings and bridges of **Vendôme** *(see p122)*.

BERRY

- **Remote rural villages**
- **Medieval Bourges**
- **La Brenne's wooded beauty**
- **Sancerre wine estates**

The rolling vineyards around the town of Sancerre

This rural area is surprisingly overlooked by many tourists. **Bourges** *(see pp150–53)*, the region's capital, is an architectural gem with a majestic cathedral. Of the many fine old buildings in this medieval city, Palais Jacques Coeur is the finest.

The region boasts a lush landscape where remote villages punctuate undulating hills, ancient woodlands and lakes, and swathes of wheat fields. Berry is a haven for nature enthusiasts, and at the **Parc Naturel Régional de la Brenne** *(see p146)*, bird-watchers can find a wide variety of species.

In the eastern corner sits **Sancerre** *(see p154)*, where you can enjoy its celebrated wines, from dry, zingy whites to soft, fruity reds made from vines that grow on chalky limestone slopes.

NORTH OF THE LOIRE

- **Great fishing and walking**
- **Cathedral city of Chartres**
- **Car racing in Le Mans**

Once the haunt of poets and painters, today this region is a paradise for anglers and walkers. The **Alpes Mancelles** *(see p161)*, with their heather-cloaked hills and stream-lined gorges, are best visited on foot. Cruising the rivers by boat is a fun way to discover pretty Loire tributaries. Fringed by trees, the Sarthe glides past the **Abbaye de Solesmes** *(see p162)*, while the Mayenne Valley offers views of hilltop villages and one of the area's main towns, **Laval** *(see p160)*.

Along the banks of the Loir, early churches mark the pilgrim trail. The magical Gothic spires of the cathedral of **Chartres** *(see pp171–5)* rising up from the surrounding wheat fields provide an unforgettable sightseeing experience. Racing enthusiasts should head for **Le Mans** *(see pp164–7)*, which also has a pretty historic centre.

LOIRE-ATLANTIQUE AND THE VENDEE

- **Vibrant Nantes**
- **Navigating the Marais Poitevin**
- **Wind-swept Atlantic coast**

Geographically this region faces out to the bracing Atlantic Ocean and turns its back on the châteaux. At the gateway to the ocean, **Nantes** *(see pp190–93)* was once the

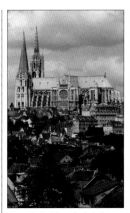
The early Gothic cathedral of Notre-Dame in Chartres

busiest port in France, and its riches were gained from ship-building and the slave trade. It is a fascinating place to explore, with many historic buildings, notably the castle and the **Musée des Beaux Arts**, *(see p192)*, but also contemporary attractions, such as **Les Machines de l'Ile** *(see p193)*, and elegant shopping streets.

Battling constantly against a sea invasion, the low-lying landscape of the **Marais Poitevin** *(see pp182–5)* is strikingly diverse, with a vast range of wildlife. The wet marsh, known as "Venise Verte", is ideally explored by *barque*, the traditional flat-bottomed boat. Punt through the maze of waterways edged by willows and take a break at one of the pretty ports.

At the Vendée coast, wide sandy beaches and thundering waves act as a magnet for both windsurfers and kitesurfers.

The beach of La Baule, in the Loire-Atlantique

Putting the Loire on the Map

The Loire Valley lies in central France, bordered by
the regions of Brittany, Normandy and the Ile de
France to the north, the Massif Central and Poitou to
the south, Burgundy to the east, and the Atlantic
Ocean to the west. The river itself, the longest
in France, flows for 1,020 km (634 miles) from
its source in the Cévennes to the Atlantic Ocean
just west of Nantes at St-Nazaire. The region
covers an area of 71,228 sq km (27,500 sq miles)
and has a population of
about 6.1 million.

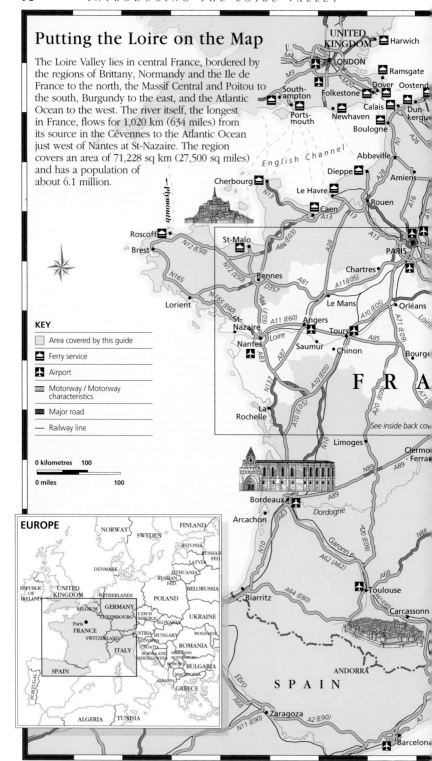

KEY

Area covered by this guide

Ferry service

Airport

Motorway / Motorway
characteristics

Major road

Railway line

0 kilometres   100

0 miles   100

EUROPE

See inside back cov

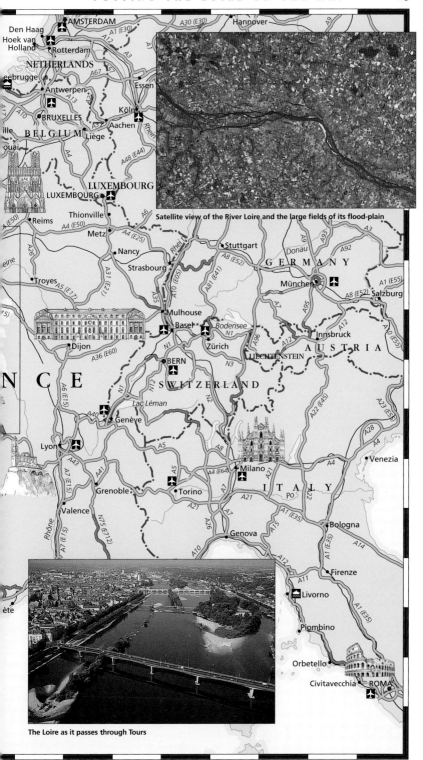

Satellite view of the River Loire and the large fields of its flood-plain

The Loire as it passes through Tours

A PORTRAIT OF THE LOIRE VALLEY

The Loire Valley, world-famous for its beautiful châteaux, has long been described as exemplifying la douceur de vivre: *it combines a leisurely pace of life, a mild climate, mellow wines and the gentle ways of its inhabitants. The overall impression conveyed by the region is one of an unostentatious taste for the good things in life.*

In this central region of France, the people have neither the brisk, sometimes brusque, demeanour of their northern counterparts, nor the excitable nature of the southern provinces. They get on peacefully with their lives, benefiting from the prosperity generated not only by the region's centuries old popularity with French and foreign visitors alike, but also by a fertile soil and a favourable climate, which rarely succumbs to extremes of heat or cold.

Cyclist on the Ile de Noirmoutier causeway

Outside of the main towns, the way of life remains in good part anchored to the traditional values of la France profonde, the country's conservative heartland – seeking to perpetuate a way of life that has proved its worth over the centuries. This is particularly true of the Berry, the easternmost region of the Loire covered in this guide. It is the geographical centre of the country – several villages claim the honour of being situated at "the heart of France" – and it seems to the visitor charmingly off the beaten track. It comes as no surprise to discover that folk traditions, including witchcraft, are recalled in some of these timeless villages.

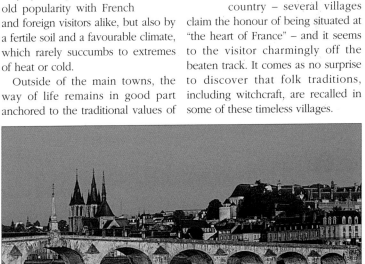

The bridge across the Loire at Blois, one of several historic bridges in the region

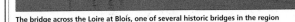

◁ Berry village in the evening

Folk dancers in costume at the Château de Blois

LOCAL STRENGTHS

The opportunity to stay in a private château is one of the many treats for visitors to the Loire Valley, where hospitality is a serious business. Even in Orléans, whose proximity to Paris has led to its reputation as a dormitory town, you can be assured of a warm welcome in hotels and restaurants. And throughout the towns and villages of Touraine and Anjou, conviviality is apparent. The many fairs, fêtes and festivals devoted to local wines and produce – garlic, apples, melons or even chitterling sausages – bear witness to the large part, even by French standards, that food and drink play in the social life of these old provinces.

They also play a major role in the region's economy: a reasonable percentage of the local population is involved in agriculture or the food industry in some way. Many a *primeur* (early fruit or vegetable) in the markets and restaurants of Paris has been transported from the fertile fields and orchards beside the Loire, and the region's melons and asparagus are sold all over the country. So are the button mushrooms, known as *champignons de Paris* (Paris mushrooms), grown in quarries near Saumur.

Although some local wines are reputed not to travel well, many of them do so very successfully, not only in France but also abroad, adding to the region's prosperity. In terms of the volume of production, the region ranks third in France but the quality and popularity of Loire wines are both increasing. Bourgueil, Chinon, Muscadet, Sancerre, Saumur and Vouvray count among the best known, but there are many more good wines available.

Just as once the nobility of France established their châteaux and stately homes in the area, wealthy Parisians have flocked to the Loire Valley to buy *résidences secondaires*. The influx has swollen with the advent of the TGV rail service, which takes less than an hour to reach the region from Paris.

Colourful summer display

RECENT DEVELOPMENTS

Since the 1990s, many of the cities along the Loire Valley have undergone spectacular

The Loire at Amboise, dotted with sandbanks

A walk along a river bank at Rochefort-sur-Loire, one of many country pursuits to enjoy

transformations. Tours has several modern developments, its cultural conference centre was designed by architect Jean Nouvel. The town continues to attract large numbers of foreign students who come to learn what's considered the "purest" French in France. By "pure", the experts mean well-modulated speech devoid of any strong accent.

Orléans, also on the Loire, has magnificently restored its historic quarter near the river, and has redesigned its broad cobbled quays. The latter had served for decades as makeshift car parks; now, they're the preserve of pedestrians and cyclists.

Angers, downstream from Tours, has also been changing on a grand scale. A contemporary quarter has emerged on the west bank of the Maine River, set around a revived port and new cultural centre.

Nearing the Atlantic, Nantes was once a massive industrial port but, as ships grew, maritime trade shifted nearer the Loire's estuary. The industrial space has now been reclaimed by the city, notably on the Ile de Nantes, a large island in the

VINS DE PROPRIETE
Dégustation
Vente

Sign offering wine-tastings

Loire just south of the centre. Here, you can admire the magical Machines de l'Ile, extraordinary outsized models of possible inventions inspired by Jules Verne.

Chinon, for several years, humorously proclaimed itself the largest medieval building site in Europe, as it embarked on the rebuilding of the huge Plantagenet fort dominating the old town. Interesting finds, unearthed during building work, are displayed in the restored fort.

Many stops along the Loire have revived their once bustling river quays, and now offer boat trips along the river, a wonderful way to see the region's stunning scenery.

Another major development for tourists has been the creation of the 800 km (500 mile) cycle path, La Loire à Vélo. The stretch from Sully-sur-Loire in the east to Chalonnes-sur-Loire was listed as a UNESCO World Heritage site in 2000.

Locally grown asparagus

From Defence to Decoration

Over the centuries, châteaux in the Loire Valley gradually developed from feudal castles, designed purely as defensive fortresses, into graceful pleasure palaces. Once the introduction of firearms put an end to the sieges that medieval castles were built to withstand, comfort and elegance became key status symbols. Many defensive elements evolved into decorative features: watchtowers became fairy-tale turrets, moats served as reflecting pools and crenellations were transformed into ornamental friezes. During the Renaissance, Italian craftsmen added features such as galleries and formal gardens, and carved decoration became increasingly intricate.

Château d'Angers in 1550, before its towers were lowered

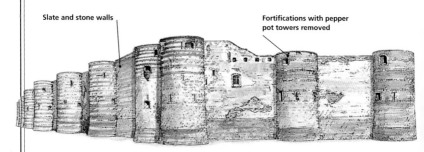

Slate and stone walls

Fortifications with pepper pot towers removed

Angers (see pp74–5) *was built between 1228 and 1240 as a mighty clifftop fortress, towering over the River Maine. Along its curtain wall were spaced 17 massive round towers. These would originally have been 30 m (98 ft) high before their pepper pot towers were removed in the 16th century.*

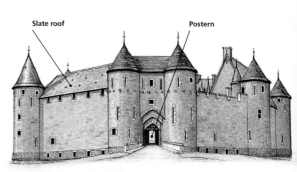

Slate roof

Postern

Ainay-le-Vieil (see p148), *dating from the 12th century, contrasts two styles. An octagonal walled fortress, with nine massive towers topped by pepper pot turrets and lit by arrow slits, was entered through a huge medieval postern gate across a drawbridge that crossed the moat. Inside, however, there is a charming, early 16th-century Renaissance home.*

Ainay-le-Vieil's delightful living quarters, hidden inside an octagonal fortress

Circular tower,
formerly defensive

Corbelled walkways,
once useful in battle

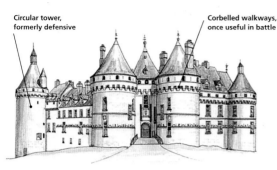

Chaumont (see p128) *stands on the site of a 12th-century fortress, destroyed in 1465 by Louis XI to punish its owners for disloyalty. The château was rebuilt from 1498 to 1510 in the Renaissance style. Although it has a defensive appearance, with circular towers, corbelled walkways and a gatehouse, these features have been lightened with Renaissance decoration.*

Chaumont's walls *are carved with the crossed Cs of Charles II d'Amboise, whose family rebuilt the château.*

Decorated
turret

Renaissance carved
windows

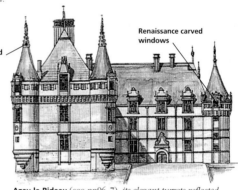

Decoration on the north façade of Azay-le-Rideau

Azay-le-Rideau (see pp96–7), *its elegant turrets reflected in a peaceful lake, was built from 1518 to 1527 and is considered one of the best-designed Renaissance châteaux. Its main staircase, set behind an intricately decorated façade with three storeys of twin bays, is very striking.*

Dormer window

Cylindrical tower

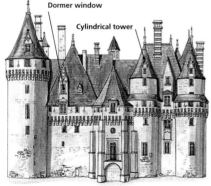

Ussé (see p101) *was built in 1462 as a battlemented fortress. Later, the walls overlooking the main court-yard were modified during the Renaissance, with dormer windows and pilasters. In the 17th century the north wing was replaced by terraced gardens.*

Château d'Ussé, once a fortress, now an aristocratic château

Inside the Châteaux

Stone carving on staircase

The typical Loire Valley château boasted several large, lavishly furnished reception rooms, adorned with luxurious tapestries and paintings and featuring decorative panelling and ceilings. The main rooms included the Grand Salon, often with an imposing fireplace, and an elegant dining room. The gallery was a focal point for host and guests to meet to discuss the events of the day, admire the views over the grounds or the paintings displayed on the gallery walls. The châtelain's private rooms, and those reserved for honoured (particularly royal) guests, were grouped in a separate wing, while servants were housed in the attics.

Apartments in one wing were for private use.

Grand Escalier (Grand Staircase)

Chairs *were often spindly – elegant but uncomfortable. The more comfortable models with armrests might be covered with precious tapestries, as with this one from Cheverny, upholstered in Aubusson.*

The Grand Salon, mostly used for entertaining, had a majestic marble fireplace carved with the owner's coat of arms, emblem or intertwined initials.

The Grand Escalier, *or Escalier d'Honneur (grand staircase), had richly carved balustrades and an elaborately decorated ceiling, such as this magnificent Renaissance staircase at Serrant (see p69). The staircase led to the owner's private suites, as well as to state guest bedrooms and rooms used on special occasions, such as the armoury.*

Main entrance

Galleries, *like this one at Beauregard (see pp130–31), were where owners and guests met to converse or to be entertained. They were often hung with family and other portraits.*

State dining rooms, *for receiving important visitors, were as sumptuously furnished and decorated as the other main reception rooms. This one in Chaumont (see p128) features Renaissance furniture.*

Château rooms were filled with costly tapestries, paintings and fine furniture, and attention was paid to detail. Decorative features, such as this French Limoges enamel plaque, or intricately carved wooden panelling were common. Even the tiles on stoves that heated the huge rooms were often painted.

The Salle d'Armes, or armoury, displayed suits of armour and weapons beside fine tapestries and furniture.

The east wing was reserved for important guests.

Dining Room

King's Bedroom

The King's Bedroom *was kept permanently ready for a royal visit. Under the droit de gîte (right of lodging), château owners were bound to provide accommodation to the king in return for a building permit. This room, at Cheverny (see p130), was used frequently.*

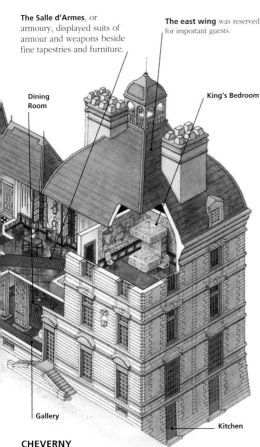

Gallery

Kitchen

CHEVERNY

A dignified Classical building in white tufa, Cheverny *(see p130)* has scarcely been altered since it was built between 1620 and 1634. The central section, containing the staircase, is flanked by two symmetrical wings, each consisting of a steep-roofed section and a much larger pavilion with a domed roof. The interior is decorated in 17th-century style.

Kitchens *were in the cellars, or separately housed. Huge spits for roasting whole carcasses were worked by elaborate mechanisms. Though often dark, the kitchens gleamed with an array of copper pots and pans, like these at Montgeoffroy (see p71).*

Churches and Abbeys

The Loire Valley has a fine array of medieval ecclesiastical architecture, ranging from tiny Romanesque village churches to major Gothic cathedrals like Chartres and Tours. In the early Middle Ages, the Romanesque style predominated, characterized by straightforward ground plans, round arches and relatively little decoration. By the 13th century, the rib vaulting and flying buttresses of Gothic architecture had emerged, enabling builders to create taller, lighter churches and cathedrals. The Late Gothic style in France, often referred to as Flamboyant Gothic, features window tracery with flowing lines licking upwards like flames.

LOCATOR MAP

① Romanesque architecture

⑨ Gothic architecture

ROMANESQUE FEATURES

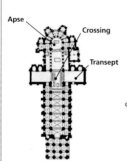

The plan of **St-Benoît-sur-Loire** *is typical of Romanesque architecture, with its cross shape and rounded apse.*

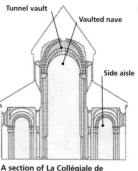

A section of **La Collégiale de St-Aignan-sur-Cher** *shows Romanesque tunnel vaulting. The vaulted side aisles provide added support for the high nave.*

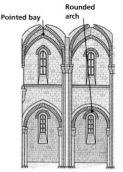

The round arches of **St-Aignan** *are typically Romanesque, while the pointed nave bays predict the Gothic style.*

GOTHIC FEATURES

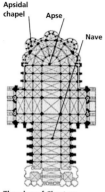

The plan of **Chartres Cathedral** *shows its very wide nave, and its apse ringed with chapels.*

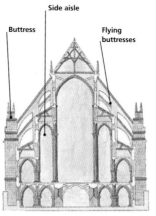

A section of **St-Etienne in Bourges** *reveals its five divisions with two aisles on either side of the nave. The building also has five portals rather than the usual three.*

Pointed arches *withstand greater stress and allow large windows, as in the nave at Bourges.*

WHERE TO FIND ROMANESQUE ARCHITECTURE

① St-Maurice, Angers *pp72–3*
② L'Abbaye St-Vincent, Nieul-sur-l'Autise *pp182–3*
③ Notre-Dame, Cunault *p79*
④ L'Abbaye de Fontevraud *pp86–7*
⑤ St-Maurice, Chinon *pp98–9*
⑥ La Collégiale, St-Aignan-sur-Cher *p129*
⑦ St-Eusice, Selles-sur-Cher *pp24–5*
⑧ La Basilique de St-Benoît-sur-Loire *p140*

WHERE TO FIND GOTHIC ARCHITECTURE

⑨ St-Etienne, Bourges *pp152–3*
⑩ St-Louis, Blois *pp124–5*
⑪ St-Hubert, Amboise, *p110*
⑫ St-Gatien, Tours *pp116–17*
⑬ La Trinité, Vendôme *p123*
⑭ Notre-Dame, Chartres *pp172–5*
⑮ St-Julien, Le Mans *p166*
⑯ Asnières-sur-Vègre *p163*

The west façade of Notre-Dame at Cunault *is simply decorated. Its machicolations and lateral towers give it a fortified appearance.*

- Bell-tower
- Machicolations
- Tympanum

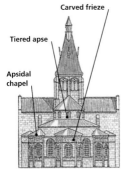

The east end of St-Eusice in Selles-sur-Cher, *with its three apsidal chapels, is decorated with friezes of carved figures.*

- Carved frieze
- Tiered apse
- Apsidal chapel

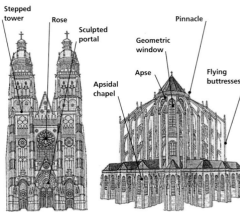

The west façade of St-Gatien in Tours *has richly carved, Flamboyant Gothic portals.*

- Stepped tower
- Rose
- Sculpted portal
- Apsidal chapel

The east end of St-Julien cathedral, in Le Mans, *has a complex arrangement of paired flying buttresses, each topped by pinnacles.*

- Pinnacle
- Geometric window
- Apse
- Flying buttresses

TERMS USED IN THIS GUIDE

Basilica: Early church with two aisles and nave lit from above by clerestory windows.

Clerestory: A row of windows illuminating the nave from above the aisle roof.

 Rose: Circular window, often with stained glass.

Buttress: Mass of masonry built to support a wall.

 Flying buttress: An arched support transmitting thrust of the weight downwards.

Portal: Monumental entrance to a building, often decorated.

 Tympanum: Decorated space, often carved, over a door or window lintel.

Vault: Arched stone ceiling.

Transepts: Two wings of a cruciform church at right angles to the nave.

Crossing: Centre of cruciform church, where the transept crosses the nave.

Lantern: Turret with windows to illuminate interior, often with cupola (domed ceiling).

Triforium: Middle storey between arcades and the clerestory.

Apse: Termination of the church, often rounded.

Ambulatory: Aisle running round the east end.

Arcade: Set of arches and supporting columns.

Rib vault: Vault supported by projecting ribs of stone.

 Gargoyle: Carved grotesque figure, often a water spout.

Tracery: Ornamental carved stone pattern within Gothic window.

Flamboyant Gothic: Carved stone tracery resembling flames.

 Capital: Top of a column, usually carved.

Writers and Artists of the Loire Valley

The valley of the River Loire is well known for its agricultural fertility, and it has also proved to be productive ground for literature, too. Over the centuries, internationally famous writers such as François Rabelais, the great lyrical poet Pierre de Ronsard and the novelists Honoré de Balzac and George Sand have lived close to the mighty river, often drawing inspiration from their native soil. Perhaps strangely, however, the pure light that so appeals to visitors to the region does not seem to have inspired as many of the country's greatest painters, although Claude Monet spent a fruitful period in the peaceful Creuse Valley.

Novelist Honoré de Balzac

Writer Marcel Proust, in a late 19th-century portrait by Jacques-Emile Blanche

WRITERS

One of the earliest authors to write in the "vulgar", or native, French tongue was born in Meung-sur-Loire in the mid-13th century. Jean Chopinel, better known as Jean de Meung, produced the second part of the widely translated and influential *Roman de la Rose*, a long, allegorical poem about courtly love. While the first half focuses delicately on two young lovers and their affair, Jean de Meung's sequel undermines the idealistic conventions of courtly love, taking a more cynical view of the world.

During the Hundred Years' War, a century and a half later, aristocratic poet Charles, Duc d'Orléans, was

Illumination from the *Roman de la Rose*

imprisoned by the English for 25 years. While in prison he was able to develop his considerable poetic skills. On his return he made his court at Blois a key literary centre. He invited famous writers and poets, among them François Villon, a 15th-century poet as renowned for the skill of his writing as for his highly disreputable lifestyle. While he was in Blois, Villon won a poetry competition with his work, *"Je Meurs de Soif auprès de la Fontaine"* ("I am Dying of Thirst by the Fountain").

François Rabelais, the racy 16th-century satirist and humanist, was born in 1483 near Chinon *(see pp98–9)* and educated at Angers. He became famous throughout Europe upon the publication of his *Pantagruel* (1532) and *Gargantua* (1535), huge, sprawling works full of bawdy humour and learned discourse in equal measure.

Pierre de Ronsard, born near Vendôme 30 years after Rabelais, was the leading French Renaissance poet, perhaps best known for his

George Sand, the 19th-century novelist

lyrical odes and sonnets to "Cassandre", "Hélène" and "Marie" (an Anjou peasant girl). Court poet to Charles IX and his sister Marguerite de Valois, he lived and died at St-Cosme Priory near Tours. Ronsard was also at the head of the Pléiade, a group of seven poets who were determined to revolutionize French poetry through the study of the classics. In the same group was Joachim du Bellay, an Anjou aristocrat and keen advocate of French literature. His *Defence and Illustration of the French Language* (1549) was a prose manifesto of the Pléiade doctrine.

Another famous native of the Loire Valley spearheaded a 17th-century intellectual revolution. Mathematician and philosopher René Descartes, born in Touraine and educated at the Jesuit college in La Flèche *(see p167)*, developed a new method of philosophical inquiry involving the simultaneous study of all the sciences. Starting with the celebrated "I think, therefore I am," he developed the rationalist doctrine known as Cartesianism in his most famous work, the *Discourse on Method*.

France's most prolific 19th-century novelist, Honoré de Balzac, often referred to his native Touraine as his favourite province. Tours, Saumur and the Indre Valley feature as settings for some of his best-known novels, all of which are keenly observant of 19th-century French mores. The work of Balzac's contemporary, George Sand (the masculine pen name of Aurore, Baroness Dudevant), is rooted in the landscapes of her native Berry, which also inspired Alain-Fournier's magical *Le Grand Meaulnes*, a romantic vision of his childhood in the region.

The hawthorn hedges and peaceful villages near Chartres provided the unforgettable setting for the early passages of Marcel Proust's impressive sequence of novels, *Remembrance of Things Past*. At the mouth of the Loire, the city of Nantes saw the birth, in 1826, of the ever-popular Jules Verne *(see pp192–3)*, whose pioneering works of science fiction have been enormously influential.

ARTISTS

Enchanting medieval wall paintings can be admired in a number of churches across the Loire Valley. In 1411 the three Limbourg brothers became court painters to the Duc de Berry in Bourges. He commissioned them to paint some 39 miniatures for *Les Très Riches Heures du Duc de Berry*. This Book of Hours remains one of the finest achievements of the International Gothic style. Some of its intricate illustrations depict scenes from life in the Loire Valley.

Jehan Fouquet, born in Tours in about 1420, was officially appointed royal painter in 1474. His portraits

A miniature from *Les Très Riches Heures du Duc du Berry*

include the famous image of the royal mistress Agnès Sorel *(see p104)* posing as the Virgin Mary.

A century after Fouquet's birth, François I persuaded the elderly Leonardo da Vinci to settle in the manor house of Cloux (now called Le Clos-Lucé, *see pp110–11*) near the royal château of Amboise. Aged 65, Leonardo was no longer actively painting, although he is known to have made some sketches of court life which have not survived. However, he was engaged in scientific investigations and inventions, the results of which can be seen in a museum in the basement of the château.

At about the time of Leonardo's death in 1519, François Clouet was born in

Henri Rousseau, in a self-portrait that typifies his naïve style

Tours. He succeeded his father, Jean, as court painter to François I and produced a string of truly outstanding portraits. His sitters included François I himself, Elizabeth of Austria and Mary, Queen of Scots. François Clouet's style, which was typical of the French Renaissance, was perpetuated by the artists and artisans in his workshop.

Anjou's most celebrated sculptor is David d'Angers, who was born in 1788. His works include busts and medallions of many of the major historical figures of his day, including a stirring memorial to the Marquis de Bonchamps, which can be found in the church at St-Florent-le-Vieil *(see pp68–9)*.

François Clouet's portrait of Mary, Queen of Scots

Exactly a century later, the Impressionist painter Claude Monet spent several weeks in the village of Fresselines in the Creuse Valley, painting the river as it passed through a narrow gorge *(see p147)*. One of these canvases, *Le Pont de Vervit*, now hangs in the Musée Marmottan in Paris.

Henri Rousseau, the quintessential naïve painter, was born in the town of Laval in 1844. Although he never left France, his best-known works are stylized depictions of lush jungles, home to all manner of wild animals. Part of the château in Laval has been converted into a Museum of Naïve Art *(see p160)* in honour of the artist.

Themed Tours of the Loire Valley

For those who wish to travel independently of tour companies, or who have a special interest in the region, self-guided themed tours provide an attractive alternative. Tourist offices produce information on routes visitors can travel in order to see the best sights on a given theme – including wine, churches, châteaux, historical buildings and beautiful botanical gardens and arboretums. Illustrated brochures and tourist maps describing each route, often in languages other than French, are available, and some of the routes are signposted along the way. Tourist office staff can assist in customizing a route for specific interests.

A la Recherche des Plantagenêts *traces the lives of Henry Plantagenet, his wife, Eleanor of Aquitaine, and their sons (see p50). The evidence of their remarkable lives, including this fortress in Loches, can be seen throughout the region.*

The Route Touristique du Vignoble (Wine Route) *guides the traveller through some of the region's prettiest wine country, including the Coteaux de la Loire. Further information is available from the tourist offices in Angers, Nantes and Saumur.*

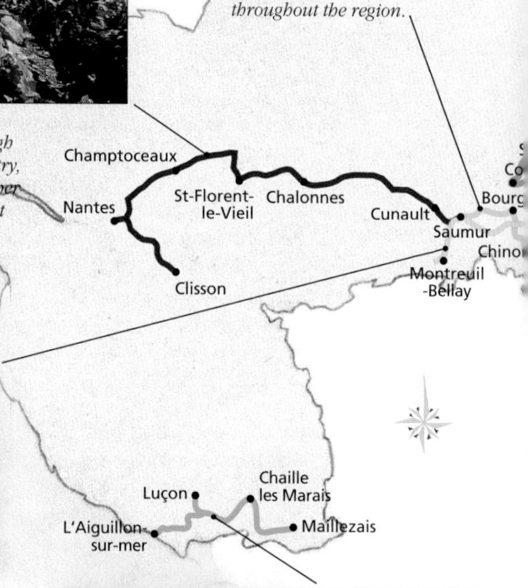

Champtoceaux
Nantes
St-Florent-le-Vieil
Chalonnes
Cunault
Saumur
Bourg
Chino
Montreuil-Bellay
Clisson

Chaille les Marais
Luçon
Maillezais
L'Aiguillon-sur-mer

The Route de la Vallée des Rois *takes motorists to many former royal residences, such as Azay-le-Rideau, as well as to cathedrals and churches along the part of the Loire known as the Valley of the Kings. Information is available from tourist offices along the route.*

The Sentier Cyclable du Marais Poitevin *is a signposted cycle route which takes in the attractions of the south Vendée, including the Marais Poitevin, to give a selection of the varied sights in this area. The tourist office at La-Roche-sur-Yon provides details.*

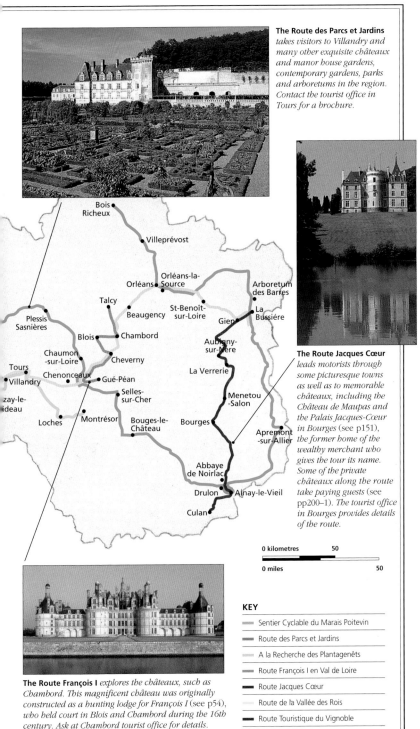

The Route des Parcs et Jardins *takes visitors to Villandry and many other exquisite châteaux and manor house gardens, contemporary gardens, parks and arboretums in the region. Contact the tourist office in Tours for a brochure.*

Bois Richeux

Villeprévost

Orléans-la-Source
Orléans

Talcy

Arboretum des Barres

St-Benoît-sur-Loire
Beaugency

La Bussiére

Gien

Plessis Sasnières

Blois • Chambord

Chaumont-sur-Loire
Cheverny

Tours
Chenonceaux • Gué-Péan

Villandry

Selles-sur-Cher

zay-le-ideau

Loches
Montrésor

Aubigny-sur-Nère

La Verrerie

Menetou-Salon

Bouges-le-Château
Bourges

Apremont-sur-Allier

Abbaye de Noirlac

Drulon • Ainay-le-Vieil

Culan

The Route Jacques Cœur *leads motorists through some picturesque towns as well as to memorable châteaux, including the Château de Maupas and the Palais Jacques-Cœur in Bourges (see p151), the former home of the wealthy merchant who gives the tour its name. Some of the private châteaux along the route take paying guests (see pp200–1). The tourist office in Bourges provides details of the route.*

0 kilometres 50

0 miles 50

KEY

━━ Sentier Cyclable du Marais Poitevin

━━ Route des Parcs et Jardins

━━ A la Recherche des Plantagenêts

━━ Route François I en Val de Loire

━━ Route Jacques Cœur

━━ Route de la Vallée des Rois

━━ Route Touristique du Vignoble

The Route François I *explores the châteaux, such as Chambord. This magnificent château was originally constructed as a hunting lodge for François I (see p54), who held court in Blois and Chambord during the 16th century. Ask at Chambord tourist office for details.*

Walking in the Loire Valley

The best way to follow the "most sensual river in France," as Flaubert called the Loire, is on foot. The *Grande Randonnée 3* (GR 3) is one of the longest marked walks in France, accompanying the Loire from its source at Gerbier de Jonc to its mouth. There are many other walking routes throughout the region, some following beautiful rivers, others focusing on themes, for example, religious paths (one passes through a route to Santiago de Compostela, or there are tracks following in St Martin's footsteps – *see p30*). A Topo-Guide *(see p224)* is a useful companion for detailed information about your walk. The Fèderation Française de la Randonnée Pédestre *(see p227)* offers more information on walking in the Loire Valley.

KEY

— Recommended walk

— Grande Randonnée de Pays

— Grande Randonnée

In the charming Alpes Mancelles, on the edge of the Parc Régional Normandie-Maine, there is a variety of walks in the valleys of the Sarthe, the Mayenne and the Orne. *(IGN 1618 OT)*

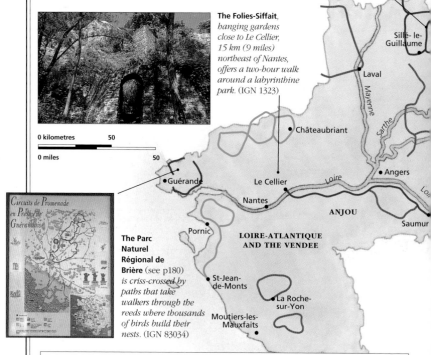

The Folies-Siffait, *hanging gardens close to Le Cellier, 15 km (9 miles) northeast of Nantes, offers a two-hour walk around a labyrinthine park.* (IGN 1323)

0 kilometres   50

0 miles   50

Circuits de Promenade en Presqu'île Guérandaise

The Parc Naturel Régional de Brière *(see p180) is criss-crossed by paths that take walkers through the reeds where thousands of birds build their nests.* (IGN 83034)

Sillé-le-Guillaume

Laval

Mayenne

Sarthe

Châteaubriant

Angers

Loire

Loir

Guérande

Le Cellier

Nantes

ANJOU

Saumur

Pornic

LOIRE-ATLANTIQUE AND THE VENDEE

St-Jean-de-Monts

La Roche-sur-Yon

Moutiers-les-Mauxfaits

ROUTE MARKERS

All the walking routes are marked with symbols painted onto trees or rocks along the paths. The different colours of the symbols indicate which kind of route you are taking. A red and white mark denotes a *Grande Randonnée* (GR) route, yellow and red are used for a regional route *(Grande Randonnée de Pays)*, and local routes *(Promenade et Randonnée)* are marked in a single colour (usually yellow).

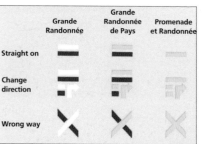

	Grande Randonnée	Grande Randonnée de Pays	Promenade et Randonnée
Straight on			
Change direction			
Wrong way			

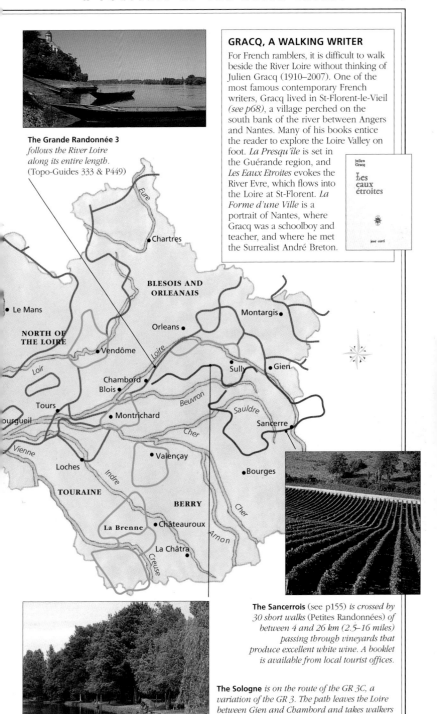

The Grande Randonnée 3
*follows the River Loire
along its entire length.*
(Topo-Guides 333 & P449)

GRACQ, A WALKING WRITER

For French ramblers, it is difficult to walk beside the River Loire without thinking of Julien Gracq (1910–2007). One of the most famous contemporary French writers, Gracq lived in St-Florent-le-Vieil *(see p68)*, a village perched on the south bank of the river between Angers and Nantes. Many of his books entice the reader to explore the Loire Valley on foot. *La Presqu'île* is set in the Guérande region, and *Les Eaux Etroites* evokes the River Evre, which flows into the Loire at St-Florent. *La Forme d'une Ville* is a portrait of Nantes, where Gracq was a schoolboy and teacher, and where he met the Surrealist André Breton.

Julien
Gracq

Les
eaux
étroites

josé corti

The Sancerrois (see p155) *is crossed by 30 short walks* (Petites Randonnées) *of between 4 and 26 km (2.5–16 miles) passing through vineyards that produce excellent white wine. A booklet is available from local tourist offices.*

The Sologne *is on the route of the GR 3C, a variation of the GR 3. The path leaves the Loire between Gien and Chambord and takes walkers on a five-day journey through this forest (see p141). For shorter walks, see the Topo-Guide P411.*

Winemaking and Vineyards

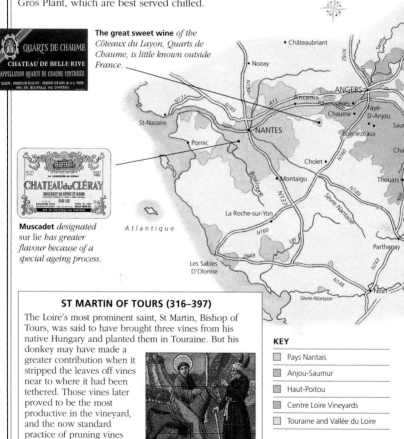

Caricature of a wine maker in "costume"

The importance of wine to life in the Loire Valley is immediately apparent. Fields of vines stretch along both banks of the river, and roadsides are lined with signs offering *dégustations*, or wine tastings *(see p212)*. Stretching 300 km (186 miles) from Nantes to Pouilly-sur-Loire, the Loire Valley is the third largest wine-producing area by volume in France and offers an unprecedented range of wine styles. The white Sancerres have an excellent reputation *(see p155)*, as do some of the rosé wines of Anjou, the sweet and sparkling Vouvrays, the full-bodied reds of Chinon and Bourgueil, and the dry *méthode champenoise* wines of Saumur. There are many more modest wines available, including Muscadet and its younger cousin Gros Plant, which are best served chilled.

Traditional vineyard cultivation

The great sweet wine *of the Côteaux du Layon, Quarts de Chaume, is little known outside France.*

Muscadet *designated* sur lie *has greater flavour because of a special ageing process.*

ST MARTIN OF TOURS (316–397)

The Loire's most prominent saint, St Martin, Bishop of Tours, was said to have brought three vines from his native Hungary and planted them in Touraine. But his donkey may have made a greater contribution when it stripped the leaves off vines near to where it had been tethered. Those vines later proved to be the most productive in the vineyard, and the now standard practice of pruning vines was born.

St Martin on his donkey

KEY

- Pays Nantais
- Anjou-Saumur
- Haut-Poitou
- Centre Loire Vineyards
- Touraine and Vallée du Loire

0 kilometres   15

0 miles   15

KEY FACTS ABOUT LOIRE WINES

Grape Varieties
The Muscadet grape makes simple, dry whites. The Sauvignon Blanc produces gooseberryish, flinty dry whites. Chenin Blanc is used for the dry and medium Anjou, Vouvrays, Savennières and Saumur, and the famous sweet whites, Vouvray, Quarts de Chaume and Bonnezeaux. Summery reds are made from the Gamay and the Cabernet Franc.

Wine Touring and Festivals
Visiting the Loire Valley's vineyards is a very popular pursuit. The diversity of wine-making across the region is such that there are almost 70 *appellations d'orgine contrôlée (AOC)* wines, produced to strict standards in precisely laid-out territories. Routes and estates are generally well signposted. Tourist offices can supply details on local wineries open to the public –

quite a large number are in stunning underground caves or beside beautiful properties. In the major cities of Tours, Saumur, Angers and Nantes, the Maisons des Vins de Loire offer introductions to the whole range of regional wines, as well as more advanced themed tastings. Wine festivals are numerous throughout the year, and often very jolly, so look out for details on those at a local level.

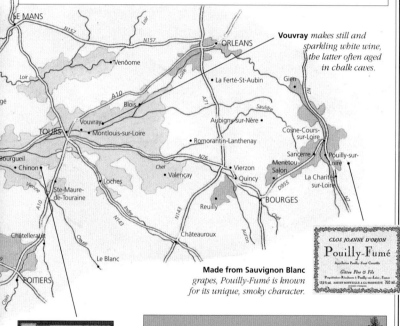

Vouvray *makes still and sparkling white wine, the latter often aged in chalk caves.*

Made from Sauvignon Blanc *grapes, Pouilly-Fumé is known for its unique, smoky character.*

Couly-Dutheil's Clos de l'Echo *is a beautiful, bright ruby wine made from Cabernet Franc grapes. The AOC wines of Chinon have an attractive, spicy aroma and age well.*

The Clos de l'Echo vineyard

A VIEW OF
THE RIVER LOIRE

A natural highway to the centre of France, the Loire was travelled from the earliest days. The remains of prehistoric canoes have been found along the river; later evidence shows that Celtic tribes and the Romans used the river extensively as a major trade route. In fact, until the development of the railway network during the 19th century, the river was a key transportation route. The growth of the French canal network from the 17th to 19th centuries, connecting the port of Nantes with Paris and the north, enhanced the Loire's importance.

See pages 34–5   See pages 36–7

The River Loire can be unpredictable and sometimes dangerous, and it was one of the first rivers that man tried to control. There is evidence that embankments were being built as early as the 12th century – and work continues – but the river remains essentially wild and is still subject to floods, freezes, shifting sands and dangerous currents. Today, the river is no longer used for commerce, except by tour boats giving visitors a unique view of the surrounding landscape. This makes an exploration of the River Loire all the more pleasant.

Sailing boats, with their typical square sails, often travelled in groups of three or more.

Steamers would use powerful winches to dip their smoke-stacks, enabling them to pass under low bridges.

Amboise's bridge traverses the river and the Ile St-Jean.

Château d'Amboise is set on a promontory above the river, safe from possible flooding.

VUE D'AMBOISE

This painting by Justin Ouvrié, now kept in the vaults of the Musée de la Poste in Paris, was painted in 1847. The bustling river scene, which includes several types of vessel, gives an indication of the importance of the River Loire to life and trade in the region, before the railways came to dominate transportation later in the century.

Barges, known in French as *chalands*, did not always have sails – sometimes they were rowed.

Everyday objects *were often decorated with river scenes, such as this 19th-century plate from the Musée de la Marine de Loire in Châteauneuf-sur-Loire.*

◁ Orléans, with the imposing Cathédrale Ste-Croix, seen from across the river

River View: St-Nazaire to Montsoreau

A pleasure barge on the River Loire

As the River Loire leaves Touraine and heads through Anjou and the Loire Atlantique, it widens and flows faster, as though rushing towards the Atlantic Ocean. Its waters are also swelled by many tributaries. Some flow alongside, creating a multitude of islands big and small; other tributaries flow north and south through the surrounding countryside. This land is rich in ancient monuments, including the Bagneux dolmen, the largest Neolithic construction of its kind, as well as fortresses built during the Middle Ages.

Champtoceaux
The village of Champtoceaux, on a cliff 80 m (260 ft) above the river, offers panoramic views. A private Renaissance château now occupies the lower part of the bluff, where a medieval citadel once stood.

St-Nazaire
At the mouth of the River Loire, where it flows into the Atlantic Ocean, St-Nazaire (see p190) is renowned for ship-building. Its graceful bridge is the westernmost river crossing.

Ancenis

Nantes' Cathédrale St-Pierre et St-Paul is Gothic style.

Nantes
Nantes was a prosperous port during the 18th and 19th centuries (see pp 190–193), the meeting point between the ocean and the inland river transportation channels.

| 0 kilometres | 20 |
| 0 miles | 20 |

Péage Fortifié du Cul-du-Moulin
This toll station was one of many constructed in the 13th century to collect revenue from passing vessels. It is one of the few still standing in France.

THE BRIDGES OF THE LOIRE

There have long been bridges across the River Loire – there was one at Orléans as early as AD 52, which was later destroyed by Julius Caesar's army. Now, with so many options for places to cross the river, it is difficult to imagine what it was like during the Middle Ages, when there were only five, or during the 15th century, when there were just 13. The bridges crossing the river today tell the story not only of the development of bridge building, but also of the region itself, its history and relationships.

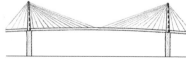

St-Nazaire
At 3,356 m (11,000 ft), St-Nazaire is one of the longest bridges in France. The central, suspended section is 404 m (1,300 ft) long. It opened for traffic in 1975. Before then, the estuary was crossed by ferry, and the nearest bridge was at Nantes.

St-Florent-le-Vieil

Once the church of a Benedictine monastery, the abbey on the promontory was the site of dramatic events during the Vendée Uprising (see p68). More than 40,000 Royalist troops and their supporters crossed the river here.

Montsoreau

Montsoreau, at the confluence of the Loire and Vienne rivers, has a 15th-century turreted château (see p85).

The Château d'Angers, with its massive towers and curtain walls, is on the River Maine, north of the Loire.

Cunault

The impressive Romanesque church in Cunault (see p79) is home to this painted 15th-century statue of St Catherine.

Angers

The Apocalypse Tapestries (see pp76–7), masterpieces of the 14th century, are displayed in the Château d'Angers.

Les Rosiers

Saumur

Saumur is famous for its cavalry school, whose fallen cadets are honoured by this memorial.

The Château de Saumur *(see p82)* rises above the town like a fairytale castle.

Ile Béhuard

This island (see p69) was once a pilgrimage site for sailors, who prayed to a sea goddess to help them navigate the sometimes treacherous waters of the River Loire. The present church was built by Louis XI who had nearly drowned here.

Chinon

Above the River Vienne, Chinon (see pp98 –100) was home to Henry Plantagenet in the 12th century.

Ancenis

The suspension bridge at Ancenis opened in 1953, replacing one destroyed in 1940. As the town is at the border of Brittany and Anjou, two coats of arms adorn either end of the bridge, one with the three lilies of Anjou and one with the ermine of Brittany.

Les Rosiers

The bridge at Les Rosiers is one of the two that cross the Loire at this point. The river is particularly wide here and has an island in the middle. The island is connected to the banks at the towns of Les Rosiers and Gennes by two bridges.

River View: Tours to Nevers

Stained glass in Gien

This is truly the royal Loire Valley. As the river flows through the regions of Touraine, Blésois and Orléanais, it passes beside many Renaissance châteaux. Some, like Chaumont, Amboise and Gien, show their fortress-like exteriors to the river, often concealing courtyard gardens and highly decorated façades. Others, like Sully, glory in their luxury. Throughout Touraine, vineyards gently slope towards the river, while the lands behind are taken up by the forests that were once the hunting grounds of kings and courtiers.

Beaugency's massive keep *(see p136)* dates from the 11th century.

Beaugency

Langeais
In the town of Langeais, (see p92) high above the river, there is a massive 15th-century château, still furnished in keeping with its period.

Blois
On the north bank of the Loire, Blois (see pp124–7) was the seat of the counts of Blois, and then the residence of François I, whose salamander emblem decorates many parts.

Château d'Amboise *(see p110),* a Renaissance château, it was built for a succession of kings.

Pagode de Chanteloup
All that remains of a once-lovely château, this strange pagoda (see p111) is 44 m (145 ft) tall.

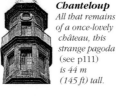

Tours
In the heart of the Loire Valley region, Tours (see pp112–17) was always a significant crossing point on the river. The lively place Plumereau, lined with 15th-century buildings, is in the Old Town.

Château de Chaumont
The great fortress of Chaumont (see p128) is softened by Renaissance touches and offers impressive views from its terrace.

Tours
When Tours' original 18th-century bridge was built, the rue Nationale, which links it to the centre of the city, became the major thoroughfare, in place of the road between the cathedral and the Old Town.

Blois
The bridge at Blois was built between 1716 and 1724, replacing a medieval bridge destroyed when a ship crashed into it. It was built to a very high standard, enabling it to survive floods and freezes.

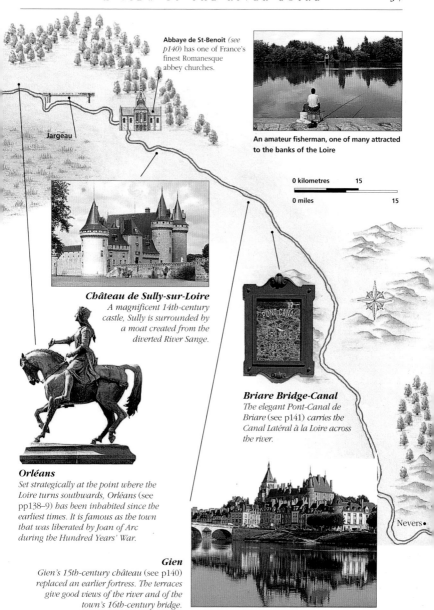

Abbaye de St-Benoît *(see p140)* has one of France's finest Romanesque abbey churches.

An amateur fisherman, one of many attracted to the banks of the Loire

| 0 kilometres | 15 |
| 0 miles | 15 |

Château de Sully-sur-Loire
A magnificent 14th-century castle, Sully is surrounded by a moat created from the diverted River Sange.

Briare Bridge-Canal
The elegant Pont-Canal de Briare (see p141) carries the Canal Latéral à la Loire across the river.

Orléans
Set strategically at the point where the Loire turns southwards, Orléans (see pp138–9) has been inhabited since the earliest times. It is famous as the town that was liberated by Joan of Arc during the Hundred Years' War.

Gien
Gien's 15th-century château (see p140) replaced an earlier fortress. The terraces give good views of the river and of the town's 16th-century bridge.

Nevers •

Beaugency
Beaugency's bridge is built in several different styles, because sections of the original 12th-century wooden structure were gradually replaced with stone. The earliest date from the 14th century.

Jargeau
The original bridge was replaced by a wooden suspension bridge in the 19th century. A steel bridge, built in the 1920s, was hit in World War II. The current bridge dates from 1988.

THE LOIRE VALLEY
THROUGH THE YEAR

Spring and early summer are often particularly beautiful in the regions bordering the River Loire. But it should not be forgotten that this is the "Garden of France", and that successful gardens need plentiful watering in the main growing season, so be prepared for some showery days. In the sultry, humid heat of July and early August, the Loire is usually reduced to a modest trickle between glistening sand banks. The châteaux can also become very crowded in the summer. Perhaps the

Spring asparagus

most pleasant season is autumn, when forests gleam red and gold in the mild sunshine, the restaurants serve succulent local game and wild mushrooms, and the grape harvest is celebrated in towns and villages with many colourful festivals. Music festivals are also very popular in the region. Concerts are staged all year round at countless venues across the region. For more information about the vast array of annual festivals, contact the local tourist offices.

SPRING

March sees the reopening of many châteaux after their winter closure, often on the Palm Sunday weekend that marks the beginning of the influx of visitors from the rest of France and abroad. The spring flowers and migrations of birds are particularly appreciated by nature lovers. Many special events, including numerous Easter egg hunts, are held on the Easter weekend

MARCH

Foire à l'Andouillette *(weekend before Easter)*, Athée-sur-Cher (nr Chenonceau). One of the earliest traditional Loire Valley festivals, with a fairground, bands and craftspeople.
Printemps Musical de St-Cosme *(last week)*, around Tours. A mainly classical music festival, held in numerous locations, notably St-Cosme priory.

APRIL

Le Printemps de Bourges *(third week)*, Bourges *(pp150–51)*. This contemporary music festival starts off the long concert season.
Carnaval de Cholet *(end Apr)*, Cholet *(p69)*. Carnival ending in a fabulous night-time parade of multi-coloured floats.

MAY

Fête de Jeanne d'Arc *(week of 8 May)*, Orléans *(pp138–9)*. One of France's oldest fêtes, begun in 1435 to celebrate the routing of the English in 1429, takes the form of a huge, colourful costume pageant.
Europajazz *(first week)*, Le Mans. One of the longest

Horse and rider from Saumur's Cadre Noir display team

established jazz festivals in the Loire Valley.
Concours Complet International *(third weekend)*, Saumur *(pp80–83)*. This international horse-riding competition takes place at the famous Cadre Noir riding school, which also hosts tattoo and equestrian displays from April until September.
Nuit Européenne des Musées *(mid-May)*, across the region. Many museums stay open late into the night and stage special events which are often free.
Le Printemps des Arts *(May and Jun)*, Nantes *(pp190–93)* and surrounding area. A Baroque dance, theatre and music festival.
Le Festival International des Jardins de Chaumont-sur-Loire *(May–mid-Oct)*, near Blois. A magnificent celebration of international horticultural innovation.

Farm workers in the fields around Bourgueil

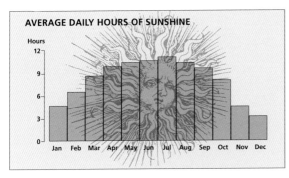

AVERAGE DAILY HOURS OF SUNSHINE

Sunshine Chart
The summer months are generally hot, with the hottest period in July. On the Atlantic coast, cool sea breezes often bring welcome relief from the heat but do not mean that sun-bathers are less likely to burn. In the spring and autumn, river areas can be misty in the mornings.

SUMMER

France's main summer celebrations include the Fête de la Musique on the longest night of the year, the Feast of John the Baptist on 24 June and Bastille Day, recalling the start of the French Revolution, on 14 July 1789. The Loire's famous son et lumière *(see pp42–3)* performances take place mainly at weekends on the long nights between mid-June and mid-August.

JUNE

Vitiloire *(first weekend)*, Tours. Touraine *vignerons* invade the town to lead the wine celebrations.
Les 24 Heures du Mans *(second or third weekend)*, Le Mans *(pp164–7)*. One of France's main events, this international 24-hour car race attracts enormous crowds.
Sardinantes *(second or third Sat)*, Nantes. Savour a plate of grilled sardines accompanied by Celtic music and dancing on the quay in old Nantes. A typical local festival.
Festival d'Anjou *(mid-Jun–mid-Jul)*. Major theatre festival held in historic sites throughout the *département*.
Avanti la Musica *(mid-Jun–mid-Aug)*, Amboise. Celebrating links between Amboise and Italy via music, theatre, cinema and more.
Fêtes Musicales en Touraine *(late Jun)*, Tours *(pp112–17)*. Started in 1964, this international festival of chamber music is held in a superb medieval tithe barn, at Parçay-Meslay, northeast of Tours.

The beach at the popular Atlantic resort, Les Sables d'Olonne

JULY

Des Lyres d'Eté, *(Jul & Aug)*, Blois. An exciting variety of theatre and music dominates the programme during this summer festival.
Bastille Day *(14 Jul)*. The celebrations for the Fête Nationale, commemorating the Storming of the Bastille in 1789, are the high point of the year in many small communities. Taking place across the region, visitors can join in the dancing and wine-quaffing, and enjoy the often very impressive firework displays.
Foire à l'Ail et au Basilic *(26 Jul)*, Tours. The headily scented garlic and basil fair is held every year on the Feast of St Anne *(p117)*.
Festival International d'Orgue *(Sun in Jul and Aug)*, Chartres Cathedral *(pp171–5)*. Internationally renowned

organists from all over the world descend on Chartres to participate in this prestigious organ festival.
Destination Moyen-Age *(third weekend)*, Chinon. This takes shape as an impressive recon-struction of a medieval settle-ment, with festivities spread over two days. It includes acrobats, musicians and street theatre, they combine to fill the historic town of Chinon.

AUGUST

L'Epopée Médiévale *(mid-Aug)*, Loches. Medieval mania takes over this fine old town.
Foire aux Vins de Vouvray *(around 15 Aug)*, Vouvray. The Feast of the Assumption is marked by numerous local festivities, with wine events predominating.
Foire aux Sorcières *(first Sun)*, Bué (nr Sancerre). The Berry was often said to be a centre of witchcraft and sorcery. On this occasion, children dressed as witches or ghosts parade through the village to a nearby field where crowds play games and watch folk groups performing.
Festival de Sablé *(last weekend)*, Sablé-sur-Sarthe *(p162)*. Over a period of five days, musicians perform in churches and manor houses around Sablé.

Folk dancers at a festival

Les Rendez-Vous de l'Erdre *(last weekend; first weekend in Sep)*, Nantes. Mixing jazz, boating and street festivities on Nantes' second river.

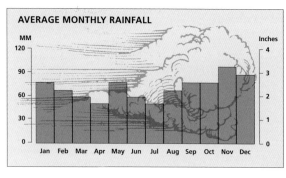

AVERAGE MONTHLY RAINFALL

	Jan	Feb	Mar	Apr	May	Jun	Jul	Aug	Sep	Oct	Nov	Dec

MM: 120, 90, 60, 30, 0 — Inches: 4, 3, 2, 1, 0

Rainfall Chart
*Spring and autumn
are the wettest times,
with the amount of
rainfall occasionally
causing the River Loire
and its many tribu-
taries to break their
banks. As you head
inland from the coast,
precipitation tends to
increase. During the
summer, rains and
violent storms are
common at night.*

AUTUMN

The golden days of autumn
attract large numbers of
Parisians to the region for
shooting weekends, espe-
cially to the forested eastern
areas. This is also the season
for the *vendanges*, or grape
harvest, and the events and
festivities associated with it,
and for fairs celebrating the
season's produce.

SEPTEMBER

Les Accroche-Coeurs (*second
week*), Angers (*pp72–3*).
During the course of three or
four days, the streets of Angers
are alive with open-air theatre,
dance, circus, concerts and all
manner of performance arts.
Jazz en Touraine (*mid-
Sep*), Montlouis-sur-Loire.
This is one of the region's
leading jazz festivals.
Festival de Loire (*mid-Sep*),
Orléans/Loiret. Joyous
gathering of Loire boats and
festivities along the river,

held every second (odd-
numbered) year.
Journées du Patrimoine
(*third weekend*). For one
weekend a year, châteaux
and other historic buildings
that are usually closed to the
public can be visited, and
concerts, exhibitions and other
cultural events are staged.
**Festival Européen de Musique
Renaissance** (*last weekend*),
Clos Lucé, Amboise. This
three-day festival, held in the
Château du Clos Lucé, features
musicians who specialize in
Renaissance music.
Entre Cours et Jardins (*last
weekend*), Le Mans. A
celebration of horticulture
across the historic old town,
with many private homes
opening their gardens to
the public.

OCTOBER

Celtomania (*first three
weeks*), Nantes. This lively
celebration of Celtic culture
includes music and theatre
performances.

High-quality local produce on sale
at the Saturday market in Saumur

Mondial du Lion (*mid-Oct*),
Le Lion d'Angers. For horse
lovers, this is a top-class
international equestrian
competition.
Foire à la Bernache (*last Sun
Oct or 1st Sun Nov*), Reugny (nr
Tours). Although it may be an
acquired taste, the *bernache*
(unfermented new wine) is
very popular with the locals.
Foire aux Marrons (*last
Tue*), Bourgueil (nr Chinon).
Chestnuts are the traditional
accompaniment to new wine,
and for this reason they
feature in many guises here.
Rockomotives (*last week; first
week in Nov*), Vendôme. The
relaxed little town on the
Loire hosts this popular
rock festival.

NOVEMBER

Marché de Noël (*last
weekend*), Château de Brissac
(*p78*). The Christmas market
in the château, featuring local
artisans and seasonal produce,
marks the beginning of the
Christmas season.

Wine-tasting at Kerhinet in La Grande Brière

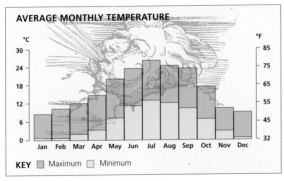

AVERAGE MONTHLY TEMPERATURE

KEY ■ Maximum ▢ Minimum

Temperature Chart
It is rare for winter temperatures to fall below freezing in the Loire Valley. In the west, the sea moderates the climate, keeping it mild. Elsewhere, summer temperatures can reach over 30˚ C (86˚ F) in the middle of the day, but the evenings are usually cooler and perfect for eating outside on terraces by the river.

WINTER

Winter is the quiet season in the Loire Valley, when a damp chill rather than a frosty cold sets in, and many of the châteaux are closed. A few Christmas markets are held, and a film festival, but in general this is a time when local people prefer the pleasures of home.

DECEMBER

Soleils d'Hiver *(through Dec)*, Angers. One of the best programmes of seasonal entertainments along the Loire, as well as a traditional Christmas market and fair-trade craft stalls.
Marché de Noël et Crèche Vivante *(through Dec)*, Cholet. A living Nativity scene, festive market and Christmas lights competition.
Noël au Fil des Siècles *(Dec–6 Jan)*, Château d'Amboise. An interesting trawl through the history of Christmas.
Foire de Noël *(first weekend)*, Richelieu *(p102–3)*. This is a traditional Christmas market

An old windmill in the Anjou countryside

selling gifts, decorations and a variety of seasonal food.

JANUARY

La Folle Journée *(last week)*, Nantes and various other towns around the region. As many as 400 classical music concerts take place in 12 different towns, all focusing on a theme that changes every year.

FEBRUARY

Fêtes des Vins d'Anjou *(last weekend)*, Chalonnes-sur Loire. The winter period is enlivened with wine fairs, such as this gathering of producers of the Saumur and Anjou appellations.

PUBLIC HOLIDAYS

New Year's Day (1 Jan)
Easter Monday
Ascension (sixth Thursday after Easter)
Labour Day (1 May)
VE Day (8 May)
Bastille Day (14 Jul)
Feast of the Assumption (15 Aug)
All Saints' Day (1 Nov)
Remembrance Day (11 Nov)
Christmas Day (25 Dec)

A concert at the Abbaye de Fontevraud

Son et Lumière in the Loire

The Loire Valley was the birthplace of son et lumière (literally "sound and light") shows, and some of the world's finest examples can be found here. The first performances, staged at Chambord in 1952, combined lighting effects and a soundtrack to emphasize the beauty of the building and to conjure up important historical figures. Today many of the shows use lasers and dramatic fireworks, as well as a cast of hundreds (often amateur actors drawn from the local community), to create a spectacular pageant. The following list includes the main regular shows, but it is worth keeping an eye open for posters advertising one-off events. Performance times may vary.

Actor at Amboise

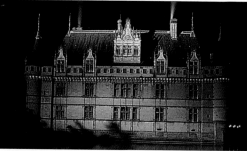

Lighting effects bringing drama to the Château d'Azay-le-Rideau

ANJOU

Saumur The Treasure of the Dukes of Anjou (1½ hours). *Tel* 02 41 83 31 31. ◯ Jul–Aug: 10:30pm Thu–Sat. 🎧 www.letresordesducs danjou.com

This entertaining show involves a British scientist creating a time-machine to go back into different centuries of Saumur's courtly history.

TOURAINE

Amboise At the Court of King François (1½ hours). *Tel* 02 47 57 14 47. ◯ late Jun–Jul: 10:30pm, selected dates; Aug: 10pm, most nights. 🎧 **Translations** Eng. www.renaissance-amboise.com

This is a celebration of the life of François I, at his favourite château (see p110). The show, enacted by local residents, re-creates the court, with sumptuous costumes, thrilling hunts and elaborate festivities.

Azay-le-Rideau The Enchanted Mirror (45 mins). *Tel* 02 47 45 42 04. ◯ Jul–Aug: 9:15pm & 10:15pm nightly. 🎧

During this fascinating promenade production, all the spectators walk around the grounds of this elegant château (see pp96–7), as they observe a succession of stage, sound and lighting effects.

Chenonceau Night-time Promenade (1½ hours). *Tel* 02 47 23 90 07. ◯ Jun: 9:30–11pm Fri, Sat & Sun; Jul & Aug: 9:30–11pm nightly. 🎧

The son et lumière production at this beautiful royal residence (see pp106–9) takes the form of a play of light and shadow orchestrated by Pierre Bideau, the designer of the Eiffel Tower illuminations. The walk leads through the gardens designed by Diane de Poitiers and Catherine de Médicis. Corelli's music adds to the romantic atmosphere.

Loches Les Mille et une Nuit (2 hours). ◯ mid-Jul–mid-Aug: 10pm, selected dates. 🎧

A dramatic nocturnal walk around the floodlit monuments and medieval streets of the town, starting from the Logis Royal. This is followed by a spectacle of fire and dance. It's cheaper to book the two events together.

Semblançay Scénoféerie (1¾ hours). *Tel* 02 47 56 66 77. ◯ Jun–mid-Aug: 9pm Fri & Sat. www.scenofeerie.fr

Some 450 actors take part in this grand historical display with a castle as the backdrop.

BLESOIS AND ORLEANAIS

Blois The Story of Blois (45 mins). *Tel* 02 54 90 33 32. ◯ Apr–May & Sep: 10pm nightly; Jun–Aug: 10:30pm nightly. 🔴 some public hols. 🎧 English performance on Wed.

Images of key moments in the history of the Château Royal de Blois (see pp126–7) are projected onto the building's façade during this sound and light show. The loves, dramas and mysteries portrayed include the visit of Joan of Arc in 1429, the poetry contest

Faces from the past projected onto the walls of Château de Blois

Fireworks and lighting effects illuminate the château of Puy-du-Fou

between Charles of Orléans and François Villon in 1457, and the assassination of the Duc de Guise in 1563. Watch the show from the château's courtyard.

Cléry-Saint-André
La Révolution Française (1¾ hours). **Tel** 02 38 45 94 06.
⬭ 3 weekends from mid-Jul–Aug: 10:15pm. **www.**cleryraconte.com

A cast of hundreds re-creates the uprising, struggles and other events of the French Revolution. These include the storming of the Bastille and the battle of Valmy. Before the show you can sit down to a Republican banquet, starting at 7pm (making an advanced reservation is advised), during which more entertainment is provided.

BERRY

Valençay Tel 🛈 02 54 00 04 42. **Spectacle Nocturne** (90 mins).
⬭ last week in Jul–mid-Aug: 10pm, selected dates. 🖼 **www.**spectacle-valencay.fr

The dramatically lit grounds of this château *(see p146)* make an ideal setting for the retelling of classic fairy tales such as *Cinderella* and *Beauty and the Beast*. There are 10 enchanting performances by the 100-strong cast, complete with elaborate period costumes and a musical score.

LOIRE ATLANTIQUE AND THE VENDEE

Le Puy-du-Fou
Cinéscénie (100 mins).
Tel 02 51 64 11 11.
⬭ Jun & Jul: 10:30pm Fri & Sat; Aug–early Sep: 10pm Fri & Sat. Arrive one hour earlier. 🖼 book in advance. **Translation** Eng. **www.**puydufou.com

The Château du Puy-du-Fou *(see p188)* hosts the Ciné-scénie, which bills itself as the world's largest permanent son et lumière spectacle. More than 1,000 actors, 250 horses, countless volunteers and various spectacular high-tech effects combine to trace the turbulent history of the Vendée from the Middle Ages to the end of World War II.

THE MAGICIAN OF THE NIGHT
The master of the modern son et lumière in France is Jean-Claude Baudoin, who is also known as *"le magicien de la nuit"*. Since 1966 he has created the sets for more than 150 musical productions, held at the châteaux of Blois, Loches Chambord and Valençay, as well as in St-Aignan-sur-Cher, Les Sables d'Olonnes and Chartres.

Producer Jean-Claude Baudoin

The history of the Vendée re-enacted in the Cinéscénie at Le Puy-du-Fou

THE HISTORY OF THE LOIRE VALLEY

The Loire's central role in French history is splendidly displayed in the breadth of its architectural styles, ranging from megalithic structures to royal and ducal châteaux.

Imposing prehistoric monuments testify to the existence of thriving Neolithic cultures as early as the third millennium BC. By the 1st century BC, the conquering Romans found sophisticated Celtic communities already established. Later, as Christianity spread, the ancient Celtic towns at Angers, Bourges, Chartres, Orléans and Tours became well known as centres of learning.

Fleur-de-lys, the royal emblem

A long period of territorial conflict began in the 9th century, first among local warlords and later between France and England, when Henry Plantagenet, count of Anjou and duke of Normandy and Aquitaine, inherited the English crown in 1154. In the 15th century, major battles between the two countries were fought in the region during the Hundred Years' War, with Joan of Arc spurring on French victories. A series of French kings made the Loire Valley their home, ruling from the magnificent châteaux. The fierce 16th-century Wars of Religion between Catholics and Protestant Huguenots brought yet more bloodshed to the area.

By the 17th century, France's political focus had shifted to Paris, although the River Loire remained a key transportation route until the advent of the railway. Later, the Vendée Uprising of 1793 was the most serious civil threat to the French republic after the 1789 Revolution.

In the 20th century, the architectural evidence of the Loire's rich history has led to the growth of the region's tourist industry. This balances with a diverse and well-established industrial base, as well as thriving agriculture, to make the valley one of the most economically stable regions of France.

16th-century views of Tours, with its cathedral, and Angers, with its slate quarries

◁ A portrait of François I, the Renaissance king (reigned 1515–47), attributed to Jean Clouet

Rulers of the Loire

In the course of the Loire's history, the power of the local nobility often rivalled that of the French throne. The dukedoms of Anjou and Blois were established when Charlemagne's territory was divided among his sons upon his death in 814. Henry Plantagenet, count of Anjou, duke of Normandy and king of England, could trace his lineage to Charlemagne. The French monarchy did not consolidate its authority until Charles VII moved from the Loire back to Paris in 1436. Another local family, the royal house of Orléans, saw two of its sons become kings.

KEY

French monarchs

Notable members of local dynasties

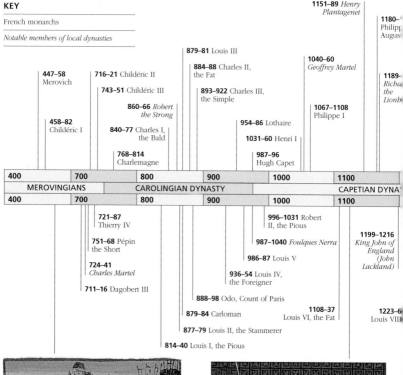

447–58 Merovich

458–82 Childéric I

716–21 Childéric II

743–51 Childéric III

860–66 *Robert the Strong*

840–77 Charles I, the Bald

768–814 Charlemagne

879–81 Louis III

884–88 Charles II, the Fat

893–922 Charles III, the Simple

954–86 Lothaire

987–96 Hugh Capet

1040–60 *Geoffrey Martel*

1067–1108 Philippe I

1031–60 Henri I

1151–89 *Henry Plantagenet*

1180– Philipp Augus

1189– *Rich the Lionh*

400	700	800	900	1000	1100
MEROVINGIANS		CAROLINGIAN DYNASTY			CAPETIAN DYNA

400	700	800	900	1000	1100

721–87 Thierry IV

751–68 Pépin the Short

724–41 *Charles Martel*

711–16 Dagobert III

996–1031 Robert II, the Pious

987–1040 *Foulques Nerra*

986–87 Louis V

936–54 Louis IV, the Foreigner

888–98 Odo, Count of Paris

879–84 Carloman

877–79 Louis II, the Stammerer

814–40 Louis I, the Pious

1199–1216 *King John of England (John Lackland)*

1108–37 Louis VI, the Fat

1223–6 Louis VIII

482–511 Clovis I

1137–80 Louis VII

1422–61
Charles VII,
the Victorious

1270–85 Philippe III

1285–1314 Philippe
IV, the Fair

1314–16 Louis X

1316–22
Philippe V,
the Tall

1322–28
Charles IV,
the Fair

1328–50
Philippe VI

1483–98
Charles VIII,
the Affable

1498–1515 Louis XII,
Father of the People

1515–47 François I

1547–59 Henri II

1559–60
François II

1643–1715 Louis
XIV, the Sun King

1774–92 Louis XVI

1804–14
Napoléon I

1300	1400	1500	1600	1700	1800

VALOIS DYNASTY | BOURBON DYNASTY

1300	1400	1500	1600	1700	1800

1430–80
*René I of
Anjou*

1350–64
Jean II,
the Good

1461–83
Louis XI, the
Spider

1364–80
Charles V,
the Wise

1226–70
Louis IX
(St Louis)

1380–1422
Charles VI,
the Fool

1560–74
Charles IX

1574–89 Henri III

1814–24
Louis XVIII

1824–30
Charles X

1830–48 *Louis-Philippe I,
Duc d'Orléans,
King of the French*

1715–74
Louis XV

1852–70
Napoléon III

1589–1610 Henri IV

1610–43 Louis XIII

Neolithic and Roman Loire

Neolithic Culture produced some of France's largest prehistoric tombs and sacred sites. Their builders had Central European roots, as did the Celts who established cities along the Loire in the Bronze and Iron Ages. Julius Caesar's conquest of the valley in 51 BC left the Celtic tribes under a light Roman rule, the basis of relative prosperity for the next 300 years. The spread of Christianity coincided with Rome's military decline and the rise of kingdoms ruled by Visigoths to the south and Germanic Franks to the north. The Frankish king, Clovis I, converted to Christianity and took power in 507 by routing the Visigoths.

Baptism of Clovis
Frankish chieftain Clovis converted to Christianity at the end of the 5th century to legitimize his rule.

The entrance porch is a distinctive feature of Angevin dolmens.

Palaeolithic Remains
Flint tools made in the Loire basin were traded by Palaeolithic tribes at least 50,000 years ago.

Celtic Art
Celtic art was not dominated by the naturalistic ideals of the occupying Romans. This bronze statuette of a young woman dates from the 1st–2nd century AD.

BAGNEUX DOLMEN
This 5,000-year-old chamber tomb in Saumur is 21 by 7 m (69 by 23 ft). The nine massive uprights were levered onto loose stones, dragged to the site, tilted and sunk into ditches 3 m (10 ft) deep.

TIMELINE

c.2500 Loire dolmens with porches set new style of Neolithic burial chamber

c.800 Celtic Carnutes found settlements at Blois, Chartres and Orléans

57–6 Romans conquer western Loire tribes

51 Julius Caesar ends Gaulish uprising that began in Orléans

Julius Caesar, first to unite Gaul

2500 BC	100 BC	AD 1	AD 100

c.1200 Loire region exports bronze weapons made using local tin resources.

Celtic helmet

31 Roman emperor Augustus sets framework for 300 years of Pax Romana (peace and prosperity) in the Loire

50 Loire Valley flourishes as border link between two Gallo-Roman provinces, Lugdenunsis and Aquitania

Celtic Armour
The warlike Celts were skilled armourers, as this bronze breastplate of 750–475 BC shows. The Romans found them formidable opponents.

An inner pillar, perhaps part of a wall, helps support a 40-tonne capstone.

Gallo-Roman Art
This beaten bronze stallion, displayed in the archeology museum in Orléans, was dedicated to Mars, god of war and guardian of agriculture.

Orthostats (upright stones) were sunk in holes 3 m (10 ft) deep and filled with sand, which was then dug out.

Fresh Water by Aqueduct
Roman pillars near Luynes supported a 2nd-century aqueduct which carried spring water to baths in Caesarodunum (Tours).

250 Gatien, Bishop of Tours, among the first Christian evangelists in the Loire

313 Emperor Constantine makes Christianity official Roman religion

372 Martin, Bishop of Tours, leads monastic growth

507 After converting to Christianity, Clovis defeats Visigoths near Poitiers

498 Clovis I takes Orléans

511 Clovis I dies; his sons divide his lands

200	300	400	500

60 Romans build amphitheatre at Gennes

275 Emperor Aurelian gives Orléans independent status

St Martin, Bishop of Tours

451 Visigoth kingdom of Toulouse helps repel Attila the Hun at Orléans

473 Visigoths capture Tours

Wine: an early Loire export

c.550 First record of wine production in the Loire region

The Early Middle Ages

In raising the massive keep at Loches, Foulques Nerra of Anjou was typical of the warlords who took power in the Loire after the 9th century. The chains of citadels they built laid the foundations for the later châteaux. The Plantagenets, who followed Nerra as rulers of Anjou, also claimed territory from Normandy to Aquitaine and then inherited the English

Royal seal of Henry II

throne. It was not until the 13th century that the French King Louis IX brought Anjou back under direct control of the crown. Throughout this period the Church was a more cohesive power than the French crown. Its cathedrals and monastic orders established schools and *scriptoria* (where manuscripts were copied and illuminated), and it was to the Church rather than the throne that feudal warlords turned to mediate their brutal disputes.

THE LOIRE AROUND 1180

☐ *Other fiefs*

▨ *French royal domain*

Gregory I codified the liturgical music sung during his reign as pope (590–604).

St Louis
Popularly called St Louis for his piety, Louis IX (1214–70) was the first Capetian monarch to inherit a relatively stable kingdom. A brave crusading knight and just ruler, he forced England to abandon claims to the Loire.

TIMELINE

687 Pépin II establishes the power of the "mayors" of the Carolingian dynasty, ancestors of Charlemagne, over Merovingian kings

732 Charles Martel drives Moors back from the Loire in decisive battle south of Tours

850 Normans lay waste to Loire Valley

866 Robert the Strong, ancestor of Capetian k killed by Normans in A

911 Chartres repe Norma

| 600 | 700 | 800 | 90 |

Charlemagne, the Frankish king

768–84 Charlemagne conquers Brittany and all Loire

796 Charlemagne's mentor, Alcuin, makes Tours a centre of Carolingian art

Coinage of Charles the Bold

Carolingian Ivory

Ivory plaques, reliquaries and book covers are among the most beautiful Frankish decorative objects to survive Norman destructions of the 10th century. Carolingian art usually served a religious or utilitarian purpose.

WHERE TO SEE EARLY MEDIEVAL LOIRE

Early churches such as the one at Cunault (*see p79*) are charged with medieval atmosphere, as are abbeys such as Noirlac (*p149*) or at Solesmes (*p162*) and Fontgombault (*p147*), where you can hear Gregorian chant. Fortress châteaux such as the one at Loches (*p104*) and ruined towers at Lavardin (*p122*) or Montrichard (*p128*) tell grimmer feudal stories.

Medieval musical notation showed variations in pitch (high and low notes). The length of each note depended on the natural rhythm of the text.

Monastic Arts

The development of the Caroline Minuscule style of calligraphy was led by the monks of Tours' Basilique St-Martin in the 9th century.

Romanesque Capitals

This Romanesque sculpture is on a capital in Cunault church.

Fine Craftsmanship

Many of the finest surviving pieces of medieval craftsmanship are worked in metal. This 13th-century funerary mask was cast in copper from the effigy of a woman and then gilded.

ILLUMINATED MANUSCRIPT

This manuscript is the first page of a 13th-century gradual, a book of plainsong sung during mass. It is typical of the style of illuminated manuscripts that were produced by the abbeys of the Loire Valley. This collection of Gregorian chant was compiled by monks of the strict Cistercian Order (*see p149*).

Hugh Capet of Orléans

Hugh, depicted here being handed the keys to Laon, was elected king in 987, ending the Carolingian dynasty. He set a precedent for kings to seek refuge in the Loire in troubled times.

1101 Founding of Abbaye de Fontevraud

1096 First Crusade launched

ugh Capet of ans becomes irst Capetian ng of France

1128 Marriage in Le Mans of Geoffrey Plantagenet and Matilda, daughter of Henry I of England

1189 Henry II's death leaves his son, Richard the Lionheart, as the Angevin rival to the French king

1000   **1100**   **1200**

Foulques Nerra

992 Bretons driven out of Anjou by Foulques Nerra

1154 Henry Plantagenet accedes to the English throne as Henry II

1214 Angevin empire ends with defeat of King John at Angers

1125 Thibaut IV of Blois and Champagne rivals Capetian power

The Hundred Years' War

14th-century knight

The destructive climax of the Middle Ages was war between the French and English crowns, flaring intermittently from 1337 to 1453. When the English besieged Orléans in 1428, the Loire region became the focus for a struggle that seemed likely to leave France partitioned between England and its powerful ally, Burgundy. Instead, the teenage heroine, Joan of Arc, inspired Orléans to fight off the English and brought the dauphin Charles VII out of hiding in Chinon. Her martyrdom in 1431 helped to inspire a French recovery. In spite of marauding soldiery and the more widespread disaster of the plague known as the Black Death, the Loire knew periods of peace and prosperity, during which medieval court life flourished.

THE LOIRE VALLEY IN 1429

☐ *French territory in the Loire*

■ *English possessions*

The English longbow was a powerful weapon, requiring strong, skilled archers.

Charles VII
Joan of Arc's dauphin, often portrayed as a weakling, was in fact a crafty man in a difficult situation. Disinherited by the French royal family in 1420, he used Joan's charisma to rally support. However, he distrusted her political judgment.

Cannons could fire stone balls that weighed as much as 200 kg (440 lb).

Jousting Tournament
The sumptuous trappings of their warlike recreations display the wealth of the ruling class in the early 15th century. Jousting was dangerous – Henri II died from a lance blow.

TIMELINE

1341 English support John of Montfort against Charles of Blois in War of Breton Succession

1346 English longbows defeat French knights at Crécy

1352 Loire begins recovery from four years of plague

Black Death depicted in a 15th-century illuminated manuscript

1325	1350	1375

1337 Philippe VI is elected first Valois king; he confiscates English lands in Guyenne, starting Hundred Years' War

Portrait of Philippe VI

1360 Anjou becomes a duchy

Apocalypse
War and the plague made the end of the world a preoccupation of 15th-century art. In this tapestry from Angers (see pp76–7), St John hears the clap of doom.

WHERE TO SEE THE LOIRE OF THE 14TH AND 15TH CENTURIES

Guérande *(p180)* is a well-preserved, 15th-century walled town. Many others, such as Chinon *(pp98–100)*, have half-timbered houses. Orléans *(pp138–9)* has a replica of the house in which Joan of Arc lodged. Le Plessis-Bourré *(p70)* exemplifies the shift towards more graceful lifestyles after the end of the Hundred Years' War.

Château de Chinon
This château is strategically positioned on a cliff above the River Vienne.

The halberd was a typical infantryman's weapon.

Siege tower

Joan of Arc
Although shown here in feminine attire, the real Joan (see p137) wore men's dress into battle.

René, Duke of Anjou
René I (1409–80) loved tournaments but was also a painter, scholar and poet. To some, he represented the ideal 15th-century ruler.

THE SIEGE OF ORLÉANS

The English first besieged Orléans in November 1428, and they quickly established their position and built major siegeworks. In February 1429, a French attempt to cut English supply lines was defeated, and it was not until 30 April that Joan of Arc's troops were able to enter the city. Within a week the English were forced to abandon the siege.

1409 Birth of René I, Duke of Anjou		**1429** Joan of Arc visits the dauphin Charles at Chinon, ends English siege of Orléans and crowns him King Charles VII at Reims	**1453** War ends without a treaty, with English retaining only Calais	
1417–32 English occupy Chartres	**1418** Charles VI burns Azay-le-Rideau			**1461** Louis XI begins his reign
400	**1425**		**1450**	
92 Louis, Duke Orléans, quires Blois	**1415** Crushing English victory at Agincourt leads to alliance between England and Burgundy	**1428** English besiege Orléans / **1435** Charles VII makes peace with Burgundy. Army reforms lead to French victories	**1438** Jacques Cœur of Bourges becomes court banker and reorganizes France's tax system	*15th-century sporting crossbow* / **1470** Silk weaving in Tours begins

Renaissance Loire

Catherine de Médicis (1519–89)

The Italian wars of Charles VIII, Louis XII and François I between 1494 and 1525 gave all three kings a taste for Italian art and architecture. At Amboise and Blois they made the Loire a centre of court life, establishing the culture of the French Renaissance. François I patronized countless artists and craftsmen who worked in the Italian style, setting an example for the aristocracy throughout France. The Loire suffered 40 years of warfare when his son's widow, Catherine de Médicis, could not persuade Catholics, led by the Guise family, to live in peace with Protestants during the reigns of her sons, Charles IX and Henri III.

Fortress of Faith
The pope is besieged by Protestants in this portrayal of the Wars of Religion.

François I
France's strongest Renaissance king made the Loire his hunting playground. His great confidence is captured here by François Clouet of Tours (see p23).

Colonnades were a feature of the Classical Renaissance style.

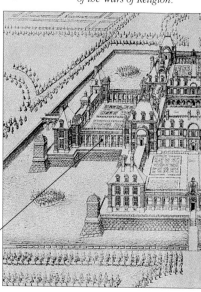

The First Tank Design
Da Vinci spent his last years at Le Clos-Lucé (see p111). This tank is a model of one of the inventions he worked on there.

THE IDEAL CHÂTEAU

From Charles VIII (1483–98) onwards, French Renaissance kings dreamt of creating the ideal château. The symmetrical vistas of this plan by Androuet du Cerceau display a late-Renaissance stylistic move towards Classical grandeur.

TIMELINE

1484 Etats Généraux, a national assembly, meets at Tours

1493 Charles VIII redesigns his birthplace, the Château d'Amboise, in Italian style

1498 Duke of Orléans is crowned Louis XII and marries Anne of Brittany

1515 François I conquers Milan and invites Italian artists to the Loire

1532 Treaty binds Brittany and Nantes to France

1475 | **1500** | **1525**

Charles VIII, France's first Renaissance king

1508 Louis XII remodels Blois as Renaissance royal capital

Cellini's saltcellar for François I (1515–47)

1519 François I begins building Chambord. Leonardo da Vinci dies at Le Clos-Lucé (see p111)

1491 Marriage of Charles VIII to Anne of Brittany links autonomous Brittany to French crown

Henri IV

Brave, astute and likeable, Henri IV of Vendôme and Navarre, France's first Bourbon king, reasserted the authority of the crown over a disintegrating kingdom within 10 years of his accession in 1589. Rubens (1577–1640) shows him receiving a betrothal portrait of Marie de Médicis.

WHERE TO SEE RENAISSANCE LOIRE

Fine Renaissance buildings can be seen throughout the region. Older châteaux that reflect the Italian influence include Amboise (p110) and Blois (pp126–7). The most delightful achievements of the French Renaissance are Chenonceau (pp106–9) and Azay-le-Rideau (pp96–7). Smaller examples, such as Beauregard (pp130–31), are widespread. Undoubtedly the most spectacular is Chambord (pp132–5).

Château de Chambord
This impressive château sits on the banks of the River Cosson.

High roofs and dormers show the persisting French influence.

An arcaded central courtyard formed the basis of 15th-century palaces in the Italian style.

Anne of Brittany's Reliquary

By marrying successively Charles VIII and Louis XII, Anne of Brittany, whose reliquary is in Nantes (see p191), welded her fiercely independent duchy to France.

Diane de Poitiers

The mistress of Henri II was flatteringly portrayed as Diana, the Roman goddess of the hunt.

1559 Death of Henri II begins power struggle between his widow, Catherine de Médicis, and anti-Protestant followers of the Duc de Guise

1572 Court moves to Fontainebleau after St Bartholomew's Day massacre of Protestants

1576 Henri, Duc de Guise, founds pro-Catholic Holy League. Meeting of Etats Généraux at Blois fails to find a peace formula

1598 Edict of Nantes establishes Protestant rights of worship

1550

1575

1547 Henri II begins reign and gives Chenonceau to his mistress, Diane de Poitiers

1562 Wars of Religion start with major battles and massacres along the Loire

1588 Holy League virtually takes over government. Henri III has Duc de Guise and his brother murdered at Blois

Coin of Henri IV "the Great"

1594 Protestant Henri IV crowned at Chartres after becoming Catholic to end the Wars of Religion

Growth and Prosperity

The Loire lost its central role in French politics when the focus of court life moved to the Paris region at the end of the 16th century. The Vendée, however, was the centre during the French Revolution of a violent popular uprising against Republican excesses, including rising taxes, the persecution of priests and conscription. River trade remained important, especially for the increasingly wealthy port of Nantes. As early as the 17th century, work had begun on canals to connect Nantes and the Loire directly with Paris, of which Eiffel's 19th-century bridge-canal at Briare was the aesthetic high point. Although industry grew slowly, the region remained predominantly agricultural.

19TH-CENTURY WATERWAYS

— *Rivers*

— *Canals built before 1900*

Cardinal Richelieu
As Louis XIII's chief minister between 1624 and 1642, Cardinal Richelieu helped to establish orderly government in France.

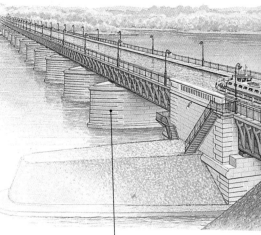

The 15 granite piers supporting the structure were bedded using early compressed-air techniques.

Winemaking in the Loire
Winemaking in the 18th century remained a pastime for the idle rich, who used badly paid peasants to harvest and press the grapes.

TIMELINE

1610–16 Regency of Henri IV's widow, Marie de Médicis, over Louis XIII

1617 Louis XIII banishes his mother to Blois. They are reconciled by Richelieu in 1620

1631 Richelieu starts building planned town and château on the Touraine border

1720s Loire again becomes a centre of country life for the nobility

1600

1650

1700

Louis XIII

1648–53 La Fronde: a series of French civil wars

17th-century watch made in Blois

1685 Saumur and other cities lose Huguenot population as these terrorized Protestants flee after Louis XIV's revocation of the Edict of Nantes

Vendée Hero
Bonchamps' plea to spare Republican prisoners (see p187) was depicted in stone by David d'Angers.

Loire "Inexplosibles"
Faced by competition from the railways, 19th-century steamboats were a last attempt to maintain the Loire's role as a great French trade route.

Graceful lamps above the wide pavements provide a Parisian boulevard touch.

Passage Pommeraye
The elegance of this 19th-century shopping arcade reflected the wealth of Nantes.

BRIARE BRIDGE-CANAL
Gustave Eiffel designed this 662-m (725-yd) bridge to carry canal traffic safely across the Loire. Opened in 1896, it completed a grand waterway system begun in the 17th century linking the Loire, Seine and Rhône rivers. The metal structure used new steel technology.

Steam Omnibus
In 1873, Amédée Bollée's l'Obéissante was the first car to be built in Le Mans.

1756 Royal College of Surgeons founded at Tours

1789 French Revolution

1793–4 Vendée Uprising

1846 Paris railway reaches Tours

1897 Opening of Eiffel's bridge-canal spanning the Loire at Briare

1852 Napoléon III crowned emperor

1856 Great flood of the Loire

750   1800   1850

1770–90 Nantes reaches peak of mercantile wealth

1804 Napoléon makes La Roche-sur-Yon the capital of pacified Vendée and funds drainage of the eastern Marais Poitevin

1829 First Loire steamboat, *Le Loire*, travels from Nantes to Angers in 16 hours

The Vendée heart emblem

1863 Last Loire steamboat company closes

1870 Franco-Prussian War drives Napoléon III into exile

1873 Amédée Bollée begins manufacturing steam-driven cars at Le Mans

The Modern Era

Fruits of the Loire Valley

Although ship-building reached a peak at Nantes and St-Nazaire in the 1920s, and light industry expanded steadily around Orléans, Le Mans and Angers, the region did not become prosperous until after World War II. Its larger cities were occupied by the Germans in 1940 and many were bombed in 1944. Since the 1960s, when the recovery gathered momentum, tourism has supplemented the Loire's traditional strength as the "Garden of France". Private châteaux have been opened to the public, and the state has funded major restoration schemes, as at the Abbaye de Fontevraud.

Wilbur Wright
The pioneer US flying ace galvanized European aviation when he demonstrated this commercial prototype near Le Mans in 1908.

Dramatic fireworks light up the night sky.

TGV Links
With stops at Vendôme, Tours, Angers and Nantes, the Loire is well served by France's TGV (Train à Grande Vitesse) network.

Orléans, 1944
Bridges across the River Loire were prime bombing targets at both the beginning and the end of World War II.

SON ET LUMIERE
Puy-du-Fou's Cinéscénie laser spectacle updates a tradition begun at Chambord in 1952 by Robert Houdin, son of a famous Blois magician. Evening performances draw thousands to Amboise, Blois, Chenonceau and other great châteaux (see pp42–3).

TIMELINE

1900	1910	1920	1930	1940	1950

1905 Loire farming in decline as falling wheat prices follow damage to vines from phylloxera

1908 Wilbur Wright stages test flights at Auvours near Le Mans

1920 Cheverny opens to the public

1923 First 24-hour race at Le Mans

1936 Renault opens Le Mans factory

1944 Liberation of Loire cities ends four-year German occupation

1959 André Malraux ma Minister of Cultural Affai He speeds up restorati work on Loire monume

Alain-Fournier (1886-1914)

1914 World War I begins. Among the first dead is the writer Alain-Fournier *(see p23)*

1929 Town of La Baule builds promenade and becomes one of France's top beach resorts

1940 German advance forces temporary government to move from Paris to Tours

1952 First son et lumière performance at Chambord

Earth Day Ecology Protests on the Loire
*Environmentally aware locals are committed to
preserving the rich natural resources of the great river.*

Nuclear Power
*The Loire was an early
resource for cooling nuclear
reactors. Avoine, near
Chinon, opened in 1963.*

Computer-controlled lighting
effects, lasers and water jets
add a modern twist.

Le Vinci
*The sensitive modernization of
Tours city centre shows how
old and new architectural
styles can be combined.*

More than 2,000 local residents
volunteer as performers, security
patrols and guides at each
Cinéscénie evening.

Le Mans
*The renowned 24-hour race at Le Mans attracts
motor enthusiasts from around the world.*

1963 First
French nuclear
power station
starts operating
at Avoine

1970s Loire wine
exports, especially
of Muscadet, soar

1989–90 Inauguration of TGV
Atlantique high-speed services
brings Angers within a mere 90
minutes of Paris

2007 Nicolas Sarkozy wins
the presidential election.
He appoints François
Fillon from the Sarthe
as Prime Minister

1970	1980	1990	2000	2010	2020

*Muscadet,
produced
east of
Nantes*

1994 Government dismantles dam
at Maisons Rouges to allow
salmon to reach spawning grounds

2000 The Loire Valley from Chalonnes-
sur-Loire to Sully-sur-Loire is inscribed
on UNESCO's World Heritage list

2002 The euro replaces
the Franc as France's
currency

2012 Socialist François Hollande becomes
French President. Jean-Marc Ayrault, mayor
of Nantes, becomes French Prime Minister.

THE LOIRE VALLEY AREA BY AREA

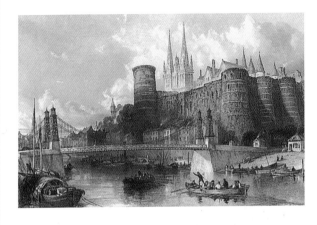

The Loire Valley at a Glance

Rich in history and architecture, the Loire Valley is best known for its sumptuous Renaissance châteaux, such as Chambord and Chenonceau. But the region has also retained the wealth of earlier ages, from Bronze Age dolmens to medieval keeps, such as the Château d'Angers, and an impressive heritage of religious architecture, including the Gothic marvels of Chartres and Bourges cathedrals. Visitors who desire a break from the past can revel in the beauty of the landscape, which contains natural surprises such as the lush Marais Poitevin. In a region packed with delights, those shown here are among the very best.

The Gothic spires of Chartres Cathedral, which tower over an attractive town *(see pp172–5)*

NORTH OF THE LOIRE

The Château d'Angers, protected by its formidable curtain walls *(see pp74–7)*

Angers •

ANJOU

• Nantes

• Cholet

LOIRE-ATLANTIQUE AND THE VENDEE

La Roche-sur-Yon •

Abbaye de Fontevraud, the largest medieval abbey complex in France *(see pp86–7)*

0 kilometres   50

0 miles   50

The Marais Poitevin, a labyrinth of shady canals contrasting with rich fields of painstakingly reclaimed land *(see pp182–5)*

◁ Tree-lined avenue at the Château de Blanville

The memorable François I Renaissance staircase of the Château de Blois (see pp126–7)

Chambord, the largest royal residence in the Loire (see pp132–5)

Bourges Cathedral, a Gothic masterpiece (see pp152–3)

Chartres

ns

Orléans

BLESOIS AND ORLEANAIS

Blois

Tours

TOURAINE

BERRY

Bourges

Châteauroux

Chenonceau, stretching languidly across the River Cher (see pp106–9)

The graceful symmetry of Azay-le-Rideau (see pp96–7)

Villandry's spectacular reconstructed Renaissance gardens (see pp94–5)

ANJOU

The landscape of Anjou is as gentle and pleasant as its climate and its people. The region's rolling plains are intersected by a network of rivers, which help to irrigate the already fertile land. North of the city of Angers, the confluence of the Sarthe, Mayenne and Loir rivers forms a great flood-plain in the winter months and is a regular port of call for thousands of migrating birds.

The creamy limestone, or tufa, used to build the great châteaux of Anjou combines with black roof slates to give Angevin architecture its distinctive look. Tufa quarrying has created hundreds of caves. Many are now used for growing mushrooms, and others have been transformed into troglodyte dwellings, some of which are open to visitors.

Some of the Loire Valley's finest fruits and vegetables are grown here. Trees and flowers also flourish; the rose gardens of Doué are legendary. The region's vines produce not just white, red and rosé wines, but also the sparkling wines of Saumur and St-Cyr-en-Bourg. Visitors can see the complicated process of the *méthode champenoise* first-hand by visiting the major wine houses around Saumur.

Anjou is steeped in the history of the powerful rival dynasties of medieval France. Then, as now, Angers, dominated by its barrel-chested fortress, was the centre of the region. The city was a feudal centre of the Plantagenets, among them Henry of Anjou, who became Henry II of England. Fifteen of the family, including Henry II, his wife, Eleanor of Aquitaine, and their famous son, Richard the Lionheart, are buried at Fontevraud Abbey. Nearby, Saumur's château formed the fairy-tale backdrop to the "September" miniature in the 15th-century masterpiece, *Les Très Riches Heures du Duc de Berry*. Other impressive châteaux in this region include Brissac, the tallest château in the Loire, and Le Plessis-Bourré, a charming pre-Renaissance château.

Château de Saumur, towering above the town and the River Loire

◁ Cattle resting in an Anjou meadow

Exploring Anjou

Northern Anjou is crossed by the Mayenne, Sarthe and Loir rivers, flowing southwards to their convergence in the River Maine. Angers, the geographical and administrative centre of the region, straddles the Maine 8 km (5 miles) before it flows into the Loire. Anjou's most famous châteaux, antiquities and troglodyte sites are located around Angers and Saumur, 50 km (30 miles) up the Loire. But there are also dozens of lesser-known châteaux, clustered around Segré in the northwest and Baugé in the northeast.

SEE ALSO

- **Where to Stay** p202
- **Where to Eat** pp214–15

Eglise St-Maurille, Chalonnes-sur-Loire

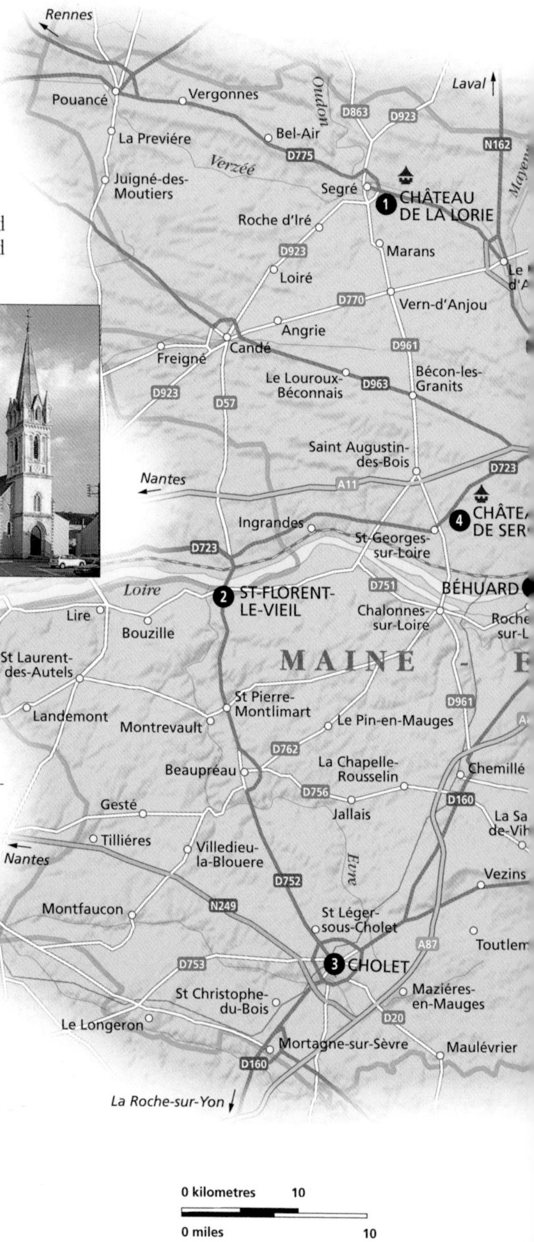

SIGHTS AT A GLANCE

Tour

Rennes

Pouancé
Vergonnes
Laval
La Previère
Bel-Air
D863 D923
N162
Juigné-des-Moutiers
Verzée
Segré ❶ CHÂTEAU DE LA LORIE
Roche d'Iré
D775
Marans
D923
Le
d'A
Loiré
Vern-d'Anjou
D770
Angrie
Freigné Candé
D961
Bécon-les-Granits
Le Louroux-Béconnais
D923 D57 D963
Nantes
Saint Augustin-des-Bois
Ingrandes
A11
D723
St-Georges-sur-Loire
❹ CHÂTE DE SER
Loire
Lire
❷ ST-FLORENT-LE-VIEIL
D751
BÉHUARD
Bouzille
Chalonnes-sur-L
Roche sur-L
St Laurent-des-Autels
MAINE - F
Landemont
Montrevault
St Pierre-Montlimart
D961
D762
La Chapelle-Rousselin
Le Pin-en-Mauges
Chemillé
Beaupréau
D756 D160
La Sa de-Vih
Gesté
Jallais
Tilliéres
Villedieu-la-Blouère
Vezins
Nantes
D752
Eure
Montfaucon
N249
St Léger-sous-Cholet
A87
Toutlem
❸ CHOLET
D753
St Christophe-du-Bois
Maziéres-en-Mauges
Le Longeron
D20
Maulévrier
D160
Mortagne-sur-Sèvre
La Roche-sur-Yon

0 kilometres 10

0 miles 10

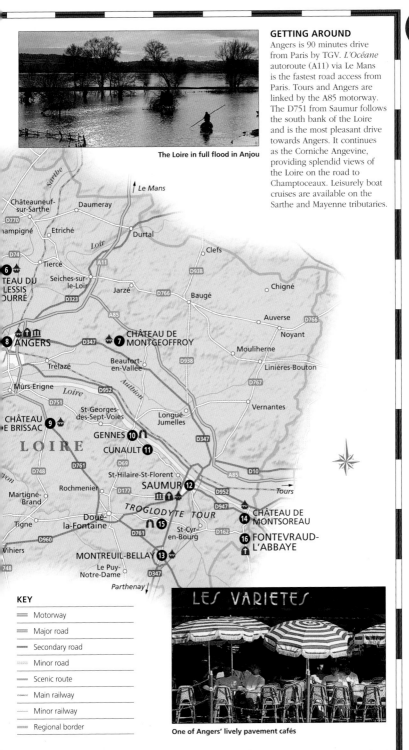

The Loire in full flood in Anjou

GETTING AROUND

Angers is 90 minutes drive from Paris by TGV. *L'Océane* autoroute (A11) via Le Mans is the fastest road access from Paris. Tours and Angers are linked by the A85 motorway. The D751 from Saumur follows the south bank of the Loire and is the most pleasant drive towards Angers. It continues as the Corniche Angevine, providing splendid views of the Loire on the road to Champtoceaux. Leisurely boat cruises are available on the Sarthe and Mayenne tributaries.

One of Angers' lively pavement cafés

KEY

═══	Motorway
═══	Major road
━━━	Secondary road
┄┄┄	Minor road
━━━	Scenic route
⌇⌇⌇	Main railway
────	Minor railway
═══	Regional border

St-Florent-le-Vieil's 18th-century church, on a hill above the old town

Château de la Lorie ❶

Road map B3. 🚌 *Segré, then taxi.*
Tel *02 41 92 10 04.* ◯ *Jul–mid-Sep: Wed–Mon; groups by appt.* 🅿️ ♿
www.chateaudelalorie.net

Elegant gardens in the 18th-century French style introduce this dry-moated château, 2 km (1 mile) southeast of the old town of Segré on the River Oudon. The original building, which is embellished by a statue of the Roman goddess Minerva over the central door, was built during the 17th century by René le Pelletier, provost-general of Anjou.

A century later, two wings were added to form a courtyard, together with an ornate marble ballroom. This *pièce de résistance* is crowned with a musicians' gallery located in an overhead rotunda. It was completed by Italian craftsmen in 1779, only a few short years before the French Revolution put an end to these types of extravagant shows of wealth and personal power.

St-Florent-le-Vieil ❷

Road map B3. 🏘️ *2,700.* 🚉 *Varades, then taxi.* 🚌 🏢 *4 pl de la Févrière (02 41 72 62 32).* 🎭 *Festival de Musique, Les Orientales (mid-Jun–mid-Jul).* **www**.ville-saintflorentlevieil.fr

A walk through the narrow streets of the old town, lined with buildings dating from the 16th to the 18th centuries, ends atop a hill with magnificent views over the Loire Valley. Here stands a large, 18th-century church, the scene of dramatic events during the Vendée Uprising. The Uprising began in March 1793, with a mass revolt against conscription into the Republican army.

Seven months later, the Royalist army, beaten at Cholet, crossed the Loire here with 40,000 troops and at least as many supporters. They planned to kill more than 4,000 Republicans held in the church, but were stopped by one of their leaders, the Marquis de Bonchamps, who cried, "Spare the prisoners," as he lay dying. Among those

---

THE CORNICHE ANGEVINE

One of the most scenic routes in the region, the Corniche Angevine (D751) curves along the cliffs above the south side of the Loire through western Anjou, offering lovely views of the islands that break up the river in this area, and of the opposite bank, with its fertile vineyards and beautiful manor houses. The road is never more than hilly and has a pleasantly rural feel as it runs alongside the Louet (a tributary of the Loire), flanked by vineyards and fields.

Chalonnes-sur-Loire, at the western end, is an ancient village with a graceful church, the Eglise St-Maurille, parts of which date back to the 12th century. The quay beside the church is a good place to stop for a picnic. Further along, La Haie Longue has particularly pretty views across the river. At the eastern end of the Corniche Angevine, the town of Rochefort-sur-Loire has a 15th-century bell-tower and a square of old turreted houses. Powerful fortresses once stood on outcrops of rock below the village, and the ruins of some of them can be explored.

The view across the river at La Haie Longue

saved was the father of the sculptor David d'Angers, whose marble statue of Bonchamps was placed in the church in 1825 *(see p57)*. Stained-glass windows in the chancel recount the story, as does the **Musée d'Histoire Locale et des Guerres de Vendée**.

🏛 **Musée d'Histoire Locale et des Guerres de Vendée**
Place J et M Source.
Tel 02 41 72 62 32. ◯ *May–Jun: Sat & Sun pm only; Jul–mid-Sep: daily pm.* 🖼

Emile Boutigny's 1899 depiction of the Vendée Uprising in Cholet

Cholet ❸

Road map B4. 🏘 *57,000.* 🚊 🚌
ℹ *14 av Maudet (02 41 49 80 00).*
🅿 *Sat.* 🎭 *Carnaval de Cholet (Apr); Festival des Arlequins (Apr–May); L'Eté Cigale (Jun–mid-Sep).*
www.ot-cholet.fr

Capital of the Mauges region and second city of Anjou, Cholet was a thriving town until 1793 when it lost half of its population in the Vendée Uprising *(see p187)*. Its revival was testimony to the strength

The tomb of the Marquis de Vaubrun in Serrant's chapel

of the area's textile industry. Cholet's red handkerchiefs with white borders are souvenirs of a crucial battle. The Vendée Uprising is commemorated in the city's **Musée d'Art et d'Histoire**.

🏛 **Musée d'Art et d'Histoire**
27 av de l'Abreuvoir. *Tel 02 72 77 23 20.* ◯ *Wed–Sun (Jul–Aug: Wed–Mon).* ◐ *1 Jan, 1 May, 25 Dec.* 🖼 ♿

Château de Serrant ❹

Road map B3. 🚊 *Angers, then taxi.*
Tel 02 41 39 13 01. ◯ *mid-Mar–Jun: Wed–Sat pm only, Sun all day; Jun–mid-Sep: daily; mid-Sep–mid-Nov: Wed–Mon.* 🖼 🎫
www.chateau-serrant.net

The most westerly of the great Loire châteaux, the privately-owned Serrant was begun in 1546 and developed in an entirely harmonious style over the next three centuries. Its pale tufa and dark schist façades, with massive corner towers topped by cupolas, create an air of dignity. Inside, the central pavilion contains one of the most beautiful Renaissance staircases in the

region. The château also has 18th-century furniture, Flemish tapestries, and a library of some 12,000 books.
Serrant's most famous owner was the Marquis de Vaubrun, whose death in battle (1675) is commemorated by a magnificent tomb in the chapel, sculpted by Antoine Coysevox. The Irish Jacobite family of Walsh, shipowners at Nantes, owned Serrant in the 18th century, and the château displays a painting of Bonnie Prince Charlie bidding farewell to Anthony Walsh, whose ship took the prince to Scotland.
In 1830 Serrant passed to the Duc de la Trémoille. His descendents still own it today.

A statue of the Madonna, set in the church wall at Béhuard

Béhuard ❺

Road map C3. 🏘 *110.* 🚌 *Baiche Maine, then taxi.* ℹ *Angers tourist office (02 41 23 50 00).*

The narrow lanes of the medieval village on this delightful island in the Loire were made for pilgrims visiting a tiny church fitted into an outcrop of rock. It is dedicated to the safety of sailors navigating the often treacherous river.
The lovely wine village of Savenniéres on the north bank of the Loire, opposite Béhuard is also worth a visit. Its vineyards produce delicious Chenin Blanc white wines that are sold at some of the gorgeous, walled properties in the area.

The south façade of Château de Serrant, with huge corner towers

Château du Plessis-Bourré ❻

Road map C3. 🚄 *Angers, then taxi.* **Tel** *02 41 32 06 72.* ⏰ *mid-Feb, Mar, Oct & Nov: Thu–Tue pm only; Apr–Jun & Sep: Fri–Tue, pm Thu; Jul–Aug: daily.* ● *Dec–Jan.* 🏛️ 📷 www.plessis-bourre.com

Set in a moat so wide it looks more like a lake, Château du Plessis-Bourré, with its silvery-white walls and dark slate roofs, seems to float on the water. Built in five years from 1468, it is the least altered and perhaps even the most perfect example of the work of Jean Bourré, whose home it was. As advisor and treasurer to

the king of France, Bourré also oversaw the creation of Langeais *(see p92)* and Jarzé and was influential in the transformation of Loire castles from fortresses into pleasure palaces. The Château du Plessis-Bourré itself is well defended, but its fortifications do not interfere with a design that is orientated towards gracious living. Its wonderful condition stands as a testament to the quality of the materials used in its construction and to the skills of the craftsmen who created it.

After crossing a long, seven-arched bridge, visitors enter the château's arcaded courtyard

Ceiling of the Salle des Gardes

by one of four working drawbridges. The state rooms are surprisingly light and airy, with finely carved stone decoration. An astounding painted ceiling in the Salle des Gardes depicts many allegorical and alchemical scenes, including a lively representation of the demon-wolf Chicheface, emaciated because she could eat only wives who always obeyed their husbands. Some furniture, mainly dating from the 18th century, is displayed. During the French Revolution, coats of arms on the library fireplace were defaced, and graffiti can still be seen.

Château du Plessis-Bourré, set in its wide moat

BIRD-WATCHING IN THE BASSES VALLÉES ANGEVINES

At the confluence of the Sarthe, Loir and Mayenne rivers, some 4,500 ha (11,100 acres) of land, the Basses Vallées Angevines, are flooded between October and May each year. Thousands of migrating birds visit the area, making it an exceptional bird-watching site.

Perhaps the rarest visitor is the elusive corncrake, which arrives in the grasslands during April. There are more than 300

breeding pairs in the area, making it one of the best sites in western Europe. Protection of this species is aided by enlightened local farming methods, such as late hay harvests.

Insects in the meadows, ditches and rivers attract swifts, hobbys, whinchats and yellow wagtails. In early summer the Basses Vallées resound with birdsong and in the evenings the strange call of the corncrake can be heard.

The flood-plains of Anjou at twilight

For hotels and restaurants in this region see p202 and pp214–15

Château de Montgeoffroy ⑦

Road map C3. 🚊 *Angers or Saumur, then taxi.* 🚌 **Tel** *02 41 80 60 02.* 🕐 *mid-Mar– mid-Nov: daily.* 📷 🎫 **www**.chateaudemontgeoffroy.com

Montgeoffroy is a masterpiece of late 18th-century style, built for the Maréchal de Contades by the architect Nicolas Barré between 1773 and 1775, and beautifully preserved by his descendants. The château is a model of balance, with subtle blue and grey harmonies of stone and paintwork, tall French windows and a lovely park.

The central building is flanked by flat-roofed pavilions, which connect two side wings to the main house. The wings are both rounded off with towers built in the 16th century. One tower houses a harness room smelling of fresh Norwegian spruce, leading to magnificent stables and a fine display of carriages. The chapel in the opposite wing is also 16th-century.

The symmetrical façade of the Château de Montgeoffroy

Hérault de Séchelles by Hubert Drouais

Next to the main house, the kitchen has a collection of 260 copper and pewter pots.

The charming principal rooms are alive with pictures, tapestries and furniture made especially for the château. An innovation in the dining room is a porcelain stove fashioned in the shape of a palm tree, brought from Strasbourg where the *maréchal* (marshal) was governor. His crossed batons are used as a decorative motif in the superbly positioned Grand Salon. The marshal's "friend", Madame Hérault, had her own rooms, where a portrait of their "natural" grandson, Marie-Jean Hérault de Séchelles, can be seen.

Montgeoffroy's stables, where the collection of carriages is housed

---

BIRD SPECIES

In winter, resident ducks, coots and cormorants are joined by geese and swans at the margins and golden plovers in the fields. February sees the arrival of the black-tailed godwits. Pintail ducks, greylag geese, lapwings and black-headed gulls also appear for a time, as do waders such as ruff, snipe, redshank and dunlin. In summer, the meadows dry out, and things are quieter.

Snipe

Lapwing

Golden plover

BIRD-WATCHER'S CHECKLIST

Road map C3. 🚊 *Angers, then taxi.* ℹ️ *Ligue pour la Protection des Oiseaux, Maison de la Confluence, 10 rue du Port-Boulet, Bouchemaine (02 41 44 44 22).* 🔦 *Day, night and weekend outings.* 📷 *By reservation for LPO programmes.* **www**.lpo-anjou.org
Best viewing area (Feb–late Jul): confluence of Loir and Sarthe rivers, southwest of Briollay. Take the D107 from Angers to Cantenay-Epinard. Turn right just before the village and follow signs for Le Vieux Cantenay. Return to the D107 via Vaux. Continue north to Noyant, where all of the little roads across the meadows lead to the River Sarthe. Return to Noyant and head for Les Chapelles and Soulaire-et-Bourg. Then take the D109 to Briollay if the road is passable.

Angers ❽

Situated on the River Maine, only 8 km (5 miles) before it joins the Loire, Angers was once the power base for Foulques Nerra (*see pp50–51*) and the other notorious medieval counts of Anjou. By the 12th century, under the rule of the Plantagenets, Angers became a key stronghold of an empire stretching as far as Scotland. Today, it is a thriving university town, with wide boulevards, beautiful public gardens and narrow older streets evocative of its long history.

Angers Cathedral carving

Exploring Angers

Angers is divided into two sections by the River Maine. The oldest part is on the east bank of the river, guarded by the fortress-like 13th-century **Château d'Angers** (*see pp74–5*). Shielded inside the château's massive walls are the Apocalypse Tapestries, the oldest and largest of France's tapestries, dating from the 14th century (*see pp76–7*). Nearby is the Maison des Vins de Loire, which offers an introduction to the region's wines, and the **Cathédrale St-Maurice**.

Angers has 46 timber-framed houses, most of them near the cathedral. The best is the **Maison d'Adam**, on place Ste-Croix. This 15th-century merchant's house is decorated with carved wooden figures of sirens, musicians and lovers.

On the right bank of the River Maine, the old quarter of **La Doutre** (*"d'outre Maine"*, or "the other side of the Maine") is well worth a visit. Its most famous building is the medieval hospital, now home to a collection of modern tapestries (*see p77*).

A rewarding stroll from rue Gay-Lussac to place de la Laiterie passes many of La Doutre's historic buildings. Included among them are the elegant **Hôtel des Pénitentes** (once a refuge for reformed prostitutes), a 12th-century **apothecary's house** and the restored church of **La Trinité**, which adjoins the ruins of Foulques Nerra's Romanesque **Abbaye du Ronceray** – a Benedictine abbey reserved for daughters of the nobility. A little way south down the Maine is Angers' old port. It has been revived and an attractive area has grown up around it, full of restaurants, and cafés. Le Quai, a major arts complex with an impressive theatre can also be found here.

🅐 Cathédrale St-Maurice
pl Freppel. **Tel** 02 41 87 58 45. ⬜ *daily.*
This striking cathedral was built at the end of the 12th century, although the central lantern tower was added during the Renaissance period. The façade's Gothic sculptures are impressive.

Maison d'Adam, the best of Angers' timber-framed houses

The elegant Angevin vaulting in the nave and the transept is one of the best, and earliest, examples of its kind, and gives a dome-like shape to the high ceiling. The cathedral's interior is lit through glowing stained glass, which includes a stunningly beautiful rose window in the northern transept that dates from the 15th century.

🏛 Musée des Beaux Arts
14 rue du Musée. **Tel** 02 41 05 38 00. ⬜ *mid-May–mid-Sep: 10am–6:30pm daily; mid-Sep–mid-May: 10am–noon, 2–6pm Tue–Sun.* 🔵 *pub hols.* 🈳 ♿
www.musees.angers.fr

The museum is arranged according to two themes: the history of Angers told through works of art from Neolithic to modern times; and fine arts from the 14th century. Don't miss the intriguing display of religious antiquities on the first floor, including a lapidary Cross of Anjou and a beautiful 13th-century copper-gilt mask of a woman.

🅐 Collégiale St-Martin
23 rue St-Martin. **Tel** 02 41 81 16 00. ⬜ *Jun–Sep: 10am–7pm daily; Oct–May: 1–6pm Tue–Sun.* 🈳 ♿
www.collegiale-saint-martin.fr
This 9th-century church was reopened in 2006 after 20 years of restoration. It now houses a superb collection of religious statues dating from the 14th century, including a delightful representation of the Virgin preparing to suckle the infant Jesus.

One of the many beautiful public gardens in Angers

COINTREAU

Angers, the city of Cointreau, produces some 15 million litres of the famous liqueur every year. The distillery was founded in 1849 by the Cointreau brothers, local confectioners well known around Angers for their exotic, curative tonics. But it was Edouard, the son of one of them, who created the original recipe. The flavour of this unique colourless liqueur is artfully based on sweet and bitter orange peels.

The Hôpital St-Jean houses *Le Chant du Monde*, a set of extraordinary tapestries, by artist Jean Lurçat *(see p77)*.

Galerie David d'Angers

33 bis, rue Toussaint. *Tel* 02 41 05 38 90. mid-May–mid-Sep: 10am–6:30pm daily; mid-Sep–mid-May: 10am–noon, 2–6pm Tue–Sun. public hols.

The glassed-over ruins of the 13th-century abbey church of Toussaint are filled with plaster casts of the work of local sculptor Pierre-Jean David (1788–1856), known as David d'Angers. His idealized busts and figures were much in demand as memorials for people such as the Marquis de Bonchamps *(see p57)*. They are forceful examples of Academic art.

Sculpture by David d'Angers

Musée Jean Lurçat et de la Tapisserie Contemporaine

4 bd Arago. *Tel* 02 41 24 18 45. mid-May–mid-Sep: 10am–6:30pm daily; mid-Sep–mid-May: 10am–noon, 2–6pm Tue–Sun. public hols.

A Gothic masterpiece in La Doutre, this graceful building functioned as a hospital until 1875, the oldest surviving one in France. It was founded in 1175 by Henry II of England, and the Plantagenet coat of arms is displayed with the Anjou heraldry inside the entrance to the grounds. A reconstruction of the dispensary occupies one corner of the Salle des Malades, and a chapel and 12th-century cloisters can also be visited.

Musée Cointreau

Bd des Brétonnières, St. Barthélémy d'Anjou. *Tel* 02 41 31 50 50. May–Oct: 11am–6pm daily; Nov–Apr: 11am–6pm Tue–Sat. Jan, 25 Dec.

From a walkway high above the alambics and bottling machines, visitors can observe the production processes involved in the creation of Cointreau here. The 90-minute tour takes you round the distillery, in the St. Barthélémy district of Angers, ending up with a *dégustation* of the famous orange-flavoured liqueur. Thousands of objects, documents, photos, publicity posters and films illustrate the long history of the company and its famous square bottle.

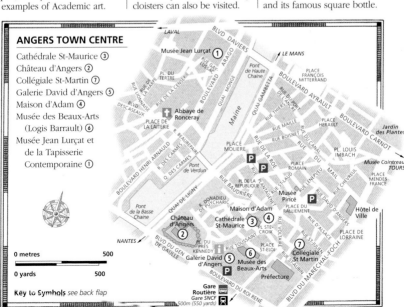

ANGERS TOWN CENTRE

Cathédrale St-Maurice ③
Château d'Angers ②
Collégiale St-Martin ⑦
Galerie David d'Angers ⑤
Maison d'Adam ④
Musée des Beaux-Arts (Logis Barrault) ⑥
Musée Jean Lurçat et de la Tapisserie Contemporaine ①

0 metres 500

0 yards 500

Key to Symbols *see back flap*

Château d'Angers

The huge drum towers and curtain walls of this powerful feudal fortress were built on the site of Count Foulques Nerra's stronghold between 1228 and 1240. The work was begun at the behest of Blanche of Castille, the mother of Louis IX and regent during his youth. Within the 650-m (2,100-ft) perimeter, later nobles developed a château lifestyle in almost playful contrast to the forbidding outer towers. The last duke of Anjou, King René I, added charming buildings, gardens, aviaries and a menagerie. After several centuries as a prison, the citadel-château now houses France's most famous tapestries.

The Logis du Gouverneur was built in the 15th century and modified in the 18th century. It now houses a restaurant and reception areas.

★ **Moat Gardens**
The dry moat, which is a remarkable 11 m (36 ft) deep and 30 m (98 ft) wide, is now filled with a series of geometric flower beds.

Fortress Towers
The 17 towers rise up to 40 m (131 ft) in height. They lost their pepper pot roofs and were shortened during the 16th century to adapt them for the use of artillery.

Formal gardens have been planted in the great courtyard.

The drawbridge leading to the Porte de la Ville (Town Gate) is the entrance to the château.

TIMELINE

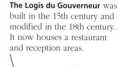

Henry III

	1200	1300	1400	1500	1600	1700	1800	1900

1230–40 Fortress built on a rocky spur, where counts of Anjou had built older castles

1410 Louis II and Yolande of Aragon reconstruct chapel and Logis Royal

1945 Allied bombers damage fortress, in use as a German munitions base

1648–52 Louis XIV turns fortress into a prison.

1360 Louis I of Anjou cuts doors and windows to relieve the grimness of the walls

1450–65 René I renovates interior, adding gardens and new buildings

1585 Fortress taken by Huguenots. Henri III wants towers demolished but governor merely lowers them

1875 Declared a historic monument

1952–54 Bernard Vitry builds gallery to house Apocalypse Tapestries

★ **Apocalypse Tapestries**
*Bernard Vitry's modern
Galerie de l'Apocalypse
displays the Apocalypse
Tapestries (see pp76–7).*

The King's Window depicts
René I, king of Naples, and his
wife, Jeanne de Laval, kneeling
before the Virgin.

VISITORS' CHECKLIST

Prom du Bout du Monde.
Tel 02 41 86 48 77. May–
Aug: 9:30am–6:30pm daily; Sep–
Apr: 10am–5:30pm. 1 Jan,
1 May, 1 Nov, 11 Nov, 25 Dec.
http://angers.
monuments-nationaux.fr

**Walkways along the wide
walls** stretch for more than a
kilometre (¾ mile). There are
fine views of the town, as well
as some beautiful gardens.

The towers
are ascended
by spiral
staircases.

The Logis Royal,
built for King René,
houses the Apocalypse
Tapestries *(see p76).*

★ **Châtelet**
*Built in 1450 by René I, the
gatehouse still retains its
charming pepper pot roofs.*

★ **Ducal Oratory**
*The ducal oratory
opens on to
the Chapelle
St-Geneviève.
Equipped with a
fireplace, it was
used by the duke
and members of
his family.*

STAR FEATURES

★ Apocalypse
Tapestries

★ Ducal Oratory

★ Moat Gardens

★ Châtelet

The Tapestries at Angers

The Apocalypse Tapestries, made in the 14th century for
Duke Louis I of Anjou, illustrate the visions of St John
from the Bible's Book of Revelation. During the French
Revolution, the tapestries were thrown out, cut up and
used for anything from bed canopies to horse blankets.
Restoration began in the mid-19th century. Acclaimed
as a masterpiece, the surviving sections of this work
stretch for 103 m (338 ft) along a specially-built gallery
in the Château d'Angers. Nearly 600 years after their
creation, they inspired Jean Lurçat to design his own
tapestry sequence, called *Le Chant du Monde*.

Detailed Work
*Each of the devils devouring
Babylon has a distinct
character. The tapestries
were woven so skilfully that
the front and the back are
almost mirror images.*

St John appears as
the narrator of
each vision.

An angel dictates to St John in one
of the best-preserved scenes.
Elsewhere, the green textiles have
faded to beige.

THE FALL OF BABYLON

The Apocalypse Tapestries were woven in 1375–83 in Parisian
workshops. Designed by Hennequin de Bruges, who was
inspired by Carolingian manuscript illuminations, they depict
the end of the world and the coming of a New Jerusalem. The
original 90 panels were arranged in 6 chapters, each with an
introductory panel and 14 scenes. Scene 66 depicts the Fall of
Babylon: "Babylon the Great is fallen, is fallen, and is become
the habitation of devils" (Rev. 18:2).

Water is changed to
poisonous wormwood
at the blowing of the
third trumpet in this
cataclysmic scene.

Mille Fleurs Tapestries
These late 15th-century Flemish tapestries are still vibrantly coloured.

Le Chant du Monde

The vast, vaulted medieval interior of the Musée Jean Lurçat *(see p73)* provides a stunning background to *The Song of the World*. This piece, which stretches for 79 m (260 ft) around three sides of the hall, was Lurçat's response to the Apocalypse Tapestries, which he saw for the first time in 1937. The

Jean Lurçat (1892–1966)

ten panels are 4 m (13 ft) high and were woven at workshops in Aubusson between 1957 and 1963. Thematically, the images move from the horrors of Nazi genocide and the bombing of Hiroshima to the conquest of space, conceived as the dawning of a new age.

"Ornamentos Sagrados" from Lurçat's *Le Chant du Monde* tapestry

THE ART OF TAPESTRY

In medieval times, tapestries were a symbol of luxury, commissioned by royal and noble families to adorn châteaux and churches. Hung on the thick stone walls, they helped to keep the vast rooms warm by preventing drafts.

Medieval tapestry weaver

Paris and Flanders were the centres of tapestry work in the 14th century, where highly skilled weavers followed an artist's full-size drawing, called a "cartoon". Threads were stretched vertically (the warp) on a loom to the length of the finished piece, then coloured threads (the weft) were woven horizontally across them.

Tapestry-making declined from the 16th century, but the 20th century has seen a revival, with artists such as Pablo Picasso and Henri Matisse experimenting in the medium.

The tumbling towers of Babylon reveal a nest of demons.

Blue backgrounds alternate with red, providing continuity through the series.

Coloured tapestry threads at the Manufacture St-Jean in Aubusson

Brissac's wine cellars

Château de Brissac **❾**

Brissac-Quincé. **Road map** C3.
🚆 *Angers, then taxi or bus.* 🚌
Tel *02 41 91 22 21.* ◯ *Apr–Jun &
Sep–Oct: Wed–Mon; Jul–Aug: daily;
Nov–Mar: by appointment only.*
● *Jan, 25 & 31 Dec.* 🎫 📷 ♿
📷 🍴 www.brissac.net

The château of the dukes of
Brissac, towering above the
River Aubance 18 km (11 miles)
southeast of Angers, is the
tallest along the Loire, and is
perhaps the grandest still in
private hands. Ownership has
passed down a long family line.

Charles de Cossé, governor
of Paris and marshal of
France, ordered the building
of a vast palace on top of
an earlier fortress, but its
completion was halted by
his death in 1621.

On the entrance façade, an
ornate, 17th-century, domed
pavilion soars to 37 m (120 ft)
between two 15th-century
towers. Fifteen of the 204
rooms are open to the public
and are filled with furniture,
paintings and tapestries.
Among the most striking is
the Salle des Gardes, which
is decorated with Aubusson
tapestries and gilded ceilings.
The room is lit through the
distinctive paned windows
that are a feature of architect
Jacques Corbineau's work.

Other memorable rooms
are Louis XIII's bedroom and
an 1883 opera theatre, still
used for concerts. In the
château's picture gallery hangs
a 19th-century portrait of
Madame Clicquot, matriarch of
the famous champagne house
and a distant ancestor of the
present duke. The castle's fine
grounds can be explored, and
its wines tasted in cellars
dating from the 11th century.

Gennes **❿**

Road map C3. 🏠 *2,000.* 🚆 *Saumur
or Les Rosiers-sur-Loire.* 🛈 *square de
l'Europe (02 41 51 84 14).* 🗓 *Tue.*
www.cc-gennois.fr

During the Gallo-Roman
period *(see pp48–9)* Gennes,
on the south bank of the
River Loire, was an important
religious and commercial
centre. The largest **amphitheatre** in western France was
built on a hillside more
than 1,800 years ago and was
used from the 1st to the 3rd
centuries for gladiatorial
contests. A restoration project
in the 1980s revealed the
sandstone walls and brick
tiers of a stadium that seated
at least 5,000 spectators and
included changing rooms and
an efficient drainage system.
In front of the arena, which
measures 2,160 sq m (2,600
sq yds), marshlands on the
Avort river were probably
flooded for aquatic combats
and displays.

The area around Gennes is
also very rich in Neolithic
sites. Among the 20 ancient
burial chambers and menhirs
nearby is the **Dolmen de la
Madeleine**, one of the largest
in France. Formerly used as a

**The medieval Eglise St-Vétérin in
the town of Gennes**

bakery, it can be found 1 km
(1,100 yds) east, past Gennes'
medieval **Eglise St-Vétérin** on
the D69.

There is a lovely panoramic
view over the Loire from
St-Eusèbe, a ruined church
dating from the 11th to the
15th centuries, sited on a
knoll above the village.
Beside the old nave is a
moving memorial to cadets
of the Saumur cavalry school
(see p83) who died trying
to prevent the German
army crossing the Loire
in June 1940.

A bronze statue of Mercury
has been discovered on the
hill, and this seems to suggest
that a temple to the Roman
god may have stood here in
the Gallo-Roman period.

♯ **Amphithéâtre**
Tel *02 41 51 94 70.*
◯ *groups only and only by
appointment.* 📷

♯ **Dolmen de la Madeleine**
◯ *daily.* ♿ *restricted.*

The Neolithic Dolmen de la Madeleine, near Gennes

Environs

At L'Orbière, 4 km (2½ miles) from Gennes, the late sculptor Jacques Warminsky created a monumental underground work, named *L'Hélice Terrestre* (*The Earth's Helix*), consisting of intriguing, interlinking carved galleries that represent the universal philosophy of the artist.

To the west, in the village of Coutures, another extraordinary underground gallery is to be found at the **Manoir de la Cailliére**. Here, the artist Richard Rak has been creating other worlds and paintings from gathered objects.

⌂ L'Hélice Terrestre
L'Orbière, St-Georges-des-Sept-Voies. **Road map** C3. 🚆 *Saumur, then taxi.* **Tel** 02 41 57 95 92. ◯ *May–Sep: daily; Oct–Apr: daily, pm only (by appt).* 📷

⌂ Manoir de la Cailliére
Coutures. **Tel** 02 41 57 97 97. ◯ *May–Sep: Tue–Sun; Oct–Apr: weekends & public hols, or by reservation.*

Cunault ⓫

Road map C3. 🏠 *1,000.* 🚌 *Saumur.* ℹ️ *Gennes (02 41 51 84 14).* 🎭 *Mois de L'Orgue (May); Les Heures Musicales (Jul & Aug).*

Cunault's pale limestone priory church, the **Eglise Notre-Dame**, has rightly been called the most majestic of all the Romanesque churches in Anjou, if not the whole of the Loire Valley. In the 12th century, Benedictine monks from Tournus in Burgundy built the church in this small village on the south bank of

Artist Jacques Warminsky at work on *L'Hélice Terrestre*

the Loire. They incorporated the bell-tower, dating from the 11th century, from an earlier building. A short spire was added in the 15th century.

Cunault is the longest Romanesque church without a transept in France. Inside, the first impression is of simplicity and elegance. The height of the pillars is impressive; they are topped with 223 carved capitals, decorated with fabulous beasts, demons and religious motifs, and are placed high enough so as not to interfere with the pure architectural lines. Binoculars are needed to see details.

Three aisles of equal width were made to accommodate the crowds of pilgrims who travelled to the church to see its relics, which included one revered as the wedding ring of the Virgin Mary, and the floor is deeply worn beside a 12th-century marble stoup at the foot of the entrance steps. Towards the chancel, the

ambulatory is floored with scalloped terracotta tiles. Traces of 15th-century frescoes remain, including a figure of St Christopher.

Other treasures include some impressive furniture in oak and ash, a 13th-century carved wooden reliquary and a painted 15th-century statue representing St Catherine.

The central aisle of Cunault's majestic 12th-century church

CULTIVATED MUSHROOMS

Around 75 per cent of French cultivated mushrooms come from Anjou. The damp, dark caves in the tufa cliffs along the Loire are the perfect environment for the *champignons de Paris*, so called because they were first cultivated in disused quarries in the Paris region before production began in the Loire Valley in the late 19th century. Today, mushroom cultivation is a thriving business, employing thousands of people in the region. Growers have been diversifying in recent years, cultivating more exotic mushrooms such as *pleurottes* and *shiitake*, in response to demand from food-lovers.

Oyster mushrooms, known as *pleurottes*

Street-by-Street: Saumur ⑫

The storybook château is set on a hill high above the
town, making it easy for visitors to locate Saumur's
old quarter, which lies mainly between the château, the
river and the main street running straight ahead from
the central bridge over the Loire. The twisting streets
that wind up and down the hill on which the château is
built merit exploration. Saumur's modest size, which
suits sightseeing on foot, is only one of the many
charms of this friendly town.

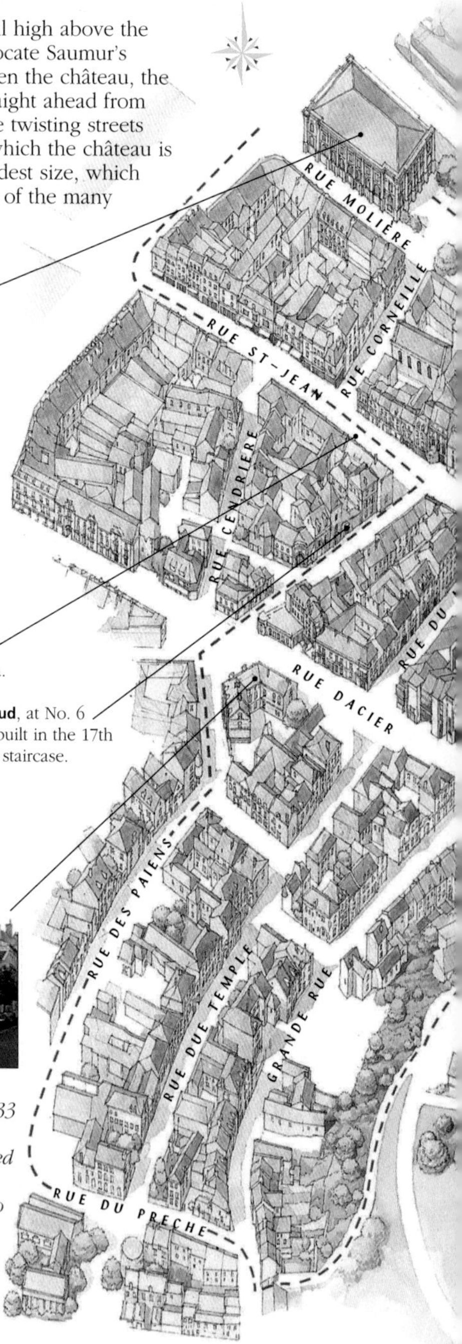

Theatre
*Saumur's theatre, which opened in
the late 19th century, was modelled
on the Odéon in Paris.*

Rue St-Jean is the heart of
Saumur's main shopping area.

The Hôtel des Abbesses de Fontevraud, at No. 6
rue de l'Ancienne-Messagerie, was built in the 17th
century and has a marvellous spiral staircase.

Maison du Roi
*This pretty Renaissance building at No. 33
rue Dacier once housed royalty but is
now the headquarters of the Saumur Red
Cross. In the courtyard is a plaque to
the cultured duke, René I of Anjou, who
often held court at Saumur.*

STAR SIGHTS

★ Château de Saumur

★ Eglise St-Pierre

---

0 metres   50

0 yards   50

For hotels and restaurants in this region see p202 and pp214–15

Hôtel de Ville
The town hall was originally a manor house forming part of the city's fortified river wall. Built in 1508, subsequent restorations and additions have been in keeping with its Gothic style.

VISITORS' CHECKLIST

Road map C3. 🚗 *30,000.*
🚉 *av David d'Angers.* 🚌 *square Balzac.* 🛈 *8 bis quai Carnot (02 41 40 20 60).* 🗓 *Sat.* 🎪 *Carrousel de Saumur (Jul); Les Grandes Tablées (Aug); Festivini (Sep).*

Place St-Pierre
Saumur's oldest half-timbered houses, dating from the 15th century, are situated in place St-Pierre (Nos. 3, 5 and 6).

★ Eglise St-Pierre
First erected in the 12th and 13th centuries, and completed during the 15th and 16th centuries, this church has a fascinating collection of tapestries.

Maison des Compagnons is a 15th-century building at the top of La Montée du Fort, which has been restored by a guild of stonemasons whose apprentices can be seen at work.

★ Château de Saumur
Saumur's château is situated next to the Butte des Moulins, a small hill that was once covered with windmills, and has great views of the surroundings, including a picturesque vineyard to one side.

KEY

 Suggested route

Exploring Saumur

Today, Saumur is best known for its wines, mushrooms and fine horse riders. It was a major power base for the medieval counts and dukes of Anjou, then a refuge for French Protestants in the 16th and 17th centuries, until the revocation of the Edict of Nantes in 1685 forced many Protestants to leave. Saumur has a rich legacy and is a vibrant town today. An excellent self-guided walking tour is available from the tourist office.

Panel from the 15th-century choir stalls in the Eglise St-Pierre

The old quarter

At the heart of Saumur's old quarter stands the **Eglise St-Pierre**, which was built in the late 12th century. Its treasures include the beautifully carved 15th-century wooden stalls in the choir, and the magnificent 16th-century tapestries of the lives of Sts Peter and Florent. The latter was an influential figure in the monastic history of the region. He is depicted being rescued from Roman

The façade of the Eglise Notre-Dame de Nantilly

persecution, slaying a dragon and founding a monastery.

Nearby, the **Grande Rue**'s limestone and slate houses reflect Saumur's prosperity in the late 16th century under Protestant rule. The "Huguenot Pope", Philippe Duplessis-Mornay, who governed the town between 1589 and 1621, owned the house at No. 45.

The oldest church in Saumur, **Notre-Dame de Nantilly**, was the town's principal place of worship for centuries. It too has a fine collection of 16th and 17th-century tapestries, as well as carved capitals and an epitaph composed by the poet-king René I (see p53) to his childhood nurse inscribed on the third pillar on nave's south side.

🏛 La Distillerie Combier

48 rue Beaurepaire.
Tel 02 41 40 23 00.
⬜ Apr, May & Oct: Wed–Sun; Jun–Sep: daily; Nov–Mar: by appt.

www.combier.fr
Since 1834 this distillery has been producing liqueurs according to traditional methods. The recipes remain a well-kept secret, but you can see the process and then have a tasting.

♣ Château de Saumur

Tel 02 41 40 24 40. ⬜ Tue–Sun.
The famous miniature of this château in *Les Très Riches Heures du Duc de Berry* (see p93) shows a white fairy-tale palace. The château was built for Louis I, Duke of Anjou, in the second half of the 14th century. It was constructed on the base of an earlier fortification. The glittering mass of chimney stacks and pinnacles was later

Skyline of the Château de Saumur

simplified to a more sturdy skyline of shortened pencil towers, but the shape of the château remains graceful. The powerful-looking outbuildings that surround the château recall its later, although less pleasant, roles as a Protestant bastion, state prison and finally army barracks.

The château has undergone extensive renovations, following the collapse of part of the ramparts in 2001. The first floor houses the **Musée des Arts Décoratifs** which comprises a collection formed by Count Charles Lair, a native of Saumur, who left it to the château in 1919. It includes paintings, many fine tapestries, furniture, statuettes and ceramics that date from the 13th up to the 19th century.

Statuette from the Musée des Arts Décoratifs

🏛 Musée de la Cavalerie

Place Charles de Foucauld.
Tel 02 41 83 69 23. ⬜ mid-Jan–mid-Dec: Mon–Thu (Mar–Nov: also Sat–Sun pm).
www.museecavalerie.free.fr
Saumur's great horse-riding traditions stem from the training of cavalry elites for the French military. In the Ancien Régime, Saumur became one of the most specialized training centres in France. This museum starts the story in the 15th century, when the first royal military riding corps was created under Charles VII, to help end the Hundred Years' War.

🏛 Musée des Blindés

1043 rte de Fontevraud.
Tel *02 41 83 69 95.* ⃝ *daily.*
🌑 *1 Jan, 25 Dec.* 🏷 ♿
www.museedesblindes.fr

Owned by the Cavalry and Armoured Vehicles School, this barn-like museum has on display more historic tanks and armoured personnel carriers in working order than any other international military collection.

Beginning with a FT 17 Renault dating from 1917 and moving through the German World War II panzers to the monsters produced today, the museum offers a chance to see at close quarters these veterans of many conflicts.

A 1917 Renault tank in the collection of the Musée des Blindés

🏚 Dolmen de Bagneux

56 rue du Dolmen, Bagneux. **Tel** 02 41 50 23 02. 🚃 *Saumur.* 🚌 ⃝ *Sep–Jun: Thu–Tue; Jul & Aug: daily.* 🏷 ♿ **www**.saumur-dolmen.com

Saumur's main street leads to the suburb of Bagneux. Here, in a local bar's garden, one unexpectedly finds one of the most impressive Neolithic burial chambers in Europe. Visitors can sip drinks in the garden, absorb the impact of the dolmen and marvel at the massive sandstone slabs, some weighing 40 tonnes, that were dragged, tilted and wedged into position 5,000 years ago *(see p48–9)*.

A signpost for the Bagneux dolmen

Environs

The village of St-Hilaire-St-Florent, 2 km (1½ miles) northwest of Saumur on the D751, is well worth a visit for its museums and the famous Cadre Noir riding school. It also has a number of wine cellars where visitors can taste and buy the famous Saumur Brut, a sparkling wine that is produced by the *champagne method*. The Maison des Vins de Loire de Saumur, next to the tourist office, provides information on local wines, vineyards and tourist routes.

🏛 Musée du Champignon

Route de Gennes, St-Hilaire-St-Florent. **Tel** 02 41 50 31 55. ⃝ *mid-Feb–mid-Nov: daily.* 🏷 ♿ **www**.musee-du-champignon.com

This unique museum takes visitors through a network of limestone caves. Displays show how mushrooms that are grown from spores in bagged or boxed compost thrive in the high humidity and constant temperature of this environment *(see p79)*. The museum has an excellent collection of live mushroom species, as well as of fossils found during quarrying. On sale, and worth tasting, is a local speciality, *gallipettes farcies*, large mushrooms stuffed with a variety of fillings.

🏛 Parc Miniature Pierre et Lumière

Route de Gennes, St-Hilaire-St-Florent. **Tel** 02 41 50 70 04. ⃝ *Feb–mid-Nov: 10am–7pm daily.* 🌑 *mid-Nov–Jan.* 🏷 ♿ **www**.pierre-et-lumiere.com

The gallery of a former underground quarry is now the setting for 20 scale models carved from the tufa rock. They represent some of the most famous – and a few less well-known – monuments, towns and villages of the Loire Valley. Among the highlights are Fontevraud Abbey, Tours cathedral and the Château d'Amboise. The models are the work of self-taught sculptor Philippe Cormand.

🏛 Ecole Nationale d'Equitation

Terrefort, St-Hilaire-St-Florent. **Tel** 02 41 53 50 50. ⃝ *Mon pm–Sat am, visits at fixed times.* 🌑 *Sun and public hols.* 🏷 ♿ **www**.cadrenoir.fr

The National Riding School, founded in 1814, is world famous for its team, known as the Cadre Noir because of the riders' elegant black and gold ceremonial uniforms. The team of riders is generally restricted to just 22 elite horsemen. The Cadre Noir's horses are trained in a distinctive style of dressage, which was first practised in the 19th century. They are taught perfect balance and control and learn choreographed movements that show their natural grace.

During the summer months, visitors can enter the academy team's quarters and watch a morning training session. There are also regular performances of the spectacular summer gala.

The 5,000-year-old Bagneux dolmen near Saumur

Montreuil-Bellay ⑬

Road map C4. 🏘 *4,500.* 🚊 *Saumur*
🚌 🛈 *pl du Concorde (02 41 52 32 39).* 🚗 *Tue am, Sun (May–Sep).*
www.ville-montreuil-bellay.com

Combining an ancient village and a fascinating feudal château, Montreuil-Bellay, 18 km (11 miles) south of Saumur, is one of the most attractive towns in Anjou. The château complex occupies a site which was first fortified in the 11th century by Foulques Nerra and besieged by Geoffrey Plantagenet during the following century. In the 13th century it was surrounded by strong walls, with a grand towered entrance (known as the Château-Vieux) and 11 other towers. Inside the ramparts is a collection of mainly late 15th-century

Frescoes in the oratory of the Château de Montreuil-Bellay

buildings, looking over landscaped terraces falling to the pretty River Thouet.

The Château-Neuf is an elegant Renaissance-fronted building, begun in the late

15th century. The turret was made famous by the infamous French noblewoman, Anne de Longueville (1619–79), who rode her horse to the top of its spiral staircase.

The château's interior is superbly furnished and has a number of fireplaces in the Flamboyant style as well as splendid painted and carved ceilings. The 15th-century frescoes adorning the oratory are currently under restoration, but the guided tour still takes in the medieval kitchens, which are said to be modelled on those of the earlier Fontevraud Abbey (*see pp86–7*).

🏰 **Château de Montreuil-Bellay**
Tel 02 41 52 33 06. ⬜ *Apr–Jun, Sep–Nov: Wed–Mon; Jul, Aug: daily.*
🎫 ✔ **www**.chateau-de-montreuil-bellay.fr

Troglodyte Tour ⑮

Caves, cut into the Tufa cliffs beside the Loire and other limestone rich areas in Anjou, are used as dovecotes, chapels, farms, wine cellars and even homes. These so-called "troglodyte" dwellings, some of which date back to the 12th century, and have hardly changed over the centuries, are fashionable again as artists' studios or holiday homes. Life in and among these caves is the subject of this fascinating tour.

Dénézé-sous-Doué ⑥
In these underground caves, carved by Protestant stonemasons during the 16th-century Wars of Religion, more than 400 figures are chiselled into the walls, floors and ceilings.

La Fosse ⑦
This inhabited troglodyte farmhouse is open to visitors.

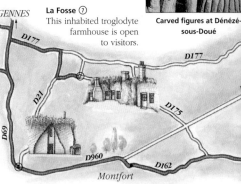
Carved figures at Dénézé-sous-Doué

GENNES
⑥
D177
⑤
D21
D69
0 kilometres 3
0 miles 3
D960
Montfort
D177
D175
D162

Troglodyte houses at Rochemenier

Rochemenier ⑤
This former troglodyte farming community has been turned into a museum displaying underground farmyards, barns, houses and a simple rock chapel.

Doué-la-Fontaine ④
The rue des Perrières was excavated from a stratum of shell marl (*faluns*); its "cathedral" vaults were dug vertically from the top. The town also has an amphitheatre cut from the rock and an outstanding zoo set in old quarries.

Château de Montsoreau ⑭

Road map C3. 🚉 *Saumur, then taxi.* ☎ **Tel** *02 41 67 12 60.*
⏰ *Apr: daily pm; May–Sep: daily; Oct–mid-Nov: daily pm.* 📷 ♿
www.chateau-montsoreau.com

This picturesque late-medieval château stands in the midst of a beautiful village. The castle was built for its lords to control the port and river toll.

In Alexandre Dumas' novel *La Dame de Montsoreau*, the jealous count, Charles de Chambes, forces his wife to lure her lover to the château, where he is murdered. This story is true, in part, and one of the exhibitions inside retells this violent tale. The focus of the other displays is the Loire, covering nature along the river, as well as the people who have

Château de Montsoreau on the River Loire

transformed it over the years.

Also in Montsoreau is the ecologically built **Maison du Parc** of the Parc Naturel Régional Loire-Anjou-Touraine, showing how the park has changed over time.

🍁 **Maison du Parc Régional Loire-Anjou-Touraine**
15 av de la Loire. **Tel** *02 41 53 66 00.*
⏰ *Mar, Nov: weekends pm; Apr, Oct: Tue–Sun; May–Sep: daily .* ♿ **www**. parc-loire-anjou-touraine.fr

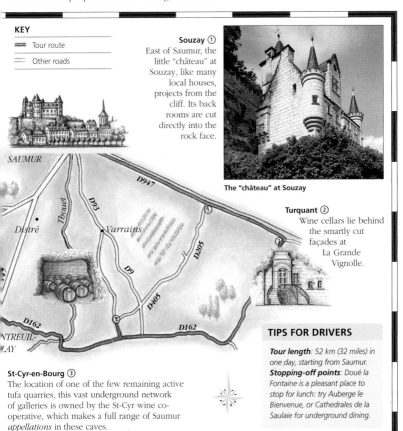

KEY

━━━ Tour route

═══ Other roads

SAUMUR

Distré

Thouet

Varrains

D947

D93

D205

D9

D405

D162

NTREUIL-LAY

Souzay ①
East of Saumur, the little "château" at Souzay, like many local houses, projects from the cliff. Its back rooms are cut directly into the rock face.

The "château" at Souzay

Turquant ②
Wine cellars lie behind the smartly cut façades at La Grande Vignolle.

St-Cyr-en-Bourg ③
The location of one of the few remaining active tufa quarries, this vast underground network of galleries is owned by the St-Cyr wine co-operative, which makes a full range of Saumur *appellations* in these caves.

TIPS FOR DRIVERS

***Tour length**: 52 km (32 miles) in one day, starting from Saumur.*
***Stopping-off points**: Doué la Fontaine is a pleasant place to stop for lunch: try Auberge le Bienvenue, or Cathedrales de la Saulaie for underground dining.*

Abbaye de Fontevraud 16

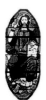

Stained glass in church

Fontevraud Abbey, founded in 1101 by the hermit Robert d'Arbrissel for both women and men, is the largest and most extraordinary of its kind in France. It was run for nearly 700 years by aristocratic abbesses, almost half of them royal-born. They governed a monks' priory outside the main walls, and four distinct communities of nuns and lay sisters, ranging from rich widows to repentant prostitutes, as well as a leper colony and an infirmary. Restoration work has removed traces of the 150 years after the Revolution when the abbey served as a prison. Now it is fully open to tourists and hosts many cultural events.

The grand refectory, with its Renaissance ribbed vaulting, is 60 m (200 ft) long.

Nursing sisters of the St Benoît order cared for invalids in this section of the abbey.

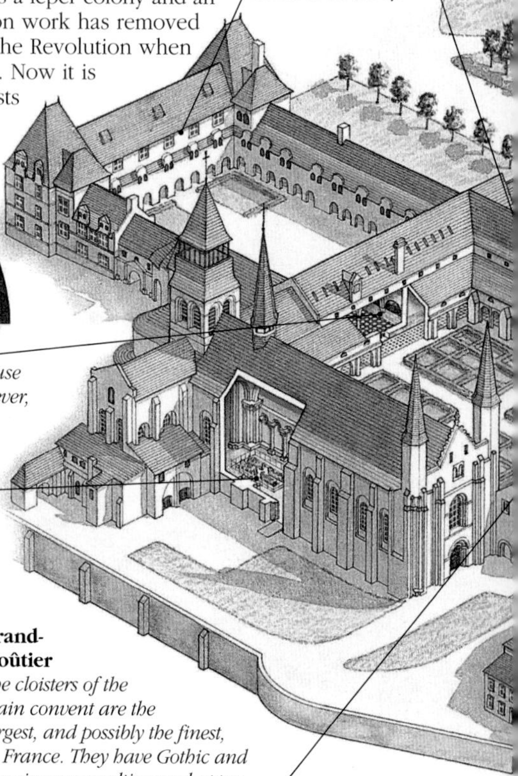

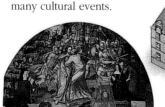

★ Chapter House Paintings
The paintings in the Chapter House date from the 16th century. However, some figures were added later.

★ Plantagenet Effigies
*These four effigies (*gisants*), each a realistic portrait, are displayed in the nave of the abbey church.*

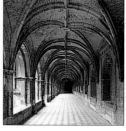

Grand-Moûtier
The cloisters of the main convent are the largest, and possibly the finest, in France. They have Gothic and Renaissance vaulting and upper galleries built in the 19th century.

STAR FEATURES

- ★ Plantagenet Effigies
- ★ Chapter House Paintings
- ★ Romanesque Kitchens

THE RESTING PLACE OF THE PLANTAGENETS

The medieval painted effigy of Henry Plantagenet, count of Anjou and king of England (1133–1189), lies beside that of his wife, Eleanor of Aquitaine, who died here in 1204. With them are the effigies of their son, King Richard the Lionheart (1157–1199), and Isabelle, wife of his brother, King John. In all, 15 of the family are buried here.

Effigies of Eleanor of Aquitaine and Henry II

For hotels and restaurants in this region see p202 and pp214–15

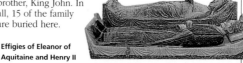

St-Lazare Priory
*Built as a hospital for lepers,
the priory is now a smart hotel.
It is undergoing restoration
work, but, upon reopening,
parts will be open to visitors.*

VISITORS' CHECKLIST

Road map C3. **Tel** *02 41 51
73 52.* ☐ *late Jan–6 Apr & Nov–
Dec: 10am–5pm; 7 Apr–Jun &
Sep–Oct: 9:30am–6:30pm; Jul–
Aug: 9:30am–7:30pm.* 🚫 📷
♿ 🎁 🍴 🎫 *Exhibitions held
throughout the year.* **www.**
abbayedefontevraud.com

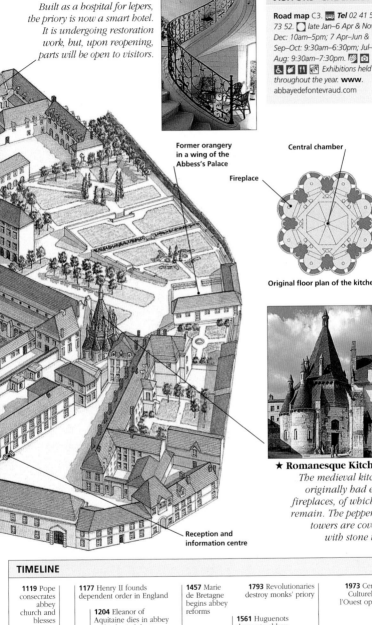

**Former orangery
in a wing of the
Abbess's Palace**

Central chamber

Fireplace

Original floor plan of the kitchens

★ Romanesque Kitchens
*The medieval kitchen
originally had eight
fireplaces, of which six
remain. The pepper-pot
towers are covered
with stone tiles.*

**Reception and
information centre**

TIMELINE

1119 Pope consecrates abbey church and blesses cemetery	**1177** Henry II founds dependent order in England	**1457** Marie de Bretagne begins abbey reforms	**1793** Revolutionaries destroy monks' priory	**1973** Centre Culturel de l'Ouest opens
	1204 Eleanor of Aquitaine dies in abbey and is buried there		**1561** Huguenots desecrate abbey	
1100	**1300**	**1500**	**1700**	**1900**
1115 First Abbess appointed to oversee each of the five orders	*17th-century abbess, Gabrielle de Rochechouart*		**1792** Order suppressed by Revolutionaries	**1804** Napoléon converts main buildings into state prison
1099–1101 Order of Fontevraud founded by Robert d'Abrissel (1047–1117)				**1963** Prison closed, restoration begins

TOURAINE

Touraine is known chiefly for the magnificent white châteaux strung out along the broad Loire and its tributaries. Added to these are its rich history and fertile landscape,, making it the archetypal Loire Valley region. The rolling terrain and lush forests that once attracted the kings and queens of France continue to work their charm over visitors from all around the world today.

The feudal castles that still exist, at Loches and Chinon for example, remind visitors that this now tranquil region was once a battle-ground for the warring counts of Blois and Anjou. It was also here, at Chinon, that the Anglo-French Plantagenet monarch, Henry II of England, held court and where, later, Joan of Arc managed to bully the future Charles VII of France into raising the army that she would lead to victory over the English.

Charles VIII, Louis XII and François I brought the influence of the Italian Renaissance to France and set a fashion in architecture that produced the unforgettable châteaux of this region. The most magical – the delicate Azay-le-Rideau, the majestic Chenonceau, and Villandry with its extraordinary formal gardens – were built during this period. However, at the end of the 16th century, Touraine ceased to be a playground for the court.

Tours, at the heart of the region, makes a natural base for visitors, who can enjoy its sensitively restored, medieval old town.

The rolling terrain and gentle climate of Touraine encourage outdoor pursuits, including hiking, boating and fishing. The area is also famous for its *primeurs*, early fruit and vegetables, such as white asparagus, grown on its low-lying, fertile soils. Its many wines, including the well-known *appellations* of Bourgueil, Chinon and Vouvray, are the perfect accompaniment to the region's excellent cuisine.

A view of the Château de Chinon, on a cliff above the River Vienne

◁ The rooftops of Le Grand-Pressigny, as seen from high on the hill on which the town is built

Exploring Touraine

Criss-crossed by rivers great and small, Touraine
sits regally at the heart of the Loire Valley.
Châteaux are distributed along the paths of
the rivers: Langeais and Amboise by the Loire
itself; Ussé, Azay-le-Rideau and Loches by
the gentle Indre; and Chenonceau grace-
fully straddling the Cher. Tours, the main
town in the region, is also on the Loire.
The Gâtine Tourangelle to the north of the
river was once a magnificent forest but was
felled progressively from the 11th century
by local people in search of wood and
arable land. However, small pockets of
woodland remain, delightful for walking
and picnicking.

Candes-St-Martin, with its
12th- to 13th-century church

KEY

▬▬	Motorway
▬▬	Major road
▬▬	Secondary road
▬▬	Minor road
▬▬	Scenic route
▬▬	Main railway
----	Minor railway
▬▬	Regional border

GETTING AROUND

Tours is the natural hub of
the region and has a small
international airport. The TGV
from Paris takes an hour to
St-Pierre-des-Corps, followed by
a five-minute shuttle service to
the centre of Tours. It is possible
to rent a car either from Tours or
St-Pierre-des-Corps. The A10 is
the fastest route from Paris by
car. The A85 is the easiest way to
get across the region. The D952
and D751 hug the Loire and pass
through attractive countryside.
The prettiest drives, however,
include those along the rivers
Cher, Indre and Vienne.

One of Touraine's renowned vineyards

SEE ALSO

- *Where to Stay* pp203–4
- *Where to Eat* pp215–16

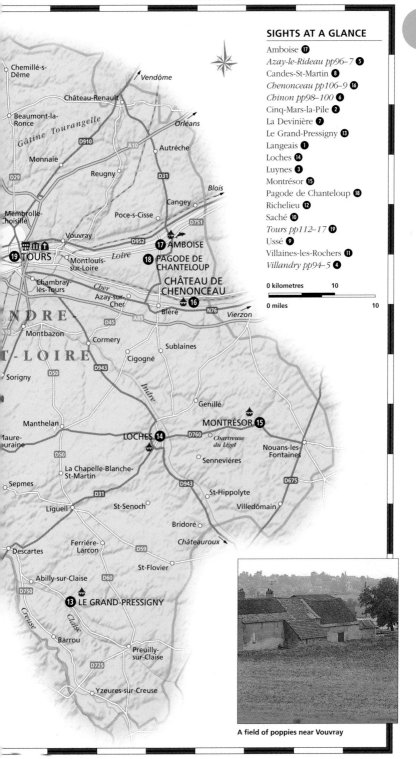

0 kilometres   10

0 miles   10

A field of poppies near Vouvray

Chapel of the Château de Langeais, with its curved, wood ceiling

Château de Langeais ❶

Road map D3. 🚉 **Tel** 02 47 96 72 60. ⬤ daily. 📷 📹
www.chateau-de-langeais.com

The feudal Château de Langeais, looming up in the centre of the small town, was built for King Louis XI between 1465 and 1490 by his treasurer,

Jean Bourré. It stands on the site of an earlier fortress built by the fearsome Foulques Nerra (see p50), of which only the rectangular keep remains – this can now be climbed up and it serves as a backdrop for historical reenactments.

Langeais' forbidding outer walls, towers, drawbridge and heavily machicolated sentry walk contrast strongly with its elegant interiors, unaltered over the centuries. Its collection of beautifully displayed 15th- and 16th-century furniture, paintings and tapestries was amassed in the late 19th century by its last private owner, the well-known Alsace banker and philanthropist, Jacques Siegfried.

Among the treasures in the castle is the wedding chest brought by the 14-year-old Duchess Anne of Brittany when she married the tiny, hunchbacked Charles VIII here in the early hours of 6 December 1491. A waxwork tableau re-creates this clandestine event – both were

already betrothed to others – and includes a copy of Anne's cloth-of-gold wedding gown, lined with 160 sable skins.

From the castle's parapets visitors can view the handsome town below, which has a good Sunday morning food market. The remodelled castle grounds, which include a remarkable treehouse, are also worth exploring.

The Gallo-Roman tower near Cinq-Mars-la-Pile

Château de Cinq-Mars-la-Pile ❷

Road map D3. 🚉 **Tel** 02 47 96 40 49. ⬤ Apr–Jun & 16 Sep–Oct: Sat & Sun; Jul & Aug: Wed–Mon. ⬤ Nov–Mar. 📷

The most famous inhabitant of the castle of Cinq-Mars was Henri Ruzé d'Effiat, Marquis de Cinq-Mars, and the eponymous hero of a novel by the Touraine writer Alfred de Vigny. The marquis, a favourite of King Louis XIII, rashly became involved in a plot against Louis' minister, Cardinal Richelieu, and was beheaded in 1642, aged 22. Richelieu ordered the castle at Cinq-Mars to be truncated – it is said that even the trees had their crowns chopped off. A pair of towers remain, each with three vaulted chambers, surrounded by an extremely wide moat. The château's fragrant, romantic gardens are adorned with topiary.

The *Pile* in the town's name refers to a strange Gallo-Roman brick tower, more than 30 m (98 ft) high, on a

Towers of the Château de Cinq-Mars-la-Pile

Luynes' imposing château, dominating the village below

ridge just east of the village. The south side of the tower, whose purpose and precise date are a mystery, was decorated with 12 multi-coloured brick panels, laid out in a geometric design, four of which are still intact today.

Luynes ❸

Road map D3. 🏘 5,000. 🚌 Tours, then bus. 🚋 ℹ 9 rue Alfred Baugé (02 47 55 77 14). 🛒 Sat. **Château Tel** 02 47 55 67 55. ☐ Apr–mid-Sep: daily. 🖼 🎫 www.luynes.fr

Brooding over this pretty little town is an imposing château, originally called Maillé after the noble owners who rebuilt it in the early 13th century. It is still inhabited by descendants of the first Duc de Luynes, who bought it in 1619, and furnished with Renaissance and 17th-century pieces. The old town developed to the south of the château, and its 15th-century wooden market hall remains.

The remaining 44 arches of a **Gallo-Roman aqueduct** can be seen 1.5 km (1 mile) northeast of Luynes. Standing in isolation amid fields, they are a striking sight.

The wealthy Maillé family also owned a feudal castle on the site of the **Château de Champchevrier**, 10 km (6 miles) northwest of Luynes. The present Renaissance manor house, with various 18th-century additions, is set in a lush forest. Its elegant rooms are beautifully furnished, with particularly fine family portraits and Beauvais tapestries. A pack of hounds is kept at the château.

⚓ **Château de Champchevrier** Cléré-les-Pins. **Tel** 02 47 24 93 93. ☐ Mid-Jun–mid-Sep: Mon–Sat, Sun pm only; mid-Sep–mid-Jun: groups by appt. 🖼 🎫 🍴 www.champchevrier.com

The Chambre du Roi in the Château de Champchevrier

LIFE IN A MEDIEVAL CHÂTEAU

During times of peace, life in a medieval château took on a pleasant routine. To fill the long winter days, nobles played board games, such as chess and draughts, or cards. Ladies, when they were not playing music or embroidering, had dwarves to entertain them, while the court jester kept banquet guests amused by making fun of everyone, even the king. Mystery plays (dramas based on the life of Christ) were very popular and cycles of these plays often lasted for several weeks. Outdoor pursuits enjoyed during the summer included bowling, archery and ball games, but it was the tournaments, with jousting and sword-play, that provoked the most excitement. Hunting was also favoured by kings and nobles and much practised in the woods and forests of the Loire Valley.

The illumination for August from Les Très Riches Heures du Duc de Berry

Château de Villandry ❹

The Château de Villandry, dating from the late Renaissance (1536), has an almost Classical elegance. But it is most famous for its superb gardens, restored since the estate was bought in 1906 by the Spanish Carvallo family. Working from 16th-century designs, skilful gardeners mixed flowers and vegetables in fascinating geometric patterns. The garden is spread between three levels: you will find the sun garden and the water garden on the highest level; a flower garden on the same level as the château; and below it, the world's largest ornamental kitchen garden *(below)*. Also explore the delightful smaller plots, such as the cross garden.

Jeune Infante by Pantoja de la Cruz

★ **Garden of Love**
Flower designs here symbolize four types of love: tragic, adulterous, tender and passionate.

A collection of **Spanish paintings** is housed in the château.

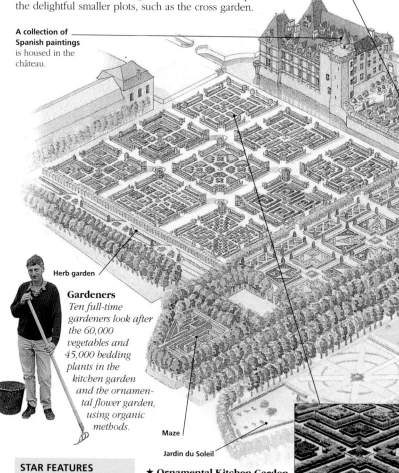

Herb garden

Gardeners
Ten full-time gardeners look after the 60,000 vegetables and 45,000 bedding plants in the kitchen garden and the ornamental flower garden, using organic methods.

Maze

Jardin du Soleil

STAR FEATURES

★ Garden of Love

★ Ornamental Kitchen Garden

★ **Ornamental Kitchen Garden**
The current state of the garden can be studied in the plan pinned up near the moat. The plant and vegetable names for each square are listed and the colours shown.

RENAISSANCE KITCHEN AND HERB GARDENS

A 16th-century French treatise on diet reveals that the melons, artichokes, asparagus and cauliflower that fill Villandry's kitchen gardens today all also commonly appeared on Renaissance dinner tables. Herbs were widely used both for their medicinal and culinary applications. They formed the borders in the kitchen gardens of monasteries, such as that at Solesmes (see p162), which were the first to feature geometric planting. Villandry has a *jardin des simples* (herb garden) on its middle level.

Knautia dipsacifolia, from a
16th-century manual on plants

VISITORS' CHECKLIST

Road map D3. **Tel** 02 47 50 02 09. 🚉 Savonnières, then taxi. ⏱ 9am–5pm daily. Château shuts 30 min earlier. Closing times vary throughout the year; Château closed early Jan–mid-Feb, mid-Nov–mid-Dec.; check the website for full details. 🎫 📷 ♿ 🍴
www.chateauvillandry.com

Shaped Pear Trees
In Villandry's gardens, nature is completely controlled. The pear trees are carefully pruned to form neat oval shapes.

The elegant stone balustrades above the kitchen garden have been restored.

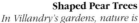

The pool for irrigating the gardens is shaped like a gilt-framed mirror.

The flower gardens, including the garden of love, level with the south façade of the château

Decorative Cabbage
Ornamental Japanese cabbages were introduced by the mother of the present owner to provide year-round colour in the kitchen garden.

Château d'Azay-le-Rideau ❺

Memorably described by Honoré de Balzac as a "faceted diamond set in the Indre", Azay-le-Rideau is one of the most popular châteaux in the Loire. Its graceful silhouette and richly decorated façades are mirrored in the peaceful waters of its lake, once a medieval moat. Azay was built from about 1518 by Gilles Berthelot, only to be confiscated by François I in 1527. The unknown architect, influenced by Italian design and innovative in his use of a straight staircase, took the defensive elements of an earlier, more warlike age and transformed them into charming ornamental features. Furnished in 16th–19th-century styles, the château has some notable tapestries and a famous portrait said to be of Henri IV's mistress, Gabrielle d'Estrées.

Kitchen
The kitchen, situated in the west wing, has rib vaulting and a huge open fireplace.

La Dame au Bain
Henri IV's haughty mistress Gabrielle d'Estrées is said to feature in the château's finest painting, done in the style of François Clouet.

STAR FEATURES

★ Central Staircase

★ South Façade

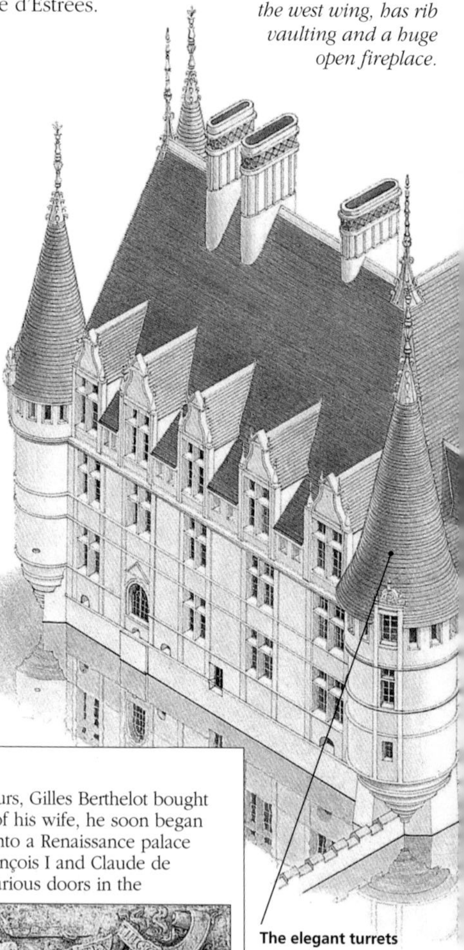

AZAY'S CREATORS

Treasurer to François I and mayor of Tours, Gilles Berthelot bought Azay-le-Rideau in 1510. With the help of his wife, he soon began transforming the medieval castle here into a Renaissance palace befitting his station. The emblems of François I and Claude de France were sculpted in stone above various doors in the château in an attempt to flatter the sovereigns. But flattery did not save Berthelot's career – about to be accused of embezzlement, he was forced to flee Azay before the building was completed.

François I's salamander emblem

The elegant turrets adorn the château's façade rather than protect it, as the sturdy towers of medieval fortresses had done in the past.

Entrance Façade
The entrance façade is dominated by the galleried stairwell topped by a tall gable. Its decoration, full of shells, medallions and candelabras, was influenced by Italian Renaissance artists.

Entrance

VISITORS' CHECKLIST

Road map D3.
Tel 02 47 45 42 04.
🚗 ⬤ *Apr–Jun & Sep:*
9:30am–6pm daily; Jul & Aug:
9:30am–7pm; Oct–Mar:
10am–5:15pm. ⬤ 1 Jan,
1 May, 25 Dec. 🎨 📷 🎧 *Son et Lumières (Jul & Aug: 9pm–midnight nightly).*
www.azay-le-rideau.
monuments-nationaux.fr

Red Room
This striking room is the antechamber to the Chambre du Roi *(the King's Bedroom). The walls are hung with portraits of, among others, François I, Henri II and Henri III.*

★ Central Staircase
Azay's most significant design feature is its central staircase, consisting of six straight flights with landings, rather than the spiral staircase that was usual for the period.

Ballroom
with
Flemish
tapestries

★ South Façade
Symmetry is the underlying motif of the exterior design, with its matching turrets and its stripe of decoration imitating machicolations

Street-by-Street: Chinon ❻

The Château de Chinon stands on a golden-coloured cliff above the River Vienne. Below it, Chinon's old crooked streets resonate with history. The travel-weary Joan of Arc *(see p137)* arrived in the town on 6 March 1429. It was here that she began her transformation from peasant girl to the warrior-saint – the saint is shown sitting astride a charger in a statue in the marketplace. In the nearby Maison des Etats-Généraux, now the Musée d'Art et d'Histoire, Richard the Lionheart lay in state in 1199. His father, Henry Plantagenet, had died a few years earlier in the château, one of the main bases from which he had ruled England as well as much of the Loire Valley.

Tour de l'Horloge
This 14th-century clock-tower stands out from the other towers along the ramparts.

★ Château
The citadel's long walls enclose three separate forts. In the royal lodgings, Joan of Arc recognized the French heir to the throne, the dauphin (see p52), a scene beautifully represented in a fine 17th-century tapestry.

0 metres   50

0 yards   50

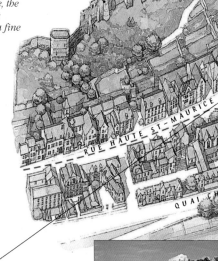

RUE HAUTE ST-MAURICE

RUE BEA

QUAI CHARLES VII

Eglise St-Maurice
Henry II rebuilt this church with Angevin vaults, retaining the Romanesque lower part of what is now the steeple.

Ramparts
The château's ramparts are an impressive sight from the opposite bank of the River Vienne.

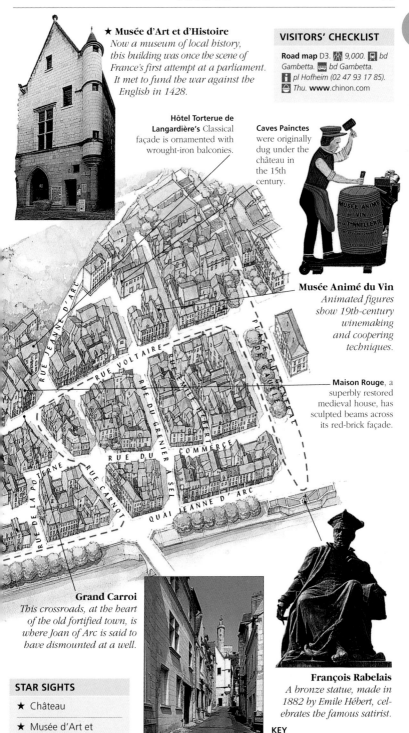

★ **Musée d'Art et d'Histoire**
*Now a museum of local history,
this building was once the scene of
France's first attempt at a parliament.
It met to fund the war against the
English in 1428.*

VISITORS' CHECKLIST

Road map D3. 🏘 9,000. 🚌 bd
Gambetta. 🚉 bd Gambetta.
🛈 pl Hofheim (02 47 93 17 85).
🛒 Thu. **www**.chinon.com

**Hôtel Torterue de
Langardière's** Classical
façade is ornamented with
wrought-iron balconies.

Caves Painctes
were originally
dug under the
château in
the 15th
century.

Musée Animé du Vin
*Animated figures
show 19th-century
winemaking
and coopering
techniques.*

Maison Rouge, a
superbly restored
medieval house, has
sculpted beams across
its red-brick façade.

Grand Carroi
*This crossroads, at the heart
of the old fortified town, is
where Joan of Arc is said to
have dismounted at a well.*

François Rabelais
*A bronze statue, made in
1882 by Emile Hébert, celebrates the famous satirist.*

STAR SIGHTS

★ Château

★ Musée d'Art et
d'Histoire

KEY

− − − Suggested route

Exploring Chinon

A walk through the narrow streets to the east of the château shows how much Chinon has to offer. High above the place Jeanne d'Arc is the remarkable Chapelle de Ste-Radegonde, carved into the limestone cliff. Behind this 12th-century frescoed chapel are ancient hermit caves and dizzying steps to an underground well. For a leisurely tour of the town, opt for a horse-drawn carriage, or board a traditional riverboat from the southbank to enjoy a different perspective from the Vienne. Heading east out of town leads to enchanting vineyards and villages, with many wineries open to visitors.

♣ Forteresse Royale de Chinon

Tel *02 47 93 13 45.* ☐ *daily all year.*
⬤ *1 Jan, 25 Dec.* 🅿 ▮
www.forteressechinon.fr
This magnificent fortress, running along the hill above the Vienne River, is closely associated with the Plantagenet kings of England, and with Joan of Arc, who helped boot the dynasty out of France at the end of the Hundred Years' War.

The huge citadel, built for King Henry II in the 12th century, fell into ruin during the Ancien Régime (*pp54-7*). However, it has since been stunningly restored and its fascinating history is brought to life using imaginative methods, including a series of short films designed to evoke key moments in the buildings history.

The citadel's western section has large towers that you can climb up and down. The views across the Vienne Valley are beautiful.

Statue of Joan of Arc by Jules Roulleau

�🏛 Musée d'Art et d'Histoire
44 rue Haute St-Maurice. **Tel** *02 47 93 18 12.* ☐ *Jun–Sep: daily pm; Oct–May: Mon–Fri pm.* 🅿
Among the treasures found in this intriguing museum of local history are a fine portrait of Rabelais by Eugène Delacroix (1798–1863), and the "Cope of St. Mexme", the first large Arab tapestry brought to France.

🏛 Caves Painctes
Impasse des Caves Painctes
Tel *02 47 93 30 44.* ▮ *only.*
Jul & Aug: 11am, 3pm, 4:30pm, 6pm Tue–Sun. 🅿
Oenology and literature come together in these wine cellars, which occupy a subterranean quarry dug under the château in the 15th century. They are the headquarters of the *Confrérie des Bons Etonneurs Rebelaisiens*, a brotherhood of wine growers who meet four times a year to celebrate Chinon wine and commemorate Rebelais's humanism and joie de vivre. The caves are allegedly inspired by the author's description of the Temple of the Divine Bottle. The price of a visit includes a wine tasting session.

🏛 Musée Animé du Vin et de la Tonnellerie
12 rue Voltaire. **Tel** *02 47 93 25 63.* ☐ *15 Mar–15 Oct: daily; 15 Oct–15 Mar: groups by appt.* ⬤ *1 Jan, 25 Dec.* 🅿
Here you can taste sharp, dry, strawberry-like Chinon red wine, while watching automated models demonstrate the various stages in wine- and barrel-making (both are important Chinon industries) using some of the museum's 19th-century implements.

FRANÇOIS RABELAIS (1483–1553)

Priest, doctor, humanist and supreme *farceur* of French literature, François Rabelais is everywhere present in "Rabelaisie", as the area around La Devinière has become known. Rabelais enthusiasts will recognize in the old farmhouse the castle of Grandgousier, besieged by the hordes of King Picrochole, but saved by the arrival of giant Gargantua on his mare, who drowns most of them by creating a flood with her prodigious urination. Rabelais' thirst for knowledge imbued his *Gargantua* and *Pantagruel* (*see p24*) with a wealth of learning that sits surprisingly easily alongside a ribald *joie de vivre*.

The infant Gargantua

The Tour de l'Horloge, leading to the middle castle

View of the Château d'Ussé from the bridge crossing the River Indre

Musée de la Devinière ⑦

Road map D3. 🚃 *Chinon, then taxi.* **Tel** *02 47 95 91 18.* ⏱ *Wed–Mon (Jul & Aug: daily).* ● *1 Jan, 25 Dec.* 🎫 🖪

The 16th-century writer François Rabelais was probably born in this modest farmhouse, 2 km (1½ miles) southwest of Chinon. It now houses a small museum devoted to the man and his contemporaries. Brought up in Chinon, Rabelais became an eminent monk, doctor and scholar, as well as the most brilliant satirist in French Renaissance literature.

La Devinière farmhouse

Candes-St-Martin ⑧

Road map C3. 🏠 *230.* 🚃 *Chinon or Port Boulet, then taxi.* 🛈 *Chinon (02 47 93 17 85).*

Beautifully situated overlooking the shimmering waters where the Loire and Vienne rivers converge, picturesque Candes is famous as the place where St Martin died in 397. Stained glass in the 12th-century church depicts the saint's body being secretly rowed to Tours for burial. The porch of the church was fortified in the 15th century and is adorned with carved heads. Inside, the ceiling is a fine example of Angevin vaulting. You can embark on a Loire boat trip from Candes.

Château d'Ussé ⑨

Road map D3. 🚃 *Chinon, then taxi (15km/9 miles).* **Tel** *02 47 95 54 05.* ⏱ *mid-Feb–mid-Nov: daily.* 🎫 🖪 *park & grd flr only.* **www**.chateaudusse.fr

With its countless pointed turrets gleaming white against the sombre trees of the Forêt de Chinon, the gorgeous Château d'Ussé is said to have inspired 17th-century French author Charles Perrault to write the fairy tale *The Sleeping Beauty*. The fortified château was begun in 1462 for the powerful courtier Jean de Bueil on the foundations of a medieval castle. In 1485 it was sold to the Espinay family, chamberlains to both Louis XI and Charles VII, who softened the courtyard façades with Renaissance features.

In the 17th century the north wing was demolished, opening up the main courtyard to views of the River Indre. Formal gardens designed by the landscape architect André le Nôtre were planted in terraces to the river and an orangery was added, completing the transformation from fortress to aristocratic country house.

The interior of the château, which is still lived in, is also decorated in a variety of styles. In one tower, visitors can see a waxwork tableau of *The Sleeping Beauty*. The chapel, stables and wine cellar are also worth a visit.

The late-Gothic exterior of Ussé's chapel

Mobile by Alexander Calder (1898–1976) in Saché

Saché **⑩**

Road map D3. 🚶 *1200*. 🚇 *Jul–Sep*. 🚌 *Azay-le-Rideau, then taxi.* 🛈 *Azay-le-Rideau (02 47 45 44 40).* **www**.*sache.fr*

The pretty village of Saché is notable for having been second home to both a writer and an artist of world fame: the 19th-century novelist Honoré de Balzac and the 20th-century American sculptor Alexander Calder, one of whose mobiles adorns the main square.

Admirers of Balzac make pilgrimages to the **Musée Balzac** in the Château de Saché. The plain but comfortable manor house, built in the 16th and 18th centuries, was a quiet place to work and a source of inspiration for many of the writer's best-known novels. The house has been well restored – one of the reception rooms has even been redecorated with a copy

of the bright green wallpaper with a Pompeiian frieze that was there in Balzac's day.

It is full of busts, sketches and memorabilia of the great man, including the coffee pot that kept him going during his long stints of writing. There are manuscripts and letters, as well as portraits of the women in Balzac's life: his mother; his first love, Madame de Berny; and his loyal friend, Madame Hanska, whom he finally married shortly before his death in 1850.

🏛 **Museé Balzac**
Château de Saché. **Tel** *02 47 26 86 50.* ⬡ *daily.* ⬤ *Tue (Oct–Mar); 1 Jan, 25 Dec.* 🖼 **www**.*musee-balzac.fr*

Villaines-les-Rochers **⑪**

Road map D3. 🚶 *930.* 🚌 *Azay-le-Rideau, then taxi.* 🛈 *Azay-le-Rideau (02 47 45 44 40).*

Since the Middle Ages, willows from the local river valleys have been made into baskets in this peaceful village. Production has been on a more substantial scale since the mid-19th century, when the local priest organized the craftsmen into one of France's first cooperatives. Everything is still hand made by the many wickerworkers (*vanniers*) in the town. This explains the relatively high prices of the attractive furniture and baskets on sale in the **cooperative**'s shop. Craftsmen and women can be watched at work in

the adjoining studio. In the summer, you can also visit a small museum with displays on the subject of basket-making, the **Musée de l'Osier et de la Vannerie**.

🏚 **Coopérative de Vannerie de Villaines**
1 rue de la Cheneillère. **Tel** *02 47 45 43 03.* ⬡ *daily (Sat, Sun: no work in progress).* ⬤ *1 Jan, 25 Dec.* ⬥
🏛 **Musée de l'Osier et de la Vannerie**
22 rue des Caves-Fortes. **Tel** *02 47 45 23 19.* ⬡ *Apr–Sep: Tue–Sun, pm only; Oct–Apr: groups by appt.* 🖼

A wickerworker in Villaines

Richelieu **⑫**

Road map D4. 🚶 *2,000.* 🚌 *Chinon, then bus.* 🛈 *7 pl Louis-XIII (02 47 58 13 62).* ⬤ *Mon, Fri.* **www**.*cc-richelieu.com*

It would be difficult to find a better example of 17th-century urban planning than the town of Richelieu, on the border between Touraine and Poitou. Its rigid design was the brainchild of Armand Jean du Plessis who, as Cardinal Richelieu and chief minister, was the most powerful man in the kingdom, not excepting his monarch, Louis XIII.

The Cardinal was determined to build a huge palace near his modest family estate of Richelieu. In 1625 he commissioned the architect Jacques Lemercier to draw up the plans and, in 1631, he received permission from the king to proceed, not only with the palace, but also with the creation of a new walled

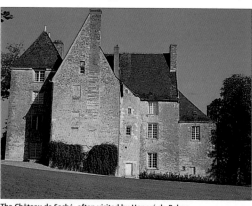

The Château de Saché, often visited by Honoré de Balzac

town. Lemercier had already designed the Palais Royal and the Church of the Sorbonne in Paris, and would later be appointed chief royal architect. His brothers, Pierre and Nicolas, were put in charge of the building work, which lasted more than a decade.

The resulting town is a huge rectangle, surrounded by walls and moats (mostly taken up with gardens today) and entered through three monumental gates. The Grande Rue, running from north to south through the centre of the town and linking two large squares, is lined with identical Classical mansions. In the south square, place du Marché, the buildings include the Classical **Eglise Notre-Dame**, the market building with its superb timber framework, and the former law courts, in which the **Hôtel de Ville** (town hall) and a small **history museum** are now housed. In the north square, the place des Religieuses, stands a convent and the Royal Academy, which was founded by Richelieu in 1640.

Richelieu clearly intended that his palace should be incomparably luxurious, and that vision was impressively realized. It was filled with priceless furniture and works of art, including paintings by Caravaggio and

Richelieu's timber-framed market hall

Andrea Mantegna. Michelangelo's *Dying Slaves*, statues that were originally designed for the tomb of Pope Julius II (now housed in the Louvre museum in Paris), adorned one of the palace's inner courtyard façades.

Extremely fearful of competition, Richelieu ordered many of the châteaux in the area to be razed to the ground. While his town managed to survive the ravages of the French Revolution intact, the sumptuous palace, ironically, was confiscated, damaged and then dismantled.

By visiting the beautiful **Domaine du Parc de Richelieu**, visitors can get an inkling of its former glory. There is also an interesting virtual

Cardinal Richelieu (1585–1642)

presentation, **Visite en 3D du Château de Richelieu** (Tel: 02 47 58 13 62), which takes place at 28 Grand Rue.

🏛 Musée de l'Hôtel de Ville
Place du Marché.
***Tel** 02 47 58 10 13.* ⬜ Mon, Wed–Fri (Jul & Aug: daily). 🌸 public hols. 📷

🌺 Domaine du Parc de Richelieu
5 pl du Cardinal. ***Tel** 02 47 58 10 09.* ⬜ daily. ♿ restricted.

Environs
Champigny-sur-Veude, 6 km (4 miles) to the north of Richelieu, boasts another stunning castle. It is not open to the public, but visitors can see the splendid Renaissance **Ste-Chapelle**, with its superb stained glass.

⛪ Ste-Chapelle
Champigny-sur-Veude. ***Tel** 02 47 95 73 48.* ⬜ May–Jun: Thu–Sun pm; Jul–Aug: daily pm; Sep: Mon & Wed–Sun pm. 📷

BALZAC AT SACHÉ

Honoré de Balzac's (1799–1850) regular stays at the Château de Saché between 1829 and 1837 coincided with the most productive period in his highly industrious career as a writer. Here, hidden well away from his creditors, he would work at least 12 hours a day. Despite starting in the early hours of the morning, he remained able to entertain his hosts, Monsieur and Madame de Margonne, and their guests in the evenings by reading aloud the latest chunk of text from his novels, acting out all the characters as he did so.

Two of Balzac's major novels, *Le Père Goriot (Father Goriot)* and *Le Lys dans la Vallée (The Lily of the Valley)*, were written at Saché. The latter is set in the Indre valley, which can be seen away from the house and does indeed have something of that "intangibly mysterious quality" to which Balzac refers with typical eloquence.

Balzac's bedroom at Saché

Le Grand-Pressigny 🔵

Road map D4. 🏛 *1,100.*
🚊 *Châtellerault, then taxi.*
🚌 *Tours.* 🚹 *pl de Savoire Villars
(02 47 94 96 82).* 🚌 *Thu.*

Perched high above the hilly
streets of the town, the **Château du Grand-Pressigny** has
lovely views over the peaceful
Claise and Aigronne valleys.
The château is part medieval
ruins, part 15th-century castle
and part Renaissance
residence. The rectangular,
12th-century ruined keep
contrasts dramatically with
the elegant 16th-century
Italianate wing.

Important prehistoric finds
have been made around
here, and various excavations
have revealed that the area
was a key centre for the
large-scale production of flint
implements, such as blades
produced from blocks known
as "pounds of butter", which
were exported as far afield as
Switzerland and Great Britain.

Many of these finds are
displayed at the **Musée de la
Préhistoire**, which has been
rebuilt, partly in startling
contemporary style, within
the ruins of the castle. The
collection includes examples
of tools and other objects
from all the prehistoric eras,
along with rock flints, large
blocks of obsidian and multi-
coloured jasper. The museum
is also home to an important
collection of plant and
animal fossils, some of which
date back 60 million years.

The museum also has a
room dedicated to temporary
exhibitions and an educa-
tional workshop on the
ground floor.

On summer afternoons
you can visit the **Archéolab**,
6 km (4 miles) northwest at
Abilly-sur-Claise, where a
transparent dome covers a
site that was inhabited by
stone cutters between 2800
and 2400 BC.

🏛 **Château du Grand-Pressigny**
Tel 02 47 94 90 20. ◯ *Apr–Sep:
daily; Oct–Mar: Wed–Mon.* ◼ *1 Jan,
25 Dec.* 🚫 🔵 **www.**prehistoire
grandpressigny.fr

🎭 **Archéolab**
Abilly-sur-Claise. *Tel* 02 47 91 07 48.
◯ *Jul–Aug: Tue–Sun, pm.* 🚫🔵

**Neolithic tool from the Musée de
la Préhistoire**

Loches 🔵

Road map D3. 🏛 *7,000.* 🚊 🚌
🚹 *pl de la Marne (02 47 91 82 82).*
🚌 *Wed, Sat.* 🎪 *Epopée
Medievale Fair (Aug).*
www.loches-tourainecotesud.com

Its medieval streets lined with
picturesque houses, the
peaceful town of Loches lies
beside the River Indre on the
edge of the Forêt de Loches.
Thanks to its strategic location,

**Agnès Sorel as the Virgin, painted
by Jehan Fouquet**

it became an important citadel
in the Middle Ages, with an
11th-century keep begun by
Foulques Nerra *(see p50)*. The
château remained in the
hands of the counts of Anjou
until 1194, when John Lackland ceded it to King Philippe
Augustus. John's brother,
Richard the Lionheart,
recaptured Loches in a surprise
attack in 1195. It took Philippe
Augustus nearly ten years to
retake the castle by force, and
eventually it became a French
royal residence. It was in the
15th-century **Logis Royal** that
Joan of Arc persuaded the
dauphin to travel to Rheims
and be crowned king of France
as Charles VII. This event is
commemorated in the tapestry-
hung Salle Jeanne d'Arc.

Also in the Logis Royal is
the tiny, late Gothic private
chapel of twice-queen Anne
of Brittany whose ermine
tail emblem recurs in the
decoration. On show in the
château are a fine *Crucifixion*
triptych by Tours painter Jehan
Fouquet (c.1420– 80) or one
of his pupils, and a copy of
his colourful *Virgin with Child*,
which was modelled on Agnès
Sorel, another woman of
influence in Charles VII's life.

The massive keep with its
surrounding towers is famous
for its torture chambers. One
of the most famous prisoners
here was Lodovico Sforza, the
duke of Milan, who died in the
Tour Martelet, where the
tempera wall paintings he
made can still be seen.

Beside the château is the
Collégiale St-Ours, a church
with four pyramid-like spires

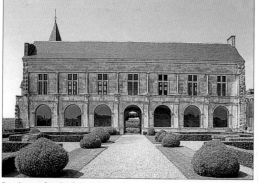

Renaissance façade of the Gallery, Château de Grand-Pressigny

For hotels and restaurants in this region see pp203–4 and pp215–16

and a Romanesque portal. Inside is the Gothic marble tomb of Agnès Sorel.

Near the Porte Royale lies the **Maison Lansyer**, birthplace of the 19th-century painter Emmanuel Lansyer. Some of his canvases are on display, along with his collection of Japanese armour and prints.

Underground, below the citadel, lie the extensive former quarries of the **Carrière Trogoldytique de Vignemont**, which are best explored with a tour guide.

🏰 **Château de Loches**
Tel **Logis Royal** 02 47 59 01 32; **Donjon** 02 47 59 07 86. ☐ *daily.* ☐ *1 Jan, 25 Dec.* 🎟️ ♿ 🎭 *Spectacle Nocturne (Aug).*

🏛️ **Maison Lansyer**
1 rue Lansyer. *Tel* 02 47 59 05 45. ☐ *Apr–Oct: Wed–Sat; Jun–Sep: Wed–Mon.*

⛏️ **Carrière Troglodytique de Vignemont**
52ter, rue des Roches. *Tel* 02 47 91 54 54. ☐ *Easter–Nov & school hols: daily.* 🎟️ 📷

Montrésor ⑮

Road map E3. 🚶 415. 🚉 *Loches, then taxi.* ℹ️ *Maison du Pays (02 47 92 70 71).*

The turreted **Château de Montrésor**, largely built in the 15th and 16th centuries, stands above this lovely village, on the site of medieval fortifications built by Count Foulques Nerra *(see p50).* It was bought in the mid-19th century by Count Branicki, an émigré Polish financier linked to the future Napoleon III. Still owned by Branicki's descendants, the château's Second Empire decor remains virtually unaltered.

As well as a fine collection of early Italian paintings and some elegant portraits, there are many gold and silver pieces. The rooms, with their mounted stags' and wolves' heads and dark panelling, retain a somewhat Central European feel. The château terrace and informal gardens offer fine views of the river.

An estate building, which used to house the château's wine press, has been converted into the Maison du Pays, an information centre and showcase for the Indrois Valley and its products.

The village's small Gothic and Renaissance church was built by Imbert de Bastarnay, lord of Montrésor, adviser to François I and grandfather of Diane de Poitiers *(see p108).* On the beautiful marble Bastarnay tomb lie *gisants* (effigies) of the lord, his lady and their son, guarded by angels and with their feet resting on greyhounds. The tomb, believed to be the work of the Renaissance sculptor Jean Goujon (c.1510–68), is decorated with statues of the apostles. There are also some wonderful Flemish and Italian paintings in the church, and a 17th-century *Annunciation* by Philippe de Champaigne (1602–74), the Baroque painter who worked on the Luxembourg palace in Paris with Nicolas Poussin.

In a lovely forest setting, to the east of the village of Montrésor, are the ruins of the **Chartreuse du Liget**, a Carthusian monastery founded by the Plantagenet king Henry II of England in

Farm buildings and poppy fields near the village of Montrésor

expiation for the murder of Archbishop Thomas à Becket. The nearby Chapel of **St-Jean-du-Liget** is decorated with 12th-century frescoes.

🏰 **Château de Montrésor**
Tel 02 47 92 60 04. ☐ *Apr–Oct: daily; Nov–Mar: Sat & Sun.* 🎟️ 📷 **www**.chateaudemontresor.fr

⛪ **Chapelle St-Jean-du-Liget**
Tel 02 47 92 60 02 *(Chartreuse du Liget).* ☐ *phone first.* ♿

Château de Montrésor, built on medieval fortifications

Château de Chenonceau 16

Chenonceau, stretching romantically across the River Cher, is considered by many the loveliest of the Loire châteaux. Surrounded by formal gardens and wooded grounds, this pure Renaissance building was transformed over the centuries from a modest manor into a palace designed solely for pleasure. The château now contains a fantastic collection of funiture and works of art. One of the latest acquisitions is a rare depiction of Henri III by the great French Renaissance painter François Clouet. The waxworks museum in one of the outbuildings focuses on the women of the château. In addition, there is also a restaurant in the old stables.

★ Cabinet Vert
The walls of Catherine de Médicis' study were originally covered with green velvet.

Chapelle
The chapel has a vaulted ceiling and pilasters sculpted with acanthus leaves and cockle shells. The stained glass, ruined by a bomb in 1944, was replaced in 1953.

Louise de Lorraine's room
was painted black and decorated with monograms, tears and knots in white after the death of her husband, Henri III.

The Tour des Marques
survives from the 15th-century castle of the Marques family.

STAR FEATURES

- ★ Cabinet Vert
- ★ Grande Galerie
- ★ Formal Gardens

The Three Graces
Painted by Charles-André Van Loo (1705–65), The Three Graces depicts the pretty Mailly-Nesle sisters, all royal mistresses.

Tapestries

As was the practice in the 16th century, Chenonceau is hung with Flemish tapestries that both warm and decorate its well-furnished rooms.

CHÂTEAU GUIDE

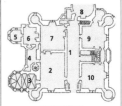

Ground floor

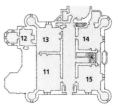

First floor

1 Vestibule
2 Salle des Gardes
3 Chapelle
4 Terrasse
5 Librairie de Catherine de' Médicis
6 Cabinet Vert
7 Chambre de Diane de Poitiers
8 Grande Galerie
9 Chambre de François I
10 Salon Louis XIV
11 Chambre des Cinq Reines
12 Cabinet des Estampes
13 Chambre de Catherine de Médicis
14 Chambre de Vendôme
15 Chambre de Gabrielle d'Estrées

★ Grande Galerie

Catherine de Médicis added this elegant gallery to the bridge designed by Philibert de l'Orme in 1556–9 for Diane de Poitiers.

Chenonceau's Florentine-style gallery, which stretches across the River Cher for 60 m (197 ft)

The Creation of Chenonceau

Chenonceau reflects the combined influence of five
women, who brought a feminine touch to this
graceful building. First came Catherine Briçonnet, wife
of the royal chamberlain, who supervised the construction of the château. Later, Diane de Poitiers, Henri
II's mistress, created a formal garden and built a
bridge over the Cher. After Henri's death, his
widow, Catherine de Médicis, reclaimed the
château and topped the bridge with a gallery.
Chenonceau survived the 1789 Revolution – because of
local respect for Louise Dupin, wife of a tax collector –
to be restored by Madame Pelouze in the 19th century.

Sphinxes
*Inscrutable stone sphinxes
guarding the entrance to
the gardens came from the
Château de Chanteloup,
which was destroyed in the
19th century (see p111).*

Diane de Poitiers
*Henri II's mistress, here
painted by François Clouet,
created a large, formal
garden, as well as the
bridge across the Cher.*

★Formal Gardens
*The current designs of the formal gardens
of Diane de Poitiers and Catherine de
Médicis date from the 19th century.*

TIMELINE

1500	1600	1700	1800	1900

1512 Thomas Bohier acquires the medieval Chenonceau. His wife, Catherine Briçonnet, rebuilds it

1559 On Henri's death, Catherine forces Diane to leave

Henri II

1913 The château is bought by the Menier family, the *chocolatiers* who still own it today

1789 Chenonceau is spared in the French Revolution, thanks to Louise Dupin

1575 Louise de Lorraine (1554–1601) marries Henri III, Catherine's son

1547 Henri II gives Chenonceau to Diane de Poitiers, his lifelong mistress

1533 Marriage of Catherine de Médicis (1519–89) to Henri II (1519–59). Chenonceau becomes a Loire royal palace

1730–99 Louise Dupin creates a salon for intellectuals at Chenonceau

1863 Madame Pelouze restores the château to its original state

1944 Chenonceau chapel is damaged in a bombing raid

Catherine de Médicis
After ousting Diane de Poitiers, Catherine de Médicis made her own mark on Chenonceau's design. She built the Grande Galerie over the Cher and added a formal garden to rival Diane's.

Louise Dupin
A well-read beauty with huge brown eyes, Louise Dupin entertained all the literary lions of her day, including Montesquieu and Voltaire. One guest, Jean-Jacques Rousseau, stayed on to tutor her children and famously praised Chenonceau's cuisine, claiming he had become "as plump as a monk".

Catherine de Médicis' emblem

Madame Pelouze bought Chenonceau in 1863 and restored it to Catherine Briçonnet's original design. Fortunately, she stopped short of taking down the Grande Galerie.

Court Festivities
Catherine de Médicis staged lavish balls and festivities at Chenonceau, some featuring plaster triumphal arches and statues designed by Francesco Primaticcio, others with living "nymphs" leaping out of the bushes chased by "satyrs".

Catherine Briçonnet
supervised the creation of an innovative château design, with rooms leading off a central vestibule on each floor.

Louise de Lorraine
Catherine de Médicis left Chenonceau to her daughter-in-law, Louise de Lorraine. Louise had her room redecorated in black upon the death of her husband, Henri III.

The Château d'Amboise, high above the town and the River Loire

Amboise ⑰

Road map D3. 🏘 *13,000.* 🚊 *quai du Général de Gaulle (02 47 57 09 28).* 🚌 *Fri, Sun.* **www**.amboise-valdeloire.com

The bustling little town of Amboise is famed for its château, and for being Leonardo da Vinci's final home.

⚜ Château Royal d'Amboise
Tel *02 47 57 00 98.* ◯ *daily.* ⚫ *1 Jan, 25 Dec.* 🖾 🖵 🚻 *Avanti la Musica (Jun–Aug); A la Cour du Roy François (Jul & Aug: Wed & Sat).* **www**.chateau-amboise.com

The late-Gothic Chapelle St-Hubert, with its highly ornate roof and spire

While much of the château has been destroyed, it is still possible to see the splendour that prevailed when first Charles VIII, then François I and, later, Henri II and Catherine de Médicis brought the Italian love of luxury and elegance to the French court.

Sculpted detail from the Logis du Roi

Amboise has also played a tragic part in history. In 1560 a Protestant plot to gain religious concessions from the young King François II was uncovered, 1,200 conspirators were slaughtered and some of their bodies strung up from the castle and town walls.

This horrifying episode was to spell the end of Amboise's glory, and the château was gradually dismantled. The enchanting, late-Gothic **Chapelle St-Hubert**, where a plaque recalls that Leonardo da Vinci was buried at the castle, has fortunately survived, perched on the ramparts of the château. Carvings on the exterior lintel of the chapel depict St

Hubert and St Christopher. The guard rooms and state rooms in the part-Gothic, part-Renaissance **Logis du Roi** are open to visitors, along with fascinating 19th-century apartments once occupied by King Louis-Philippe. Flanking the Logis du Roi is the **Tour des Minimes**, one of the original entrances to the château, with its impressive spiral inner ramp, up which horsemen could ride.

⚜ Château du Clos-Lucé
2 rue du Clos-Lucé. ***Tel*** *02 47 57 00 73.* ◯ *daily.* ⚫ *1 Jan, 25 Dec.* 🖾 ♿ *restricted.* 🚻 **http://**vinci-closluce.com

This graceful Renaissance manor house on the outskirts of Amboise was the last home of Leonardo da Vinci. In 1516 François I enticed Leonardo to the royal court at Amboise and settled him at Le Clos-Lucé, where he lived until his death in 1519.

Inside the house, da Vinci's bedroom, reception room, study, kitchen and a small chapel built for Anne of Brittany by Charles VIII are open to visitors. There are models made from Leonardo's astonishing technical drawings in the basement. More information on Leonardo's life is displayed in the outbuildings, while out in the gardens are larger models showing how some of his inventions worked.

🦈 Aquarium du Val de Loire

Lussault-sur-Loire. **Tel** *02 47 23 44 44.* ⬭ *daily.*
⬤ *2 wks Nov.* 🎫 ♿
www.aquariumduvaldeloire.com
With thousands of freshwater fish on display, the Aquarium du Val de Loire is the largest such collection in Europe.

Environs
Behind the Renaissance Château de la Bourdaisière, now also a hotel (*see p203*), hides a *potager* with 500 varieties of tomato, 150 kinds of lettuce and over 200 different herbs. Sample its produce at the Tomato Festival (mid-Sep).

⚜ Château et Jardins de la Bourdaisière

Montlouis-sur-Loire. **Tel** *02 47 45 16 31.* ⬭ *May–Oct: daily.* 🎫 📷
🖥 www.labourdaisiere.com

Leonardo da Vinci's bedroom at the Château du Clos-Lucé

Pagode de Chanteloup ⑱

Route de Bléré. **Tel** *02 47 57 20 97.*
⬭ *Feb–Mar: school hols; Apr–mid-Nov: daily.* 🎫 ♿ *park only.*
www.pagode-chanteloup.com

In the forest of Amboise, southwest of Amboise itself, stands this Chinese-style pagoda, more than 44 m (140 ft) high and built in seven stories, linked by steep spiral staircases. Each layer is smaller than the preceding one and contains an airy, octagonal room with a domed ceiling.

LEONARDO DA VINCI (1452–1519)

François I, who developed a love of Italian Renaissance art during his military campaigns there, persuaded Leonardo to join his court at Amboise, offering him an annual allowance and free use of the manor house at Clos-Lucé. The great Italian polymath arrived in Amboise in 1516 with some precious items in his luggage – three major paintings, in leather bags tied to a mule. One of them was the *Mona Lisa*, which François was to buy and place in the royal collection (hence its presence today in the Louvre in Paris).

Engraving of Leonardo da Vinci

Leonardo spent the last three years of his life at Le Clos-Lucé as the *Premier Peintre, Architecte, et Mécanicien du Roi* (first painter, architect and engineer to the king), mainly writing and drawing. As he was left-handed, the paralysis that affected his right hand was not a major handicap. Fascinated by hydrology, he produced plans to link the royal residences of the Loire Valley via waterways and even proposed rerouting the river. He also organized a series of elaborate court festivities, planning them down to the last detail with the same meticulous care he lavished on his scientific designs.

A model of Leonardo's prototype for a "car"

Seven avenues lead into the forest from the pagoda, which is reflected in a large lake.

This is all that is left of a splendid château built by Louis XV's minister, the Duc de Choiseul (1719–85). In the 1770s, Choiseul fell out with the king's mistress, Madame du Barry – he had been a protégé of her predecessor Madame de Pompadour – and was exiled from Versailles. He retreated to the château he had bought at Chanteloup in 1761 and rebuilt it. He spent his time entertaining on a large scale and dabbling in farming. After his death, the château was abandoned and then pulled down in 1823.

An exhibition in the pavilion explains the history of the once magnificent château and, for those brave enough to climb, there are impressive views of the Loire Valley from the top of the tower.

The Pagode de Chanteloup, in the heart of the forest of Amboise

Street-by-Street: Tours ⑲

The medieval old town, Le Vieux Tours, is full of narrow streets lined with beautiful half-timbered houses. Now sensitively restored, it is a lively area crammed with little cafés, bars and restaurants that attract locals as well as tourists. There are also numerous chic fashion boutiques and small shops devoted particularly to craft work and to stylish kitchen equipment. At its heart is the attractive place Plumereau, which in fine weather is filled with parasol-shaded café tables.

| 0 metres | 50 |
| 0 yards | 50 |

Place Pierre-le-Puellier
Medieval buildings surround this bustling square, which once formed part of a Renaissance cloister.

Maison des Vins de Loire
The maison offers a wonderful introduction to the wines of the Loire Valley, including tastings, for a small fee.

★ **Place du Grand Marché**
This street has undergone an exciting makeover, turning it into a very popular spot, with lovely café and restaurant terraces extending along it in warmer weather.

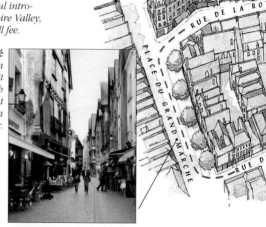

STAR SIGHTS

★ Place du Grand Marche

★ Place Plumereau

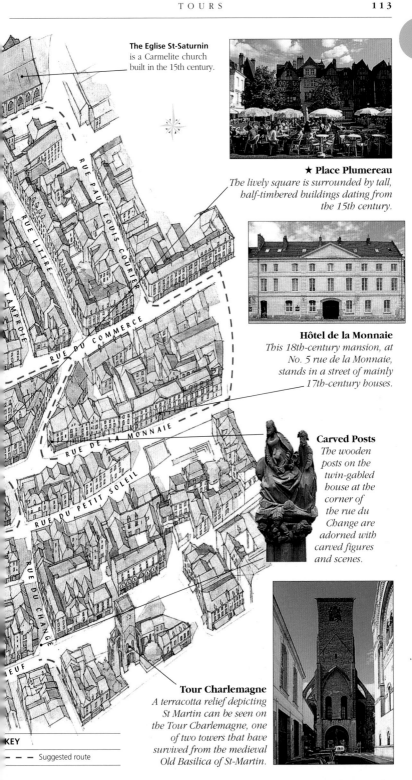

The Eglise St-Saturnin is a Carmelite church built in the 15th century.

★ **Place Plumereau**
The lively square is surrounded by tall, half-timbered buildings dating from the 15th century.

Hôtel de la Monnaie
This 18th-century mansion, at No. 5 rue de la Monnaie, stands in a street of mainly 17th-century houses.

Carved Posts
The wooden posts on the twin-gabled house at the corner of the rue du Change are adorned with carved figures and scenes.

Tour Charlemagne
A terracotta relief depicting St Martin can be seen on the Tour Charlemagne, one of two towers that have survived from the medieval Old Basilica of St-Martin.

KEY

– – – Suggested route

Exploring Tours

The pleasant Cathedral city of Tours, popular with foreign students eager to learn the country's purest French, is a perfect base for exploring Touraine. But Tours itself, its medieval heart imaginatively restored, repays exploration, too. Once a major Gallo-Roman centre, then filled with pilgrims flocking to St Martin's tomb, it became a wealthy courtly town from the mid-15th century, when the kings of France moved to the Loire. It has remained prosperous over the centuries, yet despite rapid expansion, it has kept its provincial charm.

Tours's Pont Wilson, recently rebuilt, spanning the Loire

Tours Town Centre
The area of the town close to the magnificent **Cathédrale St-Gatien** *(see pp116–17)* was part of the original Roman settlement. In the 3rd century AD, it was enclosed by a wall, the shape of which can still be seen in the rue des Ursulines, circling the cathedral and the Musée des Beaux Arts. The rue du Général-Meunier, a curving cobbled street of elegant houses once occupied by the clergy, follows the line of a Roman amphitheatre.

On the west side of Tours, a religious community grew up around the sepulchre of St Martin. The saint's tomb now lies in the crypt of the late 19th-century New Basilica, which was built on the site of the considerably larger, medieval Old Basilica. Two stone towers – the **Tour Charlemagne** and the **Tour de l'Horloge** – on either side of the rue des Halles, survive from the earlier building. Not far from the towers, the **place Plumereau**, with its charming medieval houses and tempting cafés, attracts locals, foreign students and tourists in large numbers.

Close to the cathedral, the half-timbered house at No. 39 rue Colbert bears a wrought-iron sign dedicated to the *Pucelle Armée* (the armed maid), recalling that Joan of Arc *(see p137)* bought her suit of armour here, before setting out to liberate Orléans in 1429. Nearby is the **place Foire-le-Roi**, a square where, thanks to a permit granted by the king in 1545, regular fairs were once held. The main merchandise was the silk that had been a key factor in the town's economy since the middle of the previous century. Of the gabled houses that line the square, the finest is the Renaissance Hôtel Babou de la

Bourdaisière, named after the finance minister to François I, who lived there. Slightly to the west, the 13th-century **Eglise St-Julien** stands on the site of an abbey founded in the 6th century.

The central bridge crossing the Loire, the **Pont Wilson**, is known locally as the *pont de pierre* (stone bridge). It is an exact replica of the town's original 18th-century bridge, which collapsed suddenly in 1978, making national headlines. One delight in central Tours is walking along the south quays of the Loire.

🏛 Musée des Beaux-Arts
18 pl François-Sicard. *Tel 02 47 05 68 73.* ⬜ *Wed–Mon.* ⬤ *1 Jan, 1 May, 14 Jul, 1 & 11 Nov, 25 Dec.* 🖼

The Museum of Fine Arts, conveniently situated next to the Cathédrale St-Gatien, is shaded by a cedar of Lebanon nearly two centuries old and fronted by attractive formal gardens. Once the Archbishop's Palace, the building dates mainly from the 17th and 18th centuries.

Its collections of paintings range from the Middle Ages to contemporary artists and include two celebrated altarpiece panels by Andrea Mantegna, *The Resurrection* and *Christ in the Olive Grove*, which were painted between 1456 and 1460 for the church of San Zeno in Verona.

To the right of the entrance courtyard is an outbuilding housing a huge stuffed circus elephant that died in Tours in the early 20th century.

Christ in the Olive Grove (1456–1460) by Andrea Mantegna

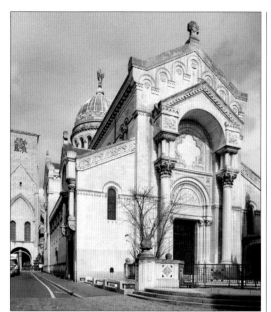

Tour's neo-Byzantine Basilique St-Martin

VISITORS' CHECKLIST

Road map D3. 🏙 *140,000.*
🚉 *pl du Général Leclerc.* 🚌 *pl du Général Leclerc.* 🛈 *78 rue Bernard Palissy (02 47 70 37 37).*
🗓 *Tue–Sun.* 🎭 *Fêtes Musicales en Touraine (early Feb); Foire à l'Ail et au Basilic (26 Jul, see p117).*
www.tours-tourisme.fr

🛈 **Basilique St-Martin**

7 rue Baleschoux. *Tel 02 47 05 63.*
◯ *daily.* **St-Martin Museum** 3 rue Rapin. *Tel 02 47 64 48 87.* ◯ *mid-Mar–mid-Nov.* 🖼

One of the greatest religious figures in French history, St Martin was born in the 4th century, in what is now Hungary. Joining the Roman army, he travelled to northern France. Moved by a naked beggar's plight there, he famously used his sword to cut his cloak in half to help the pauper. He went on to found one of France's first monasteries and become a bishop of Tours. After his death, his tomb became one of Europe's most important pilgrimage sites. This led to the building of one of the largest of all medieval churches, dedicated to him. Just two staggering towers remain from that edifice and in the late-19th century, a glittering new basilica went up in his honour. The great dome is topped by a statue of St Martin and the interior is richly styled with grand arches. Today, many Catholic pilgrims still come to pay homage to him at his tomb in the crypt. Nearby, a small museum in a Gothic chapel is dedicated to St Martin's memory and to the previous church.

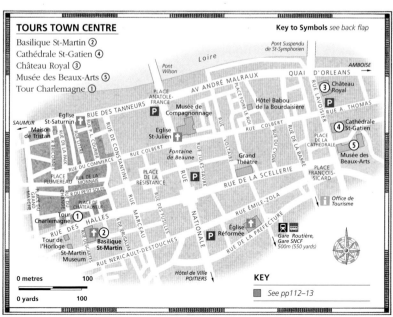

TOURS TOWN CENTRE

Key to Symbols *see back flap*

Basilique St-Martin ②
Cathédrale St-Gatien ④
Château Royal ③
Musée des Beaux-Arts ⑤
Tour Charlemagne ①

0 metres 100
0 yards 100

KEY

🟦 *See pp112–13*

Tours: Cathédrale St-Gatien

The foundation stone of Tours' Gothic cathedral, named after St Gatien, a 3rd-century bishop, was laid in the early 13th century. Because building work continued until the mid-16th century, the cathedral provides an illustration of how the Gothic style developed over the centuries. The Early Gothic chancel was the first area to be completed, while the nave and transept represent the Middle or High Gothic period and the highly decorated west façade is Flamboyant (or Late) Gothic.

Cloître de la Psalette
The cloisters, which lead off the north aisle, are made up of three galleries dating from the mid-15th and early 16th centuries.

★ West Façade
The richly carved Flamboyant west façade has three portals surmounted by a fine rose window.

Inside the North Tower is the elegant 16th-century "royal staircase".

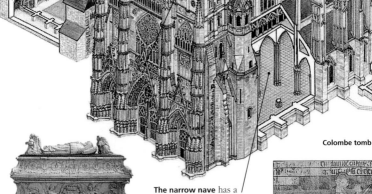

The narrow nave has a vaulted ceiling, dating from the late 15th century.

Colombe tomb

★ Colombe Tomb (1499)
The marble tomb of Charles VIII's and Anne of Brittany's infant sons features lifelike effigies by Michel Colombe or one of his pupils.

Fresco
This 14th-century fresco, restored in 1993, shows St Martin giving half his cloak to a beggar.

Colombe Statue
This statue of Tours' famous sculptor, Michel Colombe, stands in a square near the cathedral.

In the chancel, the stained-glass windows, depicting Christ's Passion and the legends of St Martin and other saints, date from around 1265.

★ **Stained-Glass Windows**
The stained glass is notable for its rich, strong colours and for the paler stained panels, or grisailles, *which let in more light than ordinary stained glass.*

STAR FEATURES

★ Colombe Tomb

★ Stained-Glass Windows

★ West Façade

⚓ **Château Royal de Tours**
25 ave André Malraux. *Tel 02 47 70 88 46.* ◯ *2–6pm Tue–Sun.* **Atelier Histoire de Tours** *(entry from church square). Tel 02 47 61 75 55.* ◯ *2–6pm Wed & Sat.* ⚫ *public hols.* ♿
The château, which served as a royal residence in the 13th and 15th centuries, was erected on top of the ancient Gallo-Roman walls, parts of which are still visible.

The Tour de Guise tower is named after the Duc de Guise, who made a daring escape while being held as a prisoner here following the assassination of his father at the Château de Blois in 1588.

In the Renaissance Logis des Gouverneurs, the exhibitions of the **Atelier Histoire de Tours** explain the city's long urban history using 3D models and plans.

🏛 **Centre de Création Contemporaine**
53 rue Marcel Tribut. *Tel 02 47 66 50 00.* ◯ *during exhibitions; Wed–Sun, pm only.* ♿ www.ccc-art.com
Occupying a modern building just a short walk southeast of the fine 19th-century railway station, this venue regularly stages shows by both internationally established contemporary artists and fresh names to the scene.

🏛 **Musée du Compagnonnage**
8 rue Nationale. *Tel 02 47 21 62 20.* ◯ *mid-Sep–mid-Jun: Wed–Mon; mid-Jun–mid-Sep: daily.* ⚫ *public hols.* 📷 ♿ www.museecompagnonage.fr
Housed in part of the abbey once attached to the medieval **Eglise St-Julien**, this unusual museum is devoted to craftsmanship. It has a fascinating collection of "master pieces" made by members of a guild of itinerant *compagnons* (journeymen) who applied to be awarded the prestigious title of Master Craftsman. Displays cover many trades, ranging from the work of stonemasons to that of clog makers, and even include some extraordinary spun-sugar creations.

A barrel on display in the Musée du Compagnonnage

GARLIC AND BASIL FAIR
On 26 July, the Feast of St Anne, the place du Grand-Marché in the Old Town, near the colourful covered market *(Les Halles)*, is the scene of the traditional Garlic and Basil Fair *(Foire à l'Ail et au Basilic)*. Pots of basil form a green carpet, and stalls are garlanded with strings of garlic heads, purple onions and grey or golden shallots.

Stalls laden with garlic and basil in the place du Grand-Marché

BLESOIS AND ORLEANAIS

T*hese two closely-linked regions are excellent starting points
for an exploration of the central Loire Valley. The area's forests
and marshlands have attracted nature lovers for centuries.
During the Renaissance, magnificent hunting lodges were built by
kings and nobles throughout the area, including the great Chambord,
the sumptuously furnished Cheverny and the charming Beauregard.*

Blésois and Orléanais remain
richly forested, with abundant game, including rabbits and hares, deer and
wild boar. The great forest
of Orléans, still magnificent,
contrasts with the heaths and marshy
lakes of the Sologne, a secretive region
of small, quiet villages and low, half-
timbered brick farmhouses. Although
a paradise for hunters and fishermen,
other visitors rarely venture into the
depths of this area.

The northern stretch of the Loire flows
through towns whose names resound
throughout the history of France.
Bridges and castles at Gien, Orléans,
Beaugency and Blois all assumed strategic significance during wars from the
Middle Ages to the 20th century.

It was at Orléans in 1429 that Joan
of Arc, lifting the English siege of the
town, galvanized the spirit of the
French army engaged in the Hundred
Years' War. The modern
city's proximity to Paris
has led to its growth as a
commercial centre, but
careful reconstruction
after the devastation of
World War II has meant that a sense
of the past survives in the old *quartier.*

During the Wars of Religion, the
château at Blois was sunk in political
intrigue. Now restored, its walls still
echo with the events of 1588, when
the Duc de Guise was assassinated
on the orders of the king, Henri III.

To the west of the region, the River
Loir, smaller than its majestic sound-
alike, flows through the countryside
of the Vendômois and also through
Vendôme itself, one of the most attractive towns in the region. Vendôme's
cathedral, La Trinité, is only one of the
memorable churches in Blésois and
Orléanais, many of them decorated
with early frescoes and mosaics.

Anglers taking part in a competition on a local canal

◁ **The nave of the Cathédrale Ste-Croix in Orléans**

Exploring Blésois and Orléanais

Orléans, the largest city in
Blésois and Orléanais, lies at
the northernmost point of the
River Loire. To the west is the
Petite Beauce, fertile, wheat-
growing land, while to the east is
the great forest of Orléans, dense
and teeming with wildlife. Blois,
downstream from Orléans, is also
surrounded by forests. To the
south, the Sologne is a land of
woods and marshes, scattered
with small lakes, or *étangs*.
The River Cher marks its
southern border, as it
flows through
charming villages.

One of the region's stone farmhouses

SIGHTS AT A GLANCE

KEY

═══ Motorway

─── Major road

─── Secondary road

┄┄┄ Minor road

─── Scenic route

╼╼╼ Main railway

─── Minor railway

─── Regional border

SEE ALSO

- ***Where to Stay*** pp204–5

- ***Where to Eat*** pp216–17

For additional map symbols *see back flap*

GETTING AROUND

The fastest route by car from Paris is *L'Aquitaine* autoroute (A10), which passes through Orléans and Blois. Some Paris-to-Tours TGVs stop at Vendôme, only a 45-minute journey. The Corail express train from Paris takes one hour to Les Aubrais (a suburb of Orléans with a connecting train to the city centre) and a further 30 minutes to Meung-sur-Loire and Blois via Beaugency. From Tours, a local line follows the Cher, stopping at Montrichard, Thésée and St-Aignan. Bus services between towns are extremely limited, especially during the school holidays. The drive along the D976, which parallels the River Cher, is very scenic, and the roads through the cool, forested areas of the region are tranquil and pleasant.

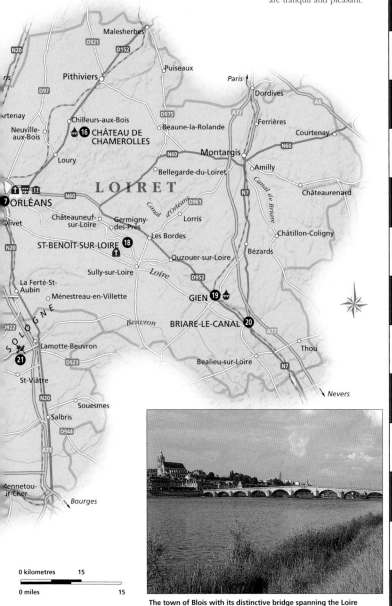

The town of Blois with its distinctive bridge spanning the Loire

0 kilometres   15

0 miles   15

Trôo's "speaking well"

Trôo **❶**

Road map D3. 🏛 *320.* 🚊 *Vendôme, then taxi.* 🚌 **ℹ** *02 54 72 87 50.* **www**.otsi-montoire.fr

On a cliff above the Loir, this village should be entered from the top through its ruined medieval gate. To the left of the gate is a covered "speaking well" with a very clear echo. During the Middle Ages, a massive fortress stood here. All that remains today is a mound, or *motte*, from the top of which there is a good view of the valley below. Parts of the **Eglise St-Martin**, nearby, date from the 11th century.

Steep paths wind down the hill, passing on the way the pretty flower gardens of a group of troglodyte dwellings, some of which are open to visitors. At the bottom of the hill is the **Grotte Pétrifiante**, a cave full of stalactites that have been developing for more than 4,000 years. The **Cave Yuccas** offers visitors the chance to explore a typical subterranean house with rooms dug out of the rock.

Across the river, the little church at **St-Jacques-des-Guérets**, built in the 12th century, is justly famous for its 13 murals, painted in a distinctive Byzantine style. They were rediscovered in 1890 during restoration work. The *Christ in Majesty* in the apse is a particularly beautiful example.

St-Gilles chapel in nearby Montoire-sur-le-Loir is also worth a visit. It has some even finer 12th-century murals, remarkable for the range of colours used. A dark day in French history, when Hitler met the collaborationist French leader, Marshal Pétain, at the former railway station is recalled at the **Musée des Rencontres**. World music is celebrated with an annual festival in August, and at the lively **Musikenfête** museum.

🏃 Grotte Pétrifiante
39 rue Arnault (Trôo). **Tel** *02 54 72 87 50.* 🕐 *Apr–Oct: daily.* 🈂

🏃 Cave Yuccas
12 rue Gouffier (Trôo). **Tel** *02 54 85 30 45.* 🕐 *Apr–Jun & Sep–Oct: Sat & Sun, weekdays pm only; Jul–Aug: daily.* 🈂

🏛 Musée des Rencontres
Av de la République (Montoire-sur-le-Loir). **Tel** *02 54 85 33 42.* 🕐 *Jul–Sep: 10am–noon, 3–6pm Mon, Thu, Sat & Sun, Wed & Fri pm only.* 🈂

🏛 Musikenfête
Espace de l'Europe (Montoire-sur-le-Loir). **Tel** *02 54 85 28 95.* 🕐 *May–Sep: 10am–noon, 2–6pm Tue–Sun; Oct–Dec: 2–6pm Tue–Sun.* 🈂 **www**.musikenfete.fr

---

Lavardin **❷**

Road map D3. 🏛 *250.* 🚊 *Vendôme, then taxi.* 🚌 **ℹ** *Montoire-sur-le-Loir (02 54 85 23 30).*

The fortifications of Lavardin's ruined **château** tower above the medieval bridge leading to the village. On the boundary between the Capetian and Angevin king-doms, the fortress was a key stronghold for centuries in battles between the French crown and the Plantagenet dynasty.

Lavardin's finest treasure is the Romanesque **Eglise St-Genest** with its fragile murals from the 12th–16th centuries.

♟ Château de Lavardin
Tel *02 54 85 07 74 (Mairie).* 🕐 *May: Sat & Sun; Jun–Sep: Tue–Sun.* 🈂 🈂

Vendôme **❸**

Road map D3. 🏛 *18,000.* 🚊 🚌 **ℹ** *47–49 rue Poterie. (02 54 77 05 07).* 🛒 *Fri & Sun.* **www**. vendome-tourisme.fr

One of the region's most scenic towns, Vendôme is built over a group of islands in the Loir, its bridges, water gates and old stone buildings forming a delightful tableau.

Situated on the border between French and English feudal territories, the town changed hands many times. It passed to the Bourbons in 1371, eventually becoming a duchy in 1515. Later, held by the Holy League during the Wars of Religion, it was recaptured by Henri IV in 1589; the skulls of his leading Catholic opponents are a grisly exhibit in the **Musée de Vendôme**. Set by an old abbey's cloisters, the museum also has a harp said to have been played by the ill-fated Marie-Antoinette, and some frescoes in the adjoining chapter house.

Vendôme's jewel is the abbey church of

Delicate murals in Lavardin's Eglise St-Genest

Ornate façade of Abbaye de la Trinité in Vendôme

La Trinité, founded in 1034 by Geoffroy Martel, son of Foulques Nerra. It stands beside a 12th-century Roman-esque bell-tower, with a spire reaching more than 80 m (260 ft). The church's bold, ornate façade was created by Jean de Beauce, who also designed the Old Bell-tower of Notre-Dame de Chartres. Its flame-like tracery is a typically virtuoso statement of the Flamboyant Gothic style.

Inside, beyond the transept, which dates from the 11th century, are choir stalls carved with amusing figures. To the left of the altar, a pretty latticework base with teardrop motifs once held a cabinet displaying a famous relic,

Wooden carving from La Trinité

which was said to be the tear supposedly shed by Jesus on the grave of Lazarus.

Shopping is centred around the place St-Martin, with its 15th-century clock-tower and carillon, and a statue of the local count of Rochambeau, who commanded the French forces during the American Revolution. There is also a graceful, *fin-de-siècle* covered market just off rue Saulnerie.

The best views of the town's old fortifications are from the square Belot. Also visible from here is the Porte d'Eau, a water gate built during the 13th and 14th centuries, which once controlled the water for the town's mills and tanneries. At certain times, you can take a boat trip on the Loire through town.

In the centre of town is the Parc Ronsard, with its 15th-century wash house, the Lavoir des Cordeliers, and the Old Oratorians College, which dates from the 17th and 18th centuries. Vendôme's ruined château stands on a bluff above the town, with the 12th-century Tour de Poitiers at one corner. The extensive garden offers some delightful panoramic views of the town.

🏛 Musée de Vendôme
Cloître de la Trinité. **Tel** 02 54 77 26 13. ◯ Wed–Mon. ⬤ Sun (Nov–Mar); 1 Jan, 1 May, 25 Dec. ⬤

Talcy's over 300-year-old wine press, still in working order

Château de Talcy ❹

Road map E3. 🚆 Mer, then taxi. **Tel** 02 54 81 03 01. ◯ Apr–Sep: daily; Oct–Mar: Wed–Mon. ⬤ 1 Jan, 1 May, 25 Dec. 🎟 🎫 also night tours Jul–Aug. 🎨 exhibition every summer. **www**.monum.fr

After the grander châteaux of the Loire Valley, Talcy comes as a delightful surprise: a fascinating, human-scale home, hiding behind a stern façade. The original building, a keep, dates from the 15th century. It was transformed by Bernardo Salviati, a Florentine banker and cousin of Catherine de Médicis, who bought it in 1517 and added to the building significantly.

In 1545, the poet Pierre de Ronsard *(see p24)* fell in love with Salviati's 15-year-old daughter, Cassandre. Over the following decade, his love for her inspired the sonnets of his famous collection, known as *Amours de Cassandre*.

Bernardo Salviati gave Talcy its feudal look, adding the crenellated sentry walk and fake machicolations to the gatehouse. In the first courtyard, with its arcaded gallery, is an elegant domed well. A 3,000-bird dovecote in the second courtyard, dating from the 16th century, is the best-preserved in the Loire.

A huge wooden wine press, over 300-years-old but still in working order, is worth a look. The château's vineyards are no longer productive, but an orchard preserves old varieties of fruit trees.

Inside the château, the charming rooms have retained their original 17th- and 18th-century furnishings.

The Lavoir des Cordeliers in Vendôme's Parc Ronsard

Street-by-Street: Blois

A powerful feudal stronghold for several
centuries, Blois became a royal city under
Louis XII, who established his court here in
1498. The town remained at the centre of
French royal and political life for much
of the next century. Now an important
commercial centre for the agricultural
districts of the Beauce and Sologne,
Blois, with its harmonious combination
of white walls, slate roofs, and redbrick
chimneys, is the quintessential Loire
town. The hilly, partly pedestrianized
old quarter, bordered by the river,
the château, and the cathedral, is
full of architectural interest.

Hôtel d'Alluye
*Blois' outstanding
Renaissance man-
sion was built in
1508 by Florimond
Robertet, treasurer
to three kings.*

| 0 metres | 10 |
| 0 yards | 100 |

Façade des Loges, the
château's most theatrical
side, has Renaissance
window bays rising in
tiers to a gallery.

★ Château de Blois
*The rich history of the Château
de Blois is reflected in its varied
architectural styles.*

Blois as seen from the Loire, with the three
spires of the Eglise St-Nicolas in the centre

★ Eglise St-Nicolas
*This striking, three-spired
church once belonged to a
12th-century Benedictine
abbey. Its high, narrow
Gothic nave leads to an
apse of magical beauty,
sheltered by elegant
Corinthian columns
and lit through lovely
blue glass.*

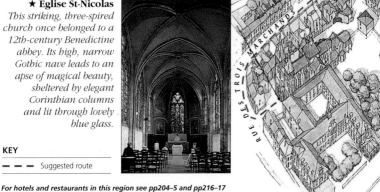

KEY

— — — Suggested route

For hotels and restaurants in this region see pp204–5 and pp216–17

Escalier Denis-Papin
Named after the native son (1647–1714) who invented the pressure cooker, these stairs provide a remarkable view over the town and the river.

VISITORS' CHECKLIST

Road map E3. 51,000.
pl de la Gare.
23 pl du Château (02 54 90 41 41). Tue & Sat.
Son et Lumière: Château de Blois (mid-Apr–mid-Sep: daily); Tous sur le Pont (music & theatre; early Jul).
www.bloischambord.com
Musée d'Histoire Naturelle & Musée d'Art Religieux
Couvent des Jacobins.
Tel 02 54 90 21 00. Tue–Sun pm. 1 Jan, 1 May, 1 Nov, 25 Dec.

Maison des Acrobates, in the place St-Louis, has carvings of medieval characters on its posts.

Couvent des Jacobins now houses museums of religious art and natural history.

Cathédrale St-Louis
Most of the original building was destroyed by a hurricane in 1678. The present cathedral was erected during the reign of Louis XIV.

★ Quartier Vieux Blois
This well-preserved area of Blois has some marvellous 16th-century buildings. This galleried town house is at the top of rue Pierre de Blois.

STAR SIGHTS

★ Château de Blois

★ Eglise St-Nicolas

★ Quartier Vieux Blois

Château Royal de Blois ❺

Porcupine emblem of the House of Orléans

Home to Kings Louis XII, François I and Henri III, no other Loire château has such a sensational history of skulduggery at court. It culminated with the stabbing, on the order of Henri III, of the ambitious Duc de Guise, leader of the formidable Catholic Holy League *(see pp54–5)*. This macabre event, which took place in the king's own bedroom, marked the end of the château's political importance. The building itself juxtaposes four distinct architectural styles dating from the 13th century, through the Gothic and Renaissance periods, to the Classical. The château has benefited from major restorations, which began in 1989.

Gaston d'Orléans Wing
Of striking Classical design, as shown in the ceiling of the entrance hall, the Gaston d'Orléans wing hosts major temporary exhibitions.

King Louis XII
A statue of Louis XII (1462–1515) is the centrepiece of the entrance archway. Known as "Father of the People", he was popular for his benevolent domestic policies.

The Tour du Foix remains from the ramparts that surrounded the 13th-century feudal fortress.

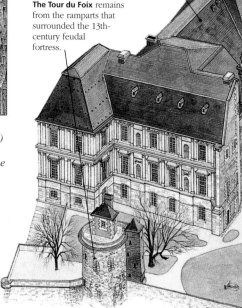

STAR FEATURES

★ François I's Staircase

★ Cabinet de Catherine de Médicis

★ Salle des Etats Généraux

TIMELINE

1200	1300	1400	1500	1600	1700	1800	1900
1200 Counts of Blois rebuild feudal fortress dating from 9th century			**1576** Etats Généraux meets in feudal hall / **1515** François I rebuilds north wing	**1788** The decaying château is turned into barracks / **1588** Etats Généraux meets again. Henri III has Duc de Guise assassinated	*Architect Félix Duban*		
	1391 Fortress passes to Louis d'Orléans, brother of Charles VI		**1498** Louis XII adds three new wings and rebuilds the St-Calais chapel / **1635** Gaston d'Orléans replaces west wing with Classical building	**1810** Napoléon makes city of Blois responsible for the château / **1843** Félix Duban begins restoration of the château			**1989** Major restoration programme begins

★ Cabinet de Catherine de Médicis
The queen's room has 237 carved panels, four with secret cupboards for her jewels, works of art or, some believed, poisons.

VISITORS' CHECKLIST

Pl du Château. 02 54 90 33 32. □ daily, opening times vary; check the website for details. ● 1 Jan, 25 Dec. 📷 📷 📷 Ainsi Blois vous est conté (see p42).
www.chateaudeblois.fr

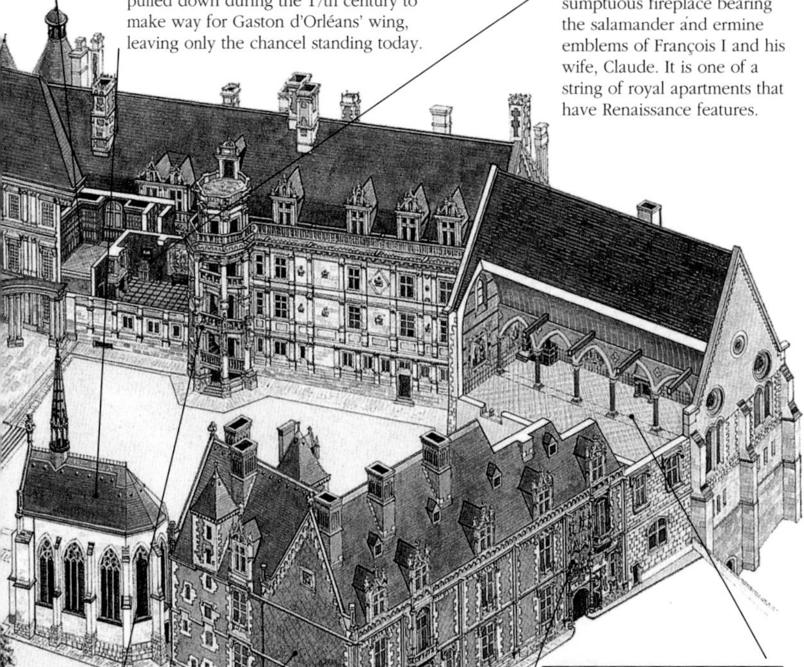

The nave of the St-Calais chapel was pulled down during the 17th century to make way for Gaston d'Orléans' wing, leaving only the chancel standing today.

The Salle d'Honneur has a sumptuous fireplace bearing the salamander and ermine emblems of François I and his wife, Claude. It is one of a string of royal apartments that have Renaissance features.

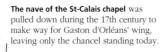

Statue of Louis XII

The Gothic Louis XII wing has intricate, decorative exterior brickwork.

★ François I's Staircase
Enclosed in an octagonal well, the staircase, with its highly ornate carving, is a Renaissance tour de force. From its open balconies, the royal family could watch events in the courtyard.

★ Salle des Etats Généraux
Used for royal receptions and Etats Généraux meetings (see pp54–5), this vast 13th-century room survives from the original fortress.

Château de Chaumont, towering above the town

Château de Chaumont ❻

Chaumont-sur-Loire. **Road map** D3.
🚉 Onzain, then taxi. 📞 02 54 20
99 22. ◯ daily. ● 1 Jan, 1 May,
1 & 11 Nov, 25 Dec. 🎟 🚻
🎭 Festival International des Jardins
(May–mid-Oct). **www**.domaine-
chaumont.fr

Chaumont, set on a wooded
hill above the Loire, appears
like a fantasy of a feudal
castle. Its tall, white towers,
built between 1466 and 1510,
were never tested in battle and
have remained in immaculate
condition. Emblems carved on
the towers include the crossed Cs of Charles II d'Amboise.

When Charles inherited
Chaumont in 1481, he made
major alterations to the pre-
existing castle, bringing the
Renaissance architectural
style to France.

Catherine de Médicis, wife
of Henri II, acquired the
château in 1560. Legend has
it that Catherine's astrologer,
Ruggieri, revealed to the
queen the tragic fate of her
three royal sons in a magic
mirror. Catherine's chamber
also has a balcony adjoining
the attractive chapel, which
was restored towards the
end of the 19th century. In
1562 Catherine gave Chaumont to Diane de Poitiers,
mistress of the late Henri II,
after forcing her out of
Chenonceau (see pp108–9).
Diane's entwined Ds and
hunting motifs are carved

on the machicolations of the
entrance and on the east wing.

Subsequent owners either
neglected the chateau or
altered it to their own
purposes. One 18th-century
owner, abandoning the
fortress design, demolished
the north wing so that the
whole courtyard was opened
up to the river
views. The
sculptor Nini also
worked here
during the period
and Benjamin
Franklin was one
famous visitor he
depicted.
Sweeping
improvements
began in 1875
when Prince
Amédée de
Broglie came to
live in the château with his
wife Marie, a sugar heiress.
Their lavish lifestyle can be
sensed not just in the castle,
but also in the handsome
stables, which once housed
an elephant, given to them on
a visit to the Maharajah of
Kapurtala in India.

The council room has
tapestries by Reymbouts and
majolica floor tiles, brought
from a 17th-century Palermo
palace, while the library has
medallions made in the

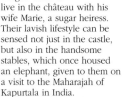

**Stained glass from the
dining room at Chaumont**

château by Jean-Baptiste Nini
in the 1700s.

The château's park was
landscaped in 1884 by Achille
Duchêne and follows the lines
of an English country garden.

Each summer, the park hosts
an extraordinarily detailed
array of miniature gardens by
leading designers. These
predominantly
cutting-edge
designs are for
the prestigious
Festival Inter-
national des
Jardins.
Chaumont has
also become the
Centre d'Arts
et de Nature,
commissioning
major works by
contemporary
artists in its
grounds. Several exciting
restaurants set up on the estate
cater to the crowds that come
for these events.

Montrichard ❼

Road map D3. 🏠 3,500. 🚉 🚌
ℹ️ 1 rue du Pont (02 54 32 05 10).
🛒 Mon pm, Fri am. **www**.office
tourisme/montrichard.com

This small town is dominated
by the remnants of its

Montrichard, seen from across the River Cher

château. The 11th-century drawbridge, archers' tower and the remains of its Renaissance apartments remain, and the keep houses the small **Musée du Donjon** on local life.

Adjoining the château is the **Eglise Ste-Croix**. Here, in 1476, the future Louis XII reluctantly wed Jeanne, the tragically deformed daughter of Louis XI. The marriage was later annulled so Louis could marry Anne of Brittany.

⛪ **Château de Montrichard & Musée du Donjon**
Tel 02 54 32 57 15.
⏰ Easter–Sep: Tue–Sun. 🖼
🎭 Spectacle du Donjon (a show with stuntmen on horseback, twice daily; mid-Jun–mid-Aug).

White tiger from Beauval Zoological Park

St-Aignan-sur-Cher ⑧

Road map E3. 🏘 3,700. 🚉 St-Aignan-Noyers-sur-Cher. 🚌
🛈 02 54 75 22 85. 📅 Sat. **www.** tourisme-valdecher-staignan.com

Once a river port, St-Aignan is now an engaging summer resort for boating, swimming and fishing. The town is dominated by the Renaissance château of the dukes of Beauvillier and the collegiate church of St-Aignan, a marvel of Romanesque art.

The château interior is not open to the public, but visitors can climb 19th-century stairs to look at its two elegant wings and enjoy the views from its courtyard terrace as a reward for their exertions. Ruined towers and

walls remain from a feudal fortress built by the counts of Blois. In rue Constant-Ragot, leading to the château and church, there is a fine half-timbered Renaissance house on the corner with rue du Four.

The **Collégiale de St-Aignan**, with its two impressive bell-towers, was begun around 1080. Its majestic chancel and sanctuary are built over an earlier Romanesque church, which now forms the crypt. Once used as a cowshed, the crypt still retains its Romanesque feel. Among the important frescoes to survive here are a portrayal of the miracles of St Gilles in the southern chapel and a rare 11th-century *Christ in Majesty* on the chancel vault.

Some of the 250 sculpted capitals in the main church are carved with scenes from the Old and New Testaments as well as allegories of sin and punishment. Others are worked with decorative motifs. In the Chapel of Our Lady of Miracles, the 15th-century ceiling paintings are equally fascinating.

The **Beauval Zoological Park**, 2 km (1¼ miles) south of the town, contains some 4,000 animals, a superb jungle

St-Aignan's Chapel of Our Lady of Miracles

house, a lagoon of piranhas, and impressive landscaped enclosures for big cats, including several magnificent prowling white tigers.

🐾 **Beauval Zoological Park**
Tel 02 54 75 50 00. ⏰ daily. 🖼 ♿
🍴 **www**.zoobeauval.com

Thésée ⑨

Road map E3. 🏘 1,300. 🚉
🛈 St Aignan (02 54 75 22 85); Mairie (02 54 71 40 20). 📅 Thu.

Just outside the charming little wine village of Thésée is the most important Gallo-Roman site in the Loire-et-Cher *département*, Les Maselles (or Tasciaca). Impressive ruined walls with brick courses testify to the skills of stonemasons who built it in the 2nd century AD. This settlement was a major staging post and ceramic-making centre on the road between Bourges and Tours. The **Musée Archéologique** within the town hall displays a quite dazzling and instructive array of jewels, coins, pottery and other interesting artifacts from this little-known site.

Fresco of Christ in Majesty, from the Eglise de St-Aignan

🏛 **Musée Archéologique**
Hôtel de Ville. *Tel* 02 54 71 40 20.
⏰ Wed–Mon. 🖼 📷 **Les Maselles**: 10am & 2:30pm.

Classical façade of the Château de Cheverny

Château de Cheverny ⑩

Road map E3. **Tel** *02 54 79 96 29.* ○ *daily.* 🚫 🚹 *grd floor & park only.* **www**.chateau-cheverny.fr

The elegance of Cheverny's white stone façade, with its pure Louis XIII lines, was achieved in a single phase of construction between 1620 and 1634, with all the finishing touches completed by 1648 *(see pp20–21)*.

Initiating a new architectural style for the châteaux of the Loire Valley, Cheverny has no defensive elements, such as large turreted towers or formidable entrances. Instead, its Classical façade is striking in its simplicity. The château stands on the site of a previous castle and is owned by the illustrious Hurault family. Henri Hurault, with his wife, Marguerite, led the château's reconstruction, and the family has retained its ownership.

Jean Mosnier worked on the interior for 10 years, using gilded beams, panels and ceilings. His finest work is in the dining room, with its scenes from Don Quixote's travels, and in the king's bedroom, where the combined effect of wall-hangings, painted ceilings and a bed canopied in Persian silk is stunning. The château's largest room, the Salle des Armes, displays a collection of arms and armour and is adorned with Mosnier's paintings.

Famous paintings in the château include a portrait of Cosimo de' Médici by Titian, Pierre Mignard's striking portrait of the Countess of Cheverny above the fireplace in the Grand Salon, and a collection of fine portraits by Jean Clouet and Hyacinthe Rigaud in the adjoining gallery.

The Cheverny hunt, which rides twice a week in winter, is famous throughout the Sologne. A visit to the kennels (open Apr–mid-Sep) is a highlight of the château, especially in the late afternoon, when 70 hungry hounds wait their turn to be fed.

The gardens can be explored by visitors, including an ornate kitchen garden and elegant English-style park. You can even hire electric buggies or an electric boat to discover more of the grounds and canals.

Fans of *Tintin* will recognize that the lovely Cheverny features as the Château de Moulinsart (or Marlinspike Hall in English) in his adventures. A special permanent exhibition reveals more.

The Grand Salon at Cheverny

Château de Beauregard ⑪

Cellettes. **Road map** E3. 🚉 *Blois,* then taxi. **Tel** *02 54 70 40 05.* ○ *Feb–Mar, Oct–Nov school hols: daily (weekdays pm only); Apr–Sep: daily.* ⬤ *Jan & Dec.* 🚫 🚹 **www**. beauregard-loire.com

Beauregard stands in a well-tended park on the edge of the Russy forest. A manor here was used as a hunting lodge for François I, but this was transformed into a graceful château in the mid-16th century for Jean du Thier, scholarly secretary of state to Henri II. It was du Thier who commissioned the king's Italian cabinet–maker, Scibec de Carpi, to make him an exquisite study panelled in gilded oak, the Cabinet des Grelots. This little room is

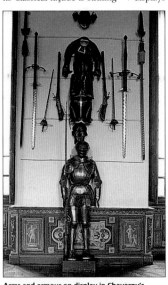

Arms and armour on display in Cheverny's Salle des Armes

Detail from Beauregard's portrait gallery

Château de Villesavin ⑫

Villesavin. **Road map** E3. 🚌 *Blois, then taxi.* **Tel** 02 54 46 42 88. ◯ *Mar: Fri–Wed; Apr–mid-Nov: daily.* ● *mid-Nov–Feb.* 📷 ♿ *grd flr only.* 🌐 www. chateau-de-villesavin.com

Renaissance Villesavin, built between 1527 and 1537 by Jean Breton, was his home while he supervised works at Chambord *(see pp132–5)* nearby. Stone carvers from the royal château ornamented Villesavin and presented Breton with the beautiful Florentine basin in the entrance courtyard.

decorated with the bells, or *grelots*, found on du Thier's crest, and has some charming paintings from the studio of Niccolo dell'Abate.

The portrait gallery, the château's most spectacular feature, was added in the 17th century by Henry IV's former treasurer, Paul Ardier. A catalogue of famous European faces from 1328 to 1643 – kings, queens, saints, explorers – is arranged in three rows around the gallery. Adding to the impact of these 327 portraits are beautiful beams and panels painted by Jean Mosnier and the largest

delft-tiled floor in Europe, which depicts an army on the move in Louis XIII costume.

Other delights include the southern gallery, with its rich Brussels tapestry and carved furniture, and the kitchen, with its flagstone floors and a table built around the central column. Above the ratchet-operated spit, a motto on the chimney breast advises that those who keep promises have no enemies.

One of Villesavin's antique carriages

This is one of the least altered of the many late-Renaissance châteaux in the Loire Valley. Villesavin, with its low walls and unusually high roofs, was built around three very spacious courtyards. The elegant southern façade ends with a large dovecote, which has 1,500 pigeonholes and a revolving ladder.

The château's essentially domestic spirit is also evident in the service court, overlooked by a spacious kitchen with a working spit. The interesting collection of old carriages on display here includes an 18-m (59-ft) long *voiture de chasse* with four rows of seats, from which ladies could watch the hunt.

Environs

Situated on the southern banks of the Beuvron river, Bracieux is worth a visit for its grand covered market, which was built during the reign of the Renaissance king François I (1515–47). At that time, the town acted as an important staging post on the routes between the towns of Tours, Chartres and Bourges.

The market is built of brick, stone and wood, with an upper tithe barn. Its original oak posts were strengthened during the 19th century. There are also 17th- and 18th-century houses here.

Garden façade of the Château de Villesavin

Château de Chambord ⑬

Henry James once said: "Chambord is truly royal – royal in its great scale, its grand air, and its indifference to common considerations." The brainchild of the extravagant François I, the château began as a hunting lodge in the Forêt de Boulogne. In 1519 the original building was razed and Chambord begun, to a design probably initiated by an Italian architect. Leonardo da Vinci has been linked with the conception of the stunning central staircase.

Statue of Diana in the Salle de Diane

By 1537 the keep, with its towers and terraces, had been completed by 1,800 men and two master masons. François I, and then his son Henri II, made further additions, including a private royal pavilion on the northeast corner and a chapel, and Louis XIV completed the 440-roomed edifice in 1685.

The Château de Chambord with the Cosson, a tributary of the Loire, in the foreground

The roof terraces include miniature spires, stair turrets, sculpted gables and cupolas.

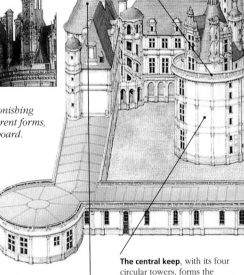

★ Skyline
Chambord's skyline is its most astonishing feature – a bizarre jumble of different forms, likened to an overcrowded chess board.

Salamander
François I's emblem appears more than 700 times in the château. It symbolizes patronage of the good and destruction of the bad.

The central keep, with its four circular towers, forms the nucleus of the château.

Chapel
Begun by François I shortly before his death in 1547, the chapel was given a second storey by Henri II. Later, Louis XIV embellished the roof.

STAR FEATURES

★ Skyline

★ Grand Staircase

François I Staircase
The external spiral staircase located in the northeastern courtyard was added at the same time as the galleries, starting in 1538.

The lantern tower, 32 m (105 ft) high, is supported by flying buttresses.

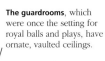

The guardrooms, which were once the setting for royal balls and plays, have ornate, vaulted ceilings.

François I's bedchamber in the east wing, as it was at his death in 1547.

Cabinet de François I
The king's barrel-vaulted study (cabinet) in the outer north tower was turned into an oratory in the 18th century by Queen Catherine Opalinska, wife of Stanislas Leszczynski (Louis XV's father-in-law and the deposed king of Poland).

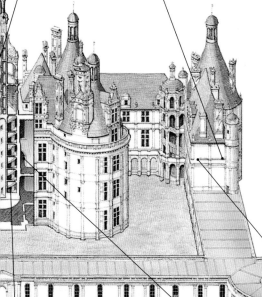

★ Grand Staircase
Seen here from the guardrooms, this innovative double staircase was supposedly designed by Leonardo da Vinci. Two flights of stairs spiral around each other.

Louis XIV's Bedchamber
The Sun King's state apartments are the grandest in the château.

The History of Chambord

Chambord, the largest château in the Loire, was a *folie de grandeur* of the young François I, whose passions included not just politics and the arts but also hunting and flirting. "He is forever chasing, now stags, now women," the Venetian ambassador once said of him. The king supervised the enclosure of the game park surrounding Chambord with the most extensive wall in France – nearly 32 km (20 miles) long. At one point, he even suggested diverting the Loire to flow in front of his château, but settled for redirecting the nearer Cosson to fill his moat.

Louis XIV portrayed as Jupiter, conquering La Fronde

François I as a young man, with various symbols of his kingship

After François I

On his father's death, Henri II took charge of François I's ambitious project. Subsequent owners, Louis XIII and Gaston d'Orléans, continued to modify the château. By the 17th century, Chambord comprised 440 rooms and had 365 chimneys, 14 main staircases and 70 smaller stairways.

Louis XIV, whose chief amusement was hunting, took Chambord very seriously. His full court retinue visited the château numerous times. With balls, plays by Molière and ballets, he re-created the glittering lifestyle of François I.

Louis XV also hawked at Chambord, but in 1725 he was ready to relinquish the château to his father-in-law, Stanislas Leszczynski. The exiled King of Poland filled in the moats to prevent malarial fevers.

The last owner to enjoy Chambord's theatricality was the Maréchal de Saxe, victor over the English troops at the Battle of Fontenoy in 1745. As well as lodging his actress mistress here, Saxe also kept two cavalry regiments whose mock battles he watched from the roof terraces.

Chambord then fell into neglect. Stripped during the French Revolution, the château was hardly used by the Bourbon pretender, Henri, Duc de Bordeaux, to whom it was given by public subscription in 1821. It was bought by the state in 1930, and a restoration programme was begun in the 1970s. The castle now contains thousands of objects, from fine portraits and tapestries to large hunting collections. It also hosts many temporary exhibitions and visitors can enjoy varied activities, including boating and cycling.

A view of Chambord (detail) by PD Martin (1663–1742)

TIMELINE

1547–59 Henri II adds the west wing and second storey of the chapel

1560–74 Charles IX continues tradition of royal hunting at Chambord and writes *Traité de la Chasse Royale*

Maréchal de Saxe

1840 Chambord declared a *Monument Historique*

1500	1600	1700	1800	1900

1670 Molière's *Le Bourgeois Gentilhomme* staged at Chambord

1519–47 The Count of Blois' hunting lodge is demolished by François I and the château created

1748 Acquired by the Maréchal de Saxe. On his death the château falls into decline

1725–33 Inhabited by exiled king of Poland

1685 Louis XIV completes the building

1970s Under Giscard d'Estaing, Chambord is restored and refurnished and the moats redug

Royal Hunting at Chambord

Under the influence of François I and his heirs, hunting and hawking were the foremost pastimes of the court during the 16th century. A Tuscan nobleman complained that the king only stayed in a place "as long as the herons last". They were quick prey for the 500 falcons that travelled with the rest of the royal retinue.

Within his vast oak forests, the king rode out at dawn to a prepared picnicking spot, there to feast and await the selection of a red deer tracked by his beaters. The quarry flushed, he would ride at full tilt in pursuit, sometimes for hours. For ladies of the court, Chambord's

St Hubert, patron saint of hunting

roof terraces offered matchless views of these exertions. François' son Henri II and grandson Charles IX were also keen and practised hunters, sometimes pursuing quarry on foot. Louis XIV favoured the English sport of following packs of hounds, but falconry was preferred by Louis XV.

Hunting was regarded as an art by the court, and for centuries it was also a favourite subject for painters and tapestry designers. The courtly importance of hunting is brought to the fore in the extensive collections of art in Chambord's Musée de la Chasse on the castle's second floor.

Matchlock

Engraved barrel

Arquebus, an early form of musket, dating from the 16th century

Wild boar was a favourite beast of the chase because of its strength and ferocity. Its head was considered a delicacy.

The crossbow was a popular hunting weapon thanks to its versatility and rapid rate of fire.

Greyhounds, prized for their speed and keen eyesight, were used as hunting dogs.

The Boar Hunt *comes from the* Traités de Fauconnerie et de Vénerie (1459), *one of many treatises on falconry and hunting to hounds. In the foreground, beaters and dogs chase their quarry. Behind them, animals and men witness the end of the hunt.*

Beaugency ⓮

Road map E3. 👥 *8,000.* 🚃 🚌
ℹ️ *3 pl du Docteur Hyvernaud (02 38 44 54 42).* 🛒 *Sat.* 🎭 *Festival de Beaugency (first & second w/end Jul).*

With the Loire racing beneath its famous 23-arch bridge, the medieval town of Beaugency makes a delightful base for exploring the Orléanais area. The town is surprisingly well preserved, although its bridge, the best on the Loire between Orléans and Blois, has attracted the attentions of a number of armies over the centuries. Restored in the 16th century, the bridge was damaged again in 1940 when the Allied army blew up its southern end to prevent the Nazis from crossing the river.

On the place Dunois at the top of rue de l'Abbaye stands a massive 11th-century keep. Opposite is the Romanesque abbey church of **Notre-Dame**, where Eleanor of Aquitaine's marriage to Louis VII was annulled in 1152, leaving her free to marry the future Henry II of England.

Higher up is the 16th-century Tour St-Firmin, near an equestrian statue of Joan of Arc. Her companion-in-arms, Jean Dunois, Bastard of Orléans and Lord of Beaugency, built the **Château Dunois**, which is undergoing restoration. Nearby, in rue des Trois Marchands, is a medieval

Beaugency's 11th-century clock-tower, once gateway to the town

clock-tower and the Renaiss-ance façade of the Hôtel de Ville. Inside is a collection of elaborate embroideries.

Meung-sur-Loire ⓯

Road map E3. 👥 *6,300.* 🚃 🚌
ℹ️ *1 rue Emmanuel Troulet (02 38 44 32 28).* 🛒 *Sun am, Thu pm.*
www.visitez-meungsurloire.fr

This pretty town, sloping down to the Loire, was the birthplace of Jean de Meung *(see p24)*, one of the authors of the 13th-century masterpiece *Le Roman de la Rose.* There has been a town on this site since Gallo-Roman times, when it was known as Magdunum.

Close to the impressive Romanesque church of **St-Liphard**, built from the 11th to the 13th century, rise the feudal towers of the **Château de Meung**. Frequently altered from the 12th century to the 18th century, the château was built in a variety of styles. The 18th-century wing has an interesting collection of furn-iture, paintings and tapestries.

More intriguing are the underground passages and dungeons of the older castle, dating from the 12th to 13th centuries and used for 500 years by the bishops of Orléans as a prison. It is said that in 1461 the poet François Villon *(see p24)*, renowned for his life of disrepute as well as his fine writing, spent five months fighting with the other condemned criminals on a ledge above a cesspool in the château's claustrophobic oubliette. Thanks to a royal pardon from Louis XI, he was the only prisoner ever to emerge alive from there.

Nearby, two gardens worth seeing are open in summer months. The Arboretum des Prés de Culands lies to the north of the centre; the Jardins de Roqulin just south across the Loire.

🏯 **Château de Meung**
Tel *02 38 44 36 47.* ⬜ *Apr–May, Sep–Oct: Tue–Sun, pm only; Jun–Aug: Tue–Sun; Dec: weekends, pm only.* 🚫 ♿ *grd flr only.* **www**. chateau-de-meung.com

Beaugency's medieval bridge, the Tour St-Firmin and the keep rising above the trees

The entrance to the Château de Chamerolles

Château de Chamerolles ⑯

Chilleurs-aux-Bois. **Road map** E2.
🚉 Orléans, then taxi. **Tel** 02 38 39 84 66. ⬜ Wed–Mon.
🌑 Jan, 25 Dec. 📷

On the edge of the huge forest of Orléans, this Renaissance château was built between 1500 and 1530 by Lancelot du Lac, Governor of Orléans (who was named after the legendary Arthurian knight).

Baccarat perfume bottle in Chamerolles' museum

Although it was built in the form of a fortress, with a drawbridge crossing a moat and a courtyard enclosed by turreted wings, Chamerolles was designed as a pleasant personal residence. Pretty Renaissance gardens, accurately reconstructed, extend to a gazebo offering views back to the château across a "mirror" lake. There is an area of rare aromatic plants, many of which were used during the 1500s for making medicines and perfumes.

A museum in the château traces the development of perfumery through the centuries, covering the variety of uses for perfumes as well as the refinement of the science of making them. This includes the laboratories of perfumers and naturalists and glittering displays of bottles, as well as a charming gift shop.

JOAN OF ARC

Joan of Arc is France's supreme national heroine, a virgin-warrior, patriot and martyr whose self-belief turned the tide of the Hundred Years' War against the English. Nowhere is she more honoured than in the Loire Valley, scene of her greatest triumphs.

Responding to heavenly voices telling her to "drive the English out of France", Joan left her home soon after her 17th birthday in 1429 and travelled via Gien to Chinon to see the dauphin, the as yet uncrowned Charles VII. He

Joan of Arc, pictured in a medieval tapestry

faced an Anglo-Burgundian alliance on the verge of capturing Orléans. Joan convinced him she could save the city, armed herself in Tours, had her standard blessed in Blois and entered Orléans with a small force on 29 April. Galvanized by her leadership, the French drove the English off on 7 May. The people of Orléans have celebrated 8 May as a day of thanksgiving almost ever since. Joan returned to Gien to urge Charles forward to Reims for his coronation in July. In 1430 she was captured and accused of witchcraft. Handed over to the English, she was burned at the stake at the age of 19. Joan's piety, patriotism and tragic martyrdom led to her canonization almost 500 years later, in 1920.

Stained-glass portrait of Charles VII from Loches

Joan of Arc Entering Orléans by Jean-Jacques Sherrer (1855–1916)

Orléans ⑰

Orléans was the capital of medieval France and a royal duchy until the 18th-century French Revolution, when it became staunchly Republican. Its historical fame might, at first glance, seem submerged by its 20th-century role as a rail junction, food processing and business centre, especially as the old quarter of the city was badly damaged during World War II. However, an area of the old town and the Loire-side quays have been attractively restored, and there are many beautiful gardens in this "city of roses".

Heroic Joan of Arc

Exploring Orléans

A sense of grandeur lingers in Vieil Orléans, the old quarter bounded by the cathedral, the River Loire and the **place du Martroi**. Dominating this square is Denis Foyatier's statue of the city's heroine, Joan of Arc *(see p137)*, whose festival on 8 May is a highlight of the year. The plinth of the statue, which was erected in 1855, is beautifully sculpted with the events of her life. Two splen-did Classical buildings, the Chancellery and the Chamber of Commerce, are also found in the square.

A few medieval buildings have survived in the narrower streets around rue de Bour-gogne, a partly pedestrianized shopping street with an astonishing range of ethnic restaurants. Other delightful and often inexpensive res-taurants can also be found close to the **Nouvelles Halles**, the city's covered market. The most sophis-ticated shopping street is the rue Royale, which leads to the 18th-century bridge, the Pont George V.

🏛 Maison de Jeanne d'Arc

3 pl de Gaulle. *Tel* 02 38 52 99 89. ◻ *May–Oct: Tue–Sun; Nov–Apr: Tue–Sun pm only.* ● *public hols.* 🖾 **www. jeannedarc.fr/maison**
A reconstruction of the half-timbered house that lodged the warrior-saint for 10 days in 1429, the Maison de Jeanne d'Arc been completely modernized. The museum now presents the life of Joan of Arc in striking contemp-orary fashion, with evocative audiovisual dioramas.

Orléans' Renaissance Hôtel Groslot, once a private residence

🏨 Hôtel Groslot

Pl de l'Etape. *Tel* 02 38 79 22 30. ◻ *Sun–Fri.* ● *Sat & public hols.* ♿
The most handsome of the many Renaissance buildings in the city, the Hôtel Groslot, built between 1549 and 1555, served until recently as the town hall.

Built out of red brick crossed with black, this was a grand residence, with scrolled stair-case pillars, caryatids and an ornately tooled interior. It was once considered fine enough to lodge the kings of France. Here, in 1560, the sickly, young François II died after attending a meeting of the Etats Généraux with his child bride, Mary, later Queen of Scots. The beautiful

statue of Joan of Arc guarding the steps was sculpted by Princess Marie d'Orléans in 1840. Walk through the building to visit a charming little park, backed by the re-erected façade of the 15th-century Flamboyant Gothic chapel of St-Jacques.

⛪ Cathédrale Ste-Croix

Pl Ste-Croix. *Tel* 02 38 24 05 05 (tourist office). ◻ *daily.* 🖾 ♿
The cathedral, set on a spacious esplanade, was begun in the 13th century. The original building was badly damaged by Huguenots in the 16th century and then restored in Gothic style between the 17th and 19th centuries. Behind the ornate façade, the towering nave is lit by the radiating spokes of the rose window dedicated to the "Sun King", Louis XIV. The chapel of Joan of Arc, whose martyrdom is portray-ed in the stained glass, features a kneeling sculpture of Cardinal Touchet, who fought for Joan of Arc's canonization. The cathedral's most famous painting, a masterly rendition of *Christ Bearing the Cross*, by the Spanish religious painter Francisco de Zurbarán (1598–1664), has temporarily been removed for restoration.

The nave of the Cathédrale Ste-Croix

The peaceful Parc Floral in Orléans-la-Source

VISITORS' CHECKLIST

Road map E2. 🚻 *116,000.*
🚊 *ave de Paris.* 🚌 *rue Marcel
Proust.* ℹ️ *2 pl de L'Etape (02
38 24 05 05).* 🛒 *Tue–Sun.*
🎭 *Fête Jeanne d'Arc: 7–8 May;
Festival de la Loire: Sep.*
www.tourisme-orleans.com

Environs
The suburbs of Orléans are
pleasant places to relax after
a day spent sightseeing in
the city centre. In Olivet, for
example, it is possible to go
boating on the River Loiret.
This river also provides
opportunities for pretty walks.
A tributary of the Loire, the
Loiret flows underground
from near the town of St-
Benoît-sur-Loire *(see p140)*
and rises in the grand **Parc
Floral** of Orléans-la-Source. A
nature reserve, the park is a
mass of blooms from April.
Adjoining the park is the 17th-
century Château de la Source.

🌸 **Parc Floral**
Orléans-la-Source.
***Tel** 02 38 49 30 00.* ⏰ *Apr–Oct:
daily; Nov–Mar: daily, pm only.*
● *1 Jan, 24, 25 & 31 Dec.* 🎫 ♿
www.parcflorallasource.com

🏛 Musée des Beaux-Arts
Place Ste Croix. ***Tel** 02 38 79 21 55.*
⏰ *Tue–Sun.* ● *public hols.* 🎫 ♿
The high standard of the
collection, which includes a
self-portrait by Jean-Baptiste-
Siméon Chardin (1699–1779)
and *St Thomas* by the young
Diego Velázquez (1599–1660),
represents the strength of
European painting from the
14th to the early 20th century.
There is a charming collection
of miniature enamelled
statuettes on the second floor,
a delightful contrast to the
heavier richness of the
19th-century paintings.

🏛 Musée Historique et Archéologique
Square de l'Abbé Desnoyers.
***Tel** 02 38 79 25 60.* ⏰ *May–Jun
& Sep: Tue–Sun pm only; Jul–Aug:
Tue–Sat & Sun pm; Oct–Apr: Wed &
Sun pm.* ● *public hols.* 🎫
The chief treasures of this
museum are the Celtic statues
discovered at nearby Neuvy-
en-Sullias in 1861, which
include a fine horse from the
2nd century AD *(see p49)*.
The museum also has
interesting pieces on
Joan of Arc and a pleasing
variety of arts and crafts from
the Middle Ages onwards.

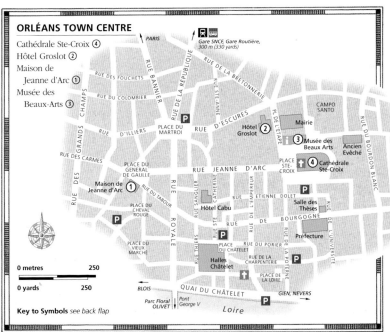

ORLÉANS TOWN CENTRE

Cathédrale Ste-Croix ④
Hôtel Groslot ②
Maison de
   Jeanne d'Arc ①
Musée des
   Beaux-Arts ③

0 metres 250
0 yards 250

Key to Symbols see back flap

The Romanesque façade of the abbey church of St-Benoît

St-Benoît-sur-Loire ⑱

Road map F3. ☒ 2,800. ☐
ℹ️ 44 rue Orléanaise (02 38 35 79 00). **www**.abbaye-fleury.com

This quiet town has one of the finest Romanesque abbey churches in France, constructed between 1067 and 1108. The most appealing feature of the façade is the belfry porch, probably built early in the 11th century by Abbot Gauzlin, son of the first Capetian king, Hugh. On the capitals of its 50 golden pillars are carved figures, including beasts and goblins.

Inside, thickset columns separate the side aisles from the rib-vaulted Gothic nave. The chancel, dating from the earlier Romanesque period, has blind arcades and a mosaic floor brought from Rome. The bas-relief head of a Norman raider is carved on the wall of the north transept. Its cheeks are pierced to expel its pagan spirit.

In the crypt, a lamplit casket contains the relics of St Benedict, the 6th-century father of Western monasticism. They were spirited here in 672 from Benedict's own monastery of Monte Cassino in Italy. By the 11th century, when the present building was begun, the Benedictine order was rich and St-Benoît-sur-Loire was renowned for its scholarship as well as its purloined relics. St-Benoît is a living monastery, and one of

the best ways to experience the spirit of the place is to attend midday mass sung in Gregorian chant.

The 9th-century church of **St Germigny-des-Prés** lies 5 km (3 miles) along the D60 from St-Benoît-sur-Loire. The small cupola of the east apse has an enchanting mosaic of angels bending over the Ark of the Covenant – a composition made up of 130,000 coloured-glass cubes probably assembled during the 6th century.

Gien ⑲

Road map F3. ☒ 16,000. ☐ ☐
ℹ️ pl Jean-Jaurès (02 38 67 25 28). ☐ Wed, Sat. **www**.gien.fr

Sensitively restored after being devastated during World War II, Gien is considered one of the Loire's prettiest towns. From its handsome quays and 16th-century bridge, houses of brick, slate and pale stone rise steeply to a château. It was built for Anne de Beaujeu, who acted as regent for her brother Charles XIII at the end of the 15th century.

Only the steeple tower of the **Eglise Ste-Jeanne d'Arc**, next to the château, survived the

Max Ingrand's stained glass

destruction of the war, but a remarkable church replaced it in the 1950s. Warm facings, composed of bricks made in Gien's famous pottery kilns, blend with the patterned red and black brickwork of the château. The interior glows with stained glass by Max Ingrand and the faïence that is a speciality of the area. A museum of fine china and earthenware is open daily (except Sundays and public holidays) at the factory, which was founded in 1821 (*see p221*).

The **château** of Anne de Beaujeu, built between 1484 and 1500 on the site of one of the Loire's oldest castles, sheltered the young Louis XIV and the Queen Mother during the Fronde civil war (1648–53). Its grand beamed halls and galleries now house a superb museum of hunting, tracing the sport's development since prehistoric times. The collection covers the weaponry, costumery, techniques and related artistry of almost every associated activity, from falconry to the royal chase. The memorable entrance hall of the château features a 17th-century painting of St Hubert, the patron saint of hunting, depicting his conversion by the vision of a resurrected

Gien's château and its 16th-century bridge across the Loire

stag carrying a crucifix between its horns. An Italian crossbow and a powder horn decorated with images of the mythical and tragic encounter between Diana and Actaeon are beautiful examples of 17th-century carving. Other prominent artists on display here include the 20th-century sculptor Florentin Brigaud, the Flemish etcher, Stradanus, and François Desportes, whose fine paintings dominate the spectacular trophy hall.

⚜ Château et Musée International de la Chasse
Tel 02 38 67 69 69. ○ *Wed–Mon (Jul & Aug: daily).* ● *Jan, 25 Dec.* ✍

A pleasure boat crossing Briare's elegant bridge-canal

Briare-le-Canal ⓴

Road map F3. 🏠 6,000. 🚍 🚌
🛈 *pl Charles-de-Gaulle (02 38 31 24 51).* ➔ *Fri.*

This small town, with its attractive marina, is the setting for a sophisticated engineering masterpiece – the longest bridge-canal in Europe *(see pp56–7).* With stonework and wrought-iron flourishes designed by Gustave Eiffel (1832–1923), the structure crosses the Loire, linking the Briare-Loing canal with the Canal Latéral. These waterways in turn join the Seine and the Rhône rivers respectively. Visitors can stroll its length, lined in the style of a Parisian boulevard with elegant lampposts, or cruise across the 662-m (2,170-ft) bridge in a *bateau-mouche.*

Fishing on one of the peaceful *étangs* of the Sologne

The Sologne ㉑

Road map E3. 🚍 🚌 *Romorantin-Lanthenay.* 🛈 *(02 54 76 43 89).*
www.tourisme-romorantin.com

Between Gien and Blois, the Loire forms the northern boundary of the Sologne, a vast area of flat heathland, marshes and forests covering nearly 5000 sq km (1,930 sq miles). The area is dotted with *étangs*, broad lakes teeming with fish, which are magnets for migratory birds and waterfowl. The forests are just as attractive to hunters and nature lovers now as they were during the Renaissance, when members of royalty chose to build their grand hunting lodges here. Much of the land is privately owned, although there are some public paths.

Romorantin-Lanthenay is the "capital" of the Sologne, which boasts 17th- to 19th-century buildings and a medieval quarter. The town is proud of its associations with

racing car manufacturers, Matra, it is also home to the **Musée de Sologne**, whose exhibits explain the economy and wildlife of the area.

The **Maison des Etangs** at St-Viâtre gives information on the Sologne lakes. This is one of several small tourist maisons on specific local themes dotted around the area. Closer to Chambord's great park *(see pp134–5)* is the Maison du Cerf, where deer can often be seen, especially in Autumn.

Another large, public nature reserve is the **Domaine du Ciran**, 25 km (15 miles) south of Orléans, near Ménestreau-en-Villette.

🏛 Musée de Sologne
Tel 02 54 95 33 66. ○ *daily.* ● *Tue, Sun am; 1 Jan, 1 May, 25 Dec.* 🚻 ⚤

✹ Maison des Etangs
Tel 02 54 88 23 00. ○ *daily (Nov–Mar: Wed, Sat, Sun & pub hols, pm only).* ● *1 Jan, 25 Dec.* ✍

✹ Domaine du Ciran
Ménestreau-en-Villette. 🚍 *La Ferté-St-Aubin, then taxi.* 🛈 *02 38 76 90 93.* ○ *daily.* ● *Tue (Oct–Mar).* ✍

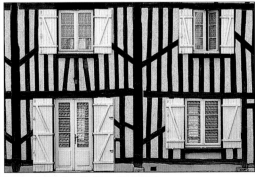
A typical, half-timbered building of La Sologne

BERRY

Berry lies in the very centre of France, south of the Paris Basin and just north of the Massif Central. It is a varied land of wheat fields, pastures and vineyards, ancient forests, rolling hills and lakes, peaceful villages and elegant manor houses. Mainly off the beaten tourist track, the region gives visitors an opportunity to experience the rural heart of France.

Bourges, the principal town of Berry, was one of the capitals of Aquitaine in the Gallo-Roman period. It then enjoyed another moment of glory in the 14th century, with the administration of Jean, Duc de Berry. This warmongering patron of the arts built a splendid palace in the city (now destroyed) and collected paintings, tapestries, jewellery and illuminated manuscripts.

In the 1420s, when Charles VII was fighting for the French crown *(see pp52–3)*, Bourges was his campaign base. Afterwards, his treasurer Jacques Cœur did much to make the kingdom financially secure. The Palais Jacques-Cœur in Bourges competes with the city's magnificent cathedral in drawing crowds of admiring visitors.

Berry is ideal for those who love the outdoors, whether walking in the many well-tended forests, fishing or bird-watching in La Brenne, or sailing and canoeing on its rivers and lakes. Among the region's literary associations are George Sand's novels *(see p24)* and Alain-Fournier's evocative tale *Le Grand Meaulnes* (1913), which combines his childhood memories of the Sologne in the north and the rolling country of the south.

The culinary highlights of Berry include dishes made from local game and wild mushrooms. To the northeast, the renowned Sancerre wine district *(see p155)* is also known for its excellent goats' cheeses, such as the famous Crottin de Chavignol.

A river view by the village of Argenton-sur-Creuse

◁ The vineyards of Sancerre

Exploring Berry

Bourges is the natural starting point
for exploring the heart of France.
From here it is only a short drive to
the edge of the Sologne *(see p141)*
in the north or La Brenne in the
southwest, both havens for wildlife.
Below Bourges is the Champagne
Berrichonne, a vast agricultural region
producing wheat, barley and oil-rich
crops such as rape and sunflowers.
The River Loire forms the ancient
border between Berry and Burgundy
to the east as it flows through the
vineyards of the Sancerrois hills.

The Palais Jacques-Cœur in Bourges

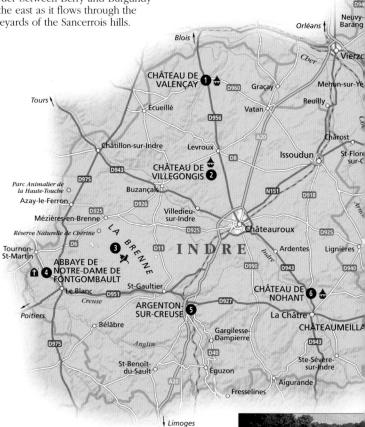

GETTING AROUND

The A71 autoroute from Orléans
passes through Vierzon, Bourges
and St-Amand-Montrond and is
an excellent route from north to
south. The A20 serves western
Berry. The TGV doesn't stop in
the region, but Corail trains from
Gare d'Austerlitz in Paris take
around two hours to either

Bourges or Châteauroux. There
are also frequent trains between
Bourges and Tours. Public
transport to the more isolated
sights is limited and a car is a
great advantage, especially
when touring the Sancerre
wine estates or La Brenne
nature reserves.

**A riverside scene, typical of the Berry
region's gentle landscape**

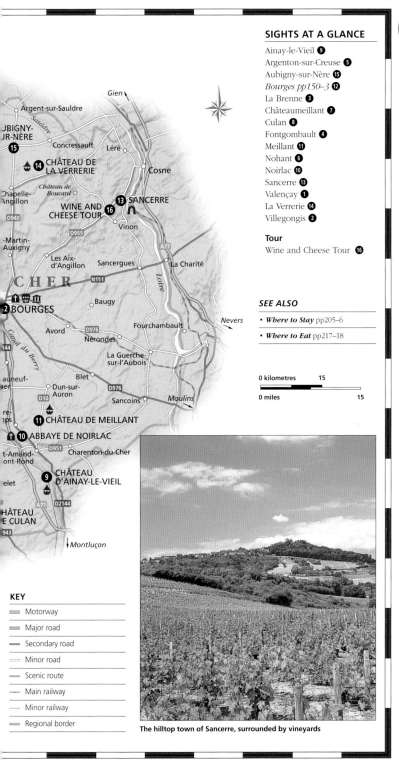

Gien

Argent-sur-Saudre

Sauldre

UBIGNY-
UR-NÈRE
⑮

Concressault   Léré

Cosne

▲ ⑭ CHÂTEAU DE
LA VERRERIE

Château de
Boucard

Chapelle-
Angillon

WINE AND ⑯
CHEESE TOUR

⑬ SANCERRE

D940

D955

Vinon

A77

-Martin-
Auxigny

Les Aix-
d'Angillon   Sancergues

La Charité

CHER   N151

Loire

Baugy

⑫ BOURGES

Fourchambault

Nevers

Avord   D976

Nérondes

144

Canal du Berry

La Guerche-
sur-l'Aubois

auneuf-
er

Blet

Dun-sur-
Auron   D976

D10

Sancoins

Moulins

re-
ps   ⑪ CHÂTEAU DE MEILLANT

⑩ ABBAYE DE NOIRLAC

D951   Charenton-du-Cher

t-Amand-
ont-Rond

elet   ⑨ CHÂTEAU
D'AINAY-LE-VIEIL

A71   D2144

HÂTEAU
E CULAN

943

↓ Montluçon

SIGHTS AT A GLANCE

Ainay-le-Vieil ⑨
Argenton-sur-Creuse ⑤
Aubigny-sur-Nère ⑮
Bourges pp150–3 ⑫
La Brenne ③
Châteaumeillant ⑦
Culan ⑧
Fontgombault ④
Meillant ⑪
Nohant ⑥
Noirlac ⑩
Sancerre ⑬
Valençay ①
La Verrerie ⑭
Villegongis ②

Tour
Wine and Cheese Tour ⑯

SEE ALSO

• *Where to Stay* pp205–6

• *Where to Eat* pp217–18

0 kilometres   15

0 miles   15

KEY

══ Motorway

▬ Major road

▬ Secondary road

▭ Minor road

▬ Scenic route

▬▬ Main railway

── Minor railway

▬ Regional border

The hilltop town of Sancerre, surrounded by vineyards

A resident peacock in front of the Château de Valençay

Valençay ❶

Road map E4. 🏛 *2,800.* 🚉 🚌
Valençay. ℹ *2 ave de la Résistance
(02 54 00 04 42).* 🛍 *Tue.* **www**.
paysdevalencayenberry.fr **Château
& Park Tel** *02 54 00 15 69.* ⭘ *mid-
Mar–mid-Nov: daily.* 🖼 ♿ *restricted.* 🎭 *There are plays at the
château in summer; themes and
dates vary. Son et Lumière: Valençay
aux Chandelles (mid-Jun–Aug).*
www.chateau-valencay.com
Musée de l'Automobile Tel *02 54
00 07 74.* ⭘ *mid-Mar–mid-Nov:
daily.* 🖼 ♿ **www**.musee-auto-
valencay.fr

From its tree-lined approach,
the Château de Valençay is a
fine sight. Started in 1510, it
took more than 300 years to
complete, but its Renaissance
and Classical elements are
convincingly blended. In
1803, it was bought by
Bonaparte's foreign minister,
Charles-Maurice de Talleyrand
Périgord. Until his death in
1838, the famous statesman
entertained many of Europe's
dignitaries here.

Valençay's rooms are richly
furnished, mostly in the
Empire style, and they display
many *objets d'art* connected
with Talleyrand. Entertaining
tours guide you through the
château, and provide details
about the statesman's beautiful mistress, his famous visitors
and his illustrious chef. Formal
gardens extend in front of the
château, while the park itself
houses an enormous labyrinth.

Next to the château, the
Musée de l'Automobile has a
private collection of motoring
memorabilia and vintage cars.

Château de Villegongis ❷

Road map E4. 🚉 *Châteauroux, then
taxi. Tel 02 54 36 63 50 (Mairie).*
⭘ *closed to public.* 🖼

Elegant and moated, the
Château de Villegongis
was probably built by Pierre
Nepveu, one of the master
masons for Chambord (*see
pp132–5*). Since the 15th
century, ownership has stayed
in the same family. Barely
touched since that time, it is
one of the purest examples of
the French Renaissance style.

The château's most striking
features are its richly decorated chimneys, which suggest
the link with Chambord, and
its cylindrical towers at either
end of the main building.

The interior is exceptionally
well furnished, with some fine
17th- and 18th-century pieces.
There is also a remarkable
carved stone staircase.

La Brenne ❸

Road map E4. 🚌 *Mézières-en-
Brenne, then taxi.* ℹ *Maison du
Parc, Rosnay (02 54 28 12 13);
Mézieres-en-Brenne (02 54 38 12
24).* **www**.parc-naturel-brenne.fr

The Parc Naturel Régional de
la Brenne, covering 1,650 sq
km (640 sq miles), is known as
the *Pays des Mille Etangs* (The
Land of a Thousand Meres). La
Brenne is a paradise for nature
lovers – more than 260 bird
species can be seen here.

Several specialist reserves are
open to visitors. The **Réserve
Naturelle de Chérine** is good
for spotting European pond
tortoises. The **Réserve de la
Haute-Touche** is home to
many endangered species
and is also close to the fine
Château d'Azay-le-Ferron. The
town of Mézières-en-Brenne
houses the **Maison de la
Pisciculture**, whose aquaria
display local fish species.

🦌 **Réserve Naturelle de
Chérine**
St-Michel-en-Brenne. 🎫 *02 54 28
11 00.* **Observatory** ⭘ *Apr–Sep:
Wed–Mon am.* 🎫 *by appt only,
Apr–Jul: Thu pm.* 🖼

🦌 **Réserve de la Haute-
Touche**
Obterre. *Tel 02 54 02 20 40.*
⭘ *Apr–Sep: daily, Oct–mid-Nov:
Wed, Sat, Sun & pub hols.* 🖼 ♿

♣ **Château d'Azay-le-Ferron**
Azay-le-Ferron. *Tel 02 54 39 20 06.*
⭘ *Apr–Sep: daily; Oct: Sat, Sun.* 🖼

🦌 **Maison de la Pisciculture**
Mézières-en-Brenne. *Tel 02 54
38 12 24.* ⭘ *Apr–Oct: Mon &
Wed–Sat, pm only; Nov–Mar:
by appt.* 🖼 ♿ *grd flr only.*

One of the many idyllic lakes in La Brenne

Abbaye de Notre-Dame de Fontgombault ❹

Road map E4. **Tel** *02 54 37 12 03.*
Hotel: *02 54 37 30 98.* ⬜ *daily.*
✝ *Mass: 10am daily; Vespers: 6pm
Mon–Sat, 5pm Sun.* ♿

This beautiful Benedictine abbey, famous for its Gregorian chant, was founded in 1091 but, by 1741, when the number of monks had dwindled to five, it was abandoned. Restored by a local priest in the 19th century, it now houses monks from Solesmes (*see p162*).

The church, with its five radiating chapels, has a richly decorated doorway, carved capitals and a much-venerated 12th-century statue known as Notre-Dame du Bien-Mourir, believed to comfort the dying. Gregorian chant is still sung during services and is more prominent in the morning service. The monks run a pottery, whose products can be bought. Accommodation is available, call the number above for details.

The radiating chapels of the Abbaye de Notre-Dame de Fontgombault

Old houses overhanging the river in Argenton-sur-Creuse

Argenton-sur-Creuse ❺

Road map E4. 🏛 *5,500.* 🚉 🚌
ℹ *pl de la République (02 54 24 05 30).* 🛍 *Thu & Sat.* 🎭 *International Folklore Festival, biennial (Jul).*
www.ot-argenton-sur-creuse.fr

This is a pretty town along the Creuse river, which winds from Fresselines to Argenton, passing through deep gorges. Streets of picturesque houses climb the hillside to Argenton's chapel of Notre-Dame-des-Bancs, dominated by its gilded statue of the Virgin Mary.

In the 19th century, the town became an important centre for the clothing industry. The informative collections of the **Musée de la Chemiserie et de l'Elégance Masculine** honour this heritage. The **Musée Archéologique d'Argentomagus**, just outside town, recalls Argenton's Gallo-Roman predecessor.

🏛 **Musée de la Chemiserie et de l'Eléga nce Masculine**
Tel *02 54 24 34 69.* ⬜ *mid-Feb–Dec: Tue–Sun.* 📷 ♿
🏛 **Musée Archéologique d'Argentomagus**
Tel *02 54 24 47 31.* ⬜ *Feb–Jun, Sep–mid-Dec: Wed–Mon; Jul–Aug: daily.* ⬤ *mid-Dec–Jan.* 📷 ♿

Château de Nohant ❻

Road map E4. **Tel** *02 54 31 06 04.*
🚉 🚌 *Châteauroux.* ⬜ *daily.*
⬤ *public hols.* 📷 🎭 *Fêtes Romantiques de Nohant (Jun); Rencontres Internationales Frédéric Chopin (Jul).*
ℹ *02 54 31 0737.*

George Sand, the *nom de plume* of the novelist Baroness Aurore Dudevant (1804–76), was largely brought up in this charming manor house. She frequently returned here during her unconventional life, to enjoy the calm beauty of her beloved Berry countryside.

Many of George Sand's novels, including *La Mare au Diable* (*The Devil's Pool*) and *La Petite Fadette* (*The Little Fairy*), are set here (*see p24*). Sand's admirers can view the boudoir where she first wrote; the stage on which she acted out her plays; the puppets made by her son, Maurice; the bedroom used by her lover, Frédéric Chopin; and the room in which she died in 1876.

MONET AT FRESSELINES

In 1889 the Impressionist painter Claude Monet travelled to the village of Fresselines, perched high above the Creuse. He visited a local beauty spot, with views plunging down into the river gorge, was captivated, and painted a series of canvases showing the scene in different lights. In February, bad weather forced him to stop painting and wait for spring. He then found that new growth had changed the view and had to pay the owner of an oak featured in five of his paintings to strip the tree of its new leaves.

Valley of the Petite Creuse **by Claude Monet**

Châteaumeillant **7**

Road Map F4. 🏘 *2,150.* 🚏
Chateauroux, then bus. 🚌 **ⅈ** *rue de
la Libération (02 48 61 39 89).* 📅 *Fri.*
www.ot.chateaumeillant.free.fr

The chief glory of this town
is the Romanesque **Eglise
St-Genès**, built between 1125
and 1150, with its elegant pink
and grey west façade. The interior is exceptionally airy, due
not only to its great height, but
also to its very wide chancel
with six apsidal chapels and
side passages that are separated by graceful double bays to
create a cloisters effect.

Châteaumeillant was once an
important Gallo-Roman centre.
The **Musée Emile-Chenon**,
based in a 15th-century manor
house, contains Roman artifacts and local medieval finds.

🏛 **Musée Emile-Chenon**
ⅈ *rue de la Victoire (02 48 61 49
24).* ◯ *Mon pm, Wed am, Thu–Sat
(Jun–Sep: daily).* ⬤ *pub hols.* 📷 ⚹

Château de
Culan **8**

Road Map F4. **Tel** *02 48 56 66 66.*
◯ *Apr–mid-Nov: daily.* 📷 ⚹
www.culan.fr

Strategically positioned on
an escarpment above the
River Arnon, this medieval
fortress dates from the 13th
and 14th centuries. Its three
conical towers are topped
by wooden siege hoardings.
A series of furnished rooms
relate the castle's long history,

The interior courtyard of the Château d'Ainay-le- Vieil

recalling famous visitors who
have stayed here, including
the Admiral of Culan, who
was a comrade-in-arms of
Joan of Arc (who also stayed
here in 1430), and the writers
George Sand *(see p24)* and
Madame de Sévigné, and
telling of an attack during the
17th-century Fronde uprising.

Lovely views over Culan's
replanted gardens and the pastoral Arnon Valley can be enjoyed from the château's terrace.

Château
d'Ainay-le-Vieil **9**

Road Map F4. 🚉 *St-Amand-
Montrond, then taxi.* **Tel** *02 48 63
50 03.* ◯ *Feb: Wed–Mon pms;
Mar, Oct & Nov: Wed–Mon; Apr–
Sep: daily.* 📷 ⚹

From the outside, Ainay-le-
Vieil has the appearance of
a fortress, with formidable
walls and its nine massive
towers, lit only by thin arrow

slits. The octagonal enclosure,
surrounded by a moat, is
entered through a huge, 13th-
century postern gate. The
exterior belies the fact that
hidden inside is a graceful
Renaissance château designed
for an elegant lifestyle, with
its richly decorated façade
enlivened by sunny loggias.

The castle changed hands
many times during its early
history. In the 15th century,
it belonged briefly to Charles
VII's treasurer Jacques Cœur
(see p151), but in 1467 it was
bought by the Seigneurs de
Bigny whose descendants still
live here today.

The Grand Salon was dec-
orated in honour of a visit by
Louis XII and Anne of Brittany
around 1500. It has a painted
ceiling and a monumental fireplace, which is said to be one
of the most attractive in the
Loire Valley. On display is a
portrait of Louis XIV's chief
minister Jean-Baptiste Colbert
and portraits of other family
members, as well as an amber
pendant that belonged to
Queen Marie-Antoinette and
several *objets de vertu*, friend-
ship gifts given by Napoleon
to General Auguste Colbert.

The tiny Renaissance chapel
has some beautiful, late 16th-
century wall paintings, which
were discovered under 19th-
century decoration. Its stained-
glass windows were made by
an artist who also worked on
the Cathédrale St-Etienne in
Bourges *(see pp152–3).*

In the park is a delightful
and sweet-smelling rose
garden. Some of the varieties
of roses which are grown here
date back to the 15th century.

The Château de Culan, set high above the River Arnon

Abbaye de Noirlac ⑩

Road map F4. 🚉 *St-Amand-Montrond, then taxi.* **Tel** *02 48 62 01 01.* ◯ *daily.* ● *23 Dec–Jan.* 🏷️ ✔️ 🎵 *Les Traversées (music festival Jun–Jul).* **www**.abbayedenoirlac.com

The Cistercian Abbaye de Noirlac, founded in 1136, is a fine example of medieval monastic architecture. The Cistercian Order's austerity is reflected in the pure lines of the partly 12th-century church and visually echoed in its sober, modern stained glass.

The chapter house, where the monks' daily assemblies were held, and the *cellier*, where the lay brothers were in charge of the food, wine and grain stores, were also built in this plain but elegant style. The cloisters, with their graceful arches and decorated capitals, date from the 13th and 14th centuries, which was a less severe period.

At **Bruère-Allichamps**, 4 km (2½ miles) northwest of the abbey, a Gallo-Roman milestone marks the alleged exact central point of France.

Château de Meillant ⑪

Road map F4. 🚉 *St-Amand-Montrond, then taxi.* **Tel** *02 48 63 32 05.* ◯ *Mar–mid-Nov: daily.* 🏷️ ✔️ ♿ *grd flr only.* **www**.chateau-de-meillant.com

Sumptuously furnished rooms and elaborate carved ceilings complement the rather

The austere lines of the Abbaye de Noirlac

exuberantly decorated façade of this well-preserved Berry château. Built for Charles d'Amboise in 1510 by skilful Italian craftsmen, the château represents a fine combination of late Gothic and early Renaissance architecture. It is dominated by the *Tour du Lion* (Lion's Tower), an octagonal three-storey staircase tower. The plainer west façade, mirrored in a moat, dates from the early 1300s.

A small grotesque carving in Meillant

Other highlights of a visit include the château's graceful chapel and its surrounding grounds in which peacocks strut. On the estate, you'll also find old horse-drawn carriages and vintage cars; the Parcours de Miniatures, featuring small-scale models illustrating ways of living through different historic periods, and a collection of dolls' houses.

LIFE IN A CISTERCIAN ABBEY

The rules of the Cistercian Order were based on the principles of austerity and simplicity. Abbeys were divided into two communities, which did not mix. Lay brothers, not bound by holy vows, ensured the self–sufficiency of the abbey by managing the barns, tilling the fields, milling corn and welcoming guests. The full, or choir, monks were the only ones allowed into the cloister, at the heart of the

A Cistercian monk labouring in the fields

complex, and could not leave the abbey without the permission of the abbot.

The monks' days started at 2am and ended at 7pm and were regularly punctuated by religious devotions, which included prayers, confession, meditation and mass. The strict rule of silence was broken only to read from the Bible or from the Rules of the Order. Many monks were literate, and monasteries played a leading role in copying manuscripts.

Bourges ⑫

The heart of modern Bourges, once the Roman city of Avaricum, is the network of ancient streets around its magnificent cathedral. The city was an important religious, courtly and arts centre in the Middle Ages. In the late 19th century, it became a prosperous industrial town. Today Bourges has a relaxed atmosphere that complements its excellent museums, housed in superb old buildings. The town is known for its music festivals including *Le Printemps de Bourges*, and *Un Eté à Bourges*, a programme of free events held during the summer.

The 16th-century *Concert Champêtre*, displayed in the Hôtel Lallemant

🏛 Hôtel des Echevins & Musée Estève

13 rue Edouard Branly. *Tel* 02 48 24 75 38. ☐ Mon, Wed–Sat; Sun pm only. ● 1 Jan, 1 May, 1 & 11 Nov & 25 Dec. ⑤

The Hôtel des Echevins (the house of the aldermen) is remarkable for its intricately carved octagonal tower and fireplaces. Built in 1489, it served as the seat of the city council that governed Bourges for more than three centuries.

The building was classified an historic monument in 1886. In 1985 work to renovate the building began, and in 1987 it became the Musée Estève, displaying paintings by the self-taught artist Maurice Estève, who was born in Culan in the south of Berry (*see p148*). The collection is mainly made up of Estève's powerful, brightly coloured canvases. However, this permanent display is augmented by temporary exhibitions of his watercolours, collages and line drawings. The collection is arranged in chronological order on three levels, connected by elegant stone spiral staircases. This modern work seems surprisingly at home in the spacious Gothic rooms.

Samsâra by Maurice Estève (1977)

🏛 Hôtel Lallemant & Musée des Arts Décoratifs

6 rue Bourbonnoux. *Tel* 02 48 57 81 17. ☐ Tue–Sat; Sun pm only. ● 1 Jan, 1 May, 1 & 11 Nov & 25 Dec.

This Renaissance mansion, which was built for a rich merchant family originally from Germany, houses the city's decorative arts museum. It still has the little chapel used by the Lallemant family, its coffered ceiling carved with alchemical symbols, and an elegant, restored courtyard. On display is a fine collection of tapestries from the 16th and 17th centuries, clocks, ceramics, glassware, miniatures, 15th- and 17th-century paintings and furniture, including a beautiful 17th-century ebony inlaid cabinet.

🏛 Musée du Berry

4–6 rue des Arènes. *Tel* 02 48 70 41 92. ☐ Mon, Wed–Sat; Sun pm only. ● 1 Jan, 1 May, 1 & 11 Nov & 25 Dec. ⑤ grd flr only.

The Musée du Berry, housed in the Renaissance Hôtel Cujas, concentrates on local history. The collections include a large display of Gallo-Roman artifacts, many of which were unearthed in the area. There is some wonderful Gothic sculpture, especially Jean de Cambrai's weeping figures from the base of the tomb of Jean, Duc de Berry, the upper section of which can be seen in the crypt of the Cathédrale St-Etienne (*see pp152–3*).

On the upper floor of the museum is a permanent exhibition of Berry's rural arts, crafts, and everyday objects, including the distinctive stoneware made in La Borne near Sancerre.

Jehan Fouquet's Angel Ceiling in the Palais Jaques-Cœur

JACQUES CŒUR

The son of a Bourges furrier, Jacques Cœur (c.1400–56) became one of the richest and most powerful men in medieval France. With his merchant fleet he sailed to the eastern Mediterranean and Far East, bringing back luxury goods such as silks, spices and precious metals, until Charles VII appointed him head of the Paris Mint, then treasurer of the Royal Household. In 1451 he was accused of fraud and falsely implicated in the death of the king's mistress, Agnès Sorel. He was arrested, tortured and imprisoned, but escaped to Rome. There he took part in the pope's naval expedition against the Turks and died on the Greek island of Chios.

The merchant Jacques Cœur

🏛️ **Palais Jacques-Cœur**
Rue Jacques-Cœur. **Tel** *02 48 24 79 42.* ⭕ *daily.* 🔴 *1 Jan, 1 May, 1 & 11 Nov, 25 Dec.* 📷 ✔️
This splendid house, built on the remains of the city's Gallo-Roman walls, is among the finest secular Gothic buildings in Europe. It was constructed at great expense between 1443 and 1451 for Jacques Cœur, one of the most fascinating men in medieval France.

The palace has a number of innovations remarkable for their period. Rooms open off corridors instead of leading into each other. Appealingly, each room is "labelled" over the doorway with carved scenes illustrating its function.

From *trompe l'oeil* figures peeping out from the turreted entrance façade to the mysterious, possibly alchemical, symbols carved everywhere, the palace offers a feast of interesting details. Hearts are a common motif – the newly ennobled Jacques Cœur naturally had hearts, *cœurs* in French, on his coat of arms.

The fireplace in the south gallery of the Palais Jacques-Cœur

Other features are a large courtyard, majestic wooden vaulting in the galleries, and the beautiful ceiling in the chapel, painted by the 15th-century artist, Jehan Fouquet (*see p25*).

Temporary exhibitions are held here annually.

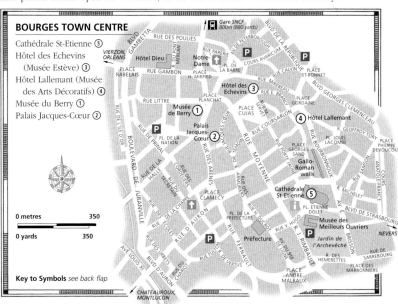

BOURGES TOWN CENTRE

Cathédrale St-Etienne ⑤
Hôtel des Echevins
    (Musée Estève) ③
Hôtel Lallemant (Musée
    des Arts Décoratifs) ④
Musée du Berry ①
Palais Jacques-Cœur ②

0 metres   350
0 yards   350

Key to Symbols *see back flap*

Bourges: Cathédrale St-Etienne

Stained-glass window detail

St-Etienne, one of France's finest Gothic cathedrals, was built mainly between 1195 and 1260. The unknown architect designed St-Etienne without transepts, which, combined with the interior's unusual height and width, makes it seem much lighter than most Gothic cathedrals. This effect is beautifully enhanced by the brilliant hues of the medieval stained glass. Also unusual are the asymmetrical west front; the double row of flying buttresses rising in pyramid-shaped tiers; and a "crypt", a lower, window-lit church, created because the ground is 6 m (20 ft) lower at the east end.

Vast Interior
The interior is 124 m (400 ft) long and 37 m (120 ft) high.

The Tour Sourde
(Deaf Tower) is so called because it has no bell.

★ **Astrological Clock**
Dating from the 1420s, this fascinating clock was designed by Canon Jean Fusoris, a mathematician.

Entrance

THE LAST JUDGMENT

The tympanum on the central portal of the west façade depicts Archangel Michael weighing souls. Those found wanting are hustled by devils into the mouth of Hell, while the elect are gathered into the bosom of Abraham. The youthful, naked dead lift up their tombstones in a dramatic Resurrection scene.

The Last Judgement portal of the Cathédrale St-Etienne

The Grand Housteau is a striking rose window, donated by the renowned patron of the arts Jean, Duc de Berry.

The five portals of the west front are surrounded by carved scenes. The doorways vary in size and shape, adding to the asymmetry of the façade.

★ Stained-Glass Windows
The medieval stained glass in the choir was sponsored by local guilds, whose members are depicted practising their crafts at the bottom of each window.

The Chapelle Jacques-Coeur has a glorious Annunciation window.

VISITORS' CHECKLIST

Pl Etienne Dolet. *Tel 02 48 23 02 60.* ☐ *8:30am–7:15pm daily (Oct–Mar: 9am–5:45pm).* 🅿️ ✝️ *6:30pm Sat, 11am Sun; Jul & Aug 6:30pm daily.* **Crypt & North Tower** ☐ *daily.* 🔲 🖊️ 📷

Praying Figures
In the crypt are statues of the Duc and Duchesse de Berry. During the Revolution the statues were decapitated and the existing heads are copies.

The crypt, or lower church, was built in the earlier Gallo-Roman moat.

The Romanesque portal on the cathedral's south side is decorated with a *Christ in Majesty* and the 12 apostles.

★ St Sépulcre
This dramatic sculpture of the Entombment of Christ was placed at the far end of the lower church in 1540.

STAR FEATURES

★ Astrological Clock

★ Stained-Glass Windows

★ St Sépulcre

Jean, Duc de Berry
The recumbent marble effigy of Jean, Duc de Berry, his feet resting on a bear, was originally part of his tomb.

A Sancerre vineyard

Sancerre ⑬

Road map F3. 🏘 *1,800.* 🚌
ℹ️ *esplanade Porte-César (02 48 54 08 21).* 🛒 *Tue & Sat.* 🎪 *Foire aux Crottins (goat's cheese fair, May); Foire aux Vins (wine fair, Whitsun); Foire aux Vins de France (French wine fair, Aug).* **www**.tourisme-sancerre.com

The ancient Berry town of Sancerre is perched on a domed hill, a rare sight in the flat landscape of the Loire Valley. Its narrow streets boast interesting 15th- and 16th-century houses. All that remains of the medieval castle that once dominated the town is the **Tour des Fiefs**, which gives a superb view of the River Loire. The town and surrounding area are famous for their dry white wines.

To learn of the winemaking traditions, visit the **Maison des Sancerre**, which also hosts cultural events. You can enjoy a tasting here and at other wineries in the area.

🏰 Tour des Fiefs
🕐 *Apr–Nov: 10am–12:30pm, 2–6pm Mon–Fri, 2–6pm Sat & Sun.*

🏛 Maison des Sancerre
Tel *02 48 54 11 35.* 🕐 *Apr–mid-Nov: daily.* **www**.maison-des-sancerre.com

Château de la Verrerie ⑭

Road map F3. 🚉 *Gien, then taxi.*
Tel *02 48 81 51 60.* 🕐 *Easter–Nov: Sat, Sun (Jul, Aug: daily); Dec–Easter: by appointment only.* 🎫 🎬 🍴 *See* **Where to Stay**, *p205.*

This fine, early Renaissance château is on the edge of the Forêt d'Ivoy. The land was given to the Scot Sir John Stewart of Darnley by Charles VII. It was a gift of thanks for defeating the English at the battle of Baugé in Anjou in 1421. John's son, Béraud Stewart, began to build on the land several decades later, and the Château de la Verrerie was eventually completed by Béraud's nephew, Robert Stewart.

La Verrerie reverted to the French crown in 1670. Three years later Louis XIV gave the château to Louise de Kéroualle. She lived here until her death in 1734 at the age of 85.

La Verrerie has a lovely Renaissance gallery adorned with beautiful 16th-century frescoes. The chapel also boasts some fine frescoes. In the 19th-century wing are four beautiful alabaster statuettes from the tomb of the Duc de Berry *(see pp152–3).*

Alabaster statuettes in the Château de la Verrerie's 19th-century wing

Aubigny-sur-Nère ⑮

Road map F3. 🏘 *6,000.* 🚌 ℹ️ *rue de l'Eglise (02 48 58 40 20).* 🛒 *Sat.* 🎪 *Fête Franco-Ecossaise (mid-Jul).* **www**.aubigny.net

Attractive Aubigny is proud of its association with the Scottish Stewart clan. In 1423 the town was given by Charles VII to Sir John Stewart of Darnley, along with nearby La Verrerie. After a major fire in 1512, the Stewarts rebuilt Aubigny in the Renaissance style and also constructed a new château.

In 1673 Louis XIV gave the duchy of Aubigny to Louise de Kéroualle. Although she spent most of her time at La Verrerie, Louise had a large garden created at the Château d'Aubigny. The Aubusson tapestries presented to her by the king are displayed in the château, which now serves as the town hall and also houses two museums. The unusual **Mémorial de l'Auld Alliance** is devoted to the Auld Alliance, the town's long ties with Scotland: Jacobite refugees settled here during the 18th century.

The 13th-century **Eglise St-Martin**, in transitional Gothic style, was largely rebuilt by the Stewarts. It has a beautiful wooden Pietà and a moving 16th-century Entombment.

Berry has a reputation for sorcery, a tradition well illustrated in Concressault's lively **Musée de la Sorcellerie**, 10 km (6 miles) east of Aubigny. Here waxworks bring to life the history of herbalism, healing and magic, and portray the gruesome fate of those accused of witchcraft during the Inquisition.

🏛 Mémorial de l'Auld Alliance & Musée Marguerite-Audoux
Château d'Aubigny. **Tel** *02 48 81 50 07.* 🕐 *May–Sep: Fri–Mon & public hols; early Apr & late Oct: weekends & public hols, pm only.* 🎫 🚻 *Mémorial de l'Auld Alliance only.*

🏛 Musée de la Sorcellerie
La Jonchère, Concressault. **Tel** *02 48 73 86 11.* 🕐 *Apr–Nov: daily.* 🎫 🚻 **www**.musee-sorcellerie.fr

The Maison de François I, one of the many old houses in Aubigny-sur-Nère

Wine and Cheese Tour ⑯

The Sancerrois in eastern Berry is renowned for its wines and goat's cheese. Gourmets can visit the top-class Sancerre cellars and taste the fresh and fragrant white wines made from the Sauvignon grape, or charming light reds and rosés made from the Pinot Noir. The flavours combine beautifully

Sancerre wine

with the sharp little goat's cheeses called Crottins de Chavignol, which are also produced locally. This rural route passes by gently hilly vineyards and fields of grazing red goats. The tour takes in many of the major producers, as well as a few local museums that explain the long history of both wine and cheese.

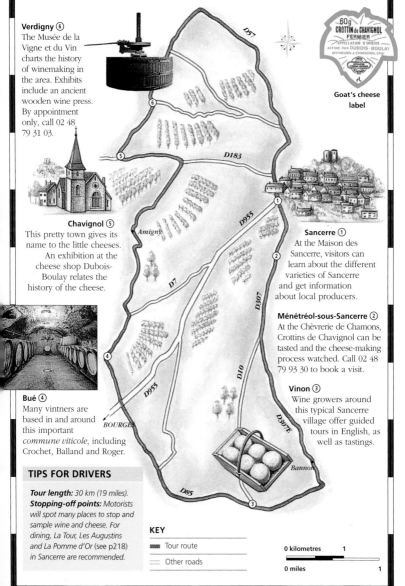

Goat's cheese label

Verdigny ⑥
The Musée de la Vigne et du Vin charts the history of winemaking in the area. Exhibits include an ancient wooden wine press. By appointment only, call 02 48 79 31 03.

Chavignol ⑤
This pretty town gives its name to the little cheeses. An exhibition at the cheese shop Dubois-Boulay relates the history of the cheese.

Bué ④
Many vintners are based in and around this important *commune viticole*, including Crochet, Balland and Roger.

Sancerre ①
At the Maison des Sancerre, visitors can learn about the different varieties of Sancerre and get information about local producers.

Ménétréol-sous-Sancerre ②
At the Chèvrerie de Chamons, Crottins de Chavignol can be tasted and the cheese-making process watched. Call 02 48 79 93 30 to book a visit.

Vinon ③
Wine growers around this typical Sancerre village offer guided tours in English, as well as tastings.

TIPS FOR DRIVERS

Tour length: 30 km (19 miles).
Stopping-off points: Motorists will spot many places to stop and sample wine and cheese. For dining, La Tour, Les Augustins and La Pomme d'Or (see p218) in Sancerre are recommended.

KEY

▬▬▬ Tour route

═══ Other roads

0 kilometres 1

0 miles 1

NORTH OF THE LOIRE

The peaceful Mayenne and Sarthe regions seem worlds away from the tourist-frequented château country of the central Loire Valley. A grouping of districts with little common history, the area north of the Loire has very different attractions from the former royal domains to the south. The rivers, hills, forests and plains abound with opportunities for fishing, boating and country walks.

River boats cruise along the quiet Sarthe, through pretty wooded scenery and meadowlands, to Sablé-sur-Sarthe, near the Abbaye de Solesmes, famous for its tradition of superb Gregorian chant.

The more dramatic scenery of the Mayenne valley, from Laval southwards, with steep cliffs and villages perched on wooded hills, makes a pleasant spot for a restful break from château-visiting. The river, studded with locks, runs into the Maine and then into the Loire, a pattern also followed by the Loir (Le Loir, which is not to be confused with La Loire).

The valley of the Loir is also very pretty, the slow-moving river flowing through peaceful villages. It is a perfect place for relaxing and enjoying the countryside. The valley also offers a few spectacular sights of its own, including the château at Le Lude, with its four imposing corner towers, and the stern-faced château of Châteaudun further upstream, which was once a stronghold of the counts of Blois. Le Mans, world famous for its 24-hour car race, also has an attractive old centre. East of Le Mans, gentle scenery gives way first to the wooded hills of the Perche and then to the vast wheat-fields on the plain of the Beauce, which is dominated by the magnificent cathedral at Chartres. Two lovely châteaux, Anet and Maintenon, were homes to royal mistresses: Diane de Poitiers *(see p55)*, mistress of Henri II, retreated to Anet, and Madame de Maintenon was the mistress of Louis XIV. Like Chartres Cathedral, these great houses stand on the edge of the Ile de France, the region around Paris, so they attract many day visitors from the country's capital.

Clog-making at the woodwork centre in Jupilles in the Forêt de Bercé

◁ The River Sarthe near the village of St-Céneri-le-Gérei

Exploring the North of the Loire

Consisting of the *départements* of Mayenne, Sarthe and Eure-et-Loire, the region north of the Loire borders Brittany, Normandy and the Ile de France. It combines characteristics of all these regions with those of the central Loire Valley. In the north, the hills of the Alpes Mancelles have more in common with the landscapes of Normandy than they do with the rolling fields further south. The rivers traversing the region – the Loir, Sarthe and Mayenne – are smaller and gentler than the mighty Loire but still very scenic. The largest towns in the region are Chartres, Le Mans and Laval, all of them worth a visit.

One of Chartres' winding, cobbled streets

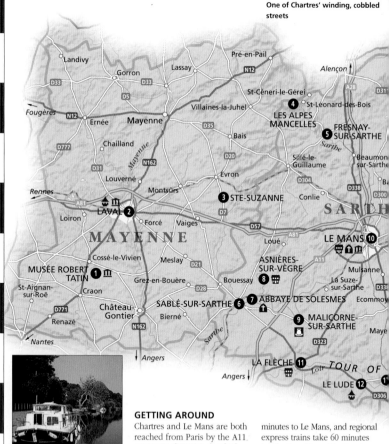

Cruising on the River Sarthe, upstream from Sablé

GETTING AROUND

Chartres and Le Mans are both reached from Paris by the A11 autoroute *(L'Océane)*, which continues to Angers. The A81 crosses the region from Le Mans to Laval, while the A28 cuts north–south from Alençon to Tours. Trains from Paris are frequent: the TGV takes 55 minutes to Le Mans, and regional express trains take 60 minutes to Chartres. From Chartres to Le Mans is about 90 minutes. Buses link most of the main towns in the region but are less regular during school holidays. Boating is one of the best ways of seeing the countryside.

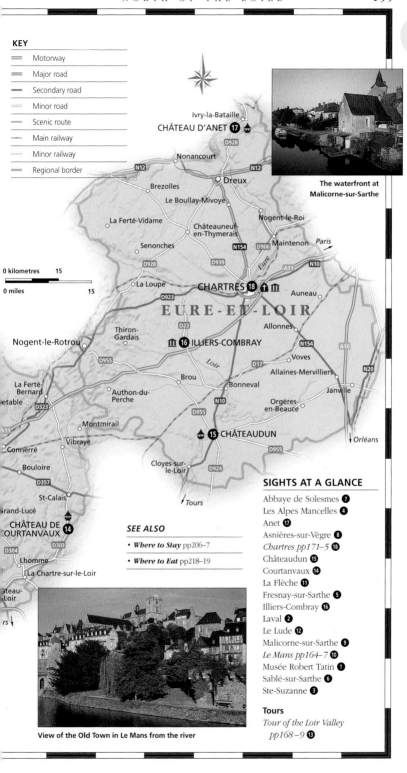

Ivry-la-Bataille
CHÂTEAU D'ANET **17**
D928
Nonancourt
N12
Dreux
N12

The waterfront at
Malicorne-sur-Sarthe

Brezolles
Le Boullay-Mivoye
La Ferté-Vidame
Châteauneuf-
en-Thymerais
Nogent-le-Roi
Senonches
Maintenon
Paris
N154 D906
Eure
A11 N10

0 kilometres 15

0 miles 15

La Loupe
CHARTRES **18**
Auneau
D928 D939
D923
EURE-ET-LOIR
Thiron-
Gardais D23
Allonnes
Nogent-le-Rotrou
16 ILLIERS-COMBRAY
N154 A10
D955
Voves
Loir
D17
Brou
Allaines-Mervilliers
N20
La Ferté-
Bernard D323
Bonneval
Orgères-
en-Beauce
Janville
etable
Montmirail
D955 N10
A11
Vibraye
Authon-du-
Perche
Connerré
15 CHÂTEAUDUN
Orléans
Bouloire
D955
D357
Cloyes-sur-
le-Loir D924
St-Calais
Grand-Lucé
Tours
CHÂTEAU DE
COURTANVAUX **14**
D304 D303
Lhomme
La Chartre-sur-le-Loir
âteau-
Loir
rs

SEE ALSO

• **Where to Stay** pp206–7

• **Where to Eat** pp218–19

View of the Old Town in Le Mans from the river

Musée Robert Tatin ❶

Road map B2. La Frênouse.
🚉 Laval. 🚌 Cossé-le-Vivien.
Tel 02 43 98 80 89. ⬜ daily
(Oct–Mar: pm only). ⬛ Jan, 25 Dec.
📷 📹 ♿ www.musee-robert-tatin.fr

The multi-talented artist Robert Tatin (1902–83) devised an extra-ordinary museum, in the little village of La Frênouse, near Cossé-le-Vivien. The building is approached via the Allée des Géants (Giants' Avenue): lining the path are huge, strange concrete figures, depicting people who impressed Tatin, including Pablo Picasso, Toulouse-Lautrec, Joan of Arc and the Gallic warrior,

Tatin's statue of Picasso at the Musée Robert Tatin

Vercingetorix. Beyond them, a statue of a huge dragon with gaping jaws stands guard. The grounds also feature themed gardens including a maze.

In the museum, awarded the coveted *"Maison des Illustres"* (Houses of the Famous) label in 2012, is a cross-section of Tatin's work: paintings, sculpture, frescoes, and ceramics. Tatin was also a cabinet-maker and much else besides. He was influenced by the megalithic monuments in Brittany as well as by Aztec art.

Laval ❷

Road map C2. 🏠 54,000.
🚉 🚌 ℹ️ 1 allée du Vieux St-Louis
(02 43 49 46 46). 🛍️ Tue, Sat.
www.laval-tourisme.com

Laval straddles the River Mayenne. On the west bank is the **Vieux Château**. This castle dates from the early 11th century, when the region was under the sway of Foulques Nerra, Count of Anjou – it formed one link in his chain of fortresses designed to keep out the invading Bretons and the Normans. The château has a collection of the equipment used by Laval native,

Ambroise Paré (1510–c.1592), known as "the father of modern surgery". It is best known, however, for its **Musée d'Art Naïf** (Museum of Naïve Art) which was inspired in part by Henri Rousseau *(see p25)*. He was known as *Le Douanier*, his nickname deriving from the period when he worked as a customs officer. His Paris studio, complete with piano, has been well reconstructed here. Although the museum has only two works by Rousseau, there are many gems here, including a painting of the ocean liner *Normandie* by the artist Jules Lefranc (1887–1972).

Laval's old town has attractive houses as well as the **Cathédrale de la Ste-Trinité**, with its Aubusson tapestries. The city became

famous for producing elaborate *retables* (altarpieces). **Notre-Dame-des-Cordeliers**, on rue de Bretagne, has several fine examples. Laval and Mayenne are also major cheese-making areas. Discover how this agricultural activity reached industrial heights at the **Lactopôle**. Laval also has a couple of France's few surviving **bateaux-lavoirs**, which now form a museum of the same name. Such floating laundries first appeared in the mid-19th century on the banks of rivers in the western Loire Valley.

🏛 **Château & Musée du Vieux Château**
Pl de la Trémoille. **Tel** 02 43 53 39 89. ⬜ Mon–Sat, Sun pm. 📷 📹

🏛 **Lactopôle**
Tel 02 43 59 51 90. ⬜ Mon–Fri.
📹 Guided tours only. www.lactopole.com

🏛 **Bateaux-Lavoirs**
Quai Paul-Boudet. **Tel** 02 43 49 46 46 (tourist office). 📷

Le Lancement du Normandie by Jules Lefranc, at the Musée d'Art Naïf

Ste-Suzanne ❸

Road map C2. 🏠 *1,000.* 🚇 *Laval, then bus.* 🏛 *1 rue du Bueil (02 43 01 43 60).* **www**.ste-suzanne.com

This village, high on a hill, is still partly surrounded by the fortifications designed as a defence against marauding Normans in the 10th century – it was sturdy enough to withstand an attack by William the Conqueror, whose former encampment site can be seen just 3 km (2 miles) outside the town. Although much of the original castle was pulled down by the English in the early 15th century, a 10th-century keep has withstood the ravages of time. The **Château de Ste-Suzanne** has been restored, with exhibitions focusing on the area's heritage. Village history is also explored at the **Musée de l'Auditoire**, with reconstructions of events and vignettes of daily life.

Church doorway, St-Léonard-des-Bois

🏛 Château de Ste-Suzanne
1 rue Fouquet de la Varenne. **Tel** *02 43 58 13 00.* ◯ *Jul–Aug: daily; Sep–Jun: Mon–Fri.* ⬤ *mid-Dec–early Jan.* 📷 🎫

🏛 Musée de l'Auditoire
7 Grande Rue. **Tel** *02 43 01 42 65.* ◯ *Apr–Jun & Sep: Sat–Sun; Jul & Aug: daily.* 📷

Les Alpes Mancelles ❹

Road map C2. 🚇 *Alençon.* 🚌 *Fresnay-sur-Sarthe.* 🏛 *19 av du Dr Riant, Fresnay-sur-Sarthe (02 43 33 28 04).* **www**.ot-alpes-mancelles.com

The name of this region of wooded hills and green meadows, between Fresnay-sur-Sarthe and Alençon, means "Alps of Le Mans". Although certainly an exaggeration, there is something faintly alpine in the landscape, with its streams winding through gorges, sheep, fruit trees and heather-clad hillsides. A large part of the area is

St-Céneri-le-Gérei's Romanesque church, perched on a hill

incorporated into the regional natural park of Normandie-Maine.

The enchanting village of **St-Céneri-le-Gérei** hides in a loop in the Sarthe. It has a wonderful Romanesque church containing medieval murals. In the 19th and early 20th centuries, artists, such as Eugene Boudin and Camille Corot, were drawn to this picturesque area. They often stayed at the **Auberge des Soeurs Moisy**, now turned into a compact museum. Exhibits focus on the history and heritage of fine art in the region. It is also worth wandering through the themed **Jardins de la Mansonière**, which includes a nuttery and a perfume garden.

The neighbouring village of **St-Léonard-des-Bois** lies south down the Sarthe. The steep slopes are appreciated by mountain-bikers and walkers;

climb to the top for grand views of the Sarthe plain leading to Le Mans. Canoeists also favour this section of the river. Located on the outside of St-Léonard-des-Bois **Domaine du Gasseau** has an equestrian centre, tree-top assault course and an art centre. A restaurant, hotel, café and a shop selling local produce can be found here too.

🏛 Auberge des Soeurs Moisy
Rue du Dessous, St-Céneri-le-Gérei. **Tel** *02 33 27 84 47.* ◯ *Apr–Sep: Wed–Sun, pm only.* 📷

♣ Jardins de la Mansonière
Route d'Alençon. **Tel** *02 33 26 73 24.* ◯ *mid-Apr–May: Fri–Sun & public hols, pm only; Jun–mid-Sep: Wed–Mon, pm only.* 📷 📱 **www**.mansoniere.fr

🏃 Domaine du Gasseau
St-Léonard-des-Bois. **Tel** *02 43 34 34 44.* ◯ *Apr–Sep: daily.* **www**.legasseau.fr

Fresnay-sur-Sarthe ❺

Road map C2. 🏠 *2,400.* 🚇 *Alençon, Sillé-le-Guillaume, La Hutte.* 🚌 🏛 *19 av du Dr Riant (02 43 33 28 04).* 🛒 *Sat am.*

From the 16th to the 19th century, Fresnay-sur-Sarthe was an important centre for cloth weaving, and its outskirts remain rather industrial. The centre of Fresnay, however, still retains a charming medieval feel, with unusual church and castle vestiges.

The River Sarthe from the town of Fresnay-sur-Sarthe

Sablé-sur-Sarthe ❻

Road map C2. 🏃 *13,000.*
🚇 🚌 🛈 *rue du Château (02 43 95
00 60).* 🅿 *Mon, Fri–Sat.* 🎵 *Festival
de la Musique Baroque (late Aug).*
www.tourisme.sablesursarthe.fr

A good base from which
to take river cruises along
the Sarthe, Sablé is pleasant,
although fairly industrial.
There is some surprising
modern sculpture in this
traditional setting: in the cobbled place Raphaël Elizé in
the town centre stands a contemporary sculpture entitled
Hymne à l'Amour, by local
sculptor Louis Derbré, and
around the square are several
piles of "cannon balls", a
rather curious modern
installation that was inspired
by an 18th-century fashion.

Sablé has some attractive
shops in the pedestrian rue de
l'Ile and in the nearby square,
where the Maison du Sablé
sells the famous shortbread-like
biscuits to which the town has
given its name.

The town's château, which
was built in the early 18th
century by a nephew of Louis
XIV's chief minister, Jean-
Baptiste Colbert, now houses
workshops for restorers of old
books and manuscripts of the
Bibliothèque Nationale, the
national library of France.

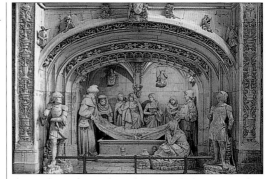

The Entombment of Our Lord, part of the "saints of Solesmes" group of
stone carvings in the church of the Abbaye de Solesmes

Although the château cannot
be visited, the pleasant park
that surrounds it is open.

On the route de Solesmes,
opposite the summer swim-
ming pool, is the Jardin Public,
from which there are views of
the Abbaye de Solesmes.

Abbaye de Solesmes ❼

Road map C2. 🚇 *Sablé-sur-Sarthe,
then taxi or walk 3 km (2 miles)
along the river.* **Tel** *02 43 95 03 08.*
Abbey Church 🕐 *daily.* 🛉 *10am
daily; vespers: varies between 4 and
5:30pm.* 🚻 **www**.solesmes.com

Services at the Benedictine
Abbaye de St-Pierre, part of
the Abbaye de Solesmes, attract
visitors who come from far and
wide to listen to the monks'
Gregorian chant. For over a
century, the abbey has been
working to preserve and
promote this ancient form of
prayer. Books and recordings
produced by the monks are
sold, outside church service
times, in the shop near the
entrance to the abbey.

Originally founded in 1010
as a priory, the abbey was
substantially rebuilt in the late
19th century in a somewhat
forbidding, fortress-like style.

The interior of the **abbey
church** has an austere beauty.
Its nave and transept are both
Romanesque, while the 19th-
century choir imitates the
medieval style. Both arms of
the transept are adorned by
groups of stone carvings made
in the 15th and 16th centuries
and known collectively as the
"saints of Solesmes". The
chapel to the left of the high
altar contains *The Entombment
of Our Lord*, with the haunting
figure of Mary Magdalene
kneeling at Christ's
feet, deep in prayer. In
*The Dormition of the
Virgin*, which can be
seen in the chapel on
the right, the lower
scenes illustrate the
Virgin Mary's death
and burial, while the
scenes above depict
her Assumption and
heavenly Coronation.

The little **parish
church**, which is locat-
ed beside the entrance
to the abbey, is worth
visiting for its interesting modern stained-
glass windows.

The imposing Abbaye de Solesmes, reflected in the River Sarthe

For hotels and restaurants in this region see pp206–7 and pp218–19

Asnières-sur-Vègre ❽

Road map C2. 🏠 380. 🚉 Sablé-sur-Sarthe, then taxi. 🈯 Sablé-sur-Sarthe (02 43 95 00 60).

This pretty village of old houses and water mills, with a 12th-century hump-backed bridge, is largely built in pinkish-yellow stone. Its church has lively wall paintings, dating from the 12th and 15th centuries, depicting scenes from medieval life and moral warnings in the shape of the damned being herded into hell by huge, slavering hounds. The 13th-century **Cour de Justice** is an impressive Gothic building, built as a meeting place for the canons of the Cathédrale St-Julien in Le Mans. The **Jardin Mosaïque**, above the village is an ecological garden. Nearby **Juigné** is on the old road from Le Mans to Sablé-sur-Sarthe. Its château was rebuilt in the early 17th century, and the park with its panoramic views of the river, is open to the public. It is possible to hire boats from Juigné's tiny harbour, from which one can see the church perched on the cliff above.

The 12th-century humpbacked bridge in Asnières-sur-Vègre

Detail from the frescoes in Asnières' church

🌿 **Jardin Mosaïque**
Tel 02 43 92 52 35. ☐ late Apr–mid-Oct: Wed–Sun & public hols, pm only.

Malicorne-sur-Sarthe ❾

Road map C3. 🏠 2,000. 🚉 Noyen-sur-Sarthe, La Suze-sur-Sarthe. 🚌 pl Désautels (02 43 94 74 45). 🛒 Fri. **www**.ville-malicorne.fr

The chief claim to fame of this little town on the Sarthe is its faïence (tin-glazed earthenware). Jean Loiseau, a potter, first set up here in 1747. At the **Faïenceries du Bourg-Joly** visitors can buy the open-work ware known as *Faïence de Malicorne*. The **Faïenceries d'Art de Malicorne**, (pottery) just outside the village, also has a factory shop, while the **Malicorne Espace Faïence**, in the centre of town, boasts an extensive pottery museum. Malicorne's small harbour is a popular spot for boaters, and both cruises and the hire of small motorboats are possible. The village also contains the pretty **Château de Malicorne**, dating from the 18th century, as well as a charming Romanesque church.

🏺 **Faïenceries du Bourg-Joly**
16 rue Carnot. **Tel** 02 43 94 80 10. **Shop** ☐ Mon–Sat & Sun pm.

🏺 **Faïenceries d'Art de Malicorne**
18 rue Bernard Palissy. **Tel** 02 43 94 81 18. **Workshop** ☐ Apr–Sep: Tue–Sat. **Shop** ☐ Mon–Sat.
🚻 ♿ 📷

🏺 **Malicorne Espace Faïence**
Rue Victor Hugo. **Tel** 02 43 48 07 17. ☐ mid-Feb–mid-Apr, Nov–Dec: Wed–Mon; mid-Apr–Oct: daily. 🚻 ♿ 📷

🏛 **Château de Malicorne**
Tel 02 43 94 84 65. ☐ Jul–Aug: Wed–Sun. 🚻 ♿ 📷

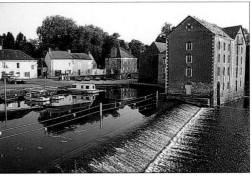

The harbour at Malicorne, surrounded by former water mills

Street-by-Street: Le Mans ➓

The hilly, picturesque old town (La Cité Plantagenêt) is best explored on foot. Its narrow, cobbled streets are lined by 15th- and 16th-century half-timbered houses interspersed with Renaissance mansions. Several of the finest buildings served as temporary residences for France's kings and queens, although the one named after Richard the Lionheart's queen Bérengère, or Berengaria, was built two and a half centuries after her death. The quarter is bounded to the northwest by the old Roman walls, which run beside the River Sarthe.

Carving on house in rue des Chanoines

Maison d'Adam et Eve
The carvings on this doctor's house illustrate the importance of astrology in 16th-century medicine.

Hôtel d'Argouges
Louis XI is said to have stayed in this 15th-century turreted mansion in 1467.

The Roman walls are among the best-preserved in Europe.

| 0 metres | 50 |
| 0 yards | 50 |

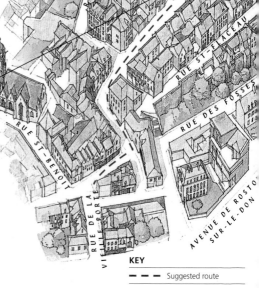

QUAI LOUIS-BLANC

RUE DE VAUX

RUE DE LA VERRERIE

GRANDE RUE

RUE ST-FLACEAU

RUE DES FOSSÉS

RUE ST-BENOIT

RUE DE LA VIEILLE PORTE

AVENUE DE ROSTO SUR-LE-DON

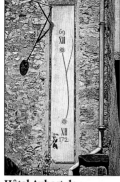

Hôtel Aubert de Clairaulnay
The sundial on the side of this late 16th-century mansion was placed there in 1789 by Claude Chappe, the inventor of semaphore.

KEY

- - - Suggested route

For hotels and restaurants in this region see pp206–7 and pp218–19

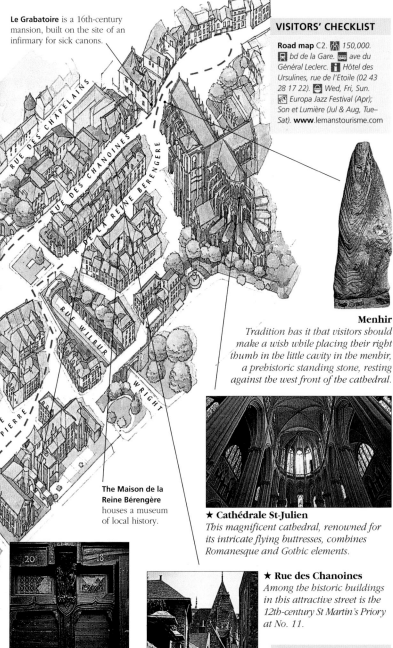

Le Grabatoire is a 16th-century mansion, built on the site of an infirmary for sick canons.

RUE DES CHAPELAINS

RUE DES CHANOINES

R DE LA REINE BÉRENGÈRE

RUE WILBUR

WRIGHT

E PIERRE

Menhir
*Tradition has it that visitors should
make a wish while placing their right
thumb in the little cavity in the menhir,
a prehistoric standing stone, resting
against the west front of the cathedral.*

**The Maison de la
Reine Bérengère**
houses a museum
of local history.

★ **Cathédrale St-Julien**
*This magnificent cathedral, renowned for
its intricate flying buttresses, combines
Romanesque and Gothic elements.*

★ **Rue des Chanoines**
*Among the historic buildings
in this attractive street is the
12th-century St Martin's Priory
at No. 11.*

STAR SIGHTS

★ Rue des Chanoines

★ Maison des Deux
Amis

★ Cathédrale St-Julien

★ **Maison des Deux Amis**
*This building is named for
its carving of two friends
holding a coat of arms.*

Exploring Le Mans

Although best known for its gruelling 24-hour motor race, Le Mans has many other attractions, not least of which is the magnificent Cathédrale St-Julien. The city's history stretches back to Roman times. The walls surrounding the old town, once the ancient city of Vindunum, date from the late 3rd and early 4th centuries. They originally stretched for some 1,300 m (1,400 yards). Eleven towers are still standing, and their massive walls are decorated with geometric patterns created by using courses of brick alternating with undressed stone in various colours. Outside the city walls, Le Mans has developed into a bustling, modern city with several memorable museums and a number of attractive churches.

The Plantagenet Enamel (1150) displayed in the Musée de Tessé

♙ Cathédrale St-Julien
Pl St Michel. **Tel** 02 43 28 28 98.
◯ daily. ♿
The best view of Cathédrale St-Julien's dramatic flying buttresses, unlike those of any other cathedral in their complex arrangement, is from the place des Jacobins. The cathedral is something of a hybrid: the 12th-century nave is essentially Romanesque, and the transepts were built a century later than the pure Gothic choir, one of the tallest in France, which dates from the 13th century. From the entrance via the Romanesque south portal, there is a striking view of the pillars in the choir. These used to be decorated with 16th-century tapestries that provided a splash of colour echoed in the medieval stained glass. These days, the tapestries are displayed only a few months a year.

The Curate's Meal (1786), from the Musée de la Reine Bérengère

⌂ Musée de la Reine Bérengère
Rue de la Reine Bérengère. **Tel** 02 43 47 38 51. ◯ May–Sep: Tue–Sun; Oct–Apr: Tue–Sun, pm. ● 1 Jan, 24–26 Dec. ⬛
This museum is set in three attractive half-timbered houses in the old town, their wooden façades lively with carved figures. Its collections of art and local history include faïence and pottery from many periods, with some examples of Malicorne ware *(see p163)*. The museum also shows furniture made in the region. On the second floor, the 19th-century paintings by local artists show how relatively little the town of Le Mans has changed over the years. Also of note is Jean Sorieul's dramatic canvas, *The Battle of Le Mans of 13 December, 1793.*

⌂ Musée de Tessé
2 av de Paderborn. **Tel** 02 43 47 38 51. ◯ Tue–Sun. ● 1 Jan, 24–26 Dec. ⬛ ♿
In a pretty park a short walk from the cathedral, the bishop's palace was converted in 1927 into Le Mans' art museum, devoted to the fine and decorative arts, as well as archaeology. The permanent collection of paintings on the ground floor ranges from the late Middle Ages to the 19th century, and the archaeology section is mainly Egyptian and Greco-Roman, with two replica Pharaonic tombs. The Tessé's most famous exhibit is the vivid Plantagenet Enamel, a medieval enamelled panel depicting Geoffroy V, known as Le Bel (The Handsome).

⌂ Musée de 24 Heures
Circuit des 24-Heures. **Tel** 02 43 72 72 24. ◯ Mar–May, Sep–Dec: Tue-Sun; Jun–Aug: daily. ● Jan, Feb. ⬛ ♿ **http://**musee24h. sarthe.com
Near Le Mans' famous race track is this museum, which displays a dazzling range of vintage, classic and modern racing cars and motorbikes. It includes some of the early designs of Amédée Bollée, an industrialist whose first pioneering car design dated from 1873. Bollée's family made the city famous for car design decades before the first 24-hour race *(see p57).*

16th-century tapestry hanging in the Cathédrale St-Julien

La Flèche ⓫

Road map C3. 🏛 16,000. 🚉 ℹ️
blvd de Montréal (02 43 94 02 53).
🛒 *Wed & Sun.* 🎭 *Festival des
Affranchis (2nd weekend in Jul).*
www.tourisme-lafleche.fr

La Flèche is an attractive
town on the Loir, with some
restored old mills in the
midst of the river. Its chief
glory is the **Prytanée
Militaire**, the French military
academy. Founded as a Jesuit
college in 1604 by Henri IV, it
was assigned its present
function by Napoléon in 1808.

On the opposite bank of the
river is Port Luneau, from
where Jérôme le Royer de la
Dauversière set off for the New
World. Nearby, the bustling
place Henri IV, with a statue of
the king, is lined with cafés.

At the heart of the town,
the 15th-century **Château des
Carmes**, the former town hall
(now hosting art exhibitions),
is reflected in the River Loir.
The charming **Théâtre de la
Halle au Blé** also presents
exhibitions as well as
engaging theatre productions.

The **Parc Zoologique de la
Flèche**, just outside town, is a
major zoo in France. It displays
a wide variety of animals and
participates in a number of
conservation programmes.

🏛 **Prytanée Militaire**
Rue du Collège. **Tel** 02 43 48 59
06. ⭕ *Jul & Aug: daily.* 🎟

🐾 **Parc Zoologique de la Flèche**
Le Tertre Rouge. **Tel** 02 43 48 19
19. ⭕ *daily.* ⛔ *1 Jan, 25 Dec.* 🎟
🍴 ♿ **www**.zoo-la-fleche.com

Place Henri IV in La Flèche, with the statue of the king in the centre

Le Lude ⓬

Road map C3. 🏛 4,200. 🚉
ℹ️ *pl F-de-Nicolay (02 43 94 62
20).* 🛒 *Thu.* 🎭 *Marché Nocturne
(night market; 3rd weekend in Jul).*
www.tourisme-bassinludois.fr

The oldest section of this
market town is the area
surrounding the **Château du
Lude**, where houses dating
from the 15th to 17th centuries line the narrow streets.
The château's 15th-century
structure has been transformed
over the centuries into a more
elegant form. The interior is
beautifully furnished, largely
in the 19th-century style,
although there are some
pieces from the 17th and 18th
centuries, including French
and Flemish tapestries. The
Oratory is decorated with
16th-century frescoes, which
depict Old Testament scenes.
The formal gardens lead
down to the River Loir.

Cyclists and keen walkers
can follow the former railway
line northwest along the
Loir, from Le Lude to the
picturesque twin villages
of **Luché-Pringé**.

⚓ **Château du Lude**
Tel 02 43 94 60 09. ⭕ *Apr–Sep:
Thu-Tue, pm only; mid-Jun–Aug:
daily pm only.* **Park** *Apr–Sep: daily.*
🎟 🚫 ♿ *ground floor.*
🎭 *Le Weekend des Jardinières
(1st w/end Jun).* **www**.lelude.com

**The imposing towers of the
Château du Lude**

LES 24 HEURES DU MANS

The name of Le Mans is known throughout
the world, thanks to its famous 24-hour car
race. Since it began on 26 May 1923, the
event has attracted huge crowds every June,
both from France and abroad – these days,
more than 230,000 spectators and 2,500
journalists watch the race. The circuit is
to the south of the city and is 13.6-km
(8½-miles) long, including some stretches on
ordinary roads. Nowadays, drivers can cover
some 5,300 km (3,300 miles) within the time
limit. Within the course is the Hunaudières
track where, in 1908, Wilbur Wright staged
the first aeroplane flight in France.

One of the early races in Le Mans

Tour of the Loir Valley ⑬

Between Poncé-sur-le-Loir and La Flèche, the River Loir passes through peaceful, unspoiled country-side and picturesque villages. An unhurried tour of the valley takes two days and allows time to try some of the numerous riverside and forest walks. Families may enjoy the sailing, riding, angling and cycling facilities available in the area, while art lovers can seek out little-known churches adorned with delicately coloured Romanesque frescoes. Wine buffs will be interested in trying some of the area's wines, which can be sipped from locally blown glass – the Loir Valley also has an excellent reputation for its crafts.

The banks of the tranquil Loir, ideal for fishing and walking

La Flèche ①
The home of the Prytanée Militaire (military academy, *see p167*), La Flèche is a charming town with wonderful views across the River Loir.

Entrance to the Prytanée Militaire

Vaas ④
The Moulin de Rotrou, on the edge of this pretty village, is a working flour mill and museum of breadmaking. In Vaas, the Eglise Notre-Dame de Vaas has fine 17th-century paintings.

Parc Zoologique de la Flèche ②
Just outside the town, this zoo is one of the largest in France, with nearly 1,200 animals (*see p167*).

TIPS FOR DRIVERS

Tour length: 103 km (64 miles).
Stopping-off points: The forests and riverbanks along the Loir are ideal for picnicking, and shops in the region sell delicacies to make a cold meal very special. This will be a doubly satisfying experience if you buy local produce from a market, such as that in Le Lude, first. If you prefer to eat in a restaurant, Le Moulin des 4 Saisons in La Flèche has local dishes on the menu. For those wishing to stay overnight, Le Relais Cicéro, also in La Flèche, is recommended.

Le Lude ③
This market town is known mainly for its spectacular château (*see p167*).

The entrance to the Château du Lude

Forêt de Bercé ⑤
This extensive forest is famous for its ancient oaks. Some in the Futaie des Clos are more than 40 m (130 ft) tall and over 350 years old. In Jupilles visitors can see traditional wooden clogs *(sabots)* being made. Also visit the fascinating Musée Carnuta, devoted to the forest.

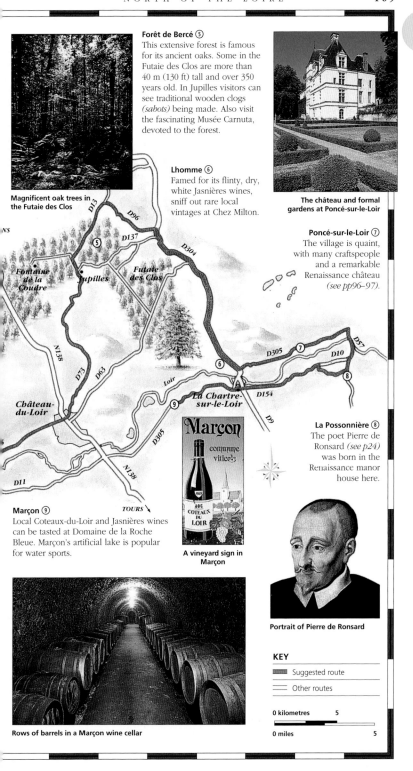

Magnificent oak trees in the Futaie des Clos

The château and formal gardens at Poncé-sur-le-Loir

Lhomme ⑥
Famed for its flinty, dry, white Jasnières wines, sniff out rare local vintages at Chez Milton.

Poncé-sur-le-Loir ⑦
The village is quaint, with many craftspeople and a remarkable Renaissance château *(see pp96–97).*

La Possonnière ⑧
The poet Pierre de Ronsard *(see p24)* was born in the Renaissance manor house here.

Marçon ⑨
Local Coteaux-du-Loir and Jasnières wines can be tasted at Domaine de la Roche Bleue. Marçon's artificial lake is popular for water sports.

A vineyard sign in Marçon

Portrait of Pierre de Ronsard

Rows of barrels in a Marçon wine cellar

KEY

Suggested route

Other routes

0 kilometres 5

0 miles 5

The Château de Courtanvaux with its towering walls

Château de Courtanvaux 🔵

Bessé-sur-Braye. **Road map** D3.
Tel 02 43 35 34 43. ⬜ Apr: Sat & Sun; May–Sep: Tue–Sun. ⬤ for private events. 🎫 📷 **Park** ⬜ daily.

Beyond Bessé-sur-Braye's unprepossessing outskirts, this Gothic and Renaissance château makes a romantic sight as it looms up at the end of a tree-lined drive. To see the Château de Courtanvaux's carefully restored interior book a place on a guided tour. The formal gardens are home to a tiny Gothic chapel, visitors are free to explore its 156 acres (63 ha) of pools and woodland.

Châteaudun 🔵

Road map E2. 🏠 14,500. 🚉 🚌
🛈 1 rue de Luynes (02 37 45 22 46). ⬤ Thu. 🎪 Foire aux Laines (medieval fair, early Jul).
www.tourisme-chateaudun.fr

Dominated by its fierce-looking **château**, the town of Châteaudun is situated above the River Loir where the Beauce plain meets the Perche district. Châteaudun was owned at one time by the aristocratic poet Charles d'Orléans (see p24), who then handed it on to his half-brother Jean Dunois, known as the bastard of Orléans and one of Joan of Arc's loyal companions-in-arms (see p137). It was Jean who began

the château's south wing in 1460, and built the beautiful late Gothic chapel, adorned with murals and life-size statues. The other wing was built half a century later.

Both wings are hung with wonderful tapestries, which date from the 16th and 17th centuries. Visitors can tour the château's living rooms, kitchens and massive keep.

Châteaudun's Old Town has a number of picturesque buildings, as well as several interesting churches: the Romanesque **Eglise de la Madeleine**, built in stages and now restored after damage sustained in 1940, and **St-Valérien**, with its tall square belfry. Situated on the far bank of the River Loir, the **Eglise St-Jean-de-la-Chaine** is also Romanesque. The **Grottes du Foulon** are located beneath the town. These large underground caves house remarkable crystallized sea creatures, preserved from the pre-historic era.

Remembrance of Things Past by Proust

🏛 **Château**
Tel 02 37 94 02 90. ⬜ daily.
⬤ 1 Jan, 1 May, 25 Dec. 🎫 📷
♿ restricted. **www**.monuments-nationaux.fr

🏔 **Grottes du Foulon**
Tel 02 37 45 19 60. ⬜ May–Jun: Tue & Thu–Sun, pm only; Jul–Aug: daily; Sep–Apr: Sat, Sun & public hols, pm only. 🎫

Illiers-Combray 🔵

Road map E2. 🏠 3,300. 🚉 🛈 5 rue Henri Germond (02 37 24 24 00). ⬤ Fri. 🎪 Journée des Aubépines (Proustian May Day, May).
www.tourisme-illiers-combray.fr

The little market town of Illiers has added the word "Combray" to its name in honour of Marcel Proust's magnificent novel, *Remembrance of Things Past*, in which it is depicted as Combray (see p25). As a child, Proust spent many happy Easter holidays in the town, walking by the banks of the River Loir, which he later portrayed in his work as the "Vivonne". The author's admirers make pilgrimages to the places described in the novel, such as the big Gothic church, and the Pré Catalan gardens, and the house once owned by Proust's uncle Jules Amiot, **La Maison de Tante Léonie**. The house is now a touching museum about the famous writer's life, complete with the kitchen where the "Françoise" of the novel (who was actually Ernestine, the family cook) reigned supreme.

🏛 **La Maison de Tante Léonie**
4 rue du Dr Proust. **Tel** 02 37 24 30 97. ⬜ Tue–Sun. ⬤ mid-Dec–mid-Jan. 🎫 📷

A view of Châteaudun's castle from across the River Loir

Carved hounds and stag on the
gateway of the Château d'Anet

Château d'Anet ⓱

Road map E1. 🚉 *Dreux, then taxi.*
Tel *02 37 41 90 07.* ◯ *Feb–Mar &
Nov: Sat–Sun pm; Apr–Oct: Wed–
Mon pm.* ◉ *Dec–Jan.* 📷 ♿ *restri-
cted* 🖥 **www**.chateaudanet.com

When the mistress of Henri
II, Diane de Poitiers, was
banished from Chenonceau
after the king's accidental
death in 1559, she retired to
Anet, which she had inherited
from her husband, and
remained here until her death
in 1566. It had been rebuilt for
her by Philibert de l'Orme,
who also designed the bridge
over the Cher at Chenonceau
(*see pp106–7*). The château
was superbly decorated and
furnished, as befitted the
woman who reigned over a
king's heart for nearly 30 years.

The château was sold after
the Revolution and, in 1804,
the new owner pulled down
the central apartments and
the right wing. However, you
can still admire the magnificent
entrance gate (the bronze
relief of Diane by Benvenuto
Cellini is a copy), the chapel,
decorated with bas-reliefs by
the Renaissance sculptor Jean
Goujon (c.1510–68), and the
richly furnished west wing.
Just beside the château stands
the mausoleum where Diane
de Poitiers is buried.

Chartres ⓲

Road map E2. 🏠 *42,000.* 🚉 🚌
🛈 *pl de la Cathédrale (02 37 18 26
26).* 🅿 *Sat.* 🎵 *Festival d'Orgue
(organ music; Jul–Aug).*
www.chartres-tourisme.com

Surrounded by the wheat
fields of the Beauce plain,
Chartres was for many years
a major market town. Visitors
who come to see the Gothic
cathedral (*see pp172–3*)
should explore the town's
old streets, particularly the
rue Chantault, the rue des
Ecuyers, the rue aux Herbes
and, over the Eure, the rue
de la Tannerie (which took
its name from the tanneries
that once lined the river).
Some of the most remarkable
buildings, including the town
hall and historic churches, are
lit up at night in extravagant
manner from mid-April to mid-
September. Pick up a leaflet
on **Chartres en Lumières** to
follow the trail after nightfall.

Beside the cathedral, the
Musée des Beaux-Arts,
occupies the elegant 18th-
century building that was
once the bishop's palace. It
has some fine Renaissance
enamel plaques, a portrait
of Erasmus in old age by
Holbein, and many 17th-
and 18th-century paintings,
by French and Flemish artists.

Half-timbered houses in the rue
Chantault in Chartres

There is also a collection
of 17th- and 18th-century
harpsichords and spinets.

Close by, the **Centre
International du Vitrail**, a
stained glass centre, is housed
in the converted attics of the
Cellier de Loëns, which was
part of the cathedral's chapter
house. Visitors can enjoy
temporary exhibitions of old
and new stained glass, as well
as changing exhibitions on
the theme of stained glass.
Beautiful stained glass can be
seen in situ in some of the
old churches around the
historic town, notably the
Eglise St-Pierre and the **Eglise
St-Aignan**.

🏛 **Musée des Beaux-Arts**
29 cloître Notre–Dame. **Tel** *02 37
90 45 80.* ◯ *Wed–Mon.* ◉ *Sun
ams & public hols.* 📷

🏛 **Centre International du
Vitrail**
5 rue du Cardinal Pie. **Tel** *02 37 21
65 72.* ◯ *daily.* ◉ *1 Jan, 25 Dec
(and between exhibitions).* 📷 ♿
www.centre-vitrail.org

IN THE FOOTSTEPS OF PROUST

No visit to Illiers-Combray is complete without
retracing the hallowed walks of Marcel Proust's childhood holidays. When he stayed with his Aunt and
Uncle Amiot, he would join in the family walks that
became, in *Remembrance of Things Past*, "Swann's
Way" and "Guermantes Way".

The first takes the walkers towards the village of
Méréglise, crossing the Loire and passing through a
park that was once Uncle Jules' Pré Catelan and
appears in the novel as "Tansonville Park". The "Guermantes" walk covers a few kilometres towards St-Eman,
following the river to its source, now trapped unroman-
tically in a wash house in the village. The walks are signposted and guides are available at the local tourist office.

Illiers-Combray's "Tansonville Park"

Chartres: Cathédrale Notre-Dame

According to art historian Emile Male, "Chartres is the mind of the Middle Ages manifest". The Romanesque cathedral, begun in 1020, was destroyed by fire in 1194; only the south tower, west front and crypt remained. Inside, the sacred Veil of the Virgin relic was the sole treasure to survive. Peasant and lord alike helped to rebuild the church in just 25 years. There were few alterations after 1250 and it was relatively unscathed by the French Revolution. The result is a Gothic cathedral of exceptional unity. Major restoration work has begun on the ochre coatings put on the internal walls in the 13th century.

Part of the Vendôme Window

Elongated Statues
These statues on the Royal Portal represent Old Testament figures.

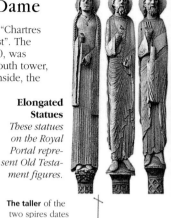

The taller of the two spires dates from the 16th century. Flamboyant Gothic in style, it contrasts sharply with the solemnity of its Romanesque counterpart.

STAR FEATURES

★ Royal Portal

★ South Porch

★ Stained-Glass Windows

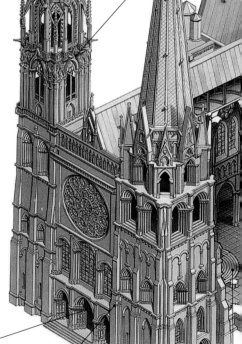

Gothic Nave
As wide as the Romanesque crypt below it, the nave reaches a height of 37 m (121 ft).

★ Royal Portal
The central tympanum of the Royal Portal (1145–55) shows Christ in Majesty.

The lower half of the west front is a survivor of the earlier Romanesque church, dating from the 11th century.

Labyrinth

THE LABYRINTH

The 13th-century labyrinth, inlaid in the floor of the nave, was a feature of most medieval cathedrals. As a penance, pilgrims used to follow the tortuous route on their knees, echoing the Way of the Cross. The journey of 262 m (860 ft), around 11 bands of broken concentric circles, took at least an hour to complete.

VISITORS' CHECKLIST

Pl de la Cathédrale. *Tel* 02 37 21 59 08. ◯ 8:30am–7:30pm daily (Jun–Aug: to 10pm Tue, Fri & Sun). ✝ 11:45am Mon–Sat; 6:15pm Mon–Fri; 7pm Sun–Fri; also 9am Fri; 6pm Sat; 11am & 6pm Sun. ◙ & ☑ check website for times. 🔊 (tours). **www**.cathedrale-chartres.org

St-Piat Chapel
Built between 1324 and 1353, the chapel houses the cathedral treasures, including the Veil of the Virgin relic and fragments of the fragile 13th-century rood screen dismantled in 1763.

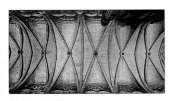

Vaulted Ceiling
A network of ribs supports the vaulted ceiling.

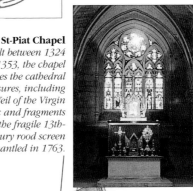

★ Stained-Glass Windows
The windows cover a surface area of over 3,000 sq m (32,300 sq ft).

★ South Porch
Sculpture on the South Porch (1197–1209) reflects New Testament teaching.

Crypt
This is the largest crypt in France, most of it dating from the early 11th century. It comprises two parallel galleries and a series of chapels, plus the 9th-century St Lubin crypt.

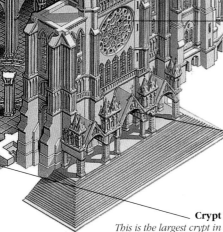

The Stained Glass of Chartres

Donated by the guilds between 1210 and 1240, this glorious collection of stained glass is world-renowned. Over 150 windows illustrate biblical stories and daily life in the 13th century (bring binoculars if you can). During both World Wars the windows were dismantled piece by piece and removed for safety. The windows have been restored and releaded thanks to generous donations.

Stained glass above the apse

Redemption Window
Six scenes illustrate Christ's Passion *and death on the* Cross (c.1210).

★ Tree of Jesse
This 12th-century stained glass shows Christ's genealogy. The tree rises up from Jesse, father of David, at the bottom, to Christ enthroned at the top.

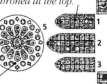

★ West Rose Window
This window (1215), with Christ seated in the centre, shows the Last Judgment.

KEY

1 Tree of Jesse	12 Noah	22 St Anthony and St Paul	33 St Theodore and St Vincent
2 Incarnation	13 St John the Evangelist	23 Blue Virgin	34 St Stephen
3 Passion and Resurrection	14 Mary Magdalene	24 Life of the Virgin	35 St Cheron
4 North Rose Window	15 Good Samaritan and Adam and Eve	25 Zodiac Window	36 St Thomas
5 West Rose Window	16 Assumption	26 St Martin	37 Peace Window
6 South Rose Window	17 Vendôme Chapel Windows	27 St Thomas à Becket	38 Modern Window
7 Redemption Window	18 Miracles of Mary	28 St Margaret and St Catherine	39 Prodigal Son
8 St Nicholas	19 St Apollinaris	29 St Nicholas	40 Ezekiel and David
9 Joseph	20 Modern Window	30 St Remy	41 Aaron
10 St Eustache	21 St Fulbert	31 St James the Greater	42 Virgin and Child
11 St Lubin		32 Charlemagne	43 Isaiah and Moses
			44 Daniel and Jeremiah

North Rose Window
This depicts the Glorification *of the Virgin, surrounded by*

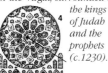

4

the kings of Judah and the prophets (c.1230).

GUIDE TO READING THE WINDOWS

Each window is divided into panels, which are usually read from left to right, bottom to top (earth to heaven). The number of figures or abstract shapes used is symbolic: three stands for the Church; squares and the number four symbolize the material world or the four elements; circles eternal life.

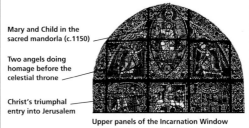

Mary and Child in the sacred mandorla (c.1150)

Two angels doing homage before the celestial throne

Christ's triumphal entry into Jerusalem

Upper panels of the Incarnation Window

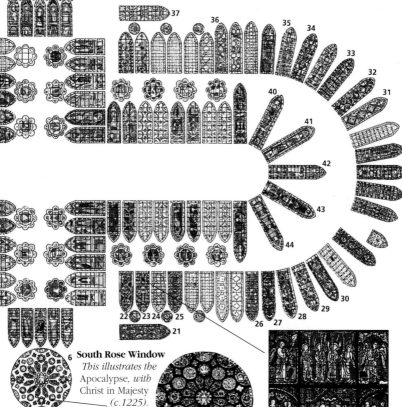

37

36

35

34

33

32

31

40

41

42

43

44

30

29

28

27

26

25

24

23

22

21

6 South Rose Window
This illustrates the Apocalypse, *with* Christ in Majesty *(c.1225).*

STAR WINDOWS

★ West Rose Window

★ Tree of Jesse

★ Blue Virgin Window

★ **Blue Virgin Window**
Scenes of The Marriage at Cana *show Christ changing water into wine at the request of the Virgin Mary.*

LOIRE-ATLANTIQUE AND THE VENDEE

The region stretching from Guérande in the north to the Marais Poitevin in the south turns away from the Vallée des Rois, the land of châteaux, to face the sea. Pale limestone gives way to darker granite and, beyond the hilly, wooded areas to the east, plains stretch into marshlands and estuaries inhabited by clouds of birds.

Here, people have for centuries won their living either from the land or from the sea. Local communities were until quite recently isolated, conservative, religious and fiercely independent. Their loyalties were the basis of the Vendée Uprising *(see p187)* which, at the end of the 18th century, threatened the new French Republic and ended in the devastation of an entire region south of the Loire. Until the 1790s, Nantes, the capital of the Loire-Atlantique, and its environs were part of Brittany, one of the last French duchies to be brought under the crown.

Nantes itself grew prosperous on the wealth generated by its maritime trade to become the seventh largest city of France in the 18th and 19th centuries. With its fine museums and elegant 18th-century *quartiers*, it remains a fascinating and likeable city.

The coast and islands of the Loire-Atlantique to the north, and the Vendée – as the region to the south is known – now draw thousands of summer visitors. Part of their charm is that most of the holiday-makers are French, since the rest of the world has barely begun to discover the beauty of the rocky headlands of Le Croisic or the beaches of golden sand that stretch from La Baule to Les Sables d'Olonne. In the south, dry summers and warm winters on the Ile de Noirmoutier have given it an almost Mediterranean look, with its whitewashed houses and Roman tiles.

In contrast, the Marais Poitevin, at the southern tip of the Vendée, is one of France's most fascinating natural environments. This land has been won back from rivers and the sea through the construction of dykes, canals and dams over hundreds of years.

An oyster gatherer in the Bay of Aiguillon

◁ Romanesque capitals in the nave of the Collégiale St-Aubin in Guérande

Exploring Loire-Atlantique and the Vendée

The mighty river Loire finally reaches the sea at St-Nazaire, in the west of the Loire-Atlantique *département*. To the northwest lies the Guérandaise Peninsula, where long expanses of sandy, south-facing beaches give way to the dramatic, rocky Atlantic coastlines. The best Atlantic beaches stretch along the Vendée coastline, from the Ile de Noirmoutier to the Marais Poitevin in the south. The Marais Poitevin, 96,000 hectares (237,000 acres) of marshland, is networked with canals. To the east lie the Vendée Hills, where the roads wind gently through towns and along the hillsides, giving lovely views of the surrounding area.

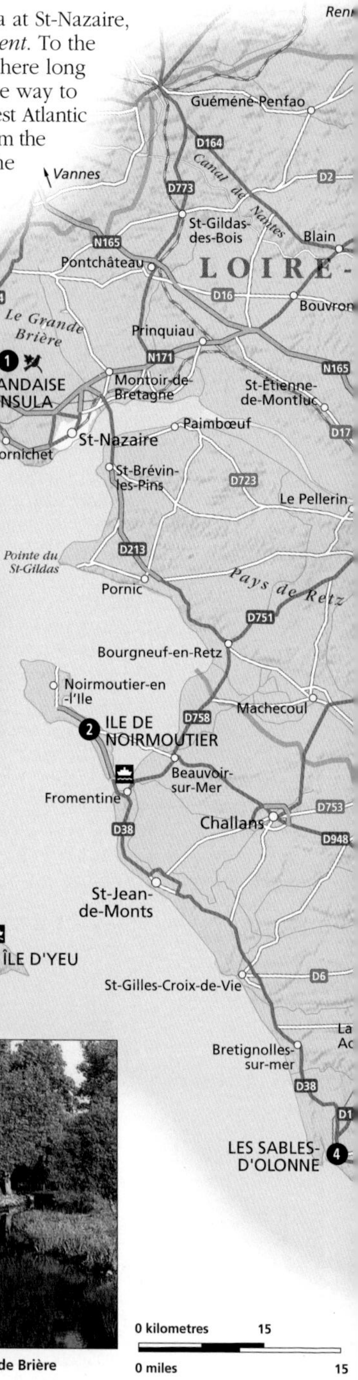

A rocky inlet at L'Aubraie on the Atlantic coast

SEE ALSO

- *Where to Stay* p207
- *Where to Eat* p219

GETTING AROUND

Nantes, with its international airport and major train station, is the transportation hub for the region. The TGV takes only two hours to reach Nantes from Paris, and some trains continue to Le Croisic, only one hour further on. The fastest route by car to Nantes is *L'Océane* autoroute (A11) via Le Mans and Angers. While the D137 is the most direct route south to the Marais Poitevin, the coastal route, stopping off at the beautiful beaches along the way, is far more scenic. Inland towards the Vendée Hills, the D960, D752 and D755 around Pouzauges are scenic drives.

A canal in La Grande Brière

0 kilometres 15
0 miles 15

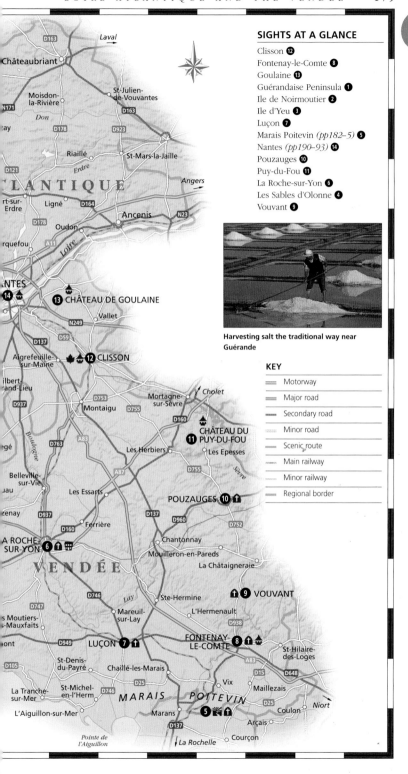

SIGHTS AT A GLANCE

Clisson ⑫
Fontenay-le-Comte ⑧
Goulaine ⑬
Guérandaise Peninsula ①
Ile de Noirmoutier ②
Ile d'Yeu ③
Luçon ⑦
Marais Poitevin *(pp182–5)* ⑤
Nantes *(pp190–93)* ⑭
Pouzauges ⑩
Puy-du-Fou ⑪
La Roche-sur-Yon ⑥
Les Sables d'Olonne ④
Vouvant ⑨

Harvesting salt the traditional way near Guérande

KEY

▬▬	Motorway
▬▬	Major road
▬▬	Secondary road
····	Minor road
—	Scenic route
▬	Main railway
—	Minor railway
▬▬	Regional border

Guérandaise Peninsula ❶

Road map A3. 🚉 *Le Croisic,
La Baule.* 🚌 *Le Croisic, La Baule,
Guérande.* 🛈 *Le Croisic (02 40 23
00 70); La Baule (02 40 24 34 44),*
www.labaule.fr; *Guérande (02 40
24 96 71),* **www**.ot.guerande.fr

La Baule, one of France's
grandest seaside resorts of the
late 19th century, has a superb
8-km (5-mile) sweep of golden
sand, now dominated by
apartment blocks. However, in
the pines behind the modern
buildings, there is a fascinating

A traditional thatched house in the Brière regional park

assortment of eccentric turn-of-
the-century villas. The resort
of Pornichet, which adjoins La
Baule, also retains some older
villas beyond a modern marina
crammed with yachts.

Le Croisic, reaching into the
Atlantic on the west, has a
wilder charm. Beyond the lively main port are miles of salty
headlands with small beaches,
pounding surf and wind-
sculpted pines. The **Océarium**
near the port is one of
France's largest aquariums.

The medieval walled town
of Guérande grew rich on its
fleur de sel – gourmet Breton
salt "farmed" on extensive
marshlands between here and
Le Croisic. Exhibitions and
a video in the **Musée des
Marais Salants** at Batz-sur-
Mer give an excellent idea of
the painstaking techniques
used to maintain its quality.

Guérande is protected by its
ramparts, which are entered
through four 15th-century
gateways. The main gate-
house, St-Michel, houses
a regional museum.
In the centre of the
town is the **Collégiale
St-Aubin**, a medieval
church with stained
glass from the 14th
and 16th centuries
and Romanesque
capitals depicting
scenes from the
lives of martyrs,
mythology
and arts.

Just 10 km (6
miles) to the east
of Guérande is
the **Parc Naturel
Régional de Brière,**

a park of 40,000 hectares
(100,000 acres) of marshlands.
Information about guided tours
by flat-bottomed boat or on
foot, bicycle or horseback is
available from the tourist office
in what was once a clog-
maker's house in La Chapelle-
des-Marais. Kerhinet, a village
of 18 restored cottages, has
displays on regional life.

🍴 Océarium
Av de St-Goustan, Le Croisic. **Tel** 02 40
23 02 44. ⬭ daily. ● first 3 weeks
Jan. 🈺 ♿ **www**.ocearium-croisic.fr

🏛 Musée des Marais Salants
Batz-sur-Mer. **Tel** 02 40 23 82 79.
⬭ Sat & Sun (Jun–Sep, school hols:
daily). ● 1–21 Dec, pub hols. 🈺 ♿

**🌿 Parc Naturel Régional
de Brière**
Road map A3. 🚉 La Baule, Le Croisic,
Pontchâteau, St Nazaire. 🚌 🛈 La
Chapelle-des-Marais (02 40 66 85
01). **www**.parc-naturel-briere.fr

Ile de Noirmoutier ❷

Road map A4. 🚌 *Noirmoutier-en-
l'Ile.* 🛈 *Noirmoutier-en-l'Ile (02 51 39
80 71).* **www**.ile-noirmoutier.com

Whitewashed Midi-style
beach villas on a long,
low island of fertile polders
(land reclaimed from the sea)
give Noirmoutier a unique
character. The adventurous
visitor arrives along a bumpy
causeway nearly 5 km
(3 miles) long, which is above
the sea for only three hours
at low tide. Cockle-collecting
locals park their cars in the
mud, but those who flirt with
the tides sometimes have to
climb to safety on platforms
(*balises*) along the causeway.
Crossing periods are posted
on the road at Beauvoir-sur-
Mer. There is also a bridge
from Fromentine.

The island's mild climate,
fishing industry and
salt marshes were the
basis of its wealth.
Now tourists come to
visit its long dunes,
pretty beaches and
the neat main village
of Noir-moutier-
en-l'Ile. The dry-
moated **Château
de Noirmoutier**
dates from the
12th century. It
has displays on
aspects of local
history, including
the bullet-riddled
chair in which the
Duc d'Elbée was

Porte St-Michel gatehouse, one of the entrances to Guérande

executed during the Vendée Uprising *(see p187)*. There is also an **aquarium** and the **Musée de la Construction Navale**, illustrating boat-making techniques and maritime traditions. **Parc Océanile**, a water park that opened in 1994, makes for a fun family outing, with water chutes and slides, pools with artificial waves, torrents and hot geysers.

♣ **Château de Noirmoutier**
Pl d'Armes. **Tel** 02 51 39 10 42.
◯ Wed–Mon (mid-Jun–mid-Sep: daily). 🖼 🈂

🐟 **Aquarium-Sealand**
Rue de l'Ecluse. **Tel** 02 51 39 08 11.
◯ mid-Feb–mid-Nov: daily. 🖼 🈂

🏛 **Musée de la Construction Navale**
Rue de l'Ecluse.
Tel 02 51 39 24 00. ◯ closed for restoration. 🖼 🈂

🏊 **Parc Océanile**
Site des Oudinières, route de Noir moutier. **Tel** 02 51 35 91 35.
◯ late Jun–early Sep: daily.
🖼 🈂 🍴

Polyprion americanas, one of the fish in Noirmoutier's aquarium

Ile d'Yeu ➌

Road map A4. 🏠 *5,000.* 🚢 from Fromentine to Port–Joinville. 🛈 Rue du Marché, Ile d'Yeu (02 51 58 32 58). **www**.ile-yeu.fr

The sandy coves and rocky coastline of this island, only 10 by 4 km (6 by 2½ miles), attract many visitors. Near the old fishing harbour of Port-de-la-Meule are a ruined 11th-century **castle** and the **Pierre Tremblante**, a giant Neolithic stone said to move when pressed at a critical spot.

The fishing village of La Chaume, near Les Sables d'Olonne

Les Sables d'Olonne ➍

Road map A4. 🏠 *16,000.* 🚊 🚌
🛈 1 promenade Marechal Joffre (02 51 96 85 85). 🈂 Tue–Sun. **www**.lessablesdolonne-tourisme.com

The justifiable popularity of the fine, curving sands has helped to preserve the most elegant beach promenade in western France. Behind the 18th-century esplanade, hilly streets lead to a lively port on the sea channel. Opposite, the fishing village of La Chaume has a chic marina.

In Les Sables itself, attrac-tions include the morning market at Les Halles (Tue–Sun; daily mid-Jun–mid-Sep), near the church of **Notre-Dame-de-Bon-Port**. Running between Les Halles and the rue de la Patrie lies France's narrowest street, rue de l'Enfer, which is only 53 cm (21 in) wide at the entrance on rue de la Patrie.

Masterly views of Les Sables in the 1920s by Albert Marquet are in the **Musée de l'Abbaye Ste-Croix**. Built as a convent in the 1600s, this now houses mainly modern paintings and Surrealist multimedia works.

🏛 **Musée de l'Abbaye Ste-Croix**
Rue de Verdun. **Tel** 02 51 32 01 16. ◯ mid-Jun–mid-Sep: Tue–Sun; Oct–mid-Jun: Tue–Sun pm only.
◯ public hols. 🖼 not first Sun of every month.

THE BEST ATLANTIC COAST BEACHES

Les Sables d'Olonne has hosted both the European surfing championship and the world windsurfing championship. It also offers family bathing at the Grande Plage. Surfers enjoy the bigger waves at Le Tanchet (Le Château d'Olonne) and L'Aubraie (La Chaume). Other good surfing beaches are Sauveterre and Les Granges (Olonne-sur-Mer) and, further north, La Sauzaie at Brétignolles-sur-Mer. Apart from Les Sables, major esplanades and beaches with fine sands and good facilities include the Grande Plage at La Baule and Les Demoiselles at St-Jean-de-Monts.

The wide, sandy beach of L'Aubraie at La Chaume

Marais Poitevin ❺

Kingfisher

The vast regional park of the Marais Poitevin stretches 96,000 ha (237,000 acres) across the south of the Vendée. In Roman times, most of it was under water. One thousand years of dyke building and drainage, first started by medieval monks, have produced the agricultural plains of the western Marais Desséché (dry marsh), which are protected from river floods inland by a complex network of canals. The enchanting aquatic mosaic of the Marais Mouillé (wet marsh), also known as the Venise Verte (Green Venice), lies to the east. Here, summer visitors punt or paddle along quiet, jade-coloured waterways under a canopy of willow, alder, ash, and poplar.

White Charolais Cattle
Prized for their meat, these cows are often transported by boat.

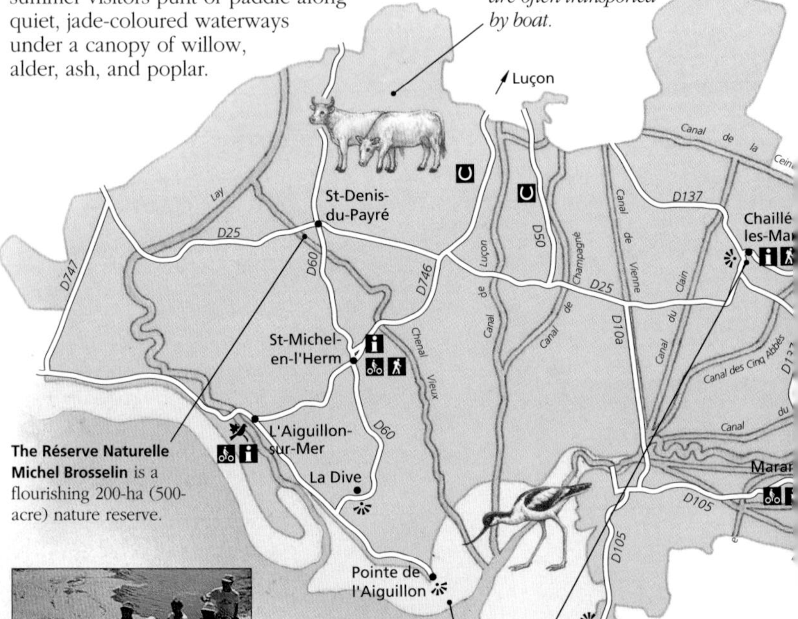

↗ **Luçon**

St-Denis-du-Payré

St-Michel-en-l'Herm

L'Aiguillon-sur-Mer

La Dive

Pointe de l'Aiguillon

Chaillé-les-Ma—

Marar—

Esnandes

The Réserve Naturelle Michel Brosselin is a flourishing 200-ha (500-acre) nature reserve.

La Maison du Maître de Digues at Chaillé-les-Marais reveals the work of the dyke builders of the area.

Flat-bottomed Barque
This typical Marais Mouillé boat has a broad bow and a chisel-shaped stern. Skilled oarsmen row or pole the boat along the canals.

Mussel Farms
Mussels are farmed on the coast around L'Aiguillon-sur-Mer. The larvae are placed on ropes strung between posts embedded in the silt, exposed to the tide's ebb and flow.

KEY

▢	Mud flats
▢	Marais Desséché
▢	Marais Mouillé
※	Viewpoint
🚶	Hiking route
◍	Horse riding
ℹ	Tourist information
🚣	Boating
🚲	Bicycles for rent
✕	Wildlife reserve

STAR SIGHTS

★ Abbaye St-Pierre-de-Maillezais

★ Coulon

★ Arçais

For hotels and restaurants in this region see p207 and p219

★ Abbaye St-Pierre-de-Maillezais

The sombre vestiges of this once-influential Benedictine abbey are impressive. Many historical figures from western France are associated with the place. Find out more on a visit or, in summer, by watching the theatrical shows staged in period costume. Also visit the 12th-century Eglise St-Nicolas in the village.

VISITORS' CHECKLIST

Road map B5. 🚆 *Niort.*
🛈 *Maillezais (02 51 87 23 01);*
Coulon (05 49 35 99 29). Good embarkation points for boating: Coulon, Maillezais, Arçais, Sansais, La Garette, St-Hilaire-la-Palud, Damvix; Tourist train: Coulon (05 49 35 02 29). Facilities for hiking tours, renting bicycles, caravans and horses.
www.parc-marais-poitevin.fr

Abbaye de Nieul-sur-l'Autise

Founded in the late 11th century, this abbey gained the patronage of Eleanor of Aquitaine in the 12th century. Remarkably, the church, cloister and monastic buildings have all survived the centuries.

0 kilometres 5

0 miles 5

Le Poiré-sur-Velluire
Nieul-sur-l'Autise
Maillezais
Maillé
Benet
Damvix
La Ronde
Arçais
Coulon
La Garette
St-Hilaire-la-Palud
Courçon
Mauzé-sur-le-Mignon

★ Arçais
This village in the Venise Verte has a small, stylish port and a 19th-century château.

★ Coulon
Coulon is the largest village in the Marais Poitevin. Its port is always crowded with the narrow, flat-bottomed boats that are traditional in this area.

Exploring the Marais Poitevin

Sign advertising trips in a *barque*

Early dykes, built to hold back the tide, did nothing to solve the problem of the rivers' annual flooding of the marshlands. So large canals were dug in the 12th and 13th centuries, under the supervision of monks who had acquired land rights to marshy areas. The Marais Mouillé (wet marsh) and the Marais Desséché (dry marsh) are still separated by one of these canals: the 13th-century Canal des Cinq Abbés, south of Chaillé-les-Marais, which was a joint effort by five abbeys. Peasants labouring for the monks were rewarded with common grazing rights, some of which are still in force. During the 17th century, Henri IV brought in Dutch engineers to improve the canals, hence the "Dutch Belt" *(La Ceinture des Hollandais)* southeast of Luçon. Current measures to control flooding on lands below high-tide level range from pressure-operated dam gates to bung holes that let water into the plains of the marais in summer.

Eastern Marais

The best way to see this area is by boat. Guided tours are available from a number of villages in the region; braver souls can hire their own boats from Arçais, Coulon, Damvix, La Garette or Maillezais.

Coulon

Road map B5. 🏠 *2,300.* 🚆 *Niort.*
🛈 *31 rue Gabriel Auchier (08 20 20 00 79).* 🛒 *Fri & Sun.* **www**.marais-poitevin.fr
With its narrow streets of old whitewashed houses and imposing 12th-century church,

Coulon is the main entry point to the Marais Mouillé. The quay on the Sèvre Niortaise river is lively in summer with punt tours and crews embarking on their day's negotiation of the maze of canals. **Coulontourisme** organises accompanied or go-as-you-please boat trips and cycle hire. You can book online. Exhibits explaining local ways of life and the history of reclamation are displayed at the **Maison du Marais Poitevin**.

🛩 **Coulontourisme**
6 rue d'Eglise. **Tel** *05 49 35 14 14.*
www.coulontourisme.com

🏛 **Maison du Marais Poitevin**
Pl de la Coutume. **Tel** *05 49 35 81 04.* ◯ *Apr–Oct: daily; Nov–Mar:groups by appointment only.* 🈂

Maillezais

Road map B5. 🏠 *1,000.* 🚌 *Fontenay-le-Comte, then taxi.* 🛈 *rue du Dr-Daroux (02 51 87 23 01).*
www.maraispoitevin-vendee.com
Maillezais was one of the most important inhabited islands in the former Gulf of Poitou. Whether from a canal boat or

---

WILDLIFE OF THE MARAIS POITEVIN

An area of diverse natural habitats, including flood-plains, copses, reclaimed agricultural land and estuaries, the Marais Poitevin supports a rich array of wildlife. It is a paradise for bird-watchers, featuring around 130 different species of nesting bird and more than 120 species of migrating and wintering birds. It also supports some 40 species of mammal, 20 species of snake, 30 species of fish and hundreds of insect species.

The stands of elms, alders, willows and hawthorns supply herons with nest sites. Birds of prey such as the European kestrel and the common buzzard are present all year round, as well as breeding pairs of black kites, hobbys and, less commonly, honey buzzards in spring and summer. At night, long-eared and tawny owls scour the marshes for small rodents.

For bird-watchers, the real interest of the area lies in migratory waders and wildfowl. These can be seen on the water meadows of the Marais Mouillé, on the drier expanses of the Marais Desséché and, especially, on the wide mud flats of the Bay of Aiguillon where the Sèvre Niortaise river reaches the sea. Birds to be seen here in autumn and winter include the common redshank, black-tailed godwit and whimbrel, and rare species such as the spotted crake.

The kestrel, one of the Marais' birds of prey

Reed warbler

The Marais Desséché is also an ideal winter refuge for frogs, toads and grass snakes, and its wide canals, bordered by thick vegetation, are home to two rare species of warbler: the great reed warbler and savi's warbler. Small numbers of another rare species, Montagu's harrier, hunt field voles in the area's reclaimed agricultural land.

The ruins of the 10th-century
Abbaye St-Pierre at Maillezais

from a viewpoint within the
town, the great ruined **Abbaye
St-Pierre**, founded in the 10th
century, is a dramatic sight.
Much of the monastery was
destroyed in 1587 by the
Protestant armies. The church
retains decorated capitals in
the 11th-century narthex, the
north wall of the nave and
the Renaissance transept.

The abbey refectory is still
standing, as is the kitchen,
now a museum. From 1524 to

1526, Rabelais sought refuge
with the monks here. To the
right of the entrance is a small
château, built in 1872 on the
ruins of the bishop's palace.

Abbaye St-Pierre
Tel 02 51 87 22 80. ☐ *daily.*
🔲 *3 weeks Jan.* 🔲 🔲 *restricted.*

Chaillé-les-Marais
Road map B5. 👥 *1,800.* ▦
🔲 *rue de l'An VI (02 51 56 71 17).*
🔲 *Thu.*

This village, beside cliffs once
washed by the tide,
was a centre for
the reclamation
works that
established the
fields of dark soil
in the Marais
Desséché. The
techniques are
explained at the
Maison du Maître de Digues,
a museum covering different
aspects of the Marais Poitevin.

Long-haired Poitou donkey

Maison du Maître de Digues
Tel 02 51 56 77 30. ☐ *Apr, Jun &
Sep: daily pm; May: public hols
only; Jul & Aug: pm daily.*
🔲 *Oct–Mar.* 🔲 🔲

Western Marais
Much of the early drainage
work in the *marais* was led
by the monks of **St-Michel-
en-l'Herm**. The Benedictine
abbey on this former island
was originally founded in 682,
but has been destroyed and
rebuilt several times since
then. Its 17th-century chapter
house and refectory are the
most important remnants.

A short drive to the south,
on the River Lay estuary, are
the ancient fishing port of
L'Aiguillon-sur-Mer and
the **Pointe d'Aiguillon**,
with its 19th-
century Dutch-
built dyke. From
here, there are
marvellous views
across the bay to
the Ile de Ré
and La Rochelle.

Shellfish farming, especially
mussels and oysters, is a
leading industry along this
part of the coast as well as in
the estuaries of the western
marais. Mussels are grown
on a forest of posts, which
are visible at low tide, or
on ropes hung from rafts in
the Bay of Aiguillon.

HABITATS
*The Marais Mouillé's extensive
network of canals provides an
ideal refuge for otters, while
its many trees provide an
ample choice of nest sites
for the purple heron.
Migrating birds,
such as garganey
ducks, and waders,
such as the lapwing, thrive
in the Marais Desséché.*

Male garganey duck

Otter

A nesting purple heron

A lapwing wintering in the Marais Poitevin

Statue of Napoléon in the main square in La Roche-sur-Yon

La Roche-sur-Yon **❻**

Road map B4. 🏠 54,000. 🚃 🚌
ℹ️ rue Georges Clemenceau (02 51 36 00 85). 🛒 Tue–Sat. 🎭 Café de l'Eté, open-air free concerts (mid-Jul– mid-Aug). **www**.ot-roche-sur-yon.fr

In 1804, La-Roche-sur-Yon was plucked from obscurity by Napoleon, who made it the administrative and military capital of the Vendée region. The rectangular grid layout was centred on a very large parade ground, now called **place Napoléon**.

The grandest 19th-century buildings include the **Eglise St-Louis** and the Classical theatre. The **Musée de la Roche-sur-Yon** covers the arts, while the older **La Maison Renaissance** is devoted to the town's history. The most popular attraction is the **Haras de la Vendée**, a smart national stud farm where you can watch equestrian shows.

🏛 **Musée de la Roche-sur-Yon**
Tel 02 51 47 48 35. ◻ Tue–Sat, pm.

🏛 **La Maison Renaissance**
Rue du Vieux-Marché. **Tel** 02 51 46 14 47. ◻ Jul & Aug: Mon–Sat, pm.

⚙ **Haras de la Vendée**
Tel 02 51 37 48 48. ◻ Apr–Jun & 1st-half Sep: Wed, Sat & Sun; Jul–Aug: daily. 🖥 **www**.haras. vendee.fr

Luçon **❼**

Road map B4. 🏠 10,000. 🚃 🚌
ℹ️ square Edouard Herriot (02 51 56 36 52). 🛒 Wed & Sat. 🎭 Les Nocturnes Océanes (every other year, mid-Jul). **www**.lucon.fr

Luçon, once a marshland port, was described by its most famous inhabitant, Cardinal Richelieu (see p56) as the muddiest bishopric in France. Sent there as a 23-year-old bishop in 1608, he went on to reorganize first the town and then the kingdom. Richelieu's statue stands in the square south of the **Cathédrale Notre-Dame**.

The cathedral has an impressive Gothic nave with Renaissance side chapels. One of these contains a pulpit and two canvases painted by Richelieu's gifted successor as bishop, Pierre Nivelle, a naturalist painter. The beautiful cloisters date from the 16th century.

Painted pulpit in Luçon cathedral

Fontenay-le-Comte **❽**

Road map C4. 🏠 15,000. 🚃 Niort. 🚌 ℹ️ 8 rue du Grimouard (02 51 69 44 99). 🛒 Sat.

Fontenay, sloping down to the River Vendée, was the proud capital of Bas–Poitou until the French Revolution. Napoléon downgraded it in favour of a more centrally-placed administrative centre, La Roche-sur-Yon, from which he could easily control the Royalist Vendée.

Although the city's castle and fortifications were destroyed in 1621, following repeated conflicts in the Wars of Religion, much of its Renaissance quarter survived, and a prosperous postwar town has sprung up around it.

The **Eglise Notre-Dame**, with its commanding spire, is a good place to begin threading through the old streets that lead down from the place Viète. The building with the corner turret at No. 9 rue du Pont-aux-Chèvres was once the palace of the bishops of Maillezais. Many Renaissance luminaries, including the poet Nicolas Rapin and François Rabelais (see p100), lived in rue Guillemet, rue des Jacobins and the arcaded place Belliard. Rabelais was later to satirize soirées he attended here during his five years as an unruly young priest in the Franciscan friary (1519–24).

Fontenay's motto "A fountainhead of fine spirits" is incised on the **Quatre-Tias** fountain in the rue de la Fontaine, which was built in the 16th century and embellished in 1899 by Octave de Rochebrune, a local artist and intellectual.

In the **Musée Vendéen**, displays range from Gallo-Roman archaeology to an excellent scale model of Fontenay during the Renaissance. Several 19th-century portraits convey the suffering of the Vendée in the wake of the 1793 insurrection. There are also displays on daily life in the *bocage*, the wooded region bordering the city.

Once a manor house, the **Château de Terre-Neuve** on the rue de Jarnigande, was converted into something

The high Gothic nave of the Cathédrale Notre-Dame in Luçon

The medieval walls surrounding Vouvant, reflected in the River Mère

more imposing for Nicolas Rapin, poet and grand provost, at the beginning of the 17th century. Two hundred years later, Octave de Rochebrune added decorative flourishes, including statues of the Muses.

The interior of the château has beautiful ceilings and two wonderful fireplaces together with a collection of fine art, furniture, panelling and a door brought from the royal study in the Château de Chambord.

🏛 **Musée Vendéen**
Pl du 137e Régiment d'Infanterie.
Tel *02 51 69 31 31.* ☐ *May–Sep: Tue–Sun, pm only; Oct-Apr: Wed, Sat & Sun, pm only.* 🎫 ♿

♟ **Château de Terre-Neuve**
Rue de Jarnigande. ***Tel*** *02 51 69 99 41.* ☐ *May–Sep: daily; Oct–Apr: groups by appt.* 🎫

Vouvant ❾

Road map B4. 🏠 *850.*
🚌 *Fontenay-le-Comte.* 🚉 *Luçon.*
ℹ *31 rue du Duc d'Aquitaine (02 51 00 86 80).* 🎪 *Fête Folklorique (2nd Sun in Aug).*

The Romanesque **Eglise Notre-Dame** in the medieval village of Vouvant has a fantastically carved twin-portal doorway, from which rows of sculptures look down on an arch decorated with a Romanesque bestiary. On the tympanum, Samson wrestles a lion as Delilah advances with her shears.

Vouvant is home to many artists and a starting point for tours of the popular Mervant-Vouvant forest with its trails and folklore surrounding the serpent-fairy

Mélusine: she tried to lead a life as a woman, but once a week her lower half would turn into a serpent's tail. The **Tour Mélusine** has splendid views of the River Mère.

The twin portals of Vouvant's Eglise Notre-Dame

Portrait of Cathelineau (1824) by Anne-Louis Girodet-Trioson

THE VENDÉE UPRISING

Although it may at times seem a footnote to the French Revolution, the Vendée Uprising has never been forgotten in this region. The Revolution outraged the conservative, Royalist people here. Rising taxes, the persecution of Catholic priests and the execution of Louis XVI in January 1793 were then followed by attempts to conscript locals for the Republican army. This triggered a massacre of Republican sympathizers in the village of Machecoul on 11 March by a peasant mob. As the riots flared, peasant leaders, such as the wagoner Cathelineau and the gamekeeper Stofflet, took charge. They were joined by nobles including Charette, Bonchamps and La Roche-jaquelain under the emblem of the sacred heart.

Using guerilla tactics, the Grand Royal and Catholic Army (Whites) took nearly all the Vendée plus Saumur and Angers by June 1793. They won several battles against Republican armies (Blues) but lost at Cholet on 17 October. Nearly 90,000 Whites fled, vainly hoping for reinforcements to join them. The Blues laid waste to the Vendée in 1794, massacring the populace. More than 250,000 people from the Vendée died.

Detail from the frieze in the church in Pouzauges

Pouzauges ⑩

Road map C4. 🏛 *5,500.*
🚉 *La Roche.* 🚌 ℹ *28 pl de l'Eglise (02 51 91 82 46).* 🛒 *Thu.*
www.paysdepouzauges.fr

This small town's ruined 12th-century castle was one of several in the Vendée owned by Gilles de Rais in the 15th century. Once Marshal of France and a companion-in-arms of Joan or Arc, de Rais' distinguished military career ended in charges of abduction and murder, and he later came to be associated with the story of Bluebeard.

The little **Eglise Notre-Dame du Vieux-Pouzauges**, with its 13th-century frescoes uncovered in 1948, is one of the treasures of the Vendée. The frescoes depict charming scenes from the life of the Virgin Mary and her family.

Château du Puy-du-Fou ⑪

Road map B4. 🚉 *to Cholet, then taxi.* **Tel** *02 51 64 11 11.*
www.puydufou.com

The brick-and-granite Renaissance château of Puy-du-Fou is 2 km (1 mile) from the little village of Les Epesses. Partly restored after its destruction in the Vendée Uprising of 1793–4, it now houses an ambitious theme park, and is the backdrop to the **Cinéscénie**, a thrilling son et lumière evening show (*see pp58–9*).

The large theme park, **Le Grand Parc**, offers plenty of entertainment. It has two reconstructed villages, one medieval and one 18th-century, with costumed "villagers" and artisans, and a market town of 1900 along the same lines. Other features include wooded walks, lakes, aquatic organ pipes and puppet theatre. Each day Le Grand Parc stages five big shows. These range from gladiatorial battles and a Viking assault to lively displays of jousting and falconry.

Environs
Northwest up the Sèvre Niortaise valley, the 12th-century **Château de Tiffauges** is another great place for families. This castle serves as backdrop for lively re-enactments of the area's history. There is also a

collection of reconstructed medieval war machines.

🎦 **Cinéscénie**
Tel *02 51 64 11 11.*
🕐 *mid-Jun–mid-Sep: Fri & Sat. Spectacle begins: Jun & Jul: 10:30pm; Aug–early Sep: 10pm (arrive 1 hour earlier); reservations required.* 🅿 🚹

🎪 **Le Grand Parc**
🕐 *Apr–Sep: daily.* 🅿 🚹

🏰 **Château de Tiffauges**
Tel *02 51 65 70 51.* 🕐 *Apr–mid-Sep: daily.* 🅿 **http://**chateau-barbe-bleue.vendee.fr

Château de Clisson, a feudal fortress now in ruins

Clisson ⑫

Road map B4. 🏛 *7,000.* 🚉
ℹ *pl du Minage (02 40 54 02 95).*
🛒 *Tue, Wed, Fri.* 🎭 *Les Médiévales (last weekend Jul).*
www.valleedeclisson.fr

Clisson, perched on two hills straddling the Sèvre Nantaise river, is notable for its Italianate beauty. After much of the town was destroyed in 1794 by punitive Republican forces following the collapse of the Vendée Uprising, Clisson was rebuilt by two brothers, Pierre and François Cacault, working with the sculptor Frédéric Lemot. Lemot's country home is now the **Parc de la Garenne Lemot**, which celebrates the style of ancient Rome with grottoes and tombs, including Lemot's own.

The evolution of defensive strategies can be followed in the massive, ruined **Château de Clisson**, dating from the 12th century and gradually

"Villagers" at work in Puy-du-Fou's Grand Parc

strengthened in stages up to the 16th century. This was a key feudal fortress for the dukes of Brittany. Peer into the dungeons, and into a well with a grisly story behind it: in the vengeful aftermath of the Vendée's defeat, Republican troops butchered and flung into it 18 people. Next to the château is a fine Renaissance covered market, it survived the destruction because it was used as Republican barracks.

The vineyards outside of this town produce Muscadet white wines.

🌿 **Parc de la Garenne Lemot & Villa Lemot**
Tel 02 40 54 75 85. ⬤ *Park* daily. *Villa Lemot* Tue–Sun pm (Jul & Aug: daily). ♿ restricted.

🏛 **Château de Clisson**
Pl du Minage. *Tel* 02 40 54 02 22. ⬤ May–Sep: Wed–Mon; Oct–Apr: Wed–Mon pm only. 🎫 📷

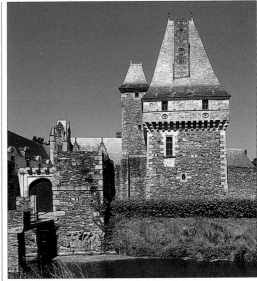

The machicolated entrance tower at the Château de Goulaine

Château de Goulaine ⑬

Road map B3. 🚆 Nantes, then taxi (15km/8 miles). 🚌 Bas Goulaine. **Tel** 02 40 54 91 42. ⬤ opening times change every year; call for details. 🎫 📷 ♿ grd fl. chât & butterfly park.
www.chateaudegoulaine.fr

Only a short distance south-east of Nantes, this is the most

westerly of all the limestone-and-slate Loire châteaux. The same family has made wine here for 1,000 years; the building dates from the 15th century with 17th-century wings. One tower survives from the 14th century. Towers rise from the central building: on one, there is a sculpture of Yolande de Goulaine, who is said to have spurred on her soldiers to repulse the besieging English by threatening to stab herself.

The château survived the Revolution because the family sold it to a Dutchman, only to recover it 70 years later. The present marquis, Robert de Goulaine, has restored the château and also opened a butterfly park where exotic species flutter about a large glasshouse. Butterflies also embellish the label of one of his *sur lie* Muscadets. At certain times of the year you can book a room for the night in this grand castle.

CINÉSCÉNIE

Puy-du-Fou's late-night show is on a grand scale, with more than 1,100 performers and 14,000 seated spectators. It was conceived as a theatre of Vendée history using the full resources of contemporary open-air multimedia techniques. Laser lighting, music, water-jets and fireworks are all carefully orchestrated by computer.

Against the backdrop of the ruined château and its lake, hundreds of locally-recruited actors form living tableaux to dance or grieve, joust or slaughter each other. Horses thunder about, fountains and fireworks soar, bells ring and the château bursts into "flames".

Although the spectacle can be enjoyed for itself, translations of the commentary are available in English, German, Italian, Spanish and Dutch to 150 of the seats on the huge stand. Warm clothing and advanced booking are advised.

A fire-eater in the Cinéscénie at Puy-du-Fou

Nantes ⑭

The ancient port of Nantes was the ducal capital of Brittany for 600 years, but is now capital of the Pays de la Loire region. Many of its fine 18th- and 19th-century buildings and houses were built on profits from maritime trade, especially in slaves, sugar, cotton and ship's supplies. The main port activities have shifted downstream towards St-Nazaire, where a modern bridge, one of the longest in France, crosses the Loire estuary *(see p34)*. Nantes is a vigorous modern city, with good museums, wide open spaces, chic restaurants, bars and shops, and some amazing visitor attractions by the Loire.

The Neo-Classical theatre in the place Graslin

Exploring Nantes

The most fashionable area of town is the **quartier Graslin**. Constructed between 1780 and 1900, the district's centre-piece is the place Graslin, with its Neo-Classical theatre approached by a steep flight of monumental steps. The architect, Mathurin Crucy, designed the place Graslin as a rectangle within a semicircle with eight streets radiating from it. The theatre is fronted by eight Corinthian columns, and statues of eight Muses look down on the square. The wall behind the columns is made of glass, allowing light to stream into the foyer during the day.

Crucy's elegant architecture is seen again in the nearby cours Cambronne, a pedestrianized avenue with fine matching houses built in the early 1800s, and in the place Royale with its splendid fountain celebrating ocean and river spirits.

On the **Ile Feydeau**, the former island where Jules Verne *(see p193)* was born, 18th-century town planning combined with middle-class trading wealth helped to produce beautiful Neo-Classical façades along streets such as allée Turenne, allée Duguay-Trouin and especially rue Kervégan where 18th-century architect Pierre Rousseau occupied No. 30. Wrought-iron balconies rise in pyramidal sequence supported by luxuriant carvings.

Just north of the Ile Feydeau is the place du Commerce and the ancient Bourse, an elegant 18th-century building, now the tourist office.

The dining room of Nantes' Art Nouveau brasserie, La Cigale

🏛 La Cigale

4 pl Graslin. **Tel** *02 51 84 94 94.* ◯ *daily.* ♿ *See Restaurants p219.*

Facing the theatre, and in dazzling counterpoint to it, stands the famous brasserie-restaurant La Cigale, opened on 1 April 1895. This *fin-de-siècle* fantasy was conceived and largely executed by Emile Libaudière. The building is crammed with Art Nouveau motifs including the cicada from which it takes its name. The rich blues of its Italian tiling, its sinuous wrought-iron, bevelled windows and mirrors, sculptures and painted panels and ceilings have made this restaurant a favourite venue for aesthetes and food-lovers for a century.

🏛 Passage Pommeraye

◯ *daily.*

To the east of place Graslin, rue Crébillon is the most elegant shopping street in Nantes. It is linked with the

The interior of the elegant passage Pommeraye

rue de la Fosse by a remarkable covered shopping arcade, the passage Pommeraye. Named after the lawyer who financed its construction, it opened in 1843 and must have astonished the bourgeoisie visiting its 66 shops.

The arcade's three galleries are on different levels, each linked by a handsome wooden staircase, lined with statues and lamps. The decoration is highly ornate. Charming sculpted figures look down on the galleries, lined with shops and rich with busts, bas-reliefs and other details in stone and metal, all beneath the original glass roof.

🏛 Musée Dobrée

18 rue Voltaire. **Tel** 02 40 71 03 50.
⬤ closed for renovations until 2015. 🎟 (except Sun).
Thomas Dobrée (1810–95), son of a rich shipowner and industrialist, spent most of his life building this collection of paintings, drawings, sculpture, tapestries, furniture, porcelain, armour, religious

Part of the carved alabaster altarpiece in the Musée Dobrée

works of art, stamps, letters and manuscripts. The impressive and palatial museum he built for them is based on a plan by the Gothic Revival architect

Eugène-Emmanuel Viollet-le-Duc. One of the reliquaries stands out – it is a gold casket, surmounted by a crown, which contains the heart of Anne of Brittany, who asked for it to be buried in her parents' tomb in Nantes cathedral (see p55). A complete 15th-century altarpiece carved in alabaster statues from Nottingham, England, is another treasure.

In a second part of the complex, a modern museum houses an archaeological collection, with Egyptian, Greek and some locally found Gallo-Roman artifacts.

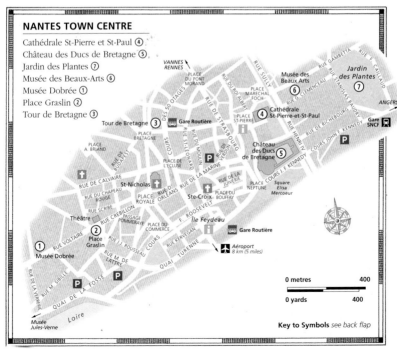

NANTES TOWN CENTRE

Cathédrale St-Pierre et St-Paul ④
Château des Ducs de Bretagne ⑤
Jardin des Plantes ⑦
Musée des Beaux-Arts ⑥
Musée Dobrée ①
Place Graslin ②
Tour de Bretagne ③

Around the Château

The Tour de Bretagne, the skyscraper built in 1976 that towers above Nantes, is a landmark dividing the city centre around place du Commerce and place Graslin to the west from the older district around the château and cathedral to the east. From the tower the cours des Cinquante Otages sweeps through the centre where the Erdre canal once flowed. This busy avenue has a memorial at the top, in place du Pont Morand, to the 50 hostages after which it is named. Their execution by the Nazis in reprisal for the assassination of the city's military commandant in 1941 turned many Nantais against the Vichy government.

The façade of the Cathédrale St-Pierre et St-Paul

♠ Château des Ducs de Bretagne

4 pl Marc Elder. **Tel** 02 51 17 49 00.
☐ Jul–Aug: daily; Sep–Jun: Tue–Sun. ● 1 Jan, 1 May, 1 Nov, 25 Dec. 🖼 château. 🗐 🕹
The château, surrounded by a landscaped moat and strong curtain walls with round bastions, in the style of the Château d'Angers *(see pp74–5)*, has been thoroughly restored. This was the birthplace of Anne of Brittany, who became duchess at 11 and then was coerced into marrying Charles VIII of France in 1491 at the age of 14. Charles died at Amboise in 1498 and, the following year, Anne married his successor, Louis XII, in the château chapel.

Anne's influence can be seen in the dormer windows and loggias of the **Grand Logis** to the right of the entrance, a graceful blend of Flamboyant and Renaissance styles. It was begun by her father, Duc François II, who built most

of the château. A smaller royal lodging lies to the west of it. It was here that Henri IV signed the 1598 Edict of Nantes, granting all Protestants permission to worship. The château now hosts a high-tech museum charting the history of Nantes from Gallo-Roman times to the present day.

♠ Cathédrale St-Pierre et St-Paul

Place St-Pierre. ☐ daily.
Nantes has the most accident-prone cathedral on the Loire. The story of its construction and destruction over centuries is vividly told in the crypt. Most recently, on 28 January 1972, a workman's match caused an explosion that blew off the roof. Following the resulting fire, a major restoration programme was undertaken. The cathedral has been left with an unusual lightness and unity.

A notable feature of this spacious Flamboyant Gothic building is the splendid black-and-white marble tomb of Duc François II and his two wives, sculpted by Michel Colombe *(see pp116–17)*.

🏛 Musée des Beaux-Arts

10 rue Georges Clemenceau.
Tel 02 51 17 45 00. ● closed for restoration. 🖼 except 1st Sun of month. 🕹 www.museedes beauxarts.nantes.fr
The grandeur of this museum and its collections is a good measure of Nantes' civic pride and wealth in the early 19th century. The galleries, undergoing restoration, are on two levels and surround a huge, arched patio, whose clean lines are an appropriate setting for contemporary exhibitions. Although the museum has some sculptures, it is known for its large collection of paintings, especially those representing key movements from the 15th to the 20th centuries.

Gustave Courbet's *The Corn Sifters* (1854) in the Musée des Beaux-Arts

Nantes' lovely botanical garden, the Jardin des Plantes

🏛 Le Lieu Unique

Quai Ferdinand-Favre. **Tel** 02 40 12 14 34. ⬚ Tue–Sat, noon–late; check the events calendar on the website. 🍴 ♿ www.lelieuunique.com

This former Lu biscuit factory, south of the castle, has been converted into a cutting-edge contemporary arts centre. It stages numerous theatrical events, from traditional theatre, through to dance, music concerts and circus acts, plus cultural and philosophical debates. It also hosts art exhibitions. There's a restaurant and boutique onsite, and even a spa. The building is signalled by an extravagant Art Nouveau tower which is a part of the factory and can be climbed for views of the city. At ground level, the café spills out onto a terrace beside the broad St-Félix canal, surrounded by modern buildings.

♣ Musée Jules Verne

3 rue de l'Hermitage. **Tel** 02 40 69 72 52. ⬚ Wed–Sat & Sun pm–Mon. ◐ public hols. 🎫 ♿ ☝

A remarkably comprehensive display representing the life and work of Jules Verne (1828–1905) starts with a room of furnishings from the house in Amiens in which he wrote most of his books. The museum is packed with mementos, splendidly bound books, cartoons, maps, magic lanterns and models.

🏛 Les Machines de l'Ile & Carrousel des Mondes Marins

⬚ mid-Feb–Mar, Nov–Dec: Tue–Sun, pm only; Apr–mid-Jul, Sep–Oct: Tue–Sun; mid-Jul–Aug: daily. ◐ 1 Jan, 6 Jan–15 Feb, 1 May, 25 Dec. 🍴 📷 www.lesmachines-nantes.fr

The enormous moving models created by Les Machines de l'Ile have helped make the western end of the Ile de Nantes a major tourist destination. These over-sized creations were dreamt up by two inventors from the region, François Delarozière and Pierre Orefice, inspired in part by that most famous of Nantais writers, Jules Verne, and his extravagant creations. You can board Le Grand Elephant, a massive mechanical elephant, for a leisurely, pleasureable tour of this corner of the island.

The Carrousel des Mondes Marins, likened to a "huge mechanical aquarium", is a giant 25-m-high (82-ft-high) carousel containing all manner of marine creatures. Visitors can explore three levels, the ocean floor, the depths and the ocean surface.

Also enter La Galerie des Machines, the ever-changing "workshop" space. Visitors are invited to get hands-on as they learn about the latest mechanical dreams on the drawing board that are turning, gradually, into reality.

THE WORLD OF JULES VERNE

Just past the Pont Anne de Bretagne is a disused section of cobbled quay which, in 1839, was lined with boats. It was here that the 11-year-old Jules Verne slipped aboard a ship to see the world. He got as far as Paimbœuf, a short trip down river, before his father caught up with him. Later, while studying law, Verne started to publish plays and librettos. His science-fiction novels, including *A Journey to the Centre of the Earth* (1864), *Twenty Thousand Leagues Under the Sea* (1870) and *Around the World in Eighty Days* (1873), have been hugely successful, and he is among the most widely read and translated authors in the world.

Bust of Jules Verne (1906) by Albert Roze

TRAVELLERS' NEEDS

WHERE TO STAY

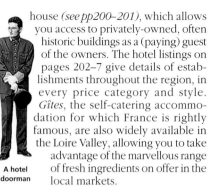

Loire Valley hotels are as charming as their surroundings. Family-style inns predominate, with dining rooms that are also popular with locals and comfortable, sometimes old-fashioned, bedrooms. The region also boasts some prestigious *Relais et Châteaux* establishments, often mansions or châteaux converted into luxury hotels with elegant rooms, superb cuisine – and prices to match. A fascinating alternative is staying in a private château or manor

A hotel doorman

house *(see pp200–201)*, which allows you access to privately-owned, often historic buildings as a (paying) guest of the owners. The hotel listings on pages 202–7 give details of establishments throughout the region, in every price category and style. *Gîtes*, the self-catering accommodation for which France is rightly famous, are also widely available in the Loire Valley, allowing you to take advantage of the marvellous range of fresh ingredients on offer in the local markets.

THE CITY HOTEL

The main towns and cities across the Loire Valley have at least one long-established *grand hôtel* in the centre. These large hotels typically have spacious entrance halls and public rooms, but some of the once large bedrooms may well have been carved up to allow for en suite bathrooms. Rooms are liable to vary somewhat in quality, so it is advisable to ask to see the room offered if you have not made a booking in advance. When you make a reservation, be sure to specify a room away from a main

road or busy square (most of these city hotels have some much quieter rooms, which overlook a courtyard). Bars are likely to be frequented by members of the local business community, who also entertain clients in the hotel restaurant, where you can expect classic French cuisine as much as regional dishes.

THE CHÂTEAU HOTEL

A number of châteaux and manor houses in the Loire Valley have been converted into expensive hotels. Often set in well-kept grounds and offering outstanding cuisine, they

range from Renaissance manor houses to huge, turreted 19th-century piles. The **Relais et Châteaux** association, of which many are members, publishes an annual brochure.

Rooms in these beautiful establishments are usually spacious and elegant, with some suites available. Some château hotels also offer more modest accommodation in outbuildings or even in bungalows in the grounds. If you prefer to stay in the main building, it is advisable to specify this when you make a booking – in many cases, advance reservations are essential.

THE CLASSIC FAMILY HOTEL

These typically French small hotels, often run by the same family for several generations, are to be found throughout the Loire Valley. The bar and dining room are likely to be widely used by locals, especially for Sunday lunch in the country districts. The atmosphere is usually friendly, with helpful staff able to provide leaflets and other information about local sightseeing and shopping.

Most of these hotels have only a small number of rooms, often reasonably spacious and pleasantly furnished with well-worn antiques and flowery wallpaper. Plumbing may be erratic, although many hotels of this type have made efforts to spruce up their bathrooms. Few family hotels in the rural

The elegant Domaine des Hauts-de-Loire hotel in Onzain *(see p204)*

◁ Lively Place Plumereau in Tours

The grand staircase of the Hôtel de l'Univers in Tours *(see p204)*

areas have single rooms, but these are more common in the region's towns.

Many family hotels belong to the **Logis de France** association, which publishes an annual booklet listing more than 3,000 family-run hotels in France. *Logis* hotels are proud of their restaurants, which tend to specialize in regional cuisine. Most are basic roadside inns, with only a few listed in the main towns, but off the beaten track you can find charming farmhouses and inexpensive hotels.

Many family-run hotels are shut in the afternoon and do not like visitors to arrive then, although hotel guests have keys. Their restaurants are also shut at least one day a week (except possibly in the tourist season).

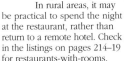

Logo of the Logis de France association

THE MODERN CHAIN HOTEL

France has an increasing number of modern chain hotels, on the edges of towns or close to motorways.

The cheapest are the one-star, very basic **Formule 1** motels. Two-star chains, which are widely used by French families on a low budget, include **Ibis, Campanile** and **Inter Hôtel**. More comfortable, but lacking in regional charm, are the **Kyriad, Novotel** and **Mercure** three-star chains. All the chain hotels offer some family rooms or connecting rooms, and in some hotels children can sleep in their parents' room without charge. Most have restaurants where the food is adequate.

THE RESTAURANT-WITH-ROOMS

A few of the well-known and expensive restaurants in the Loire Valley region also have rooms available for overnight guests. The rooms may be as chic as the restaurant. However, they might be modest bedrooms left over from the days before the restaurant was a gourmet's magnet and will therefore allow you to spend an inexpensive night to make up for a budget-busting meal.

In rural areas, it may be practical to spend the night at the restaurant, rather than return to a remote hotel. Check in the listings on pages 214–19 for restaurants-with-rooms.

MEALS AND FACILITIES

Because most visitors to the Loire Valley choose to tour around, few hotels offer full-board rates to those who settle in for holidays. However, for more than three nights in one place, it may be possible to obtain *pension* (full-board) or *demi-pension* (half-board). But half-board may apply only to lunch, which makes sightseeing difficult, and the meals for full-board guests are likely to be less interesting than the fixed-price menus. Always check whether the room rate includes breakfast. If not, you may prefer to have your breakfast in a nearby café.

Traditionally, family hotel rooms offer double beds, but twin beds are more likely to be found in city and chain hotels. Prices are usually fixed per room, but single travellers may be allowed a small reduction. Bathrooms with a shower rather than a bath make the room less expensive. Those with only a *cabinet de toilette* (an alcove containing basin and bidet) are the cheapest.

It is perfectly acceptable to ask to view the room before making a decision.

GRADINGS AND PRICES

French hotels are officially graded into one, two, three, four and five stars. These categories take account of facilities such as telephones, televisions and ensuite bathrooms, but do not necessarily indicate the quality of the decor or service. A few very modest hotels do not rate a star ranking.

Prices rise as the number of stars increases. Rooms may vary in quality within an establishment, so it is not easy to classify hotels solely by price. Rates for a double room start at around €60 per night without breakfast, although they may start at €150 in château hotels. A very small local tax *(taxe de séjour)* will be added to your bill, but service will already be included. It is usual to leave a small tip for the chambermaid.

Typical Loire Valley manor house hotel

The Domaine des Hautes Roches at Rochecorbon *(see p204)*

BOOKING

Reserve well in advance for hotels in popular tourist areas during main holiday periods, especially in July and August. It may be necessary to give a credit card number or send a fax confirmation. You may need to speak French to make a telephone booking for some hotels, but letters in English are normally acceptable. Local tourist offices can supply listings of hotels and sometimes provide a reservation service.

BED AND BREAKFAST

French bed-and-breakfast accommodation, called *chambres d'hôte*, can vary widely from modest rooms above a hayloft to an elegant room in a manor house. Local tourist offices keep lists of those families willing to take in guests. Some hosts will cook dinner if given advance warning. Many such rooms are registered and inspected by the **Gîtes de France** organization – look out for their green and yellow logo.

SELF-CATERING

Gîtes de France and **Clévacances** are the best-known organizations monitoring and booking self-catering accommodation. Run by the French government, Gîtes de France offers predominantly rural accommodation, ranging from a cottage to an entire wing of a château. Brochures are available from the *départ ement* offices of Gîtes de France, from the Paris head office or via the Internet *(see Directory)*. Booking is essential.

Local tourist offices also have lists of properties for rent within the surrounding area, but it is important to book early.

The lower-priced *gîtes* have only very basic facilities. For more luxury properties, the best way forward is to scour the major US and European newspapers, specialist magazines and the Internet, or use a letting agency. Whatever the price, a holiday in a *gîte* is a great way to experience Loire Valley life.

DIRECTORY

HOTELS

Campanile, Kyriad
Tel 08 25 02 80 38.
www.louvrehotels.com

Formule 1
Tel 08 92 68 56 85.
www.hotelformule1.com

Ibis, Novotel, Mercure
Tel 08 25 01 20 11.
www.accorhotels.com

Inter Hôtel
Tel 08 26 10 39 09.
www.inter-hotel.fr

Logis de France
83 av d'Italie, 75013 Paris. *Tel* 01 45 84 83 84.
www.logis-de-france.fr

Relais et Châteaux
UK: *Tel* (0800) 2000 0002.
US: *Tel* (800) 735 2478.
www.relaischateaux.com

BED & BREAKFAST

Gîtes de France
59 rue St. Lazare, 75009 Paris. *Tel* 01 49 70 75 75.
www.gites-de-france.fr

SELF-CATERING

Clévacances
54 boulevard de l'Embouchure, 31022 Toulouse.
Tel 05 61 13 55 66.
www.clevacances.com

CAMPING

Les Castels
Manoir de Terre Rouge, 35270 Bonnemain.
Tel 02 23 16 03 20.
www.les-castels.com

CAMPING CARNETS

The Camping and Caravanning Club (UK)
Tel (0845) 130 7631.
www.campingand caravanning.co.uk

Family Campers & RVers (US)
Tel (800) 245-9755.
www.fcrv.org

HOSTELS

CNOUS
69 quai d'Orsay, 75007 Paris.
Tel 01 44 18 53 00.
www.cnous.fr

Fédération Unie des Auberges de Jeunesse
27 rue Pajol, 75018 Paris.
Tel 01 44 89 87 27.
www.fuaj.org

YHA (UK)
Tel 01629 592 700.
www.yha.org.uk

AYH (US)
Tel 301 495 1240.
www.hiusa.org

DISABLED TRAVELLERS

Association des Paralysés de France
17 bd Auguste Blanqui 75013 Paris.
Tel 01 40 78 69 00.
www.apf.asso.fr

Mobility International USA
132 E.Broadway, Suite 343, Eugene OR 7440.
Tel (541) 343 1284.
www.miusa.org

Tourism for All
c/o Vitalise Holidays, Shap Road, Kendal, Cumbria LA9 6NZ.
Tel (0845) 124 9971.
www.tourismforall.org.uk

TOURIST OFFICES

French Govt Tourist Office (UK)
Maison de la France, Lincoln House, 300 High Holborn, London WC1V 7JH. *Tel* 09068 244 123.
www.uk.franceguide.com

French Govt Tourist Office (US)
825 Third Ave, 29th floor, New York, NY 10022.
Tel (514) 288 1904.
www.franceguide.com

CAMPING

Camping is a cheap and fun way of seeing the Loire Valley. Information on campsites can be obtained from *département* tourist offices. Some of these do not accept visitors without a special camping *carnet* (available from the AA and RAC and from the addresses listed in the Directory). French campsites are graded into four starred categories, but even one-star sites have lavatories, public telephones and running water (although this may be only cold). The top-ranked sites are remarkably well equipped. Always book ahead where possible.

The Gîtes de France organiza- tion has a guide to unpretentious sites on farm land (ask for *camping à la ferme*), and *camping sauvage* (camping outside official sites) is occasionally possible if you come to an agreement with the landowner. **Les Castels** is an up-market association of sites within the grounds of châteaux and manor houses.

Gîtes de France logo

HOSTELS

Hostels provide budget accommodation, but for two or more people sharing a room, an inexpensive hotel will probably cost the same. To stay in a youth hostel, you need to purchase a membership card from the **Youth Hostel Association (YHA)** in your own country, or buy a *carte d'adhésion* card from **Fédération Unie des Auberges de Jeunesse (FUAJ)**. Prices include breakfast and linen hire. The website of the FUAJ, the national youth hostel organization, provides useful information on becoming a member, booking and prices as well as listing addresses and contact informa- tion for hostels all over France. **CNOUS**, the Centre National des Oeuvres Universitaires, provides details of university rooms available during the summer vacation. Gîtes de France is once again a valuable source of information: ask for the *Gîtes d'étape* guide to dormitory accommodation in farmhouses for those on walking, riding or cycling holidays.

DISABLED TRAVELLERS

In the UK, **Tourism for All** publishes lists of accessible accommodation and sights in France and provides information on transportation and financial help available for taking holidays. In the US, **Mobility International USA** publishes several gen- eral guides to foreign exchange and travelling abroad with disabilities.

In France, information about accommodation with

Youth hostel in the centre of Tours old town

facilities for disabled travellers is available from the **Association des Paralysés de France**, which has also teamed up with Gîtes de France and Logis de France to recommend country *gîtes*, guest houses and other places to stay that are suitable for people with physical disabilities. These places are listed on a national register that is available free of charge from its website or from the head office of Gîtes de France, and they also appear in listings for each *département*. The Association des Paralysés de France also has branches in each *département*.

SOURCES OF INFORMATION

The useful guide *The Traveller in France,* listing hotel chains, booking agencies and tour operators specializing in travel to and in France, is published regularly by the **French Government Tourist Office**. The tourist office is also able to supply brochures and booklets for Logis de France hotels, Gîtes de France and other types of accom- modation. Regional Tourist Committees will send lists of hotels, hostels, campsites and private self-catering accommodation. The regional Loisirs Accueil centre and *Département* Tourist Committees (in the major city of each *département*) are also useful sources of information. When you are in the Loire Valley, contact local tourist offices *(see p231)* for hotel lists and details of local families taking in guests.

Camping in a forest in the Loire Valley

Staying in a Château

The establishments featured here have been
selected from our listings of recommended
places to stay on pages 202–7. They offer a
great opportunity to experience the style of life
in a private Loire Valley château, spending a
night within walls steeped in history, but often
with all the comforts of a modern hotel. At
many, you will be greeted like a house guest,
and efforts are made to make you feel part of
the owner's family, who may have lived in the
château for generations. They may also create
the atmosphere of a private party at dinner,
which can be booked and paid for in advance.

Château de Monhoudou
*The Monhoudou family have been
living in this lakeside château for 19
generations. Peacocks and swans
walk the grounds.* (See p207.)

Château des Briottières
*This 18th-century château,
furnished in period and
lived in by the same
family for six gener-
ations, has attractive
grounds and a heated
pool.* (See p202.)

| 0 kilometres | 50 |
| 0 miles | 50 |

Château de la Millière
*Close to Les Sables d'Olonne, this
19th-century château is set in
extensive grounds, complete with
an outdoor pool.* (See p207.)

Château de Rochecotte
*An elegant hotel since the late 1980s, this
château set in woodland near Langeais was
the residence of Prince Talleyrand.* (See p204.)

The Suite Marin de Vanssay in the Château de la Barre is decorated with 17th- and 18th-century antiques and luxurious fabrics.

Château de la Verrerie
The "Stuarts' château" (see p154), magically reflected in a lake and surrounded by dense woodland, has spacious, comfortable rooms and an attractive cottage-style restaurant on the grounds. (See p205.)

Château de la Barre
Twenty generations of the Counts of Vanssay have resided in this 15th-century château, set in peaceful grounds. (See p206.)

Château de Jallanges
An energetic couple have turned this brick-and-stone Renaissance dwelling, with a period garden and pretty chapel, into a charming home. (See p204.)

Château de la Bourdaisière
A princely greeting (from one of the Princes de Broglie) awaits you in this beautifully modernized château, the birthplace of Gabrielle d'Estrées. (See p203.)

Château du Boisrenault-Indre
With a choice of rooms, suites and apartments, this 19th-century Renaissance-style château is a good base for exploring either Berry or Touraine. (See p206.)

Choosing a Hotel

Hotels have been selected across a wide price range on the basis of their facilities, good value and location. All rooms have private bath or shower. Hotels in the Loire Valley are generally not air-conditioned unless stated here. Check ahead also for disabled facilities. For map references *see inside back cover*.

PRICE CATEGORIES
The following price ranges are for a standard double room and taxes per night during the high season. Breakfast is not included, unless specified:

€ Under €60
€€ €60–€90
€€€ €90–€120
€€€€ €120–€160
€€€€€ over €160

ANJOU

ANGERS Hôtel du Mail
P €€
8 Rue des Ursules, 49100 **Tel** *02 41 25 05 25* **Fax** *02 41 86 91 20* **Rooms** *26* **Map** *C3*

A charming hotel in a quiet corner of the city centre, this 17th-century building with tastefully decorated bedrooms was once part of a convent. A particularly good breakfast is served in the dining room, and there is also a shaded parking area. Friendly owners. **www.hoteldumail.fr**

ANGERS Hôtel d'Anjou
€€€€
1 Blvd du Maréchal Foch, 49100 **Tel** *02 41 21 12 11* **Fax** *02 41 87 22 21* **Rooms** *53* **Map** *C3*

The interior of this city-centre hotel is eclectically decorated with Art Deco mosaics, 17th- and 18th-century fixtures, ornate ceilings and stained-glass windows. The rooms are spacious and elegantly furnished. The on-site Le Salamandre restaurant is recommended. Parking available. **www.hoteldanjou.fr**

CHAMPIGNÉ Château des Briottières
€€€€
Route de Marigné, 49330 **Tel** *02 41 42 00 02* **Fax** *02 41 42 01 55* **Rooms** *16* **Map** *C3*

A family-run 18th-century château set in a vast English-style park. The rooms (ten in the château and six in a charming cottage) all feature luxurious furnishings, with canopied beds and rich fabrics. Romantic dinners are on offer, as well as cooking classes. Reservations required. **www.briottieres.com**

CHÊNEHUTTE-LES-TUFFEAUX Le Prieuré
€€€€€
49350 **Tel** *02 41 67 90 14* **Fax** *02 41 67 92 24* **Rooms** *36* **Map** *C3*

This former priory, dating from the 12th century, has magnificent views over the River Loire. The bedrooms have a romantic, refined decor; two also have cosy fireplaces. The elegant restaurant serves gourmet cuisine prepared with the best regional produce, like pike poached in a Chinon wine sauce. **www.prieure.com**

FONTEVRAUD-L'ABBAYE La Croix Blanche
€€€
7 Place des Plantagenêts 49590 **Tel** *02 47 51 71 11* **Rooms** *23* **Map** *C3*

Just outside the abbey walls is this 17th-century coaching inn, it is set around a wonderfully flowery courtyard. There's a wide range of rooms available, some very luxurious, plus there are three tempting restaurants to choose from, including a smart dining room and a more casual brasserie. **www.fontevraud.net**

MONTJEAN-SUR-LOIRE Le Fief des Cordeliers
€€
Bellevue, 49570 **Tel** *02 41 43 96 09* **Rooms** *5* **Map** *B3*

This lovely traditional manor lies in a beautiful rural location just east of town, with views of nearby vineyards and the Loire. Rooms are spacious, nicely furnished and good value, especially as breakfast is included. The grounds are perfect to roam around and there's a pool for guests to take a relaxing dip. **http://logis.lefiefdescordeliers.com**

MONTREUIL-BELLAY Relais du Bellay
€€
96 Rue Nationale, 49260 **Tel** *02 41 53 10 10* **Fax** *02 41 38 70 61* **Rooms** *43* **Map** *C4*

The 17th-century main building and stylishly furnished annexe house the guest rooms. All are calm and quiet. Facilities include a swimming pool, sauna and a Turkish bath. A Jacuzzi and gym are also available. There are two rooms with disabled access. **www.hotelrelaisdubellay.fr**

SAUMUR La Croix de la Voulte
€€€
Route de Boumois, St-Lambert-des-Levées, 49400 **Tel** *02 41 38 46 66* **Fax** *02 41 38 46 66* **Rooms** *4* **Map** *C3*

This manor house outside Saumur dates from the 15th century. Built at a crossroads (*croix*), it was the turning point for the royal huntsmen. The bedrooms are all different, with classic furnishings; two also have original Louis XIV fireplaces. In fine weather, breakfast is served at the side of the pool. **www.lacroixdelavoulte.com**

SAUMUR Hôtel Anne d'Anjou
€€€€€
32–33 Quai Mayaud, 49400 **Tel** *02 41 67 30 30* **Fax** *02 41 67 51 00* **Rooms** *45* **Map** *C3*

The decor in this elegant mansion, sitting between the River Loire and the château, is sophisticated and romantic. The fine building features an impressive façade, grand staircase and painted ceiling; it also has guest rooms decorated in Empire or contemporary style. Breakfast is served in the courtyard. **www.hotel-anneanjou.com**

Key to Symbols *see back cover flap*

TOURAINE

AMBOISE Belle-Vue
€€

12 Quai Charles-Guinot, 37400 **Tel** *02 47 30 33 78* **Rooms** *32*
Map *D3*

This is an old-style French hotel overlooking the Loire and very close to the Château d'Amboise. Established in the 1800s, the inn consists of four houses that have been joined together. The rooms have quirky character and some have great river views. The hotel also has a friendly bar. **www.hotel-bellevue-amboise.com**

AMBOISE Manoir St-Thomas
P ⑪ ≋ 🗏 €€€€

1 Mail St-Thomas, 37400 **Tel** *02 47 23 21 82* **Rooms** *10*
Map *D3*

You'll feel like part of the Royal court at this sumptuous manor house converted into a luxurious hall. The rooms are exceptionally elegant and well equipped, connecting rooms are offered to families. Enjoy the fine restaurant, plus there's a heated pool in the well-kept grounds. **www.manoir-saint-thomas.com**

AZAY LE RIDEAU Le Grand Monarque
P ⑪ 🗏 🖼 €€€€

3 Place de la République, 37190 **Tel** *02 47 45 40 08* **Rooms** *26*
Map *D3*

This charming hotel is based around two buildings, one a former posting inn built in the 18th century, the other an elegant 19th-century home. Rooms are decorated in a variety of styles. On site there's a good restaurant where diners are able to make the most of the hotel's lovely shaded courtyard. **www.legrandmonarque.com**

CHENONCEAUX Hôtel La Roseraie
P ⑪ ≋ 🗏 €€€

7 Rue du Dr Bretonneau, 37150 **Tel** *02 47 23 90 09* **Rooms** *19*
Map *D3*

Simpler and cheaper than other local options but still packed with charm, La Rosarie offers tastefully decorated rooms some with terraces leading onto a pretty garden. There is also a pool in the grounds, and a well-regarded restaurant. **www.hotel-chenonceau.com**

CHENONCEAUX Auberge du Bon Laboureur
P ⑪ ≋ 🏃 🗏 €€€€

6 Rue du Dr Bretonneau, 37150 **Tel** *02 47 23 90 02* **Fax** *02 47 23 82 01* **Rooms** *25*
Map *D3*

Near the famous château, this inn is set in its own park. The bedrooms are located in a series of 18th-century stone dwellings. They are small but well equipped, and they all have designer bathrooms. Some are suitable for disabled guests. The oak-beamed restaurant serves good food. **www.bonlaboureur.com**

CHINON Hostellerie Gargantua
P ⑪ €€

73 Rue Voltaire, 37500 **Tel** *02 47 93 04 71* **Fax** *02 47 93 08 02* **Rooms** *7*
Map *D4*

This hotel, located in the ancient Palais du Bailliage, with its pointed roof and turret, is a local landmark. The guest rooms are comfortable, if somewhat cramped. Each has a theme, from Jeanne d'Arc to the Empire period. Modern and classic cuisine is served in the restaurant with its pleasant dining room and terrace. **www.hotel-gargantua.com**

CHINON Château de Marçay
🖫 P ⑪ ≋ 🏃 €€€€€

37500 **Tel** *02 47 93 03 47* **Fax** *02 47 93 45 33* **Rooms** *33*
Map *D4*

This elegant hotel is housed in a restored 15th-century fortified château. From the well-appointed bedrooms, guests can enjoy the lovely views over the surrounding parkland and vineyards. Refined and aristocratic atmosphere, impeccable service and cuisine. **www.chateaudemarcay.com**

LOCHES Hôtel de France
P ⑪ 🗏 €

6 Rue Picois, 37600 **Tel** *02 47 59 00 32* **Fax** *02 47 59 28 66* **Rooms** *17*
Map *D4*

In an elegant former staging post built of local tufa stone with a traditional slate roof, this hotel is situated near the historic medieval gate. The rooms are simply furnished, comfortable and well maintained. The restaurant serves good regional dishes, such as home-smoked salmon. **www.hoteldefranceloches.com**

LOCHES La Maison de l'Argentier du Roy
P 🖼 €€€

21 Rue Saint-Ours, 37600 **Tel** *02 47 91 62 86* **Rooms** *6*
Map *D4*

Converted into a memorable B&B this enchanting Renaissance manor stands in a dramatic location in the heart of the old town, just below the citadel. Rooms are reached via a fine spiral staircase and vary in style; all benefit from lovely views. Breakfast is included. **www.argentier-du-roy.eu**

LUYNES Domaine de Beauvois
🖫 P ⑪ ≋ 🏃 🗏 €€€€€

Route de Cléré-les-Pins, 37230 **Tel** *02 47 55 50 11* **Fax** *02 47 55 59 62* **Rooms** *34*
Map *D4*

This Renaissance manor house built around a 15th-century tower overlooks its own lake. The park is so vast that the pathways have to be signposted. Rooms are large and comfortable, with splendid marble bathrooms. Guests can enjoy a romantic candlelit dinner in the acclaimed restaurant. **www.beauvois.com**

MONTLOUIS-SUR-LOIRE Château de la Bourdaisière
🖫 P ≋ €€€€€

25 Rue de la Bourdaisière, 37270 **Tel** *02 47 45 16 31* **Fax** *02 47 45 09 11* **Rooms** *20*
Map *D3*

This château was the favourite residence of Gabrielle d'Estrées, mistress of Henri IV. Now refurbished as luxury accommodation, the hotel has elegant, lavish guest rooms, some of which feature period furniture. The pavilion in the grounds houses six bedrooms. The gardens are open to the public. **www.labourdaisiere.com**

ROCHECORBON Domaine des Hautes Roches

🔲 **P** 🍽 ≋   €€€€€

86 Quai de la Loire, 37210 **Tel** *02 47 52 88 88* **Fax** *02 47 52 81 30* **Rooms** *14*   **Map** *D3*

Surrounded by Vouvray vineyards, near Tours, this hotel was once a monks' residence. Fully restored, it boasts all modern comforts. The underground rooms, hewn into the tufa chalk, are spacious and characterful. The restaurant has one Michelin star, and you can dine in the château or alfresco, on the terrace. **www.leshautesroches.com**

ST-PATRICE Château de Rochecotte

🔲 **P** 🍽 ≋ 🏊 🕴   €€€€€

St-Patrice, Langeais, 37130 **Tel** *02 47 96 16 16* **Fax** *02 47 96 90 59* **Rooms** *35*   **Map** *D3*

Situated a short way from Langeais, Prince Talleyrand's château was completely renovated, and it opened as an elegant hotel in 1986. It is set in a charming, tranquil park with woodland. The interior is decorated sumptuously; the guest rooms are large, and each has a view. **www.chateau-de-rochecotte.fr**

TOURS Le Manoir

P   €€

2 Rue Traversière, 37000 **Tel** *02 47 05 37 37* **Rooms** *20*   **Map** *D3*

This hotel has pleasant, well-priced rooms in an elegant house in the very heart of town. Guests can choose from singles, doubles or triples, and there is some private parking, which is an added bonus. The breakfast buffet is lavish and is served in an unusual painted chamber. **http://hotel.manoir.tours.voila.net**

TOURS Hôtel de l'Univers

🔲 **P** 🍽 📖   €€€€

5 Boulevard Heurteloup, 37000 **Tel** *02 47 05 37 12* **Fax** *02 47 61 51 80* **Rooms** *85*   **Map** *D3*

Statesmen and royals have stayed at this luxurious hotel; a picture gallery depicts the most famous guests since 1846. The elegant architecture continues in the large, prettily furnished bedrooms, some of which are accessible to wheelchair users. The restaurant serves classic gourmet cuisine, and there is a private garage. **www.hotel-univers.fr**

VEIGNE Domaine de la Tortinière

P 🍽 ≋   €€€€€

10 Route de Ballan, 37250 **Tel** *02 47 34 35 00* **Rooms** *30*   **Map** *D3*

On the Indre River about 15 km (10 miles) south of Tours, this magical-looking little Loire-style château lives up to first impressions. Rooms are utterly charming, a few even set in the towers. The gorgeous grounds have a pool and lead down to the Indre. You can go boating from the hotel's own boathouse. **www.tortiniere.com**

VOUVRAY Château de Jallanges

P ≋ 🕴   €€€€€

37210 **Tel** *02 47 52 06 66* **Fax** *02 47 52 11 18* **Rooms** *5*   **Map** *D3*

This imposing Renaissance brick château, now a family home, offers comfortable rooms furnished with style. Guests are taken on a guided tour from the private chapel to the top of the turrets, from where there is a superb view. The *table d'hôte* caters for guests on reservation only. A good base for exploring Touraine. **www.jallanges.com**

BLESOIS AND ORLEANAIS

BEAUGENCY Hôtel de la Sologne

P   €€

6 Place St-Firmin, 45190 **Tel** *02 38 44 50 27* **Fax** *02 38 44 90 19* **Rooms** *16*   **Map** *E3*

This typical Sologne stone building on the main square overlooks the ruined castle keep of St-Firmin. The bedrooms are small, but cosy and bright, and simply furnished. There is a pretty flower-decked patio where breakfast can be taken. Private parking is also available. **www.hoteldelasologne.com**

BLOIS Le Monarque

P 🍽 📖   €

61 Rue Porte Chartraine, 41000 **Tel** *02 54 78 02 35* **Fax** *02 54 74 37 79* **Rooms** *27*   **Map** *E3*

Located near the Tour Beauvoir, the château and main shopping area, Le Monarque has an exceptionally convivial atmosphere. The rooms are comfortably furnished, smartly decorated and well equipped, with Internet access. Two family rooms also available. The restaurant serves traditional French cuisine. **http://annedebretagne.free.fr**

BLOIS Côte Loire Auberge Ligérienne

🍽   €€

2 Place de la Grève, 41000 **Tel** *02 54 78 07 86* **Fax** *02 54 56 87 33* **Rooms** *8*   **Map** *E3*

Well placed in the former mariners' quarter at the centre of town, this cheerful, small hotel is close to the Loire and is a 2-minute walk from the Château de Blois. The 16th-century building has pleasant rooms, a lovely restaurant and a charming courtyard, ideal for dining al fresco. **www.coteloire.com**

BRIARE Domaine des Roches

🔲 🍽 📖 ≋ 🍷 🕴   €€€€

2 Rue de la Plaine, 45250 **Tel** *02 38 05 09 00* **Fax** *02 38 05 09 05* **Rooms** *26*   **Map** *D3*

This gorgeous 19th-century manor house lies in secluded grounds perched above Briare. It's been well converted into a hotel offering spacious rooms and suites, as well as private cottages with up to four bedrooms. There are many luxury features, including a pool and steam bath, and a gourmet restaurant. **www.domainedesroches.fr**

CHAMBORD Du Grand St-Michel

P 🍽   €€€

Place St-Louis, 41250 **Tel** *02 54 20 31 31* **Fax** *02 54 20 36 40* **Rooms** *40*   **Map** *E3*

Across the lawn from the château, this country house has simple but comfortable rooms, some with views. The vast restaurant is decorated with trophies, photographs and pictures, all related to hunting. There is also a lovely terrace from where guests can enjoy views of the château. Closed for a few weeks in winter. **www.saintmichel-chambord.com**

Key to Price Guide *see p202* **Key to Symbols** *see back cover flap*

COUR CHEVERNY Le Béguinage

€€   Map E3

41700 **Tel** *02 54 79 29 92* **Rooms** *5*

This excellent B&B offers a handful of rooms in an 18th-century house as well as a small *gîte independant* (cottage). The scenic grounds are bordered by a river. The rooms are good value for the space and charm, and breakfast is included in the price. **www.lebeguinage.fr**

LA FERTÉ-ST-AUBIN L'Orée des Chênes

€€€€   Map E3

Route de Marcilly, 45240 **Tel** *02 38 64 84 00* **Fax** *02 38 64 84 20* **Rooms** *26*

This hotel-restaurant complex lies in the heart of the Sologne countryside and reflects local architecture. Located in its own parkland, it is an ideal base for fishing and walking. The comfortable rooms are furnished with style and have Internet access. The restaurant serves regional dishes. Sauna available. **www.loreedeschenes.fr**

MONTLIVAUT La Maison d'à Côté

€€   Map

26 Route de Chambord, 41350 **Rooms** *9*

Located near the local church in an understated village close to Chambord, this hotel offers guests snug but contemporary rooms, some of which overlook the flower-filled terrace. It also has a well-regarded restaurant that serves delicious cuisine in a stylish setting. **www.lamaisondacote.fr**

ONZAIN Domaine des Hauts de Loire

€€€€€   Map D3

41150 **Tel** *02 54 20 72 57* **Fax** *02 54 20 77 32* **Rooms** *32*

This fomer hunting lodge with large grounds retains its grandeur, with richly furnished, bright and comfortable guest rooms. This is an unashamedly expensive place to relax. The Michelin-starred restaurant offers cutting-edge and classic dishes, and a superb selection of local wines. There is also a tennis court. **www.domainhautsloire.com**

ORLÉANS Jackotel

€€   Map E2

18 Cloître St-Aignan, 45000 **Tel** *02 38 54 48 48* **Fax** *02 38 77 17 59* **Rooms** *61*

Standing in the medieval centre of Orléans, near the cathedral, this hotel is surrounded by a good selection of restaurants. A former cloister, it features a charming inner courtyard that leads you to the Place St-Aignan, just in front of the church. Very comfortable rooms. Parking is also available. **www.jackotel.com**

ROMORANTIN-LANTHENAY Grand Hôtel du Lion d'Or

€€€€€   Map E3

69 Rue G Clémenceau, 41200 **Tel** *02 54 94 15 15* **Fax** *02 54 88 24 87* **Rooms** *16*

This former Renaissance mansion house is now a gastronomic must in this historic town. From the outside, the building is unimpressive, but the interior has instant charm. The luxury bedrooms lead off from a cobbled courtyard, and the decor is authentic Napoleon III. Formal gardens. **www.hotel-liondor.fr**

SOUVIGNY-EN-SOLOGNE Ferme des Foucault

€€   Map F4

Ménestreau-en-Villette, 45240 **Tel/Fax** *02 38 76 94 41* **Rooms** *3*

Deep in the forest in the Sologne countryside is this attractive redbrick-and-timber farmhouse. The immense bedrooms are cosy, with superb bathrooms; one even has a wood-burning stove. The other rooms are decorated with paintings by the owner's daughter. Friendly, relaxed atmosphere. **www.ferme-des-foucault.com**

VENDÔME Capricorne

€   Map D3

8 Boulevard de Trémault, 41100 **Tel** *02 54 80 27 00* **Fax** *02 54 77 30 63* **Rooms** *40*

A standard hotel near the train station. The rooms are brightly decorated; although not spacious, they are well equipped, and many overlook a pretty interior courtyard. There is also a good choice of restaurants: one serves traditional cuisine, while the other offers a buffet menu. Closed Christmas to early Jan. **www.hotelcapricorne.com**

BERRY

ARGENTON-SUR-CREUSE Manoir de Boisvillers

€€   Map E4

11 Rue du Moulins de Bord, 36200 **Tel** *02 54 24 13 88* **Fax** *02 54 24 27 83* **Rooms** *16*

A surprising find in the heart of the Old Town, this is an 18th-century manor house with an ivy-clad façade and a cosy atmosphere. Its tree-lined garden centres around the outdoor pool. The rooms are spacious and charming, with tasteful furnishings. Most of them have a view of the Creuse Valley. Closed Jan. **www.manoir-de-boisvillers.com**

AUBIGNY-SUR-NÈRE Château de la Verrerie

€€€€€   Map F3

Oizon, 18700 **Tel** *02 48 81 51 60* **Fax** *02 48 58 21 25* **Rooms** *12*

Hidden away in forests southeast of Aubigny-sur-Nère, is this early Renaissance château. The hotel is set beside a tranquil lake, on which guests can go boating, and is surrounded by spacious grounds where it's possible to go cycling or even hunting in the right season. **www.chateaudelaverrerie.com**

BOURGES Hôtel d'Angleterre

€€€€   Map F4

1 Place des 4 Piliers, 18000 **Tel** *02 48 24 68 51* **Rooms** *31*

Brilliantly located in the heart of the medieval quarter of Bourges, this modern hotel is set in a historic building. It offers guests comfortable, well-appointed rooms with good facilities, including free Wi-Fi. Breakfast is included in the price. **www.bestwestern-angleterre-bourges.com**

BRINON-SUR-SAULDRE La Solognote   🅿 🍽   €€
34 Grande Rue, 18410 **Tel** *02 48 58 50 29* **Fax** *02 48 58 56 00* **Rooms** *13*   **Map** *F3*

A charming family-run inn made up of three buildings housing comfortable, tastefully decorated rooms. All overlook the pretty courtyard garden, where breakfast can be taken. The restaurant is airy and bright, with exposed oak beams and antique furniture, and it serves excellent regional cuisine. Closed 3 weeks Mar. **www.lasolognote.com**

BUZANCAIS Château Boisrenault   🎚 🅿 🍽 🏊   €€
Buzançais 36500 **Tel** *02 54 84 03 01* **Fax** *02 54 84 10 57* **Rooms** *7*   **Map** *F2*

This 19th-century Renaissance-style château, outside a little town between Chateauroux and Tours, is a handy base for the Brenne nature reserve. As well as the spacious bedooms – four of which are suites – there are two self-catering apartments. Entertainment includes a piano, library and games. **www.chateaux-du-boisrenault.com**

ISSOUDUN La Cognette   🅿 🍽 🗒   €€€
26 Rue des Minimes, 36100 **Tel** *02 54 03 59 59* **Fax** *02 54 03 13 03* **Rooms** *20*   **Map** *E4*

Each room in this attractive hotel with flower-laden window boxes is individually decorated: there's an immaculate white decor for the Blanche de Castille room and flamboyant red for the Balzac and Madame Anska. Most open out on to a pretty terrace garden, where breakfast can be enjoyed in summer. Wi-Fi equipped. **www.la-cognette.com**

LE BLANC Hôtel du Théâtre   🅿   €
2 bis Avenue Gambetta, 36300 **Tel** *02 54 37 68 69* **Rooms** *19*   **Map** *D4*

Guests will find simple, pleasant rooms in this former theatre that has been converted into a hotel. It is conveniently located in the centre of a quiet provincial town, on the edge of the Brenne regional nature park. There are a number of triple rooms for families, and free Wi-Fi. **www.hotel-theatre-36.fr**

MAISONNAIS Prieuré d'Orsan/La Maison d'Orsan   🅿 🏊   €€€€€
Orsan, 18170 **Tel** *02 48 56 27 50* **Fax** *02 48 56 39 64* **Rooms** *3*   **Map** *F4*

This former monastery that has been transformed into a luxury residence, surrounded by enchanting gardens, which are open to the public. As well as sumptuous accommodation, guests can relax in the sitting room and library, or cycle around the grounds. Closed Jan–early Feb & Dec. **www.prieuredorsan.com**

ST-CHARTIER Château de la Vallée Bleue   🅿 🏊 🎿   €€€€
Route de Verneuil, 36400 **Tel** *02 54 31 01 91* **Fax** *02 54 31 04 48* **Rooms** *15*   **Map** *E4*

This 19th-century château is now a luxury hotel with two pools (one for children) and a putting green. The best rooms are on the first floor of the main building; but there is also a suite in the ancient dovan tower. Try to secure rooms in the main building rather than the annexe. Closed mid-Nov–mid-Mar. **www.chateauvalleebleue.com**

SANCERRE La Côte des Monts Damnés   🍽 🗒   €€€€
Chavignol, 18300 **Tel** *02 48 54 01 72*   **Map** *F3*

Set in a village known for its wine, and less than 5 km (3 miles) west of Sancerre town, this hotel is surprisingly chic, with stylish, contemporary rooms. Choose from two excellent restaurants, the gastronomic option offering top-class dining, while the bistro turns out simpler but very tasty regional fare. **www.montsdamnes.com**

VALENÇAY Relais du Moulin   🎚 🅿 🍽 🏊 🎿 🍷   €€
94 Rue Nationale, 36600 **Tel** *02 54 00 38 00* **Fax** *02 54 00 38 79* **Rooms** *54*   **Map** *E4*

The guest rooms at this hotel complex beside an ancient mill are functional, with simple modern furnishings, soundproofing and Internet access. The dining room has an attractive terrace overlooking the garden, and the restaurant serves traditional cuisine. Closed mid-Nov–Mar. **www.hotel-lerelaisdumoulin.com**

NORTH OF THE LOIRE

CHARTRES Hôtel Châtelet   🎚 🅿 ♿ 🖨   €€€
6 Ave Jehan-de-Beauce, 28000 **Tel** *02 37 21 78 00* **Fax** *02 37 36 23 01* **Rooms** *48*   **Map** *E2*

On the edge of the historic centre, within easy walking distance of the cathedral, this hotel has been stylishly modernized and offers very spacious bedrooms. Some of the rooms on the higher floors have spectacular views of the upper sections of the cathedral. **www.hotelchatelet.com**

CHARTRES Le Grand Monarque   🎚 🅿 🍽   €€€€
22 Place des Epars, 28000 **Tel** *02 37 18 15 15* **Fax** *02 37 36 34 18* **Rooms** *55*   **Map** *E2*

This large, stylish, historic inn is a Chartres institution, set on a big roundabout a short distance from the cathedral. A typical French hotel-restaurant, it has comfortable rooms, a lovely gastronomic restaurant and a fun brasserie and bar. It also has a spa for guests to enjoy. **www.bw-grand-monarque.com**

CONFLANS SUR ANILLE Château de la Barre   🅿   €€€€€
Château de la Barre, 72120 **Tel** *02 37 18 15 15* **Fax** *02 37 36 34 18* **Rooms** *5*   **Map** *D2*

Stay as a guest of the Count and Countess de Vanssay, the 20th generation of the family who live in this 15th-century château in the wooded hills of the Perche, between Chartres and Tours. Breakfast and afternoon tea are served daily; candlelit dinners are available by reservation. Apartments are available for longer rents. **www.chateaudelabarre.com**

Key to Price Guide *see p202* **Key to Symbols** *see back cover flap*

LA CHARTRE-SUR-LE-LOIR Hôtel de France
P ⊞ 🏊 🏃 €€

20 Place de la République, 72340 **Tel** *02 43 44 40 16* **Fax** *02 43 79 62 20* **Rooms** *24* **Map** *D3*

This ivy-clad hotel in the city centre has a delightful garden bordering the river. The good-value standard-sized bedrooms are simply furnished but comfortable. The bar and the brasserie are also basic, but the dining room is pleasant and serves generous portions of good food. Pretty garden terrace. **www.hoteldefrance-72.fr**

LE MANS Demeure de Laclais
€€€

4 bis Place du Cardinal Grente, 72000 **Tel** *02 43 81 91 78* **Rooms** *3* **Map** *C2*

In the centre of Le Mans's old town, opposite the entrance to the cathedral, is this beautiful hotel housed in a well-renovated 17th-century building. Rooms have great character and have been stylishly decorated. They also benefit from wonderful views of the town. Breakfast is included in the price. **www.lademeuredelaclais.fr**

LE MANS Domaine de Chatenay
P 🏃 €€€€

St-Saturnin, 72650 **Tel** *02 43 25 44 60* **Fax** *02 43 25 21 00* **Rooms** *8* **Map** *C2*

Situated in the countryside outside Le Mans, this elegant 18th-century manor house surrounded by parkland is the ideal place to relax. The spacious rooms are stylishly furnished with period furniture. Breakfast is taken in the First Empire dining room, and candlelit dinners can be booked in advance. Internet access. **www.domainedechatenay.com**

LOUÉ Hôtel Ricordeau
📶 P ⊞ 🏊 €€€

13 Rue de la Libération, 72540 **Tel** *02 43 88 40 03* **Fax** *02 43 88 62 08* **Rooms** *13* **Map** *C2*

A former coaching inn, this lovely stone building has comfortable rooms, each decorated in a different style; all are well equipped and have Internet access; some have air-conditioning. The superb garden leads down to the River Vègre. Breakfast is copious, with cold meats, cheeses, fruit and home-made jams. **www.hotel-ricordeau.fr**

MONHOUDOU Château de Monhoudou
P ⊞ 🏊 🏃 €€€€

72260 **Tel** *02 43 97 40 05* **Fax** *02 43 33 11 58* **Rooms** *5* **Map** *D2*

The 19th generation of the de Monhoudou family still owns and runs this delightful 18th-century château. Guests can stroll in the gardens among horses, sheep, swans and peacocks. The vast rooms, all with views of the park, are furnished with antiques, and some bathrooms have spa baths. **www.monhoudou.com**

LOIRE-ATLANTIQUE AND THE VENDEE

LE CROISIC Fort de l'Océan
P ⊞ 🏊 🖳 €€€€€

Pointe du Croisic, 44490 **Tel** *02 40 15 77 77* **Fax** *02 40 15 77 80* **Rooms** *9* **Map** *A3*

Seventeenth-century ramparts enclose this former fortress facing the sea, but nothing remains of the harsh military lifestyle. Comfort is key, and the guest rooms are stylish and plush; one is equipped for disabled visitors. The restaurant serves wonderful seafood. **www.hotelfortocean.com**

LES SABLES D'OLONNE Château de la Millière
📼 P 🏊 €€€

St-Mathurin, 85150 **Tel** *02 51 22 73 29* **Fax** *02 51 22 73 29* **Rooms** *5* **Map** *A4*

This elegant 19th-century château with a vast area of parkland is situated close to both the Atlantic coast and the town centre. The rooms are beautifully furnished with hangings and antiques. The library/billiard room is available to guests, and there is also on-site fishing in the private lake. Closed Oct–May. **www.chateau-la-milliere.com**

MISSILLAC Domaine de la Bretesche
📶 P ⊞ 🏊 🏃 📺 🖳 €€€€€

Domaine de la Bretesche, 44780 **Tel** *02 51 76 86 96* **Fax** *02 40 66 99 47* **Rooms** *32* **Map** *A3*

One of the most beautiful hotel-restaurants in the area. The rooms are located in the converted outbuildings beside a majestic castle. Attractive decor and rich furnishings create a truly sumptuous ambience. Facilities include a spa, parkland, a lake to swim in, tennis courts and a golf course. Closed Feb. **www.bretesche.com**

NANTES Hôtel La Pérouse
📶 📺 🖳 €€€

3 Allée Duquesne, 44000 **Tel** *02 40 89 75 00* **Fax** *02 40 89 76 00* **Rooms** *46* **Map** *B3*

This chic hotel has a wonderful Zen atmosphere. The rooms have glossy wooden flooring and crisp contemporary furniture; they are reasonably quiet. The breakfast buffet is good, and there is free Wi-Fi Internet connection and free access to a nearby gym for guests. Municipal parking is available nearby. **www.hotel-laperouse.fr**

NANTES Hôtel Pommeraye
€€€€

2 Rue Boileau, 44000 **Tel** *02 40 48 78 79* **Rooms** *50* **Map** *B3*

This hotel is located by the elegant 19th-century shopping mall, Passage Pommeraye, and is in the best area for smart shops and restaurants. Rooms range in size and some have better views than others. Prices vary considerably, but breakfast is served in generous portions. **www.hotel-pommeraye.com**

NOIRMOUTIER-EN-L'ILE Hotel Fleur de Sel
P ⊞ 🏊 €€€€

Rue des Saulniers, 85330 **Tel** *02 51 39 09 07* **Fax** *02 51 39 09 76* **Rooms** *35* **Map** *A4*

This hotel stands in a vast landscaped Mediterranean-style garden with a swimming pool. Some guest rooms are decorated with English-style pine and face the pool; others have a marine theme and a private terrace. Tennis courts, practice golf and bikes are available. The chef serves some of the best cuisine in the Vendée. **www.fleurdesel.fr**

WHERE TO EAT

In this generally prosperous region, with its excellent local produce, eating out is popular, and interest in cuisine is high even by the standards of this food-loving country. Lunch remains the main meal of the day: even in larger towns such as Tours, Orléans or Nantes, many office workers return home during their two-hour lunch break. Restaurants serve lunch from about noon, and it can be hard to find one willing to serve

A café sign in Berry

a meal if you arrive after 1pm, although cafés and brasseries in the towns are more flexible. Dinner is served from about 8pm onwards (sometimes earlier in the main tourist areas). Beware of last orders, which may be as early as 9pm, especially in country districts. The restaurants on pages 214–19 have been carefully selected for their excellence of food, decor and ambience, and cover all price ranges.

An outdoor café in the historic heart of Richelieu

TYPES OF RESTAURANT

In country districts and small towns, the most pleasant restaurants are often to be found in hotels, especially if they belong to the **Logis de France** association, which puts particular emphasis on good (and good value for money) regional cooking. Larger towns offer a broad range of places to eat, from basic pizzerias and *crêperies* to chic, gourmet establishments via cafés and brasseries. Cafés are handy for a snack, coffee or aperitif, or as places from which to watch the world go by, and brasseries are good for quick meals. Unlike restaurants, brasseries and cafés generally serve a limited range of dishes outside regular mealtimes.

The Loire also has an ever-widening choice of restaurants specializing in foreign cuisines (most commonly Vietnamese and North African).

VEGETARIAN FOOD

True vegetarians do not fare well in France. It can be more convenient to head for a *crêperie* or a pizzeria, although in some of the university towns, the occasional vegetarian restaurant may be found. A few large cafés or brasseries in the tourist districts of major towns sometimes offer a small number of vegetarian dishes, and omelettes and other egg-based dishes are usually available. Alternatively, ask the chef for the meat or fish to be left out of a salad. In full-scale restaurants, it is essential to enquire in advance whether it is possible to have a vegetarian dish specially prepared. Non-meat-eaters need have no fears: Loire Valley restaurants serve excellent fish dishes, and cafés and brasseries usually offer at least one fish dish on the menu.

READING THE MENU

The vast majority of Loire Valley restaurants offer at least one fixed-price menu. You will often find a range of menus, culminating in an expensive *menu gastronomique* (gourmet meal), which may be available only if all members of your party choose it. Look out for a *menu régional* or *menu du terroir*, which will feature a selection of regional specialities.

The less expensive menus often feature starters such as local *charcuterie* (pork specialities), a salad or *crudités* (raw vegetables), whereas gourmet menus offer more complex dishes. Vegetables are often served separately.

Cheese is considered a separate course, served between the main course and dessert – local goats' cheeses are likely to predominate.

A typical Loire Valley restaurant terrace

Many restaurants, especially in country districts, do not have a *carte* from which individual dishes may be selected. If they do, eating *à la carte* almost always works out to be more expensive than choosing from a fixed-price menu, since it is not considered acceptable to skip the starter and order only a main dish (skipping dessert is more acceptable).

Cafés and brasseries offer a *plat du jour* (dish of the day), often with a regional flavour, along with standard French fare such as steak or fish with fried potatoes, complemented by a range of salads or vegetables.

The rustic Auberge de la Petite Fadette in Nohant *(see p218)*

Auberge du Moulin de Chaméron at Bannegon in Berry *(see p217)*

MAKING RESERVATIONS

It is always advisable to book tables in advance at restaurants near the well-known châteaux, especially during the main tourist season (Easter to late September). If you enjoy eating alongside the residents at local restaurants in towns, which rarely take reservations over the telephone, make sure you arrive early. Restaurants in country districts are often closed on Sunday evenings as well as for at least one whole day during the week.

DRESS CODE

Most French people take considerable trouble with their appearance but, with the exception of a few very chic and expensive places, formal dress is not required, and ties are rarely a necessity even in the top restaurants, providing you are neatly turned out.

HOW MUCH TO PAY

It is difficult to classify restaurants by price, as most offer a range of fixed-price meals. Prices can be as low as €12 or as high as €100, but good, copious meals can be had everywhere for between €25 and €35.

A service charge of 15 per cent is usually included in the prices on menus, which are posted up outside for you to study before venturing in. It is usual to leave an extra euro or two as an additional tip. In more expensive restaurants, cloakroom attendants are given about €1 and lavatory attendants expect a small tip of about 30 cents.

Visa and MasterCard credit cards are widely accepted. Check first with the restaurant to find out whether American Express or Diners Club cards can be used.

CHILDREN AND PETS

Children are well received everywhere in the region, but they should be discouraged from leaving their seats and wandering about during the meal. High chairs are sometimes available. Some restaurants offer special low-priced children's menus *(repas d'enfant)*.

Since the French are great dog lovers, well-behaved small dogs are usually accepted at all but the most elegant restaurants (but are often banned from food shops). Do not be surprised to see your neighbour's lapdog sitting on the next door *banquette*.

WHEELCHAIR ACCESS

Because few restaurants make special provision for wheelchairs, it is wise when booking to mention that you or one of your party need space for a *fauteuil roulant*. This will ensure you get a conveniently located table and assistance, if needed, when you arrive. A list on page 198 gives names and addresses of various organizations that offer advice to disabled travellers to the Loire Valley region.

SMOKING

Since 2008, French law has banned smoking in all public places including, somewhat controversially, *lieux de convivialité*, such as bars, cafés and restaurants. Smoking is permitted at outside tables and a few establishments have special enclosed indoor spaces for smokers, which are heavily ventilated in accordance with health regulations.

The elegance of the Michelin-starred Château de Noirieux *(see p214)*

The Flavours of the Loire Valley

This huge area can take pride in a truly diverse range
of top-quality produce. The seafood from its Atlantic
coastline, the freshwater fish from its rivers and lakes, the
game birds from its forests, the bounty of fresh vegetables
and the tiny white mushrooms that flourish in the darkness
of its caves, have all helped to create a cuisine fit for kings.
Many of the Loire's typical fish and meat dishes have
become classics, now found all over France. Others
remain very much local treats, using the region's finest
and freshest produce, to be sought out and savoured in
its many fine restaurants.

Young carrots

**Fresh hake for sale, direct from the
port, in the Loire-Atlantique**

MEAT AND CHARCUTERIE

Free-range chickens are
raised in the Sarthe, Touraine
and Orléanais, and duck in
the Vendée. Anjou and
Mayenne are home to grass-
fed cattle, and the Berry to
hardy sheep. The forests of
the Sologne are well known
for deer, hare, wild boar,
pheasant and partridge.

The main charcuterie is
rillettes (shredded and potted
slow-cooked pork), a
speciality of Tours and the
Sarthe. *Rillons* (large chunks
of crunchy fried salted belly
pork) are also popular. The
Vendée produces some
excellent cured ham. The
Sologne is noted for its
terrines, Chartres for its
excellent game pies and the
Berry for a pâté that comes
baked in a pastry with slices of
hard-boiled egg.

FISH

The ports of the Loire-
Atlantique and the Vendée
offer up a variety of fish and
shellfish. La Turballe is the
main sardine port on the
Atlantic coast. The Ile de
Noirmoutier is known for
line-caught fish, lobster and
oysters, as well as farmed
turbot. But best of all is the
region's freshwater fish,
including pike-perch, shad,
tench, eels and lampreys.

Globe artichokes

Asparagus

Shallots

Watercress

Broccoli

Radishes

A selection of the superb vegetables grown in the Loire Valley

LOCAL DISHES AND SPECIALITIES

Meals often start with a terrine or pâté,
spread thickly on crusty bread. Creamy
vegetable soups, such as asparagus or
pumpkin, are also popular, as are
grilled sardines and shellfish along the
coast. Main courses include fish
baked in a salt crust or simply
poached and served with a creamy
beurre blanc sauce. Superb poultry
may also be on offer, roasted or
prepared as a fricassée with cream
and butter. The region produces
excellent beef and lamb: tender *gigot
de sept heures* is a menu favourite. Game dominates the
winter table in the Sologne, commonly served with the wild
mushrooms that flourish in the area. Many desserts are
based on fruit, often baked in a tart or poached in wine.

Ste-Maure cheese

Gigot de Sept Heures *A leg
of lamb is cooked slowly until
tender with carrots, bacon,
garlic, herbs and wine.*

A cheese stall in the market at Loches in the Touraine

along the banks of the Loire, tiny button mushrooms are cultivated. Samphire is gathered from the salt marshes near Nantes, and the Ile de Noirmoutier is famous for its new potatoes. The Sologne produces fine asparagus and lentils are grown in the Berry.

Orchards across the Loire Valley are noted for their apples and pears; Comice pears originated near Angers. Other quality fruit includes the succulent plums of Touraine and sweet strawberries from Saumur.

CHEESE

The Touraine and Berry produce some of France's finest goats' cheeses. The creamy, ash-covered Ste-Maure-de-Touraine is available both freshly made or matured in damp cellars. Selles-sur-Cher is a mild, flat, rounded, cindered cheese. Valençay, shaped into an ash-covered pyramid, is firmer with a stronger taste, and Pouligny-St-Pierre, a narrower pyramid, is mottled and blueish on the outside and white within. Most strongly flavoured are the small round Crottin de Chavignol cheeses.

Cows' milk cheeses of note include Feuille de Dreux, a flat, soft cheese with a chestnut leaf on the top, ash-covered Olivet and the washed-rinded Port-Salut.

FRUIT AND VEGETABLES

Thanks to the mild climate, winter vegetables thrive in the Nantes area. Much of France's salad vegetables are grown here, as well as peas, radishes, turnips, early leeks and carrots. In damp caves

A busy vegetable stall in the daily market at Saumur

ON THE MENU

Alose à l'oseille Shad in a sorrel hollandaise sauce

Canard nantais Roast duck with Muscadet wine sauce

Civet de marcassin Hearty casserole of wild boar

Géline à la lochoise Géline hen in a cream sauce

Porc aux pruneaux Pork fillets cooked with prunes in a wine and cream sauce

Potage d'asperges Creamy puréed asparagus soup

Prunes au Vouvray Plums stewed in Vouvray wine

Ragoût d'anguilles et cuisses de grenouille A stew of eel and frogs' legs

Tarte aux rillettes Open savoury tart with a filling of potted pork, eggs and cream

Lapin Chasseur *Rabbit is simmered with tomato and mushrooms to make this traditional hunters' stew.*

Sandre au beurre blanc *A poached pike-perch is served with a* beurre blanc *sauce of butter, cream and shallots.*

Tarte Tatin *This upside-down tart of caramelized apples on a puff pastry base may be offered plain or with cream.*

What to Drink in the Loire

The Loire Valley is a major wine region *(see pp30–31)*, so naturally the traditional tipple in cafés and bars is *un coup de rouge* or *un coup de blanc* (a small glass of red or white wine). The light rosés, such as Rosé d'Anjou or Rosé de Touraine, are drunk chilled, either in the afternoon with a slice of cake or as an apéritif. In November, bars and cafés serve *bernache*, the greenish, fermented juice left after the grapes have been pressed for winemaking. There is also a wide variety of other alcoholic drinks, including *eaux de vie* made with local fruits and light, lager-style beers, as well as non-alcoholic drinks such as coffees, teas and juices.

A waiter in a Loire Valley bar

White Sancerre

Red Bourgueil

Sparkling wine

WINE

Wine usually accompanies meals in the Loire, as it does throughout France. Local wine is often served in carafes. Ordering a *demi* (50 cl, approximately ½ pint) or *quart* (25 cl) is an inexpensive way to try out a wide variety of the wines of the region before buying any to take home *(see pp30–31)*.

French law divides domestic wines into four classes, in ascending order of quality:

Vin de Table, *Vin de Pays*, *Vin Délimité de Qualité Supérieure* (VDQS) and finally *Appellation d'Origine Contrôlée* (AOC). *Vin de Table* wines are rarely found in good restaurants. If in doubt, order the house wine *(la réserve)*. Very few restaurants will risk their reputation on an inferior house wine, and they often provide good value for money.

APÉRITIFS AND DIGESTIFS

A glass of locally-produced sparkling wine can be an excellent apéritif or a pleasant accompaniment to the dessert course. Slightly sparkling Vouvray *pétillant* is popular, and further west in Anjou you will find Saumur sparkling wine, made by the *méthode traditionnelle*. Keep an eye open, too, for Crémant de Loire, another good local sparkling wine.

A *kir* – white wine with a touch of *crème de cassis*, a

HOW TO READ A WINE LABEL

Even the simplest label will provide a key to the wine's flavour and quality. It will bear the name of the wine and its producer, its vintage if there is one, and whether it comes from a strictly defined area *(appellation d'origine contrôlée* or AOC) or is a more general *vin de pays* or *vin de table*. The shape and colour of the bottle is also a guide. Most good-quality wine is bottled in green glass, which helps to protect it from light. The label's design may be appealing, but does not necessarily indicate a quality product.

The property or producer

Estate-bottled, rather than a blend from a merchant or growers' co-operative

Pictures may be accurate or fanciful

Capacity of the bottle

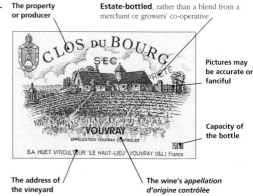

The address of the vineyard

The wine's *appellation d'origine contrôlée*

blackcurrant liqueur – is a popular apéritif, and an appealing variation, often served as the house apéritif, combines sparkling wine with raspberry or peach liqueur. Bars, cafés and restaurants also stock the usual range of French apéritifs as well as international gins, sherries, ports and whiskies.

After dinner, a little glass of clear fruit brandy made from local raspberries, pears or plums may appeal. Cointreau, Combier and Giffard are also produced in the Loire Valley. Other traditional *digestifs*, such as cognac or calvados, are also drunk after meals in the region.

BEER

The locals drink mostly lager-style draught beer in cafés – ask for *un demi*. A range of bottled beers can also be found, both French (which is considerably cheaper) and imported.

Café crème, often served at breakfast with a fresh croissant

COFFEE AND TEA

Cafés, still the main focus of community life, serve good strong *express* (a tiny cup of black coffee). White coffees are prepared with hot milk and come in two sizes: small *(petit crème)* and large *(grand crème)*. Together with fresh croissants, they make a good breakfast.

Tea served in cafés is often of the teabag variety (with a slice of lemon, it is *un thé citron*). Tearooms in towns, however, are more likely to use tea leaves. Many cafés also offer a range of exotic fruit and herb teas, which are caffeine-free. In restaurants an infusion of limeflower leaves *(tilleul)*, mint *(menthe)* or camomile *(camomille)* is often drunk after dinner as an aid to digestion.

OTHER DRINKS

Children enjoy the colourful drinks served in tall glasses known as *menthe à l'eau* (green, minty syrup with tap water) and *grenadine* (a red fruit syrup), but these may be too sweet for adult tastes. Served with Vittel mineral water, for example, they become *Vittel menthe, Vittel grenadine,* and so on. *Vittel citron amer* (with bottled, still bitter lemon) is more refreshing than *Vittel citron* (with lemon syrup). Best of all for quenching the thirst – but also more expensive – is a *citron pressé:* freshly-squeezed lemon juice served with a carafe of water and packets of sugar to mix to taste. *Orange pressée* is orange juice served in the same way. Bottled fruit juices *(jus de fruits)* are also available everywhere.

Tap water is safe to drink, but many people prefer mineral water *(eau minérale)*, either sparkling *(gazeuse)* or still *(non-gazeuse)*.

Locally-made apple juice

WHERE TO DRINK

Cafés are the traditional place to pop in for a coffee or beer, to meet a friend or watch the world go by. City centres have bustling cafés on every corner, and many squares are crowded with outdoor tables when the weather is fine. However, the traditional café, with its long bar counter lined by regulars, is gradually being super-seded, at least in towns, by more elaborate places.

Bars and *bars à vin* (old-style wine bars) are often the haunts of more hardened drinkers and of late-night revellers, although hotel bars can attract a more eclectic clientele. In larger towns,

A wood-panelled hotel bar in Touraine

many new-style wine bars, often with high-tech decor, serve wine by the glass, with light meals, plates of *charcuterie* or cheeses with crusty bread. Traditional *salons de thé* (tea-rooms), which serve coffee, tea and hot chocolate, are mainly frequented by women. They also serve *pâtisseries* and choc-olates, which can be bought to take away. The newer version offers light lunches and a variety of sweets, cakes and tarts to a younger, mixed clientele.

People enjoying a break in a stylish café in Orléans

Choosing a Restaurant

The restaurants in this section have been selected across a wide price range for their excellent food, good value and interesting location. Most restaurants in the Loire Valley offer set menus which may work out cheaper than the price category. For *Flavours of The Loire Valley* see pp210–11. For map references *see inside back cover*.

PRICE CATEGORIES
The following price ranges are for a three course meal for one, including a half-bottle of house wine, tax and service:
€ Under €30
€€ €30–€45
€€€ €45–€65
€€€€ €65–€80
€€€€€ Over €80

ANJOU

ANGERS Mets et Vins
€€€

44 Boulevard Ayrault, 49000 **Tel** *02 41 87 03 35*
Map *C3*

The modern and stylish dining room of this renowned restaurant is decorated with rows of wine bottles, and has a spectacular glass ceiling. The European cuisine is refined, there is an emphasis on the fish of the day, while the menu also includes classics like *crème brûlée*. Unsurprisingly, there is a wide choice of delicious wines to accompany the food.

ANGERS Une Ile
€€€

9 Rue Max Richard, 49000 **Tel** *02 41 19 14 48*
Map *C3*

A highly rated, stylish restaurant run by a chef who describes his cuisine as a combination of what ingredients are in the market, what is in season and his own whims. Great emphasis is placed on presentation, and there is a particularly good seafood menu. The grilled *foie gras* is also an excellent choice. Closed Sat and Sun.

BOUCHEMAINE A la Pointe
€€

La Pointe de Bouchemaine, 49080 **Tel** *02 41 77 14 96*
Map *C3*

Located in a hamlet on the confluence of the rivers Loire and Maine, this restaurant has a stunning panoramic view. The menu features freshly caught eels, pikeperch, salmon and other freshwater fish. Classic dishes, such as *sandre au beurre blanc* (pikeperch in butter), are excellently prepared.

BRIOLLAY Château de Noirieux
€€€€€

26 Route du Moulin, 49125 **Tel** *02 41 42 50 05*
Map *C3*

This elegant Michelin-starred hotel-restaurant is located in a splendid château set in grounds overlooking the River Loir. The chef prepares flawless classic dishes, such as sole with morel mushrooms and Racan pigeon pot-roasted with local wine. The exclusivity of the setting is worth the expense. The wine list is extensive.

DOUÉ-LA-FONTAINE Auberge de la Bienvenue
€€€

104 Route de Cholet, 49700 **Tel** *02 41 59 22 44*
Map *C3*

A pretty inn situated in this town of roses. The menu offers elaborate savoury preparations, such as langoustines in saffron sauce, or calf's liver in port and pepper sauce. Other dishes revolve around local products, including pikeperch, crayfish, lamb and wild mushrooms.

FONTEVRAUD-L'ABBAYE La Licorne
€€€

Allée Ste-Catherine, 49590 **Tel** *02 41 51 72 49*
Map *C3*

Next to the splendid abbey, this popular restaurant has a pretty courtyard terrace and elegant Louis IV dining room. The menu includes creations such as prawns and basil ravioli in morel sauce and, for dessert, warm chocolate soufflé or pears poached in red wine. Good selection of Saumur wines. Book ahead.

GENNES Auberge du Moulin de Sarré
€

Route de Louerre, 49350 **Tel** *02 41 51 81 32*
Map *C3*

After taking a tour of the 16th-century watermill (the only working one in the region), try either the menu of *fouées* (warm bread puffs made from flour ground at the mill) with fillings such as goat's cheese or *rillettes* (duck pâté), or the fresh trout (caught from the mill itself). Reservations are required.

MONTSOREAU Diane de Méridor
€€€

12 Quai Philippe de Commines, 49730 **Tel** *02 41 51 71 76*
Map *C3*

While dining at Diane de Méridor, you have a view of the château, which was the setting for the celluloid interpretation of *La Dame de Montsoreau* by Alexandre Dumas. Carved out of tufa rock, this restaurant is classic-modern, with exposed beams and an open fireplace. It specializes in freshwater fish dishes cooked to perfection.

SAUMUR Bistrot de la Place
€

16 Place St-Pierre, 49400 **Tel** *02 41 51 13 27*
Map *C3*

Located on a glorious historic square near the town's château, this restaurant provides not just good-quality French cuisine, but also an excellent array of local wines. Menu highlights include caramelized duck breast with lemon and sage. It has a charming terrace for dining in warmer weather that makes it perfect for people-watching. Closed Sun.

Key to Symbols *see back cover flap*

THOUARCÉ Le Relais de Bonnezeaux

Route Angers, 49380 **Tel** *02 41 54 08 33* **Map** *C3*

This large, pleasant dining room is located in a converted railway station overlooking the vineyards – this is sweet-wine country. Imaginative cuisine is created with regional produce in dishes such as eels cooked in Coteaux du Layon, and calf sweetbreads braised in Savennières.

TOURAINE

AMBOISE Le Choiseul

36 Quai C Guinot, 37400 **Tel** *02 47 30 45 45* **Map** *D3*

The Michelin-starred Choiseul is an elegant 18th-century mansion with a pretty garden and views of the Loire from the airy dining room. The sophisticated menu changes seasonally; in spring, a meal might include asparagus; in summer, roast pikeperch with mustard, or *cassoulet* of crayfish. Good Touraine wines and many other regional wines.

BOURGUEIL Le Moulin Bleu

7 Rue du Moulin-Bleu, 37140 **Tel** *02 47 97 73 13* **Map** *D3*

The house at the foot of this pretty blue mill has two vaulted dining rooms where traditional dishes are served in a friendly, convivial atmosphere. The cuisine remains faithful to the region, with Touraine-reared veal served with a Vouvray butter sauce. There are several good Bourgueil producers on the wine list.

CHINON Les Années 30

78 Rue Haute St Maurice, 37500 **Tel** *02 47 93 37 18* **Map** *D3*

The chef at this elegant little eatery, on the way up to the château, has created an exciting menu that changes seasonally. You might sample dishes such as a *tartare* of oysters with a seaweed tempura, pikeperch served with leeks or red peppers flavoured with ginger. Good local wines are available to accompany your meal.

FONDETTES Auberge de Port Vallières

Route de Langeais, 37230 **Tel** *02 47 42 24 04* **Map** *D3*

On the banks of the River Loire, this former fisherman's pub has heaps of rustic charm. Regional dishes, such as beef cooked in Chinon wine and local freshwater fish, are prepared by chef Bruno Leroux. There is also a good choice of local wines.

MONTBAZON Olivier Arlot – La Chancelière

1 Place des Marronniers, 37250 **Tel** *02 47 26 00 67* **Map** *D3*

Modern, sophisticated cuisine prepared with precision and skill is on offer at La Chancelière. This restaurant proposes savoury dishes such as oyster ravioli with a champagne sauce, or pan-fried escalope of *foie gras*. The well-selected wine list features good Vouvray and Bourgueil producers.

LE PETIT PRESSIGNY Restaurant Dallais – La Promenade

11 Rue du Savoureux, 37350 **Tel** *02 47 94 93 52* **Map** *D4*

Located in the village centre, the Michelin-starred Dallais has a striking contemporary decor in the dining room. The cuisine is exceptional. Delicately prepared savoury dishes include roast morel mushrooms, *foie gras* and local green asparagus. The sommelier gives good advice on the wide selection of wines on offer.

ROCHECORBON Les Hautes Roches

86 Quai de la Loire, 37210 **Tel** *02 47 52 88 88* **Map** *D3*

The dining room in this extraordinary château-hotel is decorated in contemporary tones, and the chef serves modern, Michelin-starred cuisine to match, including irresistible dishes, such as a terrine of *lapin*, Racan pigeon with lemon confit, and Grand Marnier soufflé. The cellar has wonderful wines from the best local producers.

SACHÉ Auberge du XII Siècle

1 Rue du Château, 37190 **Tel** *02 47 26 88 77* **Map** *D3*

In a historic building, a stone's throw from the Balzac Museum, is Auberge du XII Siècle. The main dining room has a rustic atmosphere with exposed beams. There is a good choice of fixed-price menus with classic dishes, such as snail Parmentier, roasted bass with purée of artichokes and *foie gras*, and chocolate tart with cherry coulis.

SALBRIS Domaine de Valaudran

Rue de Romorantin, 41300 **Tel** *02 54 97 20 00* **Map** *E3*

Salbris is reputed to be the best place in Sologne to hunt. In season, this restaurant in an 18th-century country house benefits from superb game, which finds its way in dishes such as stuffed pigeon breast with apple sauce. Other fine dishes include bass wrapped in cabbage with a citrus sauce, or scorpion fish with mushrooms, shallots and *foie gras*.

ST-OUEN LES VIGNES L'Aubinière

29 Rue Jules Gautier, 37530 **Tel** *02 47 30 15 29* **Map** *D3*

North of Amboise, this small rustic restaurant opens on to a pretty garden that leads down to the river. Enjoy the creations of chef Jacques Arrayet, who serves outstanding dishes including *foie gras* and lobster, a caramel of beetroot with pistachio oil, and steamed bass with herbs and Paimpol beans.

TOURS L'Atelier Gourmand

37 Rue Etienne Marcel, 37000 **Tel** *02 47 38 59 87*

€

Map D3

A charming small restaurant in a 15th-century building in the old part of Tours. Fabrice Bironneau presents a competitively priced, interesting menu. Seasonal dishes include goat's cheese and red pepper flan, veal sautéed with garlic and black olives, and fondant of chocolate. Warm, homely ambience.

TOURS L'Arche de Meslay

14 Rue des Ailes in Parçay Meslay, 37210 **Tel** *02 47 29 00 07*

€€

Map D3

Worth the 9-km (6-mile) detour from the city centre, this refined, contemporary restaurant has a kitchen in full view. Watch the chef prepare a delicious lobster salad with chipped vegetables, *bouillabaisse tourangelle* (a regional fish stew) or bass with Indian spices.

TOURS Charles Barrier

101 Avenue de la Tranchee, 37100 **Tel** *02 47 54 20 39*

€€€€

Map D3

This restaurant, on the north bank of the river, has been an institution in Tours since 1870. The cuisine is inventive and the menu changes regularly. If you want a cheaper meal try the adjacent annexe, Le Bistrot de la Tranchee. Closed Sat lunch and Sun.

VEIGNÉ Moulin Fleuri

Route de Ripault, 37250 **Tel** *02 47 26 01 12*

€

Map D3

Classic cuisine is beautifully presented by the chef in an ancient watermill on the banks of the River Indre. The menu focuses on local ingredients such as Racan pigeon, *rillettes de Tours*, *andouillette* (chitterling sausage), goat's cheese and Richelieu truffles. There is also a decent children's menu.

VILLANDRY L'Etape Gourmande La Giraudière

Route de Druye, 37510 **Tel** *02 47 50 08 60*

€€

Map D3

There are three dining rooms with original features in this 17th-century farmhouse near the château. Domaine de la Giraudière is a working farm of mainly goats, a fact that is reflected in the menu – goat's cheese marinated in herbs, kid goat and goat's milk fromage for dessert. Home-produced pâtés, charcuterie and tarts.

VOUVRAY La Cave Martin

66 Rue de la Vallée Coquette, 37210 **Tel** *02 47 52 62 18*

€

Map D3

In this famous wine village, this restaurant carved into the tufa rock has a rustic menu with *andouillettes* (chitterling sausages), duck breast and confit, and a decent choice of salads. Start with a glass of local fizzy wine, and finish with an unctuous sweet Vouvray to accompany your dessert. Book ahead.

BLESOIS AND ORLEANAIS

BEAUGENCY Le P'tit Bateau

54 Rue du Pont, 45190 **Tel** *02 38 44 56 38*

€€

Map E3

Near the château, Le P'tit Bateau is the most appealing restaurant in town. Popular with locals, it offers traditional cuisine in a rustic dining room with exposed beams and open fireplace. Fresh fish, game (in season) and wild mushrooms all feature on the menu. There is a courtyard terrace for alfresco dining on sunny days. Book ahead.

BLOIS Au Rendez-Vous des Pêcheurs

27 Rue du Foix, 41000 **Tel** *02 54 74 67 48*

€€€

Map E3

This restaurant is famed throughout the region for its menu, which focuses on Loire fish and seafood creations, including pike stuffed with chestnuts, and bream with prawns. There is also Sologne game (in season) and a good selection of wines from the Loire Valley. Book ahead.

BLOIS L'Orangerie du Château

1 Avenue Jean Laigret, 41000 **Tel** *02 54 78 05 36*

€€€€

Map E3

Housed in the 15th-century château's former winter garden, L'Orangerie has a fine setting, which is matched by the outstanding food and wine. The menu features traditional regional favourites, such as roast pikeperch and white asparagus from the Sologne. The dependable wine list includes good Touraine producers.

CHAUMONT-SUR-LOIRE La Madeleine de Proust

33 Rue du Marèchal Leclerc, 41150 **Tel** *02 54 46 41 22*

€

Map D3

This is a traditional kind of rustic village restaurant that may not look much on the outside, but which offers a delightful surprise on the plate. The excellent regional cooking includes treats such as caramelised chicory and goats cheese tart. The low price is an additional bonus. Closed Mon–Tue.

GIEN Côte Jardin

14 Route de Bourges, 45500 **Tel** *02 38 38 24 67*

€€€

Map F3

Book ahead to secure a table at this pleasant and relaxed restaurant, south of the river, it is well known for its high-quality gastronomy. The dishes are seasonal French cuisine, done to perfection. Choice is confined to just two set menus. Despite the name, there is no garden. Closed Tue–Wed.

Key to Price Guide *see p214* **Key to Symbols** *see back cover flap*

LAMOTTE-BEUVRON Hôtel Tatin
€€€

5 Avenue de Vierzon, 41600 **Tel** *02 54 88 00 03*
Map *E3*

This elegant hotel-restaurant serves traditional fare made with fresh local produce. The menu includes *foie gras*, salad of home-made pâté and warm goat's cheese, pikeperch, pigeon, steak and the famous *tarte tatin* (which must be ordered in advance). There is a good selection of quality Sancerre and Cheverny wines.

ORLEANS Chez Eugène
€€

24 Rue Sainte Anne, 45000 **Tel** *02 38 53 82 64*
Map *E2*

This chic restaurant serves delicious, innovative cuisine with Mediterranean touches. It's set in a smart quarter just east of the main shopping street, Rue de la République, in the centre of Orléans. The atmosphere is refined, the service excellent, and the price reasonable for this quality of food.

ORLEANS Le Lift
€€€

20 Place de la Loire, 45000 **Tel** *02 38 53 63 48*
Map *E2*

Chef Philippe Bardau's restaurant is housed in a modern building set in a garden overlooking the city. The tables on the terrace have magnificent views of the Loire river to the south and of old Orléans to the north. The interior design and cuisine are both contemporary and creative. On Sundays, brunch is served between 11am and 3pm.

ROMORANTIN-LANTHENAY Le Lion d'Or
€€€€€

69 Rue Georges-Clemenceau, 41200 **Tel** *02 54 94 15 15*
Map *E3*

This hotel-restaurant is set in a beautiful Renaissance manor house. Classic cuisine is prepared by a talented chef, and the subtle, elegant dishes use the best local game, vegetables and fish according to what is in season. The service is precise and professional, and there is a good selection of wines from all regions.

ST-BENOIT-SUR-LOIRE Grand Saint Benoît
€€

7 Place St André, 45730 **Tel** *02 38 35 11 92*
Map *F3*

This is the renowned restaurant of the Hotel du Labrador, which stands on the village square facing the 11th century church (*see p140*). The decor is contemporary, and the cuisine modern with some reasonably priced set menus on offer. Booking is advised. Closed lunch, Sun evening and Mon.

VENDOME Sous Les Arbres
€€

Route de Tours, Villérable, 41100 **Tel** *02 54 77 16 60*
Map *D3*

Within a short drive south from Vendôme, this lovely restaurant occupies a 19th-century house that has been renovated to modern standards. The cooking is both contemporary and generous. The wine list is small but well chosen, and there's a beautiful terrace on which you can eat on warmer days and evenings. Closed Tue–Wed, Sun pm.

BERRY

BOURGES Le Bourbonnoux
€€

44 Rue Bourbonnoux, 18000 **Tel** *02 48 24 14 76*
Map *F4*

A husband and wife team run this bright restaurant decorated with many ducks. It's both smart and quite fun, with great regional cuisine and good-value menus. The reasonably priced wine list includes local Loire specialities. Le Bourbonnoux is popular with locals as well as tourists so booking in advance is recommended.

BOURGES Le d'Antan Sancerrois
€€€€€

50 Rue Bourbonnoux, 18000 **Tel** *02 48 65 96 26*
Map *F4*

A brilliant restaurant, set on an historic street just down from the cathedral, it is run by two brothers. One cooks, the other looks after customers and selects the wine list. The cuisine is seasonal, wonderfully inventive and beautifully presented. The drinks menu is very good, too.

CHATEAUROUX Le P'tit Bouchon
€

64 Rue Grande, 36000 **Tel** *02 54 61 50 40*
Map *D4*

This cheerful little restaurant is a pleasure, serving good, simple seasonal fare at very reasonable prices. In summer, you can eat on the terrace and watch the world go by. Also a wine bar, its wine list includes hundreds of bottles that can be enjoyed by the glass. Closed Sun–Mon.

DREVANT Le Saint-Jean II
€€

Ilot de la Godine, 18200 **Tel** *02 48 96 39 82*
Map *F4*

Beautifully located by the Cher and its canal, between the town of St-Amand-Montrond and the Château d'Ainay-le-Vieil, this is a charming restaurant. On warm days you can dine on the terrace beside the canal, but the smart dining room also shares the view. The menu is small, with the chef concentrating on seasonal dishes.

LA CHATRE Le Lion d'Argent
€

2 Av du Lion d'Argent, 36400 **Tel** *02 54 48 11 69*
Map *E4*

This former 19th-century coaching inn still serves as a welcoming hotel and also houses a traditional restaurant. Here you can sample French classics, including regional specialities, at a very decent price. The setting is old-fashioned and the place is run with charm.

SANCERRE Auberge la Pomme d'Or €€

Place de la Mairie, 18300 **Tel** *02 48 54 13 30* **Map** *F3*

This small restaurant in a former coaching inn serves classic dishes created with seasonal produce from the region. Enjoy the simplicity of the Chavignol goat's cheese, pikeperch, Sologne pigeon in honey or shredded duck with raspberry vinegar.

SANCERRE La Tour €€€

31 Nouvelle Place, 18300 **Tel** *02 48 54 00 81* **Map** *F3*

This well-liked restaurant has two large dining areas, the room upstairs has views to the vineyards beyond the town. The ambiance is warm, and the cuisine excellent. Often frequented by Sancerre's winemakers, the wine list offers a great range of regional wines. The local cheeses are a highlight too.

THENAY Auberge de Thenay €€

23 Rue Rene d'Helbingue, 36800 **Tel** *02 54 47 99 00* **Map** *E3*

Set in a charming historic building in the village of Thenay, by the Creuse River, is this delightful simple inn. The choice of dishes is limited but none should disappoint. Inside the restaurant diners can see the fireplace where meats are spit-roasted. Frechwater fish also features on the menu, as do delicious local cheeses.

NORTH OF THE LOIRE

CHARTRES Les Feuillantines €€

4 Bourg, 28000 **Tel** *02 37 30 22 21* **Map** *E2*

Located on a steep street descending to the River Eure, Les Feuillantines restaurant is decorated in a simple and minimalist manner. It benefits from having a delightful terrace for fair-weather dining. Les Feuillantines is a good place to sample well-executed and well-priced French cuisine such as *foie gras* or chocolate mousse.

CHARTRES Le Parvis €€

13 Place de la Cathédrale, 28000 **Tel** *02 37 21 12 12* **Map** *E2*

Le Parvis offers the choice of dining in a provincial-style restaurant or al fresco on the terrace, the latter has fantastic views of the cathedral. Food is also served in the atmospheric cellars, of which there are three levels. The menu features French cuisine and is great value for money. There are jazz evenings and also rooms tfor overnight stays.

CHÂTEAUDUN Aux Trois Pastoureaux €€

31 Rue André Gillet, 28200 **Tel** *02 37 45 74 40* **Map** *E2*

The dining room of this well-established restaurant has warm tones; the walls are hung with paintings by a local artist. The chef's dishes combine classic produce and contemporary tastes. Try the melon accompanied by duck breast with *foie gras*, braised veal, and the chocolate and raspberry tart. Good choice of wines by the glass.

EVRON Relais du Gué de Selle €€

Route de Mayenne, 53600 **Tel** *02 43 91 20 00* **Map** *C2*

Located in the heart of the Mayenne countryside, this hotel-restaurant, in a typical old farmhouse, serves regional classic dishes that retain a pleasant rusticity. Locally sourced ingredients, such as Ernée *foie gras* served with a gelée flavoured with sweet Layon wine, Loué chicken and Maine rib of beef are some of the specialities.

LAVAL Le Bistro de Paris €€€

67 Rue du Val de Mayenne, 53000 **Tel** *02 43 56 98 29* **Map** *B2*

Set in a charming old house in the city centre, close to the Mayenne River, the interior of this restaurant looks like the architype of a smart, French Art Nouveau bistro, which is, of course, what it is. The cuisine is refined, and the prices not unreasonable for the quality. The service is excellent and the cheese selections is highly recommended.

LE MANS Le Nez Rouge €

107 Grand-Rue, 72000 **Tel** *02 43 24 27 26* **Map** *C2*

A charming timbered restaurant in the medieval part of Le Mans. The chef has trained in some of the best restaurants in France, and his dishes are based on the freshest produce, such as lobster and veal sweetbreads. The dining room is cosy and intimate, and there is a terrace across the road. Excellent value. Book ahead.

LE MANS Le Beaulieu €€€€

34 bis Place de la République, 72000 **Tel** *02 43 87 78 37* **Map** *C2*

Located in the town center, this gastronomic restaurant has a menu that changes with the seasons. To enjoy the exquisite cuisine by chef Olivier Broussard there is the seven-course Chef's Surprise menu. Diners looking for a more affordable price should try the special weekday lunchtime offers.

MALICORNE-SUR-SARTHE La Petite Auberge €€

5 Place Duguesclin, 72270 **Tel** *02 43 94 80 52* **Map** *C3*

In summer, you can dine on the riverside terrace and watch the boats go by; in winter, take refuge around the magnificent medieval fireplace. Enjoy classic cuisine with an innovative twist, including delicious gratin of scallops with smoked salmon or perfectly cooked steak with a red Bourgueil wine sauce.

Key to Price Guide *see p214* **Key to Symbols** *see back cover flap*

SOLESMES Grand Hôtel de Solesmes

🅿️ €€€

16 Place Dom-Gueranger, 72300 **Tel** *02 43 95 45 10*

Map *C2*

This venerable old inn stands opposite the entrance to Solesmes's famed abbey. It offers a range of set menus catering to different budgets and tastes, options from these include *fricaséed* snails and prawns in seaweed butter. The modern version of classic French dishes are expertly cooked, and the staff are very friendly.

LOIRE-ATLANTIQUE AND THE VENDEE

CHALLANS Château de la Vérie

€€€

Route de Soullans, 85300 **Tel** *02 51 35 33 44*

Map *A4*

A couple of kilometres (1.5 miles) south of Challans, this little château is home to both a hotel and a restaurant. The property is set in delightful grounds and the dining rooms have retained their period charm. Langoustine *tartare*, oysters and artichokes all feature on the menu, where the emphasis is on seasonal produce.

CLISSON La Bonne Auberge

📋 🖼️ €€€

1 Rue Olivier de Clisson, 44190 **Tel** *02 40 54 01 90*

Map *B4*

This comfortable auberge in the city centre has three attractive dining areas, including one set in a conservatory with garden views. The specialities include pan-fried *foie gras*, sea bass with truffle-flavoured potatoes, and tart of ceps and scallops. The desserts are delicate, and the Muscadet is good.

LA ROCHE SUR YON Le Rivoli

🍴📋🖼️ €€

31 Boulevard Aristide-Briand, 85000 **Tel** *02 51 37 43 41*

Map *B4*

Located in the heart of the Vendée, this restaurant overflows with originality. The decor is colourful, and the cuisine is refined yet simple. Dishes include a *tartare* of fish with coriander, venison in red wine, and a delicious strawberry crumble. The wine list is simple but well chosen.

LES SABLES D'OLONNE La Pilotine

€€€

7 Promenade Georges Clemenceau, 85100 **Tel** *02 51 22 25 25*

Map *A4*

At this stylish little restaurant facing the town hall, the menu is based around the catch of the day. The chef prepares inventive fish and shellfish dishes, such as casserole of lobster and Noirmoutier potatoes, or salad of langoustines with asparagus and marinated *foie gras* "chips". Be sure to book ahead.

NANTES La Cigale

🍴🍷🖼️ €

4 Place Graslin, 44000 **Tel** *02 51 84 94 94*

Map *B3*

This ornate Belle Epoque brasserie dates from 1895, when it was frequented by celebrated writers and the Nantes elite. The quality of the cuisine matches the exceptional interior. Oysters, *carpaccio* (thin, quasi-raw slices) of salmon and beef *à la plancha* (cooked on a hot plate) are among the dishes to try. Extensive wine list. Open all day.

NANTES Les Enfants Terribles

€

4 Rue Fénelon, 44000 **Tel** *02 40 47 00 38*

Map *B3*

This is a warm, welcoming and artistically decorated old apartment in the heart of Nantes, just a short walk west of the Château des Ducs de Bretagne. The cooking is excellent and the menu inexpensive. There are occasional daily specials to keep things fresh. Dishes from the main menu can vary from duck spring rolls to monkfish casserole.

NANTES La Poissonerie

📋 €€€

4 Rue Léon Maître, 44000 **Tel** *02 40 47 79 50*

Map *B3*

Not a fish shop, as the name implies and the nautical decoration emphasizes, but a lovely fish restaurant. Located in the eastern end of the Ile Feydeau quarter, prices vary considerably depending on the seafood you opt for – expect to pay a premium for the lobster. Overall, the quality and value are excellent. Closed middle weeks of Aug.

NANTES L'Atlantide

🔖📋🍷 €€€€€

16 Quai Ernest-Renaud, 44100 **Tel** *02 40 73 23 23*

Map *B3*

One of the very best places to eat in town, with a dining room on the fourth floor that offers a superb view. Exotic, innovative cuisine is served up by the well-travelled chef, whose menu includes ray with mango and avocado, and red tuna with a bergamot sauce. Remarkable wine list.

PORNIC La Poissonnerie du Môle

€

30 Rue de la Marine, 44210 **Tel** *02 40 21 04 86*

Map *A3*

Located a short walk from the central inner port is this wonderul little fish restaurant. Its compact menu focuses on deliciously fresh ingredients with main courses such as a duo of shark and swordfish. The welcome is warm and genuine, and so is the atmosphere. This is a popular *poissonnerie*, so it's best to book ahead.

ST-JOACHIM La Mare aux Oiseaux

🔖🍴🅿️🍷🖼️ €€€€

162 Île de Fédrun, 44720 **Tel** *02 40 88 53 01*

Map *A3*

Attractive auberge in the centre of the Marais de Brière. The spontaneous and imaginative cuisine uses the best from the marshlands – pigeon, eel, duck, frog and wild mint – and from the nearby sea – sardines, crab and edible seaweed. The specialities include pigeon and frogs' legs in mint sauce.

SHOPS AND MARKETS

Bourges shop sign

Shopping for specialities of the Loire Valley is always a pleasure, and the region's towns and cities also offer many opportunities to purchase the goods that France is famous for – fashion accessories and clothes, kitchenware, porcelain and crystal, and particularly food. Specialist shops are everywhere, and visiting the region's open-air and indoor food markets gives the visitor a wonderful opportunity to buy a vast range of local produce and culinary specialities. This section provides guidelines on shopping in the Loire Valley, and pages 222–3 show some of the best regional foods, wines and other specialist goods available.

Chocolates on display in La Livre Tournois, a *confiserie* in Tours

OPENING HOURS

Small food shops in the Loire region open early – around 7:30 or 8am – and close at around 12:30 for lunch, then reopen at about 3:30 or 4pm until 7 or 8pm. Other small shops are open from roughly 2 to 6:30 or 7pm on Mondays (many remain closed all day), 9am to noon and 2 to 6:30 or 7pm, Tuesday to Saturday. Small supermarkets generally take a long lunch break, but department stores and large supermarkets do not close for lunch. Sales are usually held in late-June and January.

Open-air food markets take place one, two or three mornings a week, often including Sundays, while the large indoor food markets *(les halles)* are usually open from Tuesday to Saturday for the same hours as small food shops. This guide lists the market days for each town featured.

SPECIALIST SHOPS

Despite the mushrooming of supermarkets and large superstores, small specialist shops have continued to thrive in France, and they add enormously to the pleasure of shopping trips. Food shops in particular often specialize in a single theme. *Boulangeries* sell fresh bread, but they may be *boulangeries–pâtisseries*, which means that tempting cakes and pastries will also be on offer. *Traiteurs* sell prepared dishes, while *épiceries* are small grocers. *Crémeries* specialize in dairy products, *fromageries* sell only cheese and *charcuteries* specialize in cooked and cured meats with a few prepared, cold dishes. An *épicerie fine* focuses on high-class groceries and is a good source of gifts to take home, such as local mustards or vinegars in attractive jars or bottles.

An *alimentation générale* (general food store) may have a self-service system. In small villages, this is sometimes the only shop, although fresh bread will always be available either there or from the local café. A travelling van also supplies fresh bread in some regions.

Cleaning products are bought in a *droguerie*, hardware from a *quincaillerie*, books from a *librairie* and stationery (much of which is particularly stylish in France) from a *papeterie*.

The area has some specialist shops that focus on a single product, such as umbrellas or walking sticks, chess sets or stamps, or in a single field such as militaria or natural history books. Their owners are usually extremely knowledgeable about their particular subject, and they enjoy sharing it if you show an interest. Antique shops *(magasins d'antiquités)* tend to be very pricey. Head instead for a *brocante* (bric-à-brac shop), or try hunting for bargains in local flea markets.

TASTING AND BUYING WINE

The Loire Valley is famous for its wines and the region is scattered with producers.

Signs beside the road saying *"dégustation"* mean that tastings are available at the winery. It is important to remember that the local *vigneron* will expect a modest purchase of a few bottles after you have drunk several experimental glasses. In Saumur it is possible to tour the wine growers' own cellars with the minimum of sales pressure. Best of all, visit the *Maisons des Vins de Loire* in most major towns, where the information and often free tastings are very helpful and interesting.

Sign for a *charcuterie*

HYPERMARKETS AND CHAIN STORES

Superstores and the larger hypermarkets (*hyper-marchés*) are usually situated on the outskirts of towns, often as part of a *centre commercial* (shopping complex) that may also include small boutiques, a DIY outlet and a petrol station. Many of these big stores belong to the Auchan, Carrefour or Super U chains.

The old-style *grand magasin*, or department store, found in the region's towns has generally either been converted into a series of boutiques or taken over and modernized by the up-market Nouvelles Galeries or Printemps national chains. These chic stores are good for clothes, accessories and perfumes. The popular Monoprix stores are worth visiting if you are looking for inexpensive stationery, lingerie and cosmetics. Many of them also have a reasonably priced food department.

A flower-seller and customer at the village market in Luynes

MARKETS

Open-air food markets are one of the delights of the Loire Valley. Their offerings are mouth-watering: mounds of succulent vegetables, *charcuterie* specialities, goats' cheeses and plump poultry and game. Of this excellent fare, most is produced locally, often in small-scale market gardens owned and worked by the stall-holder. Produce that has

Fresh local produce on sale in the market in Saumur's place St-Pierre

been grown locally is labelled *du pays*. Look out for unusual specialities, such as the strangely-shaped squashes and pumpkins, wild mushrooms and flavoured honeys. Honey stalls often sell honey-flavoured confectionery and honey soap, too. Spice and herb stalls are also interesting, providing a wealth of gift ideas. Some markets have stalls selling clothes or shoes and leather goods. Look out also for local craft work.

Flea markets (*marchés aux puces*) are regular events in many towns and are often held in small towns and villages in countryside districts during the summer holiday season.

VAT REBATES

Since the advent of the Single European Market, rebates of value-added tax (*taxe à la valeur ajoutée* or *TVA*) are only available to those not resident in a European Union country. They apply only to purchases totalling at least €175 in a single shop, on the same day, and taken out of the EU within three months. The export sales form you receive on purchase must be handed to the customs officer as you leave the EU. Reimbursements usually go directly to your bank. Not all articles qualify for rebates. In stores frequented by foreign tourists, staff are familiar with the process.

Local goats' cheese for sale in Amboise market

What to Buy in the Loire Valley

The best buys in the Loire tempt the eye as well as the stomach. A gourmet's paradise, the food shops and open-air markets of the region attract visitors with their delicious scents and sights. Local producers are justifiably proud of their goods and pack them with respect, in attractive crates or pottery jars. But gourmet treats are not the only local goods worth looking for. The region has long been famous for its china from Gien and for the fabric and lace of the Touraine, evocative of the remarkable history of the Loire.

A beautifully wrapped package of sweets

CONFECTIONERY

Local confectionery specialities make good gifts to take home, especially when they are so prettily packaged. The region is well-known for its wide range of sweets, which are available from tearooms and specialist confectioners, and many towns also have their own mouth-watering treats.

Forestines from Bourges

Macaroon biscuits from Cormery

Pruneaux fourrés, prunes stuffed with marzipan

Chocolates resembling traditional slate tiles

Fruit-flavoured sweets

SOUVENIRS

The châteaux and museums of the Loire Valley have well-stocked shops that sell an array of appealing souvenirs. In addition to the usual booklets and posters, many sell gifts with an historical theme, such as replica playing cards or tapestries. Wine bought direct from a local vineyard is another special souvenir (*see pp30–31*).

Playing cards with historical figures

Wine made at Chenonceau

THE FLAVOURS OF THE LOIRE

It is impossible to visit the Loire without being amazed by the abundance of delicious food. Much comes perfectly packaged for travelling. Near the game-filled forests of the Berry, you can buy jars and tins of pâtés and terrines. Goats' cheeses are moulded into a variety of shapes, and the firmer varieties travel successfully. Heather honey from Berry's heathland and wine vinegars from Orléans are also specialities of the region.

Confiture de vin, jelly made from wine

Poulain chocolate made in Blois

Pickled samphire

Sainte Maure

Goats' cheese

Sea salt from Guérande

Crémant de Loire, sparkling wine

Cotignac, quince jelly from Orléans

LOCAL CRAFTS

Traditional crafts survive throughout the Loire Valley, and you can often visit craftsmen and women at work in their studios. Many towns in the region have long been renowned for their craft specialities, such as Malicorne for its lattice-work faïence, Villaines-les-Rochers for its baskets or Gien for its china.

Pottery from La Borne in Berry

Gien china side plate

Wicker basket from Villaines

Dinner plate from Gien

ACTIVITIES IN THE LOIRE VALLEY

A holiday in the Loire Valley can combine the cultural highlights of visits to the spectacular châteaux with enjoyment of the region's wealth of natural environments. The gentle terrain and beautiful forests are perfect for exploration on foot, horseback or mountain bike, and the clear waters of the lakes and rivers – not to mention the spectacular Atlantic coastline – are enticing spots for swimming or boating. Here is a selection of the activities on offer in the region. For more information contact the regional and county *(département)* tourist boards *(see p227)*, which focus on leisure activities, or the local tourist offices in towns and villages.

WALKING

The Loire Valley is renowned for its many accessible and scenic walks, which are called *Randonnées (see pp28–9)*. Although these routes are generally clearly signposted, it is a good idea to carry a large-scale map or a Topo-Guide. These are only available in French but do contain maps, a description of the itinerary, details of sites of architectural or natural interest to be found along the route, an estimate of the time it will take you to complete the walk and the addresses of local hotels, restaurants, hostels and camp sites. Most Topo–Guides cost around €15. A complete list is available from the **Fédération Française de la Randonnée Pédestre**.

You will never be more than a day's walk away from a town or village where you will be able to find food and accommodation, so it is not necessary to carry a large amount of equipment, but, as always, you should wear good, strong walking shoes. Remember that some paths can be damp and muddy during the spring and autumn.

CYCLING

The generally flat landscape of the Loire Valley makes it perfect for cyclists. Because many of the châteaux are so near to each other, it is easy to visit several by bicycle in only a few days. Mountain bike enthusiasts will enjoy riding the clearly signposted paths through the region's forests and nature reserves.

Motorways and some major roads are forbidden to cyclists; the sign has a white background with a red border and a cyclist in the middle. Cycle lanes, when they exist, are compulsory. Bicycles must have two working brakes, a bell, a red rear reflector and yellow reflectors on the pedals, as well as a white front light and a red rear light after dark. It is also advisable to wear a helmet and to carry essential spare parts in case of breakdown. While bicycle shops are common, foreign spare parts may not be available.

It is possible to hire touring bicycles and mountain bikes throughout the region. Local tourist offices will be able to provide you with a list of cycle hire centres.

Transporting your bicycle on local trains is free in most cases, although on major train routes the SNCF requires you to register your bicycle and will levy a small charge. The booklet *Train et Vélo*, available at most train stations, gives more information on carrying bikes on trains, and you can also visit the useful website, www.velo.sncf.com *(see p240)*.

Among the many excellent itineraries for cyclists, the most ambitious is *Loire à Vélo*, a trail tracking the River Loire from Cuffy, near Nevers, to Saint-Nazaire. The route has a dedicated website, www. cycling-loire.com. There are numerous bike hire outlets along the trail, with the possibility of one-way rentals. Hotels, camp sites and *chambres d'hôte* marked with the *Accueil Vélo* sign welcome cyclists and will forward luggage to the next stop if required. A handbook with maps and accommodation listings is available from local tourist offices or seek out specialist information via the regional and county *(département)* tourist boards *(see pp227 and 240)*.

The **Fédération Française de Cyclisme** is the umbrella organization for more than 2,800 cycling clubs in France. They can provide advice and cycling itineraries if you contact them well in advance.

Cycling, one of the most pleasant ways to see the Loire Valley

A riverside pony trek in the beautiful Vendée region

HORSE RIDING AND PONY TREKKING

Horse lovers will enjoy a visit to the National Riding School in the equestrian town of Saumur, where the world-famous Cadre Noir riding team perform in regular displays *(see p83)*, or to the national stud farm, Le Haras de Vendée, in La Roche-sur-Yon.

The forests of the Loire Valley, with their well-maintained networks of trails and well-marked bridle paths, are ideal for riding. Topo-Guides are as useful for riders as they are for walkers.

Experienced riders can hire horses by the hour, half-day or day from numerous stables in the region. A sign reading *Loueur d'Equidés* means that horses are for hire without an instructor. If you prefer to be accompanied when riding, you should search out an *Ecole d'Equitation* or a *Centre Equestre* (riding school).

Many stables offer longer treks on horseback, called *randonnées*, which last between a weekend and a week. Small groups are accompanied on the trek by an experienced guide, and accommodation is usually in quite basic hotels or hostels, although some luxury tours are also available.

The rental of old-fashioned horse-drawn caravans is becoming increasingly popular in the Loire Valley. Travellers sleep in the carriage overnight and journey at a slow, leisurely pace during the day. Generally caravans come in two sizes: the smaller one carries four adults or two adults and three children; the other carries six to eight people. There are also larger, open wagons, driven by a guide, that are used for group excursions of up to 15 people.

FISHING

The rivers of the Loire Valley are teeming with freshwater fish, including bream, bullhead, carp, grey mullet, perch, pike, roach and zander. There are also trout in some of the faster-running tributaries of the Loire.

Freshwater fish

To fish in private waters, you must make arrangements with the owner. To fish in state–controlled waters, you must buy a permit, which is available from many tackle shops. Applicants must provide proof that they are a member of an angling association at home and pay a fishing tax.

There are two kinds of fishing tax: the basic tax covers fishing with worms in rivers that do not have trout runs; the special tax covers spinning, fly-fishing, and fish-bait fishing in all rivers, including those with trout. You cannot fish more than half an hour before sunrise or after sunset. There are set seasons for certain fish and limits on their size.

The **Fédération Nationale pour la Pêche en France**, which represents more than 4,000 local fishing associations, provides information on the regulations regarding fresh-water fishing and the starting dates of the different fishing seasons in France. Ocean fishing is free from any tax as long as you do not use nets, although there are restrictions on the equipment a boat can carry.

Fly–fishing on the tranquil River Loir

GOLF

Evidence of the growing popularity of golf in France can be seen throughout the Loire Valley, which has many beautiful and challenging courses. Some of the region's golf courses are set in the grounds of châteaux. Details of specific courses and regulations are available from the **Fédération Française de Golf**.

In the Loiret, many courses around Orléans have joined up to provide a golf pass that combines greens fees for the different courses and the added option of accommodation in nearby two- or three-star hotels (see the website www.golf tourismloiret.com). This is just one of such deals on the website catering to golfing tourists.

A similar deal is available in the Western Loire, where a pass offers reductions at golf courses near Nantes such as Golf Nantes Erdre (tel 02 40 59 21 21) and Golf Nantes Carquefou (tel 02 40 52 73 74). Contact the Nantes tourist office (see p231) or the participating golf courses for more information.

BOATING AND WATER SPORTS

Because the Loire Valley is criss-crossed with beautiful rivers, most visitors cannot resist the temptation to take at least one boat trip. A wide variety of short excursions are available from riverside *ports de plaisance* (marinas) throughout the Loire region, and in general they do not require advance booking.

The marshes of the Marais Poitevin *(see pp182–5)* are best viewed from its canal network in a *barque* (the traditional, flat-bottomed boat).

One option is to base your entire visit on the water by renting a houseboat or a cruiser for a period of a few days or for one or two weeks. Boats of different sizes and styles are available, from old-fashioned canal boats to sophisticated modern cruisers. Most prices are for round trips and include bedding, kitchen equipment and full training, and it may also be possible to rent bicycles or canoes, or to make a one-way *(simple)* trip. Further information is available from the main tourist offices.

If you are looking for a more adventurous way of enjoying the region's rivers, try canoeing or kayaking. It is best to take a guided tour. Although a river may look calm, there can be dangerous undercurrents and obstacles. **Fédération Française de Canoë-Kayak** can help to provide information.

Kayaking on the River Mayenne

There are good activity centres beside many of the rivers and lakes in the Loire Valley, and there may also be facilities for renting pedaloes, canoes and yachts – some centres even offer water-skiing. A good place to source information on sailing and surfing is the **Fédération Française de Voile**. There are also many Atlantic resorts where visitors are able to hire windsurfing equipment.

Swimmers should stay in the approved areas. While the sand banks may look inviting, there are risks from strong currents and shifting sands. Further information on water safety is given on pages 234–5.

Windsurfing at La Tranche-sur-Mer on the Atlantic Coast

THE LOIRE FROM THE AIR

One of the most luxurious ways to see the Loire Valley is from a hot-air balloon (*montgolfière* in French). There are daily flights in the summer, weather permitting, from Tours, Nantes and Amboise. **France Montgolfières** will put together custom-made excursions.

You can also take a tour in a helicopter or light aircraft. In addition to major airports at Tours and Nantes, there are many other airfields throughout the region. The tourist offices provide complete information. Flying lessons are also available at some of these centres. Learning to fly in France can be much cheaper than elsewhere. Details can be obtained from the **Fédération Française Aéronautique**. Visitors interested in gliding or hang-gliding should contact the **Fédération Française de Vol Libre**.

Ballooning over Le Plessis-Bourré in Anjou

DIRECTORY

SERVICES LOISIRS ACCUEIL

Cher
5 rue de Séraucourt,
18014 Bourges.
Tel 02 48 48 00 18.

Eure-et-Loir
10 rue Docteur Maunoury, 28000 Chartres.
Tel 02 37 84 01 01.

Indre
Centre Colbert, place Eugène Rolland Bat 1, 36003 Châteauroux.
Tel 02 54 27 70 49.

Indre-et-Loire
Val de Loire Tourisme, 75 av de la République, 37714 Chambray-les-Tours. *Tel 02 47 27 27 31.*

Loire-Atlantique
11 rue du Château de l'Eraudière, 44306 Nantes.
Tel 02 51 72 95 31.

Loiret
8 rue d'Escures, 45000 Orléans.
Tel 02 38 62 04 88.

Mayenne
84 av Robert Buron, 53003 Laval.
Tel 08 20 15 30 53.

Sarthe
31 rue Edgar Brandt, 72000 Le Mans.
Tel 02 43 40 22 60.

WALKING

Fédération Française de la Randonnée Pédestre
64 rue du Dessous des Berges, 75013 Paris.
Tel 01 44 89 93 93.
www.ffrandonnee.fr

CYCLING

Fédération Française de Cyclisme
Bâtiment Jean Monnet, 5 rue de Rome, 93561 Rosny-sous-Bois Cedex.
Tel 01 49 35 69 00.
www.ffc.fr

HORSE RIDING

Fédération Française d'Equitation
81–83 av Edouard Vaillant, 92517 Boulogne Billancourt **Tel** 01 58 17 58 17. **www**.ffe.com

FISHING

Fédération Nationale pour la Pêche en France
17 rue Bergère, 75009 Paris. **Tel** 01 48 24 96 00. **www**.federationpeche.fr

GOLF

Fédération Française de Golf
68 rue Anatole France, 92300 Levallois Perret.
Tel 01 41 49 77 00.
www.ffgolf.org

BOATING AND WATERSPORTS

Fédération Française de Canoë-Kayak
87 quai de la Marne, 94344 Joinville le Pont Cedex. **Tel** 01 45 11 08 50. **www**.ffcanoe.asso.fr

Fédération Française de Voile
17 rue Henri-Bocquillon, 75015 Paris.
Tel 01 40 60 37 00.
www.ffvoile.org

THE LOIRE FROM THE AIR

Fédération Française Aéronautique (FFA)
155 av de Wagram, 75017 Paris. **Tel** 01 44 29 92 00. **www**.ff.aero.fr

Fédération Française de Vol Libre
4 rue de Suisse, 06000 Nice. **Tel** 04 97 03 82 82 **www**.ffvl.fr

France Montgolfières
24 rue Nationale, 41400 Montrichard.
Tel 02 54 32 20 48.
www.france-montgolfieres.com

SURVIVAL
GUIDE

PRACTICAL INFORMATION

The Loire Valley is very well prepared to meet the practical needs of its many visitors, providing accommodation ranging from five-star hotels and private châteaux to small camp sites, as well as a selection of excellent restaurants. Because of the profusion of places of great historical, aesthetic or natural interest, from stunning châteaux and cathedrals to windswept Atlantic beaches and wild marshlands, it is a good idea to draw up

FNOTSI

National logo for tourist information

a list of priority sites you would like to visit and activities you want to experience before you travel. Also, check the entries in this guide of the places you plan to visit, or their websites, to make sure they won't be closed for seasonal breaks or for restoration work.With a wide variety of both outdoor and indoor pursuits available, the Loire Valley has something to offer all visitors. The following tips and suggestions will help you make the most of your visit.

Sun seekers enjoying the beach at La Baule

WHEN TO GO

As elsewhere in France, the peak holiday period in the Loire Valley is from mid-June to the end of August, when the region's many festivals and *son et lumière* shows are in full swing *(see p39).* On the downside, main attractions may be crowded and inland temperatures can soar into an uncomfortable range – the maximum temperature can reach up to 38 °C (100 °F). In May, September and October, the weather is generally mild and sunny, although you may need an umbrella; November through to April are the rainiest months. When packing, think of layers of clothing you can easily add or remove during the day. While the winters are warmer than in Paris, they are still grey, cold and often wet. The advantage of this season, however, is having the famous châteaux that remain open, practically to yourself.

VISAS AND PASSPORTS

There are no visa requirements for citizens of the European Union. Tourists from the United States, Canada, Australia and New Zealand who are staying in France for less than 90 days need not apply for a visa. After 90 days, a *visa de long séjour* is required. Visitors from Non-EU countries should request visa information from the French authorities in their own country before departure. Those intending to spend a good length of time in other European countries belonging to the Schengen agreement may want to apply for a 3-, 6- or 12-month Schengen visa, instead of obtaining individual visas for each country.

CUSTOMS INFORMATION

There is no limit to the amount of money visitors may take in or out of France. However, if you are carrying cash worth more than €10,000 you should declare it to French customs. There are no longer restrictions on the quantities of duty-paid and VAT-paid goods you are allowed to take from one EU country to another, as long as you are over 18 and the goods are for your own use (not for resale). Customs officers may ask you to prove that the goods are for your personal use if they exceed 10 litres of spirits, 90 litres of wine, 110 litres of beer and 800 cigarettes.

If you are resident outside the EU, you can reclaim the TVA (VAT or sales tax) on certain goods, as long as you spend more than €175 (including tax) in the same shop in one day (exceptions are food and drink, medicines, tobacco, cars and motorbikes).

Ask for *un bordereau de vente à l'exportation* (an export sales form) when making your purchases. It consists of two sheets that must be signed by the retailer and yourself. Present both form and goods at customs when leaving the EU. On returning home, send the pink sheet back to the retailer (who must receive it within six months of the sale), and the refund will be sent on to you, usually via your bank.

French perfumes, available tax-free

◁ **Château de Noirmoutier viewed from the quayside**

Tourist information office in Fontenay-le-Comte

TOURIST INFORMATION

Most towns have a tourist information office, known either as the *Syndicat d'Initiative* or the **Office de Tourisme**. This guide provides the address, telephone number and website of the tourist office in each town featured in its pages. Smaller villages often have inter-communal offices and websites. Tourist offices supply free maps, advice on accommodation (which can include booking hotels), and offer information on regional recreational and cultural activities, as well as details on upcoming concerts, festivals and other events. For a list of the main branches, *see p233*. You can also obtain details from French Government Tourist Offices before leaving your own country.

Local papers and magazines can provide details of festivals and sporting events as well as the regional weather forecast. They are available at newsagents *(maisons de la presse)* and some tobacconists' shops *(tabacs)*.

ADMISSION PRICES

Churches and cathedrals sometimes ask for a donation or charge a small admission fee to visit cloisters, bell towers and cyrpts. Museums, attractions and châteaux generally charge admission, from around €3 to €20. There are numerous special passes for museums and monuments, generally available from local tourist offices. In some cases,

online discounts are offered if you book in advance. Some museums and monuments are free for one day a month, usually the first Sunday; some may also offer reductions on particular days. Call ahead or check the relevant website before you depart.

There are usually discounts available for students who have valid International Student Identity Cards (ISIC) *(see p232)*. Anyone aged under 18 years of age can also be eligible for a price reduction, and EU citizens under 25 are admitted free to French national monuments. A few sites offer discounts for seniors too.

OPENING HOURS

Most shops, banks, museums and attractions are open from 8:30 or 9am until noon, and from 2 or 3pm until 4:30pm (shops usually stay open longer until 6:30 or 7:30pm), Tuesday to Saturday. In larger towns, however, many shops, chain stores and supermarkets are open all day, as are the more popular museums and châteaux, especially in the summer. Restaurants may close for one day a week, so do check before setting off *(see pp208–19)*.

Off season, some seaside resorts, as well as many châteaux, smaller sites and museums, close down; telephone ahead or check the website for details.

Cathedrals and churches open daily but may shut for lunch or be closed to visitors during religious services. National museums and sights

normally close on Tuesdays, with a few exceptions that close on Mondays. Opening times can also vary considerably by season, especially for country châteaux, estates and gardens. Most are closed on Christmas Day and New Year's Day, and many also close on the public holidays of 1 May and 1 and 11 November.

ETIQUETTE AND LANGUAGE

It is important to respect the French rituals of politeness. When you are introduced to someone, it is correct to shake hands with them. In shops, say *bonjour* to the assistant before asking for what you want, and then *merci* when you receive your change and finally *au revoir, bonne journée* (good-bye, have a nice day) when you depart. The usual greeting among friends of either gender is generally two or three 'air' kisses on the cheek.

Particularly in smaller communities, all efforts by English speakers to make enthusiastic use of their French, however limited, and to show a real interest in the area will be met with encouragement by the locals.

When visiting a church or religious institution, dress respectfully (avoid short skirts and shorts and bare shoulders).

Smoking in France is banned inside bars, restaurants, trains and stations, but still allowed in outdoor cafés. Many hotels are non-smoking or have non-smoking rooms. It's illegal for anyone under 18 to buy cigarettes or alcohol.

Friends greeting each other with two or three kisses

PUBLIC CONVENIENCES

Free public and wheelchair accessible *toilettes publiques* (WCs) are most often found in town centres. They can be located by a *mairie* (town hall) or covered market, in train stations and in public parks. Larger cities have modern, self-cleaning toilets on street corners, which usually charge a small fee. Always carry a small packet of tissues with you.

Museums and shopping centres also have free public toilets, while cafés and bars often reserve their facilities for customers only.

TAXES AND TIPPING

In France, sales (or value-added) taxes are incorporated into prices. For most goods the tax rate is 19.6 per cent; food, books and restaurant meals are taxed at 5.5 per cent. The city tax on accommodation *(taxe de séjour)* can be up to €1.50 per person per day. At cafés and restaurants, a 15 per cent service charge is included in the bill, but an extra few coins for good service is appreciated. Round up taxi fares and tip porters a couple of euros. It's customary to give a small tip to theatre ushers and tour guides.

TRAVELLERS WITH SPECIAL NEEDS

Although the steep, narrow streets in Loire Valley's medieval villages can be a problem, wheelchair access in the region is generally good. A number of châteaux and museums offer special services for disabled visitors; phone ahead and check before your visit. Access to and within hotels and restaurants has greatly improved, and well-marked disabled parking spaces are easy to find.

The **SNCF Accessibilité Service** and **Association des Paralysés de France (APF)** are good resources for practical help and information about facilites. **Les Compagnons du Voyage** provides companions to accompany disabled travellers on train journeys. **Handitec-Handroit's** website (in French) provides information about the legal provisions in France for disabled travellers, and lists other useful websites.

TRAVELLING WITH CHILDREN

The Loire Valley is an ideal destination for families. Many châteaux and gardens have play areas and provide activities for children, as well as offering family discounts. There is a wide range of accommodation for families to choose from: campsites, self-catering *gîtes*, hotels and B&Bs with family or connecting rooms.

Nearly all restaurants offer children's menus (*menus enfants*). Many families choose to eat their biggest meal at lunch because prices are lower, and most restaurants don't serve dinner until 7:30 or 8pm, which may be late for small children.

STUDENT AND SENIOR TRAVELLERS

Students who hold a valid **International Student Identification Card** (ISIC card) can benefit from discounts of 50 per cent or more at museums, theatres, cinemas and many public monuments, as well as the same discounts available to everyone in France aged 25 or under.

Senior travellers are eligible for discounts on trains and buses throughout the region and occasionally at museums and monuments; carry

An ISIC international student card

identification just in case. For extensive travel, a senior rail pass (€56; valid for a year) is a worthwhile purchase as it offers savings of 25 to 50 per cent on train tickets. However, for a relatively short visit to the region the best way to save money is through the SNCF Prem's tickets *(see p243)*.

TIME

The Loire Valley is one hour ahead of Greenwich Mean Time (GMT). France is in the same time zone as Germany, Italy, Spain and other Western European countries.

The French use the 24-hour clock (they do not use the am and pm system): after midday, just continue counting 13, 14 and so on to provide the 24-hour clock time. For example, 1pm = 13:00.

ELECTRICITY

The voltage in France is 220 V. The plugs on French electrical appliances have two small round pins; the heavier-duty appliances have two large round pins. Some up-market hotels offer built-in adaptors for shavers only.

Multi-adaptors, which are useful because they have

A family rowing passed the embankment of Arcais harbour in Marais Poitevin

both large and small pins, can be bought at most airports before departure. Standard adaptors can be purchased from most department stores.

CONVERSIONS

Imperial to metric
1 inch = 2.54 centimetres
1 foot = 30 centimetres
1 mile = 1.6 kilometres
1 ounce = 28 grams
1 pound = 454 grams
1 pint = 0.6 litre
1 gallon = 4.6 litres

Metric to imperial
1 millimetre = 0.04 inch
1 centimetre = 0.4 inch
1 metre = 3 feet 3 inches
1 kilometre = 0.6 mile
1 gram = 0.04 ounce
1 kilogram = 2.2 pounds
1 litre = 1.8 pints

RESPONSIBLE TOURISM

With its wide, green spaces and mild climate, the Loire Valley is known as the garden capital of France. As such, the region is dedicated to maintaining its beautiful landscape and is involved with conservation schemes including the Loire Nature scheme, which works to restore the region's river and nature reserves and conserve its biodiversity.

As well as the dozens of parks, formal gardens and vegetable gardens to visit, the region is also home to Europe's first horticultural theme park, **Terra Botanica**, designed to make botany fun and to provide education on the environment.

The area is also a leader in the *bio* (organic) movement. Two organizations, **Biocentre**

and **Bio Pays de la Loire**, provide detailed lists of markets, farms and other suppliers of organic products. Many towns also have a **Bio-coop**, which sell organic food.

The Loire Valley offers visitors the chance to stay and eat on local farms, where families prepare meals using their own produce. An easy way to locate farms that provide these services is through two umbrella organizations: **Accueil Paysan** and **Bienvenue à la Ferme**. Another way to support the local economy is to stay at locally owned B&Bs, *gîtes* or at one of the growing number of eco-lodges. **It's a Green Green World** is a great resource for visitors as it has a comprehensive catalogue of eco-friendly accommodation.

DIRECTORY

CUSTOMS INFORMATION

Info Douane Service
Tel 08 11 20 44 44.
www.douane.gouv.fr

CONSULATES AND EMBASSIES

Australia
4 rue Jean Rey, 75724 Paris. *Tel* 01 40 59 33 00.
www.france.embassy.gov.au

Canada
35 av Montaigne, 75008 Paris. *Tel* 01 44 43 29 00.
www.canada international.gc.ca

Ireland (Eire)
12 Ave Foch 75016.
Tel 01 44 17 67 50.
www.embassyofireland.fr

New Zealand
7ter Rue Léonard de Vinci 75016. *Tel* 01 45 01 43 43. www.nzembassy. com/france

United Kingdom
16 rue d'Anjou, 75008 Paris. *Tel* 01 44 51 31 00.
http://ukinfrance.fco. gov.uk

United States
4 av Gabriel, 75382 Paris.
Tel 01 43 12 22 22.

http://france.us embassy.gov

TOURIST OFFICES

Angers
7 pl Kennedy.
Tel 02 41 23 50 00.
www.angersloire tourisme.com

Blois
23 pl du Château.
Tel 02 54 90 41 41.
www.blois paysdechambord.com

Bourges
21 rue Victor–Hugo.
Tel 02 48 23 02 60.
www.bourges-tourisme. com

Chartres
Pl de la Cathédrale.
Tel 02 37 18 26 26.
www.chartres-tourisme.com

Le Mans
Rue de l'Etoile.
Tel 02 43 28 17 22.
www.lemanstourisme.com

Nantes
2 pl St Pierre.
Tel 08 92 46 40 44.
www.nantes-tourisme.com

Orléans
2 pl de l'Etape.
Tel 02 38 24 05 05.
www.tourisme-orleans.com

Tours
78 rue Bernard Palissy.
Tel 02 47 70 37 37.
www.tours-tourisme.fr

Tourists Offices Abroad

Australia
Tel (02) 9231 5244.
http://au.franceguide.com

Canada
Tel (514) 288 2026.
http://ca-en.franceguide. com

United Kingdom
Tel 09068 244 123.
http://uk.franceguide.com

United States
http://us.franceguide.com

TRAVELLERS WITH SPECIAL NEEDS

Association des Paralysés de France
Tel 02 51 89 45 00.
www.apf.asso.fr

Handitec-Handriot
www.handroit.com

Les Compagnons du Voyage
Tel 01 58 76 08 33.
www.compagnons.com

SNCF Accessibilité
Tel 08 90 64 06 50.
www.accessibilite.sncf.com

STUDENT TRAVELLERS

International Student Identification Card
www.isic.org

RESPONSIBLE TOURISM

Accueil Paysan
Tel 04 76 43 44 83.
www.accueil-paysan.com

Bienvenue à la Ferme
Tel 01 53 57 11 50.
www.bienvenue-a-la-ferme.com

Biocoop
www.biocoop.fr

Bio Pays de la Loire
Tel 02 41 18 61 40.
www.biopaysdelaloire.fr

Biocentre
Tel 02 38 71 90 52.
www.bio-centre.org

It's a Green Green World
www itsagreengreen world.com

Terra Botanica
Rte de Cantenay-Epinard 49106 Angers.
Tel 02 41 25 00 00.
www.terrabotanica.fr

Personal Security and Health

On the whole, the Loire Valley is a safe place for visitors, but it is always a good idea to take the normal precautions of keeping an eye on your possessions at all times, and avoid isolated and unlit urban areas at night. If you fall ill during your stay, pharmacies are an excellent source of advice, while the emergency services can be contacted for any serious medical problems. Consular offices can also offer help in an emergency.

French police officers

POLICE

Violent crime is not a major problem in the Loire Valley, but as in any destination it is advisable to be on your guard against petty theft, especially in cities. If you are robbed, lose any property or are the victim of any other crime, you must report the incident as soon as possible at the nearest police station (*commissariat de police*). In an emergency, dialling 17 will also connect you to the police, but you will still have to go to a station to make a statement. In small towns and villages, crime is reported to the *gendarmerie*, the force responsible for rural policing.

At police stations you will be required to make a statement, called a *procès verbal (PV)*, listing any lost or stolen items. You will need your passport and, if relevant, your vehicle papers. (Keep copies of your passport and papers in a different part of your luggage, in case the originals are lost or stolen.) Remember to keep a copy of your police statement for your insurance claim.

WHAT TO BE AWARE OF

As with elsewhere, if travelling late at night it is a good idea, especially for women, to remain within busy, well-lit areas and to be careful about talking to, or accompanying, strangers. If you are involved in a dispute or car accident, avoid confrontation, try to stay calm and speak French if you can to diffuse the situation.

Most of the beaches on the Atlantic coast are guarded in the summer by life-guards (*sauveteurs*). There are a number of good family beaches where bathing is not generally dangerous. Look for the system of coloured flags: green flags mean that bathing is permitted and is safe; orange flags warn that bathing may be dangerous and usually that only part of the beach is guarded. The guarded area is marked out by flags, beyond which you should not swim. Dangerous conditions (high waves, shifting sands and strong under-currents) are denoted by red flags, which mean that bathing is strictly forbidden. Many of the region's beaches also display blue flags, used throughout the European Union to indicate cleanliness.

The River Loire and its tributaries may tempt summer bathers but, generally, avoid the temptation, as treacherous currents and shifting sands are associated with these rivers.

IN AN EMERGENCY

The phone number for all emergency services is 112, but in practice it is often quicker to call the relevant authority direct on their traditional two-digit numbers. In a medical emergency call the **Service d'Aide Médicale Urgente** (SAMU), who will send an ambulance. However, it can sometimes be faster to call the **Sapeurs Pompiers** (fire service) who also offer first aid and can take you to the nearest hospital. This is particularly true in rural areas, where the fire station is likely to be much closer than the ambulance service based in town. If you do call out an ambulance the paramedics are called *secouristes*.

LOST AND STOLEN PROPERTY

In big cities, try not to carry conspicuous valuables with you and only take as much cash as you will need. In major towns, most multi-storey car parks are kept under surveillance by video cameras. Parking there will reduce the threat of anything being stolen from your car and avoids the risk of parking in an illegal space and being towed away to a police pound.

Police car

Fire engine

Ambulance

For lost or stolen property, it may be worth returning to the police station where you reported the incident to check if they have retrieved anything. In addition, all French town halls have a *Bureau d'Objets Trouvés* (lost property office), although they are often inefficient. Lost property offices can also be found at larger train stations, which will be open during office hours. In all cases, leave a contact name and number in case the item is found.

Pharmacy sign

If your passport is lost or stolen, notify your consulate immediately. The loss of credit or debit cards should also be reported as soon as possible to avoid fraudulent use.

HOSPITALS AND PHARMACIES

All EU nationals holding a European Health Insurance Card (EHIC) are entitled to use the French national health service. Under the French system patients must pay for all treatments up front and then reclaim most of the cost from their health authorities. Therefore, non-French EU nationals who use health services in France will need to ensure they keep the statement of costs *(fiche)* that is provided by the doctor or hospital. The statement should include stickers for any prescription drugs, which must be affixed to the statement by the pharmacist once you have made your purchase. Around 80 per cent of the cost can be claimed back – follow the instructions provided with your EHIC card or by taking the paperwork to the nearest *Caisse Primaire d'Assurance Maladie* (CPAM; French National Health Service) office; there is one in each *département* (county) capital.

Non-EU nationals must have full private medical insurance and pay for services in the same way, claiming their costs back later on insurance.

All cities have hospitals with emergency departments *(urgences* or *service des urgences).* If your hotel cannot direct you to one, call the ambulence or fire service. Your consulate should be able to recommend an English-speaking doctor if you need one; in Paris, there are both American and British private hospitals.

Pharmacies can be identified by an illuminated green cross, and there are many located throughout the region. French pharmacists are highly trained and can diagnose minor health problems and suggest treatments.

MINOR HAZARDS

The summer sun in the Loire Valley is strong, so don't be caught out: use at least SPF 30 sunscreen and wear a hat.

Mosquitoes can be nuisances in the summer, especially in campsites, so come prepared. In July and August, gardens, lawns and meadows can be infested with red harvest mites or chiggers *(aoûtats),* which are too tiny to see but attach themselves to the skin, causing red bumps and a terrible itch. Avoid them by wearing loose clothing and taking showers as soon as possible after walks in the country; if bitten, apply benzyl benzoate (available at pharmacies) to clean the area.

TRAVEL AND HEALTH INSURANCE

All travellers in France should have a comprehensive travel insurance policy providing adequate cover for any eventuality, including potential medical and legal expenses, theft, lost luggage, accidents, travel delays and the option of immediate repatriation by air in the event of a major medical emergency. Adventure sports are not covered by standard travel policies so if you are planning to undertake any extreme sports in the Loire Valley you will need to pay an additional premium to ensure you are protected. All insurance policies should come with a 24-hour emergency number.

Banking and Local Currency

The easiest way to pay bills or convert money is by using credit or debit cards. Most French banks no longer exchange foreign currency or traveller's cheques, but be aware that withdrawing cash from an automated teller machine (ATM) may incur extra charges. It is possible to save on transaction fees by using Travel Money Cards, which provide a safe and convenient way to access your holiday savings.

BANKS AND BUREAUX DE CHANGE

Generally speaking, banks open from 9am to noon and from 2 to 4:30pm, Tuesday to Saturday. Most are closed on Mondays. Over public holiday weekends, banks may be shut from noon Friday until Tuesday morning. Be aware that opening hours can be more limited in smaller towns.

If you need to exchange cash, look for *bureaux de change* offices in airports and busy tourist areas. Desks in central post offices will also exchange foreign currency into euros. Exchange rates can be quite variable.

In some banks, it is also possible to withdraw cash from debit and credit cards at the counter, although there may be charges from your bank. You will need your passport or some form of identification to make the transaction.

An automatic teller machine (ATM)

ATMS

The simplest and most convenient way to obtain cash in France is by using a credit or debit card in one of the many automatic teller machines (ATMs) found at airports, train stations, banks and shopping malls, as well as other places. To withdraw money, you will need to enter your four-digit PIN (Personal Identification Number, or *code confidentiel*). ATM instructions are usually given in several languages, including English.

It's always a good idea to tell your bank that you are travelling overseas, and the country or countries you plan to visit, so your card isn't blocked for security reasons. Also ask if your bank has a partnership with a French bank, allowing you to withdraw cash from their ATMs without paying transaction fees.

CREDIT AND DEBIT CARDS

In France, the most common credit cards are **Visa** and **MasterCard**, while **American Express** cards are not always accepted. Keep a spare credit card in a different place as an emergency backup and keep a record of your cards' 16-digit number (found on the front of the card). If your card is lost or stolen, ring to cancel it as soon as possible; knowing the card number will make the replacement process much easier.

French credit and debit cards operate on a chip-and-PIN system so you will need to know your PIN *(code personnel)*. If you have a North American card that does not use chip-and-PIN technology you must ask that your card be swiped. Most ATMs and retailers have machines that read both smart cards and older magnetic strips in a *bande magnétique* (magnetic reader).

Very few banks will cash Traveller's cheques, and so, for the most part, they have now been replaced by prepaid Travel Cards (or Cash Passports). Available from Visa, MasterCard and other companies, these cards can be topped up online in the local currency. Like credit and debit cards, they come with PIN numbers that allow users to access cash in ATMs and are protected if stolen or lost. Bear in mind, however, that ATMs may run out of notes during weekends.

DIRECTORY

BUREAUX DE CHANGE

Angers
Office de Tourisme, 7 pl Président, Kennedy. *Tel 02 41 23 50 00.*

Blois
La Poste, 2 rue Gallois.
Tel 02 54 57 17 17.

Bourges
La Poste Principale, 29 rue Moyenne. *Tel 02 48 68 82 82.*

Chartres
Ghislaine Laufray Brisson, 3 rue Bethlem. *Tel 02 37 36 42 33.*

Nantes
Le Change Graslin, 17 rue Jean-Jacques. *Tel 02 40 69 24 64.*

Orléans
La Poste, pl de Gaulle.
Tel 02 38 77 35 35.

Tours
La Gare (train station), pl du Maréchal Leclerc.
Tel 02 47 66 78 89.

LOST AND STOLEN CARDS

American Express
Tel 01 47 77 70 00.

MasterCard
Tel 0800 90 13 87.

Visa
Tel 0800 90 11 79.

THE EURO

The euro (€) is the common currency of the European Union. It went into general circulation on 1 January 2002, initially for 12 participating countries. France was one of those countries, and the franc was phased out by March 2002. EU members using the euro as sole official currency are collectively known as the Eurozone. Several EU members opted out of joining.

Euro notes are identical throughout the Eurozone countries, each one including designs of fictional architectural structures and monuments. The coins, however, have one side identical (the value side) and one side with an image unique to each country. Both the notes and coins are exchangeable in the participating countries.

Bank Notes

Euro bank notes have seven denominations. The €5 note (grey in colour) is the smallest, followed by the €10 note (pink), €20 note (blue), €50 note (orange), €100 note (green), €200 note (yellow) and €500 note (purple). All notes show the 12 stars of the European Union.

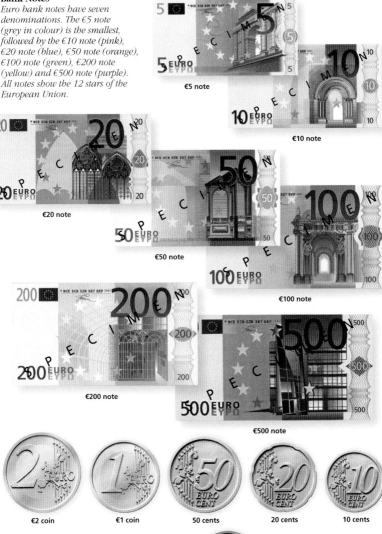

€5 note

€10 note

€20 note

€50 note

€100 note

€200 note

€500 note

€2 coin   €1 coin   50 cents   20 cents   10 cents

Coins

The euro has eight coin denominations: €1 and €2; 50 cents, 20 cents, 10 cents, 5 cents, 2 cents and 1 cent. The €2 and €1 coins are both silver and gold in colour. The 50-, 20- and 10-cent coins are gold. The 5-, 2- and 1-cent coins are bronze.

5 cents   2 cents   1 cent

Communications and Media

Mobile top-up card

French telecommunications are among the most advanced in the world, with high speed Internet available in most hotels, cafés and Wi-Fi hotspots. Although public telephones are rare, mobile networks are far-reaching and efficient. Post offices, or *bureaux de poste*, are identified by the blue-on-yellow La Poste sign. Foreign newspapers are available in most large town newsagencies, and some TV channels broadcast English-language programmes.

INTERNATIONAL AND LOCAL TELEPHONE CALLS

All French public phone boxes take phone cards *(télécartes)* and most accept credit cards. Phone cards are sold in units of either 50 or 120 minutes, and have easy-to-use instructions. They can be purchased at post offices, tobacconists *(tabacs)* and some newsagents. With the advent of mobiles phones, however, pay phones have become hard to find, apart from at airports and train stations, and most villages still have at least one phone box located centrally.

To call a number in France, simply dial the 10-digit number, always including the two-digit area code. Landline numbers in the Loire Valley begin with 02. Cheap rates operate from 7pm to 8am Monday to Friday, as well as all day Saturday, Sunday and public holidays. French mobile numbers begin with 06, and 08 indicates a special rate number.

To make an international call from France, dial 00 and then the country code. Avoid making international calls from hotels, as they tend to add a hefty surcharge.

MOBILE PHONES

French mobile phones use the European-standard 900 and 1900 MHz frequencies, so most European mobiles will work if they have a roaming facility enabled. North American mobile phones will only operate in France if they are tri- or quad-band; otherwise, another option is to buy a GSM phone and insert a French SIM card. Always check roaming charges with your service provider before

An Orange France mobile phone shop and Wi-Fi hotspot

travelling. Some companies offer "packages" for foreign calls, which can work out cheaper.

If you expect to use your phone frequently it can be more economical to get a pay-as-you-go French mobile from one of the local providers such as **Bouygues Télécom**, **SFR**, **Orange France** or **Free Mobile**, who have shops in most towns. You can top-up your phone in post offices, supermarkets and at ATM machines. It is possible to use a local SIM card in your own phone if it has not been blocked by your service provider.

INTERNET

France has an extensive network of Wi-Fi Internet hotspots (sometimes called *point Wi-Fi* or *borne Wi-Fi*), making it easy for visitors with laptop, notebook or tablet devices to get online and stay in touch through VoIP services such as **Skype** and **Viber**. Inevitably, Wi-Fi hotspots are concentrated in cities rather than the countryside. Most hotels provide Wi-Fi access

for the use of guests (check if there is a fee before use), while other hotspots can be found in airports, train stations, motorway service areas and libraries. Internet cafés are on the decline and are being replaced by conventional bars and cafés offering wireless Internet access. If you need to find Wi-Fi access, there are online resources such as the **Wi-Fi Hotspot Directory** that can direct you to your closest hotspot. A fee may be charged for Internet access, check the directory first for more information. **Orange WiFi** has a pay-as-you-go service, which is easy to use and widely available.

If you need to use a cable connection (which may be the case in a holiday home), note that the French modem socket is incompatible with US and UK plugs. Adaptors are available, but it is often cheaper and easier to buy a French modem lead.

Mail boxes throughout France are
a distinctive yellow

POSTAL SERVICE

The postal system in France
is fast and usually reliable.
There are main offices in all
cities, and branches in every
town; in villages, however,
there may just be a substation
(Relais Poste) in a local shop,
identified by a small **La Poste**
sign. Postage stamps *(timbres)*
are available at La Poste offices
and tobacconists, sold either
individually or in a *carnet*
(book of ten stamps). Letters
are dropped into yellow mail
boxes, which often have three
slots – one for the town you
are in; one for the surrounding
département (the Loire Valley
is divided into 11 *départements*,
each with its own postcode)
and one for other destinations
(autres destinations).

La Poste sell useful parcel
boxes *(colissimo)*, including
special wine bottle packaging.
Also, large branches have
Internet terminals. To use them,
buy a rechargeable pre-paid
card at the counter.

Post office hours vary. The
minimum hours are from 9am
to 5pm from Monday to Friday
with a two-hour lunch break
from noon to 2pm. On Satur-
days they are open from 9am
until noon. Post offices in
larger towns may open on
weekdays from 8am until 7pm.

The postal service offers
Chronopost courier services,
guaranteeing next-day delivery
for domestic mail and "as soon
as possible" for international.
For rapid worldwide delivery
consider a private courier
such as **DHL**, which has a
wide presence in France and
offices in Nantes and Orleans.

NEWSPAPERS AND MAGAZINES

Newspapers and magazines
can be bought at newsagents
(maisons de la presse) or
newsstands *(kiosques)*.
Regional newspapers such as
Ouest France and *La Nouvelle
République* tend to be more
popular than Paris-based
national papers such as the
conservative *Le Figaro*, weighty
Le Monde or leftist *Libération*.

English-language newspapers
such as the *International
Herald Tribune*, the *Guardian*
and the *Financial Times* are
often available for sale on the
day of issue. Other English
newspapers as well as Swiss,
Italian, German and Spanish
titles are sold on the day of
publication in summer months
and a day later out of season.

Many *départements* have
listings magazines, usually in
French and often free, which
can be found at tourist offices.
Websites listing Loire Valley
events include Culture Pays
de la Loire (www.culture.pays
delaloire.fr); also check the
"What's On" listings on the
AngloInfo websites (http://
loire.angloinfo.com and
http://centre.angloinfo.com).
Les Inrocks (www.lesinrocks.
com) has information on
music, film and arts events
for the whole of France.

TELEVISION AND RADIO

France has digital television
rather than analogue, so there
is a large range of free-to-air
channels available. The most
popular are commercial
stations TF1 and M6, followed
by the government channels
France 2 and France 3, the
latter offering daily regional
programming. The Franco-
German channel ARTE
broadcasts programmes and
films from all over the world,
often in the original language
with French subtitles. A film
shown in its original language
is listed as *VO (Version
Originale)*; a film dubbed
into French is indicated as *VF
(Version Française)*.

Canal Plus (or *Canal+*) is
a popular subscription-only
channel that offers a broad
mix of programmes, including
live sports and a good range
of films in English with
French subtitles. Many hotels
and holiday homes subscribe
to *Canal+* and also pick up
BBC World, CNN, Sky, MTV
and other satellite channels.

UK radio stations available in
France include *Radio 4* (198
long wave). Details for the BBC
World Service can be found at
www.bbc.co.uk/worldservice.
Voice of America can be found
at 90.5, 98.8 and 102.4 FM.
Radio France International
(738 AM) usually gives daily
news in English from 3 to 4pm.

TRAVEL INFORMATION

Forming a broad band about 110 km (70 miles) south of Paris and stretching from the centre of France in the east to the Atlantic coast in the west, the Loire Valley is well served by international airports, motorways and rail links. The city of Nantes has a major international airport with flights operating to many major European cities; airlines from Britain and Ireland also serve Tours and Angers. For travelling across the region, the TGV rail service *(see pp242–4)* is a swift option; and the motorways are excellent, if a little crowded in summer. There are also many more green travel options to explore, such as cycling through the region.

angers Loire aéroport

Sign for Angers airport

GREEN TRAVEL

The Loire Valley offers a number of ways to lighten your carbon footprint. Rather than fly, travel by train or coach. It may take longer but there's no baggage surcharge and both coaches and trains go direct to city centres.

The regional train service is excellent, however, bus services beyond main towns are patchy. An exception is the shuttle between the châteaux of Blois, Chambord, Cheverny and Beauregard run by **Transports du Loir-et-Cher** from April to September. Tourist boards also offer green initiatives such as the "Loire Valley Without a Car" package, organised by the **Tourist Office of Blois Pays de Chambord**, where tourists are taken on a three-day tour of the region, travelling by horse-drawn carriage, coach and a return train-journey. Accommodation is included in the price.

The Loire is ideal for cycling. There are bike-rental schemes in Nantes and Orléans (**Bicloo** and **Vélo'+**), and excellent bike trails and **Voies Vertes** (paths along former railway lines) in rural areas. A network of lanes link Niort and the Marais Poitevin; while **La Loire à Vélo** follows the Loire river and is part of the **EuroVelo6** route that will one day link the Atlantic to the Black Sea. Along the way, bike-friendly hotels (*Velotels*), campsites (*Velocamps*) and *gîtes* (*Velogite*) offer bike garages, repair kits and cycle hire. The **Châteaux à Velo** website has more information.

Among the many other self-guided cycling tours are Châteaux à Velo, **Loire Life Cycling Holidays** and **Randovelo**, which both arrange cycling tours in the region.

ARRIVING BY AIR

The Loire Valley has three airports but Paris can be just as convenient an arrival point, particularly if you plan to start your visit in the east of the region. **Angers Airport** and **Tours Airport** receive flights from Ireland and the UK. However, the region's main gateway is **Nantes-Atlantique Airport**, which has flights from many European cities and Canada.

From Canada, **Air Canada** and **Air France** fly direct to Paris; while **Air Transat** flies from Montreal to Nantes (May to October). Several airlines fly direct to Paris from the US. **Qantas** provides connecting flights to Paris from Australia and New Zealand. If flying into London Heathrow to transfer onto a flight to the Loire Valley, be aware that connecting flights may leave from one of London's four other airports; check carefully before booking your tickets to allow yourself enough time.

British Airways operates from London Heathrow to Paris, and from London City to Angers. Air France flies to Paris from Dublin, Edinburgh and regional English airports; it also has transfers from Paris to Nantes. **easyJet** flies to **Paris Charles de Gaulle** from a number of British airports; and, in summer, from London Gatwick to Nantes.

Ryanair links Nantes to Shannon and Dublin; and also Tours to Dublin, London Stansted and other English city airports in peak season. **Flybe** connects Manchester and London Gatwick to Nantes, and Southampton to Tours and **Paris Orly**.

TICKETS AND FARES

European budget airlines Ryanair, Flybe and easyJet offer the cheapest flights, especially if booked well in advance. Low-season promotional fares can cost next to nothing – at least until check-in and baggage fees are added. Fares on full-service airlines, such as British Airlines and Air France, can be reasonable too if booked early; prices are at their highest over the Easter period and in July and August. Long haul prices tend to shoot up in July and August as well; save money by shopping around online well in advance.

Travellers check departure boards at Paris Orly Airport

ON ARRIVAL

French airport formalities are usually straightforward. All arrivals must be in possession of a valid passport and, if necessary, a visa *(see p230)*. Non-EU citizens have to fill out a landing card to hand over at passport control. If you want to bring anything unusual into the country (especially large amounts of cash), check French embassy websites regarding prohibited items *(see p233)*. There is no departure tax.

Air France airbus 380

TRANSPORT FROM PARIS AIRPORTS

From Charles de Gaulle or Orly airports you can get to the Loire Valley by public transport, hire car or a domestic flight. If you hire a car, however, Orly is a better option as the airport is closer to the Loire Valley than Charles de Gaulle is.

Charles de Gaulle has its own TGV (high-speed train network) station in Terminal Two, linked to the other terminals by a free shuttle. From there, trains go directly to the Loire Valley. From Orly, take an Air France shuttle bus to Montparnasse station in Paris, then take a TGV train to your destination.

TRANSPORT FROM REGIONAL AIRPORTS

Buses leave every half hour from Nantes Airport to the main train station (€7.50). After each Ryanair flight lands at Tours, a coach take passengers to the city centre (€5). There is no public transport from Angers Airport. Taxi services to central Angers will cost about €45, to Nantes €40 and to Tours €35. Car rental companies have outlets at all airports.

PACKAGE DEALS

If you flying with Air France into Charles de Gaulle Airport, save time and money by purchasing a combined flight-train TGVAir ticket to Angers, Le Mans, Nantes or Tours (for further details see the Air France website). Other companies, such as **Cresta Holidays** and **VFB Holidays**, offer tailor-made package holidays in the Loire Valley with flights, car hire and accommodation all included. **InnTravel** offer self-guided walking, cycling and skiing package deals.

DIRECTORY

Travelling Around by Rail

Travelling to the Loire Valley by train is fast and efficient. The French state railway, the *Société Nationale des Chemins de Fer Français* (SNCF), is one of Europe's best equipped and most punctual. The journey from Paris to Nantes or Tours is quick – *Trains à Grande Vitesse* (TGV) travel at up to 300 km/h (185 mph) and reach Nantes in 2 hours and 10 minutes; Tours in just 55 minutes. With the Eurostar high-speed service running through the Channel Tunnel, London to the Loire Valley by train takes around 4 to 5 hours.

Automatic ticket machine

RAILWAY NETWORK

The main train routes to the Loire Valley from northern Europe pass through Paris. If arriving in Calais, the **TGV** network links the port with Paris Gare du Nord station. From there, passengers must transfer to Gare Montparnasse, before continuing their journey on the TGV Atlantique to the main towns in the Loire region. **Eurostar** passengers can change at Lille Europe station and transfer directly to a TGV for the Loire Valley, eliminating the need to change stations in Paris. Check schedules online.

SNCF logo

Intercité express trains to Nantes also leave from Gare Montparnasse, while Intercité express trains to all other Loire Valley destinations leave from Gare d'Austerlitz. Tickets from London to towns within the Loire Valley, travelling via the Eurostar, hovercraft or ferry, are available online from the English version websites of **Rail Europe** and **SNCF**. From southern Europe, trains run to Nantes from Madrid (with a journey time of around 18 hours) and Milan (around 11 hours).

Within the Loire Valley, the scenic route along the River Loire via Nantes, Angers and Orléans is popular, so reserve tickets in advance on this and other main rail lines *Grandes Lignes*.

MAIN STATIONS

Located in the city centre, Nantes train station *(Gare de Nantes)* has two station exits: the Sortie Sud (south exit)

brings you out in the Cité des Congrès district; the Sortie Nord (north exit), in the Jardin des Plantes.

In Tours, most trains stop at the suburban station of St-Pierre-des-Corps, from which a navette *(shuttle train)* takes passengers into the town centre station in 10 minutes.

A similar shuttle service operates in Orléans, where many main line trains arrive at Les Aubrais station, 3 km (2 miles) outside the town centre. In both cases, the price of the shuttle is included in the cost of the train ticket, and shuttles are timed so they coincide with main line services. Before boarding, check whether the departure time given on your ticket is for the shuttle or the main line train.

RESERVATIONS

Europe's main railways share a computer system, making it easy to check timetables and book Eurostar and French trains online through the Rail Europe website. If you need to alter your return date, you may have to pay for another reservation unless you book a more expensive flexible ticket. When purchasing tickets, especially for travel out of the peak Easter or summer holiday seasons, check the Eurostar website for package deals that combine train travel with hotel stays and hire cars.

Besides ticket counters, there are also automatic ticket and reservation machines (with English instructions) at main stations. A reservation differs from a ticket as it only reserves a seat, whereas you always need a valid ticket to travel. A ticket reservation is necessary when travelling on TGV, but this can be made as little as five minutes before the train leaves. Ticket prices for all trains rise at peak times, and reservations are compulsory during public holidays.

TGVs have two price levels for second class, normal and

SNCF train arriving at Tours train station

peak, and a single level for first class. The cost of the obligatory seat reservation is included in the ticket price. Tickets for other trains have just one price level for both first and second class. Seat reservations, where available, are included.

You can pick up reserved tickets from the counters or machines in the station, print them out at home or have them posted to you for free.

TICKETS

The best way to save money on TGV travel is by buying Prems tickets, available 120 days to 14 days before travel. Those who book earliest get the biggest discounts; if you have to change plans, however, the cheapest tickets may not be refundable. Sometimes there are last-minute specials

on certain destinations; check the rail websites *(see p244)*.

If you intend to take several journeys while in France, you may be better off purchasing a discount travel card or a rail pass online. SNCF rail cards *(cartes)* give up to 50 per cent discount on fares for qualifying passengers. The *Carte Enfant+* is for children up to the age of 12; the *Carte 12–25* is for those between 12 and 25 years of age; the *Carte Escapades*, for ages 26–59; and the *Carte Senior* is for anyone over 60. SNCF also caters for travellers with special needs *(see p232)*.

Rail passes give unlimited travel within a specified period of time for a one-off fee but they must be purchased in your own country before you arrive in France. They come in two varieties: "global" cards that cover several European

countries and "one country" passes that are just for travel within one country. For European residents these passes are called Interrail and to non-European residents Eurail. See the Rail Europe website for further details.

BICYCLES

On **TER** trains (part of the SNCF network), bicycles are carried free. On TGVs and Intercités, they should be dismantled, placed in a bag and stored in luggage spaces. If your train has a bicycle symbol next to its timetable listing, it will have designated areas for bikes, which you can book for €10. In Les Sables d'Olonne, Tours, Chinon, Amboise, Blois, Langeais, Beaugency and Onzain, it is possible to pre-book a bicycle *(Train + Vélo)* to await you at your destination.

TGV RAIL SERVICE

Trains à Grande Vitesse, or high-speed trains, travel at up to 300 km/h (185 mph). Their speed and comfort make them relatively expensive. You must always reserve a seat in advance, the cost of which depends on your destination and the time and date of your journey.

KEY

━━━ High speed lines

─── Other lines

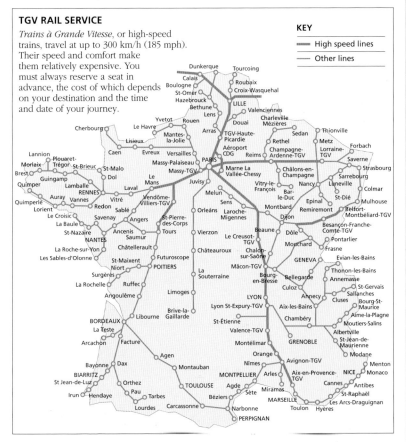

Eurostar train speeding through the French countryside

TIMETABLES

Timetables change twice a year, and leaflets for main routes are free at train stations.When reading French train timetables, pay particular attention to any footnotes, which may be indicated by a number or letter at the top of the column. *Circule tous des jours* means a train runs every day; *Sauf dimanche et jours fériés* translates not on Sundays or public holidays. Double-check the train time when you arrive at the station in case there is a delay. Coaches replace trains if lines are being repaired, or when not many passengers are expected (look for a bus symbol on the time-table). The status of the train will be displayed on a panel over the entrance to the plat-forms. If train workers have voted for strike action *(grève)* it will always be announced days in advance. If your TGV or Intercité train is more than 30 minutes late, and it's the fault of the SNCF, you are eligible for a 25 per cent refund; 50 per cent if the train is over 2 hours late or 75 per cent if over 3 hours late. Ask for an *enveloppe régularité*, or down-load the form online (http://aide.voyages-sncf.com).

Yellow validating machines *(composteur)* are located in station halls and on platforms. Before boarding, insert tickets and reservations separately, printed side up, and it will punch your ticket and print the time and date on the back. A penalty may be imposed by inspectors if you fail to do this.

EUROSTAR

Eurostar currently runs about 15 services per day between London's St Pancras International Station and the Gare du Nord in Paris. Each train has two classes: Standard, and Standard Premier or Business Premier (both First Class) which includes Wi-Fi access and waiter-served meal. All passageners have access to a buffet car where refreshments can be bought. The journey takes 2 hours and 15 minutes. Tickets must be booked in advance and checked in at least 20 minutes before the departure time. For a variety of discount schemes check the Eurostar website.

Children under 4 travel for free (on your lap), and there are special rates for ages 4–11, 12–25 and over 60. To book, contact the Rail Europe office in London, ring the Eurostar bookings line or visit their website. You can also download a free mobile app for smartphones that allows passengers to make bookings and check in using paperless mobile tickets.

EUROTUNNEL

The **Eurotunnel** shuttle-service carries cars and coaches and their passengers through the Channel Tunnel in 35 minutes. Tickets can be booked through travel agents, by calling the Eurotunnel Customer Service Centre or online. You can also purchase a ticket for the next train when you arrive at the terminals in Folkstone or Calais, but it is advisable to prebook your tickets. Fares are per car, with up to nine passengers allowed; special trains are reserved to carry large caravans (book in advance). Check online for discounted offers; the best fares will always be in the off-peak period (from Folkstone, 4pm to 5.59am; from Calais, midnight to 1.59pm). There are four trains an hour during peak times and every 2 hours during the night. All terminals have shops and restaurants. Before boarding you go through passport and customs controls for both countries.

Travelling Around by Road

France is a motorist's paradise, and the main routes to the Loire Valley are via an excellent, if expensive, tolled *autoroute* (motorway) network. There are many beautiful roads in the Loire region, particularly those running along the banks of the rivers. Popular routes, especially along the Atlantic coast and the roads leading between the châteaux, can be busy in high season. The minimum age for driving in France is 18 and for renting a car is 21.

WHAT TO TAKE

If you are taking your own car, it is compulsory to take the original registration document, a current insurance certificate and a valid driving licence. You should also carry a passport or identification card. If your car is not fitted with number plates showing the country of registration, a sticker indicating this must be displayed on the rear of the vehicle. The headlights of right-hand drive cars must be adjusted – kits for this are available at most ports. You must also have in the car a red warning triangle and a reflective jacket (both inside the car, not in the boot), as well as a breathalyzer kit. Other accessories you should take include spare headlight bulbs, a first-aid kit and a fire extinguisher.

The best general maps of the Loire Valley are the orange **Michelin** regional maps (No. 517 for the Pays de la Loire and No. 518 for Centre). **IGN** (*Institut Géographique National*) also produces two good touring maps covering this area: Central France (R08) and Pays de la Loire (R07).

Town plans are usually provided free by local tourist offices. More detailed town maps are published by Michelin or **Blay Foldex**. In the UK, **Stanfords** in London is famous for its range of maps and travel books. Those with tablet, smart phone or andriod devices will find a wide choice of map apps online.

GETTING TO THE LOIRE VALLEY

Travellers from the UK arriving at Calais and Boulogne can avoid Paris by taking the A16 motorway south to Abbeville and then the A28 via Rouen to Le Mans. At Le Mans, take the A11 for Chartres, Angers and Nantes, or head across country to Tours, Blois and Orléans. Alternatively, brave Paris and take the A1 south, skirt around the city centre and connect with the A10 for Orléans and Tours, and the A11.

From western Spain, take the A8 from San Sebastian to the border, the A63 to Bordeaux and the A10 to Tours and Orléans. From the eastern Spanish coast you can reach Orléans on the A9, A62 and A20, via Narbonne and Toulouse. From Italy take the A8 and A7 or the A43 to Lyon, where the A72 and A71 head north to Bourges and Orléans. From anywhere in Germany, the quickest way to get to the Loire Valley is via Paris.

There is three main motorways in the Loire Valley: the A11 (*L'Océane*) from Nantes to Chartres via Angers; the A10 (*L'Aquitaine*) from Tours to Orléans via Blois; and the A71 from Orléans to Bourges. There are police stations located at motorway exits. In high season, the motorways get crowded and, if you have time, it may be worth taking more minor (and often more attractive) roads. Try not to travel over the first weekend in July and the last weekend in August when French holidays start and finish and hordes of holidaymakers are on the roads.

RULES OF THE ROAD

Remember to drive on the right. Also be aware of *priorité à droite* in French towns, meaning traffic coming from streets to your right, unless halted by a white line and/or stop sign, has right of way. Seat belts are compulsory for both front and back seats.

Overtaking when there is a single solid centre line is heavily penalized. Instant fines are issued for speeding, and driving with over 0.05 per cent of alchohol in the blood is illegal. There are numerous speed cameras along French roads. Signs warn drivers that they are coming up, but in future these signs may disappear.

Unless otherwise signposted, speed limits are as follows:
- **Toll motorways** 130 km/h (80 mph), 110 km/h (68 mph) in wet weather;
- **Dual carriageways and non-toll motorways** 110 km/h (68 mph), 100 km/h (60 mph) in wet weather;
- **Other roads** 90 km/h (56 mph), 80 km/h (50 mph) in wet weather;
- In **towns** and in **heavy fog** 50 km/h (30 mph).

No entry for any vehicles

One-way system

VOUS N'AVEZ PAS LA PRIORITÉ

Give way at roundabouts

Right of way ends, give way to right

AUTOROUTE TOLL

When you drive through a tollway to join an **autoroute**, take a ticket from the machine. This identifies your starting point on the tollway; you do not pay until you reach an exit tollbooth (*gare de péage*). Charges are made according to the distance travelled and the type of vehicle.

Major toll areas have two or three staffed booths, allowing you to pay with coins, notes and debit or credit cards. The majority of the area, however, is lined with automated machines that accept credit or debit cards and rarely coins as well. Insert your ticket into the machine and the price of your journey will be displayed in euros.

The scenic D751 route around Champtoceaux

GREAT DRIVES

One of the pleasures of touring the Loire Valley is turning off the main routes onto the far more scenic country roads. The RN (*Route Nationale*) and D (*Départementale*) roads are marked in yellow or white on maps, and are often a good alternative to motorways. They are generally well sign-posted, however it is wise to carry a 1:250,000 map or a GPS. Popular drives include the riverside stretch of the D951, the D751 from Chambord to Tours, and the 800km (497 miles) of meandering wine roads, the *Routes Touristique du Vignoble* (see the **Vins Val de Loire** website for a map and guide).

Bison futé (crafty bison) signs indicate alternative routes to avoid heavy traffic, and can be helpful during French school and public holiday periods, known as *grands départs*.

PARKING

Parking in large towns is strictly regulated. If you are illegally parked, your car may be towed to a police pound and you will have to pay a stiff fine to release the car. For on-street parking, many towns in the Loire Valley have pay-and-display machines (*horodateurs*). Parking is free from noon to 2pm daily, overnight (7pm–9am), and on Sundays and public holidays.

Even if legally parked, you may find yourself hemmed in when you return to your car: the French usually honk their horn to attract the guilty party.

PETROL

Petrol (*essence*) is relatively expensive in France, especially on autoroutes. Large supermarkets and hypermarkets tend to offer discounts so are more reasonable.

Many petrol stations in France are self-service (*libre service*). If otherwise, ask to the attendant to "*faire le plein*" (fill the tank).

Petrol stations sell two different qualities of unleaded petrol (*sans plomb*) as well as diesel (*gazole* or *gasoil*). Leaded petrol is no longer available, though some stations offer lead-replacement petrol (Super ARS) or a lead-substitute additive, if needed. LPG gas is also widely available.

Not all stations are open 24 hours, especially away from the big towns. Out of shopping hours, you can self-serve at supermarket petrol stations using a credit card at the pump.

BREAKDOWNS AND ACCIDENTS

If you've had a breakdown, turn on your hazard lights, put on your reflective jacket and set up the red warning triangle 30 m (100 ft) behind the vehicle. On French motorways you are *not* expected to set out the triangle; get out of the right hand side of the vehicle and onto the other side of the safety barrier as soon as possible. There are SOS phone boxes every 2 km (1 mile); walk to the nearest one, staying on the far side of the barrier. Pressing

the button on the emergency phone will put you through to the emergency services. If you can't reach a box or have broken down off the motorway, dial 112 from a mobile phone to get help from the nearest *dépannage* (breakdown garage).

If your car is involved in a traffic accident with a French car, the driver should produce a form called a *constat à l'amiable* (European Accident Statement), which is used to record an agreed statement of events. If your French isn't up to filling this out, wait for a translator. Both drivers sign it and keep a copy. Post this to your insurer within five days of the accident.

Dial 17 for the police (*gendarmerie*) if someone is hurt or there is a dispute. You may have to accompany the other driver to the police station to make a statement (*procès-verbal* or *PV*). In case of a serious accident, dial 15 or 18 for an ambulance.

CAR HIRE

Requirements for car hire vary, but in general you must be over 21 years old and have held a driving licence for at least a year. You will need to present your driving licence, passport and a credit card against a deposit. If you want automatic transmission, book well in advance.

Europcar, Avis, Budget, Hertz and **National/Citer** are the main companies in the region and all have offices in both Paris airports. It is worth contacting a number of firms before you leave for France, as there are often special offers if you pre-pay or book online. Price comparison websites, such as **Last Minute, Auto Europe** and **Car Rentals**, can also be useful for finding good deals. Other options include fly-drive packages, and train and car-hire deals from the SNCF, with collection from main train stations (*See p244*).

To hire a moped or motorbike, find the nearest **Holiday Bikes** outlet. Several companies rent out camper vans and motor homes, including **Avis Caraway** and **Hertz Trois Soleils**.

COACH AND BUS TRAVEL

Eurolines operates coach services on Wednesdays and Fridays from London Victoria coach station to Tours, Angers and Nantes. The earlier you book, the cheaper the tickets. **Ze Bus** is a hop-on, hop-off service targeted mainly at backpackers and has routes from west Spain, Munich and Paris to the Loire Valley.

Local buses operate from most towns' *gare routière* (bus station), often located near the main train station. Although bus services in the region are relatively good, timetables in rural areas tend to be geared towards the needs of local workers and schoolchildren. As a result, morning departures tend to be very early and services may not run on a daily basis. For more details on bus routes and timetables, contact local tourist information offices (*see p233*).

TAXIS

Many taxis in rural areas are white and blue, and may double as an ambulance. In cities and large towns, vehicles can be various distinctive colours. Hailing a taxi is not customary in the Loire Valley; you must go to a taxi rank or book a car over the phone.

Prices for taxis tend to vary from one *département* to the next. The pick-up charge is usually €2, followed by €1 or more for every kilometre (0.6 mile), depending on the time and day, and up to €30 per hour if stuck in traffic. There is an extra charge for luggage or for calling out a radio taxi. All taxis are required to carry wheelchair users for no extra charge and must use a meter (*compteur*). Most taxi drivers will accept four passengers.

Taxis de France is useful for ordering taxis, and lists the rates for each *département*.

HITCHHIKING

Hitchhiking in France is legal except on motorways, although it is possible to hitch from one service station to another. A safer option is to use **Allostop**, an organization that puts you in touch with cars travelling in France and Europe. After paying an initial fee, determined by the length of the trip, hitchhikers pay the driver a fixed rate (for instance, €5 for 51–100 km/32–62 miles) to cover petrol costs and motorway tolls. The organization keeps records of all drivers' and hitchhikers' details for security purposes.

A local bus driving through the streets of Nantes

DIRECTORY

WHAT TO TAKE

Blay Foldex
www.blayfoldex.com

IGN
107 rue la Boétie, 75008 Paris.
Tel 01 43 98 80 00.
www.ign.fr

Michelin
www.michelinonline.co.uk/travel

Stanfords
12–14 Long Acre, London WC2E 9LP.
Tel (020) 7836 1321.
www.stanfords.co.uk

AUTOROUTE TOLL

Autoroutes
www.autoroutes.fr

GREAT DRIVES

Bison Futé
www.bison-fute.equipement.gouv.fr

Vins Val de Loire
www.vinsvaldeloire.fr

CAR HIRE

Auto-Europe
www.auto-europe.co.uk

Avis
France: *Tel* 0821 230 760.
Nantes: *Tel* 0820 611 676.
Orléans: *Tel* 02 38 62 27 04.
UK: *Tel* 0870 581 0147.
www.avis.fr

Avis Caraway
www.aviscaraway.com

Budget
France: *Tel* 0825 00 35 64.
UK: *Tel* 0844 544 3407.
www.budget.fr

Car Rentals
www.carrentals.co.uk

Europcar
France: *Tel* 0825 358 358.
Nantes: *Tel* 02 40 83 29 56.
Orléans: *Tel* 02 38 63 88 00.
UK: *Tel* 0871 384 1087.
www.europcar.com

Hertz
France: *Tel* 0825 861 861.
UK: *Tel* 0870 844 8844.
www.hertz.com

Hertz Trois Soleils
Tel 04 75 82 02 02.
www.trois-soleils.com

Holiday Bikes
Tel 01 41 27 49 00.
www.holiday-bikes.com

Last Minute
www.carhire.lastminute.com

National/Citer
Tel 0871 384 1140.
www.nationalcar.fr

COACH AND BUS TRAVEL

Eurolines
France: *Tel* 0892 899 091.
UK: *Tel* 0871 81 81 78.
www.eurolines.com

Ze Bus
www.ze-bus.com

TAXIS

Taxis de France
www.taxis-de-france.com

HITCHHIKING

Allostop
Tel 01 53 20 42 42.
www.allostop.net

General Index

Acknowledgments

Dorling Kindersley would like to thank the following people whose assistance contributed to the preparation of this book.

Main Contributor
Jack Tresidder has been living and writing in France since 1992. A former newspaper journalist and theatre critic, he has edited and written books on art, cinema and photography as well as travel.

Editorial Consultant
Vivienne Menkes-Ivry.

Contributors and Consultants
Sara Black, Hannah Bolus, Patrick Delaforce, Thierry Guidet, Jane Tresidder.

Additional Photography
Andy Crawford, Tony Gervis, Andrew Holligan, Paul Kenward, Jason Lowe, Ian O'Leary, John Parker, Jules Selmes, Clive Streeter.

Additional Illustrators
Robert Ashby, Graham Bell, Stephen Conlin, Toni Hargreaves, The Maltings Partnership, Lee Peters, Kevin Robinson, Tristan Spaargaren, Ed Stuart, Mike Taylor.

Cartography
Lovell Johns Ltd, Oxford.

Technical Cartographic Assistance
David Murphy.

Design and Editorial
Duncan Baird Publishers
MANAGING EDITOR Louise Bostock Lang
MANAGING ART EDITOR David Rowley
PICTURE RESEARCH Jill De Cet, Michèle Faram
RESEARCHER Caroline Mackenzie
DTP DESIGNER Alan McKee

Dorling Kindersley Limited
SENIOR EDITOR Fay Franklin
SENIOR MANAGING ART EDITOR Gillian Allan
DEPUTY EDITORIAL DIRECTOR Douglas Amrine
DEPUTY ART DIRECTOR Gaye Allen
MAP CO-ORDINATORS Michael Ellis, David Pugh
PRODUCTION David Proffit

PROOF READER Sam Merrell
INDEXER Brian Amos

Revisions Team
Claire Baranowski, Sonal Bhatt, Tessa Bindloss, Poppy Body, Sophie Boyack, Imogen Corke, Dana Facaros, Anna Freiberger, Rhiannon Furbear, John Grain, Richard Hansell, Matt Harris, Nicholas Inman, Lisa Jacobs, Gail Jones, Laura Jones, Nancy Jones, Maite Lantaron, Hayley Maher, Ciaran McIntyre, Rebecca Milner, Emma O'Kelly, Lyn Parry, Pollyanna Poulter, Erin Richards, Philippa Richmond, Ellen Root, Zoe Ross, Sands Publishing Solutions, Susana Smith, Jill Stevens, Conrad Van Dyk, Alison Verity, Dora Whitaker.

Special Assistance
Mme Barthez, Château d'Angers; M Sylvain Bellenger, Château de Blois; Tiphanie Blot, Loire-Atlantique Tourisme; M Bertrand Bourdin, France Télécom; M Jean-Paul and Mme Caroline Chaslus, Abbaye de Fontevraud; M Joël Clavier, Conseil Général du Loiret; Mme Dominique Féquet, Office de Tourisme, Saumur; Katia Fôret, Nantes Tourisme; M Gaston Huet, Vouvray; Mme Pascale Humbert, Comité Départemental du Tourisme de l'Anjou; M Alain Irlandes and Mme Guylaine Fisher, Atelier Patrimoine, Tours; Mme Sylvie Lacroix and M Paul Lichtenberg, Comité Régional du Tourisme, Nantes; M André Margotin, Comité Départemental du Tourisme du Cher; M Jean Méré, Champigny-sur-Veude, Touraine; Séverine Michau, Comité Régional du Tourisme Centre; Mme Marie-France de Peyronnet, Route Jacques-Cœur, Berry; M R Pinard, L'Ecole des Ponts et Chaussées, Paris; Virginie Priou, Comité Régional du Tourisme des Pays de la Loire; Véronique Richard, Vallée du Loir; Père Rocher, Abbaye de Solesmes; M Loïc Rousseau, Rédacteur, *Vallée du Loir*; M Pierre Saboureau, Lochois; Bertrand Sachet, Fédération Régionale de Randonnée Pédestre, Indre; M de Sauveboeuf, Le Plessis- Bourré; M Antoine Selosse and M Frank Artiges, Comité Départemental du Tourisme de Touraine; Mme Sabine Sévrin, Comité Régional du Tourisme, Orléans; Mme Tissier de Mallerais, Château de Talcy.

Photography Permissions
Dorling Kindersley would like to thank the following for their assistance and kind permission to photograph at their establishments: M François Bonneau, Conservateur, Château de Valençay; M Nicolas de Brissac, Château de Brissac; Caisse Nationale des Monuments Historiques et des Sites; Conseil Général du Cher; Marquis and Marquise de Contades, Château de Montgeoffroy; M Robert de Goulaine, Château de Goulaine; Mme Jallier, Office de Tourisme, Puy-du-Fou; Château de Montsoreau, Propriété du Département de Maine-et-Loire; Musée Historique et Archéologique de l'Orléanais; M Jean-Pierre Ramboz, Sacristain, Cathédrale de Tours; M Bernard Voisin, Conservateur, Château de Chenonceau and all other churches, museums, hotels, restaurants, shops and sights too numerous to thank individually.

Corn Sifters Gustave Colbert 192b; Musée Condé, Chantilly 25t, 47bc, 47bl, 52tl, 93b, *Gabrielle d'Estrées in her Bath* French School 17th century 96c; Musée d'Orsay, Paris *Marcel Proust* Jacques-Emile Blanche c.1891–2 24tc; Musée de la Venerie, Senlis *Diane de Poitiers as Diana the Hunter* Fontainebleau School 16th century 55crb; British Museum 54–5; MICHAEL BUSSELL'S PHOTOGRAPHY: 29tl and br.

CAHIERS CIBA: 77crb; CAMERA PRESS: 77tr; CEPHAS: Stuart Boreham 63bl; Hervé Champollion 63cra, 152tr; Mick Rock 29crb; JEAN-LOUP CHARMET, PARIS: 45b, 51b, 57cra; CHÂTEAU D'ANGERS: Centre des Monuments Nationaux / Damien Perdriau 75bl; CHÂTEAU DE CHAMEROLLES: 137cbl; CHÂTEAU DE LA BARRE: 201tl; CHÂTEAU DE MONHOUDOU: 200tr; CHÂTEAU DE MONTGEOFFROY: 71cl; CHÂTEAU DE NOIRIEUX: 209br; CHÂTEAU DE ROCHECOTTE: 200br; CHÂTEAU DE VILLANDRY: 94br; CHÂTEAU DU BOISRENAULT: 201br; CHRISTIE'S IMAGES, LONDON: 53b; BRUCE COLEMAN: NG Blake 71bc; Denis Green 185cr; Udo Hirsch 185bl; Hans Reinhard 184bl; Uwe Walz 71bl, 71br, 185br; COMITÉ DÉPARTEMENTAL DU TOURISME DU CHER: 27cra, 231tl; COMITÉ RÉGIONAL DU TOURISME, NANTES: 226t and b, JP Guyonneau 227tl, J Lesage 225tr; COMITÉ DU TOURISME DE L'ANJOU: 84b, JP Guyonneau 84c; CORBIS: Gianni Dagli Orti 4br; Adam Woolfitt 11tr; Xinhua Press/Gao Jing 236clb.

DIATOTALE: Château de Chenonceau 106t.

EDITIONS GAUD: Château de Villandry *Jeune Infante* Pantoja de la Cruz 94tl; C ERRATH: 26br, 182tr, 183bl; ET ARCHIVE: 50bl, 100br; Eurostar: 244tl; MARY EVANS PICTURE LIBRARY: 9inset, 24tl, 53cl, 61inset, 151tl, 195inset, 227inset; EXPLORER: F Jalain 56cl.

FÉDÉRATION NATIONALE DE LOGIS DE FRANCE: 197c; FÉDÉRATION UNIE DES AUBERGES DE JEUNESSE: 199tr; FNOTSI: 230c, 230tc; FONTENAY-LE-COMTE OFFICE DE TOURISME: 230cl; FONTEVRAUD ABBEY: 41b, 87b; FONTGOMBAULT ABBEY: Frère Eric Chevreau 147C.

GETTY IMAGES: AFP 240br; GIRAUDON, PARIS: 48tr and bl, 76tr and c, 135c; Archives Nationales, Paris 50tl; Bibliothèque Municipale, Laon 50–51cr; Château de Versailles *Louis XIII – Roi de France et de Navarre* after Vouet 47br, 56bl; Musée Antoine Lécuyer 134bl; Musée Carnavalet, Paris 30tl, *Madame Dupin de Francueil* 109tr; Musée Condé, Chantilly 52br, 108b; Musée d'Histoire et des Guerres de Vendée, Cholet *Henri de la Rochejaquelein au Combat de Cholet le 17 Octobre 1793* Emile Boutigny 69cl; Musée de Tessé, Le Mans 166tr; Musée des Beaux-Arts, Blois 169crb; Musée du Vieux Château, Laval 160b (all rights reserved); Telarci 51cla; Victoria & Albert Museum, London 95tl; GÎTES DE FRANCE: 199ct; LA GOÉLETTE: JJ Derennes *The Three Graces* Charles-André Van Loo 106br.

SONIA HALLIDAY PHOTOGRAPHS: 53tl; ROBERT HARDING: 37br; Paolo Koba 17br; Sheila Terry 102b; D HODGES: 167b; KIT HOUGHTON: 38c; HULTON-DEUTSCH COLLECTION: 46tr, 111tc, 134cla.

IMAGE BANK: 34clb; David W Hamilton 32; Image de Marc 16b, 90c, 103b, 117b; NICOLAS INMAN: 234bl; INVENTAIRE GÉNÉRAL: Musée du Grand-Pressigny 48cla, 104c.

JERRICAN/BERENGUIER: 13bl.

LONELY PLANET IMAGES: John Elk III 10br; Diana Mayfield 10cla.

MAIRIE DE BLOIS: J-Philippe Thibaut 42b; MANSELL COLLECTION: 30b; T MEZERETTE: 28t, 29tl; MUSÉES D'ANGERS:

18t, 51clb, 57crb, 77cra; COLLECTION MUSÉE D'ART ET D'HISTOIRE DE CHOLET: 57b, Studio Golder, Cholet *Jacques Cathelineau* Anne-Louis Girodet-Trioson 1824 187b; MUSÉE D'ARTS DÉCORATIFS ET MUSÉE DU CHEVAL, CHÂTEAU DE SAUMUR: 82cr; MUSÉE DES BEAUX-ARTS DE RENNES: Louis Deschamps *Bal à la Cour des Valois* 109cbr; MUSÉE DES BEAUX-ARTS, TOURS: *Vue Panoramique de Tours en 1787* Pierre-Antoine Demachy 8–9; P Boyer *Christ in the Olive Grove* Andrea Mantegna 114b; MUSÉE DE BLOIS: J Parker 126c, 127br; MUSÉES DE BOURGES: Musée des Arts Décoratifs, Hôtel Lallemant *Concert Champêtre Instrumental* French-Italian School 150t; MUSÉE DOBRÉE, NANTES: 55clb, 191tl; COLLECTION MUSÉE ESTÈVE © ADAGP/DACS: Dubout *Samsâra* Maurice Estève oil on canvas 150b; COURTESY, MUSEUM OF FINE ARTS BOSTON: *Valley of the Petite Creuse* Claude Monet 1889 oil on canvas Bequest of David P Kimball in Memory of his Wife, Clara Bertram Kimball (© 1995. All rights reserved) 147br; MUSÉE HISTORIQUE D'ORLÉANS: 48clb; MUSÉES DU MANS: 166c; MUSÉE DES MARAIS SALANTS, BATZ-LOIRE-ATLANTIQUE: G Buron 179cr; COLLECTION DU MUSÉE DE LA MARINE DE LOIRE, CHÂTEAUNEUF-SUR-LOIRE (LOIRET): 33bc.

NHPA: Manfred Danegger 185cl; M GARWOD: 79b; Helio & Van Ingen 182tl; R Sorensen & JB Olsen 184br; NATIONAL MOTOR MUSEUM, BEAULIEU: 57tr.

ORANGE FRANCE TELECOM: Frederic Bukajlo - abacapress.com pour Orange 238tl, 238ca.

PARC NATUREL RÉGIONAL DU POITEVIN: 185tr; JOHN PARKER: 1c, 20bc, 26bl, 27tl, 35crb, 36crb, 37ca and cl, 38bl, 51cra, 54clb, 55cra, 58tl, 63br, 72tl, 73c, 75bc, 87tc, 95bc, 106cla, 107cb, 110bl, 111br, 115c, 116tr, 117cr, 121br, 126cl, 127bl, 128tl, 130tl and bl, 131tc and bc, 132tl, cl, clb and br, 133tc, cr, bc and br, 144tr, 170br, 171br, 220cl; PHOTOGRAPHERS' LIBRARY: 159b; 199b; BY KIND PERMISSION FROM PUY DU FOU: 43t.

RUNION DES MUSÉES NATIONAUX, PARIS: Château de Versailles *Château de Chambord* PD Martin © (Photo RMN) 134crb; REX FEATURES/SIPA PRESS: Riclafe 59tr, Tall 58bl; ROUTE HISTORIQUE JACQUES CŒUR: 18b; DAVID ROWLEY: 83b.

THE SCIENCE MUSEUM/SCIENCE & SOCIETY PICTURE LIBRARY, LONDON: 56br; SCIENCE PHOTO LIBRARY/CNES: 11tr; SNCF - SOCIETY NATIONAL DES CHEMINS DE FER: 242c; SPECTRUM COLOUR LIBRARY: 137cr; TONY STONE WORLDWIDE: 63tl and tr, Charlie Waite 154t; SUPERSTOCK: Photononstop 247cl.

TELEGRAPH COLOUR LIBRARY: Jean-Paul Nacivet 26cla; TIPSIMAGES: Photononstop 246tl; TRH PICTURES: 58tr.

VILLE D'AMBROISE: Musée de la Poste 33cb; VINS DE LOIRE: 112clb; ROGER VIOLLET: 52bl, Bibliothèque Nationale 56clb, 137tr, Musée d'Orléans *Entrée de Jeanne d'Arc à Orléans* Jean-Jacques Scherrer 137br.

J WARMINSKI: 79t; C WATIER: 67t, 70b; WILDLIFE MATTERS: 94tr, 95c and br; WYSE TRAVEL CONFEDERATION: 232cr.

Front endpaper: all commissioned photography.

Jacket: Front - ALAMY IMAGES: incamerastock/ICP; Back - 4CORNERS: SIME/Luca Da Ros tl; ALAMY IMAGES: Yadid Levy cl; DORLING KINDERSLEY: Paul Kenward clb, John Parker bl.

All other images © Dorling Kindersley.

For further information, see: www.dkimages.com

SPECIAL EDITIONS OF DK TRAVEL GUIDES

DK Travel Guides can be purchased in bulk quantities at discounted prices for use in promotions or as premiums. We are also able to offer special editions and personalized jackets, corporate imprints, and excerpts from all of our books, tailored specifically to meet your own needs.

To find out more, please contact:
(in the United States) **SpecialSales@dk.com**
(in the UK) **travelspecialsales@uk.dk.com**
(in Canada) DK Special Sales at
general@tourmaline.ca
(in Australia)
business.development@pearson.com.au

Phrase Book

In Emergency

Help!	**Au secours!**	oh se**koor**
Stop!	**Arrêtez!**	aret-**ay**
Call a doctor!	**Appelez un médecin!**	apuh-**lay** uñ meds**añ**
Call an ambulance!	**Appelez une ambulance!**	apuh-**lay** oon oñboo-**loñs**
Call the police!	**Appelez la police!**	apuh-**lay** lah poh-**lees**
Call the fire brigade!	**Appelez les pompiers!**	apuh-lay leh poñ-**peeyay**
Where is the nearest telephone?	**Où est le téléphone le plus proche?**	oo ay luh tehleh**fon** luh ploo **prosh**
Where is the nearest hospital?	**Où est l'hôpital le plus proche?**	oo ay l'**opee**tal luh ploo **prosh**

Communication Essentials

Yes	**Oui**	wee
No	**Non**	noñ
Please	**S'il vous plaît**	seel voo **play**
Thank you	**Merci**	mer-**see**
Excuse me	**Excusez-moi**	exkoo-**zay** mwah
Hello	**Bonjour**	boñ**zhoor**
Goodbye	**Au revoir**	oh ruh-**vwar**
Good night	**Bonsoir**	boñ-**swar**
Morning	**Le matin**	mat**añ**
Afternoon	**L'après-midi**	l'apreh-**meedee**
Evening	**Le soir**	swar
Yesterday	**Hier**	ee**yehr**
Today	**Aujourd'hui**	oh-zhoor-**dwee**
Tomorrow	**Demain**	duh**mañ**
Here	**Ici**	ee-**see**
There	**Là**	lah
What?	**Quel, quelle?**	kel, kel
When?	**Quand?**	koñ
Why?	**Pourquoi?**	poor-**kwah**
Where?	**Où?**	oo

Useful Phrases

How are you?	**Comment allez-vous?**	kom-moñ talay voo
Very well, thank you.	**Très bien, merci.**	treh byañ, mer-**see**
Pleased to meet you.	**Enchanté de faire votre connaissance.**	oñshoñ-**tay** duh fehr votr kon-ay-**sans**
See you soon.	**A bientôt.**	Ah byañ-**toh**
That's fine.	**C'est parfait**	say parf**ay**
Where is/are...?	**Où est/sont...?**	oo ay/soñ
How far is it to...?	**Combien de kilomètres d'ici à...?**	kom-**byañ** duh keelo-**metr** d'ee-**see** ah
Which way to...?	**Quelle est la direction pour...?**	kel ay lah deer-ek-**syoñ** poor
Do you speak English?	**Parlez-vous anglais?**	par-**lay** voo oñg-**lay**
I'm sorry.	**Excusez-moi.**	exkoo-**zay** mwah
I don't understand.	**Je ne comprends pas.**	zhuh nuh kom-**proñ** pah

Could you

Could you speak slowly please?	**Pouvez-vous parler moins vite s'il vous plaît?**	poo-**vay** voo par-**lay** mwañ veet seel voo play

Useful Words

big	**grand**	groñ
small	**petit**	puh-**tee**
hot	**chaud**	show
cold	**froid**	frwah
good	**bon**	boñ
bad	**mauvais**	moh-**veh**
enough	**assez**	as**say**
well	**bien**	byañ
open	**ouvert**	oo-**ver**
closed	**fermé**	fer-**meh**
left	**gauche**	gohsh
right	**droite**	drwaht
straight on	**tout droit**	too drwah
near	**près**	preh
far	**loin**	lwañ
up	**en haut**	oñ oh
down	**en bas**	oñ bah
early	**de bonne heure**	duh bon **urr**
late	**en retard**	oñ ruh-**tar**
entrance	**l'entrée**	l'on-**tray**
exit	**la sortie**	sor-**tee**
toilet	**les toilettes, les WC**	twah-let, vay-**see**
free, unoccupied	**libre**	leebr
free, no charge	**gratuit**	grah-**twee**

Making a Telephone Call

I'd like to place a long-distance call.	**Je voudrais faire un appel interurbain.**	zhuh voo-dreh fehruñ apel añter-oorbañ
I'd like to make a reverse charge call.	**Je voudrais faire une communication PCV.**	zhuh voo**dreh** fehr oon **syoñ** komoonikah-peh-seh-veh
I'll try again later.	**Je rappelerai plus tard.**	zhuh rapel-**eray** ploo tar
Can I leave a message?	**Est-ce que je peux laisser un message?**	es-**keh** zhuh puh leh-**say** uñ mehs**azh**
Hold on.	**Ne quittez pas, s'il vous plaît.**	nuh kee-**tay** pah seel voo play
Could you speak up a little please?	**Pouvez-vous parler un peu plus fort?**	poo-**vay** voo par-**lay** uñ puh ploo for
local call	**la communication locale**	komoonikah-**syoñ** low-**kal**

Shopping

How much does this cost?	**C'est combien s'il vous plaît?**	say kom-**byañ** seel voo play
I would like ...	**je voudrais...**	zhuh voo-**dray**
Do you have?	**Est-ce que vous avez?**	es-**kuh** voo zav**ay**

I'm just looking.	**Je regarde seulement.**	zhuh ruh**gar** suhl**moñ**
Do you take credit cards?	**Est-ce que vous acceptez les cartes de crédit?**	es-**kuh** voo zaksept-**ay** leh kart duh kreh-**dee**
Do you take traveller's cheques?	**Est-ce que vous acceptez les chèques de voyage?**	es-**kuh** voo zaksept-**ay** leh shek duh vwa**yazh**
What time do you open?	**A quelle heure vous êtes ouvert?**	ah kel urr voo zet oo-**ver**
What time do you close?	**A quelle heure vous êtes fermé?**	ah kel urr voo zet fer-**may**
This one.	**Celui-ci.**	suhl-wee-**see**
That one.	**Celui-là.**	suhl-wee-**lah**
expensive	**cher**	shehr
cheap	**pas cher, bon marché**	pah shehr, boñ mar-**shay**
size, clothes	**la taille**	tye
size, shoes	**la pointure**	pwañ-**tur**
white	**blanc**	bloñ
black	**noir**	nwahr
red	**rouge**	roozh
yellow	**jaune**	zhohwn
green	**vert**	vehr
blue	**bleu**	bluh

Types of Shop

antique shop	**le magasin d'antiquités**	maga-**zañ** d'oñteekee-**tay**
bakery	**la boulangerie**	booloñ-**zhuree**
bank	**la banque**	boñk
book shop	**la librairie**	lee-**brehree**
butcher	**la boucherie**	boo-**shehree**
cake shop	**la pâtisserie**	patee-**sree**
cheese shop	**la fromagerie**	fromazh-**ree**
chemist	**la pharmacie**	farmah-**see**
dairy	**la crémerie**	krem-**ree**
department store	**le grand magasin**	groñ maga-**zañ**
delicatessen	**la charcuterie**	sharkoot-**ree**
fishmonger	**la poissonnerie**	pwasson-**ree**
gift shop	**le magasin de cadeaux**	maga-**zañ** duh ka**doh**
greengrocer	**le marchand de légumes**	mar-**shoñ** duh lay-**goom**
grocery	**l'alimentation**	alee-moñta-**syoñ**
hairdresser	**le coiffeur**	kwa**fuhr**
market	**le marché**	marsh-**ay**
newsagent	**le magasin de journaux**	maga-**zañ** duh zhoor-**no**
post office	**la poste, le bureau de poste, le PTT**	pohst, boo**roh** duh pohst, peh-teh-teh
shoe shop	**le magasin de chaussures**	maga-**zañ** duh show-**soor**
supermarket	**le supermarché**	soo pehr-**marshay**
tobacconist	**le tabac**	tabah
travel agent	**l'agence de voyages**	l'azhoñs duh vwayazh

Sightseeing

abbey	**l'abbaye**	l'abay-**ee**
art gallery	**le galerie d'art**	galer-**ree** dart
bus station	**la gare routière**	gahr roo-tee-**yehr**
cathedral	**la cathédrale**	katay-**dral**
church	**l'église**	l'ayg**leez**
garden	**le jardin**	zhar-**dañ**
library	**la bibliothèque**	beeb**leeo**-tek
museum	**le musée**	moo-**zay**
railway station	**la gare (SNCF)**	gahr (es-en-say-ef)
tourist information office	**les renseignements touristiques**	roñsayn-**moñ** too-rees-**teek**, sandee-**teev**
town hall	**l'hôtel de ville**	l'oh**tel** duh veel
private mansion	**l'hôtel particulier**	l'oh**tel** partikoo-**lyay**
closed for public holiday	**fermeture jour férié**	fehrmeh-**tur** zhoor fehree-**ay**

Staying in a Hotel

Do you have a vacant room?	**Est-ce que vous avez une chambre?**	es-kuh voo-**zavay** oon shambr
double room	**la chambre pour deux personnes**	shambr poor duh pehr-**son**
with double bed	**avec un grand lit**	avek un gronñ lee
twin room	**la chambre à deux lits**	shambr ah duh lee
single room	**la chambre pour une personne**	shambr poor oon pehr-**son**
room with a bath, shower	**la chambre avec salle de bains, une douche**	shambr avek sal duh bañ, oon doosh
porter	**le garçon**	gar-**soñ**
key	**la clef**	klay
I have a reservation.	**J'ai fait une réservation.**	zhay fay oon rayzehrva-**syoñ**

Eating Out

Have you got a table?	**Avez-vous une table libre?**	avay-**voo** oon tahbl leebr
I want to reserve a table.	**Je voudrais réserver une table.**	zhuh voo-**dray** rayzehr-**vay** oon tahbl
The bill please.	**L'addition s'il vous plaît.**	l'adee-**syoñ** seel voo **play**
I am a vegetarian.	**Je suis végétarien.**	zhuh swee vezhay-**tehryañ**
Waitress/ waiter	**Madame, Mademoiselle/ Monsieur**	mah-**dam**, mah-demwah**zel**/ muh-**syuh**
menu	**le menu, la carte**	men-**oo**, kart
fixed-price menu	**le menu à prix fixe**	men-**oo** ah pree feeks
cover charge	**le couvert**	koo-**vehr**
wine list	**la carte des vins**	kart-deh vañ
glass	**le verre**	vehr
bottle	**la bouteille**	boo-**tay**
knife	**le couteau**	koo-**toh**
fork	**la fourchette**	for-**shet**

spoon	**la cuillère**	kwee-**yehr**
breakfast	**le petit déjeuner**	puh-**tee** deh-**zhuh-nay**
lunch	**le déjeuner**	deh-**zhuh-nay**
dinner	**le dîner**	dee-**nay**
main course	**le plat principal**	plah prañsee-**pal**
starter, first course	**l'entrée, le hors-d'œuvre**	l'oñ-**tray**, or-duhvr
dish of the day	**le plat du jour**	plah doo zhoor
wine bar	**le bar à vin**	bar ah vañ
café	**le café**	ka-**fay**
rare	**saignant**	**say**-noñ
medium	**à point**	ah **pwañ**
well done	**bien cuit**	byañ **kwee**

Menu Decoder

l'agneau	l'anyoh	lamb
l'ail	l'eye	garlic
la banane	ba**nan**	banana
le beurre	burr	butter
la bière	bee-**yehr**	beer
la bière pression	bee-**yehr** pres-**syoñ**	draught beer
le bifteck, le steack	beef-**tek**, stek	steak
le bœuf	buhf	beef
bouilli	boo-**yee**	boiled
le café	kah-**fay**	coffee
le canard	kan**ar**	duck
le chocolat	**shoko**-lah	chocolate
le citron	see-**troñ**	lemon
le citron pressé	see-**troñ** press-**eh**	fresh lemon juice
les crevettes	kruh-**vet**	prawns
les crustacés	**kroos**-ta-**say**	shellfish
cuit au four	kwee oh foor	baked
le dessert	deh-**ser**	dessert
l'eau minérale	l'oh **meeney**-ral	mineral water
les escargots	leh zes-kar-**goh**	snails
les frites	freet	chips
le fromage	from-**azh**	cheese
le fruit frais	frwee freh	fresh fruit
les fruits de mer	frwee duh mer	seafood
le gâteau	gah-**toh**	cake
la glace	glas	ice, ice cream
grillé	gree-**yay**	grilled
le homard	om**ahr**	lobster
l'huile	l'weel	oil
le jambon	zhoñ-**boñ**	ham
le lait	leh	milk
les légumes	lay-**goom**	vegetables
la moutarde	moo-**tard**	mustard
l'œuf	l'uf	egg
les oignons	leh zonyoñ	onions
les olives	leh zoleev	olives
l'orange	l'oroñzh	orange
l'orange pressée	l'oroñzh press-**eh**	fresh orange juice
le pain	pan	bread
le petit pain	puh-**tee** pañ	roll
poché	posh-**ay**	poached
le poisson	pwah-**ssoñ**	fish
le poivre	pwavr	pepper
la pomme	pom	apple

les pommes de terre	pom-duh tehr	potatoes
le porc	por	pork
le potage	poh-**tazh**	soup
le poulet	poo-**lay**	chicken
le riz	ree	rice
rôti	row-**tee**	roast
la sauce	sohs	sauce
la saucisse	soh**sees**	sausage, fresh
sec	sek	dry
le sel	sel	salt
la soupe	soop	soup
le sucre	sookr	sugar
le thé	tay	tea
le toast	toast	toast
la viande	vee-**yand**	meat
le vin blanc	vañ **bloñ**	white wine
le vin rouge	vañ **roozh**	red wine
le vinaigre	vee**naygr**	vinegar

Numbers

0	**zéro**	zeh-**roh**
1	**un, une**	uñ, oon
2	**deux**	duh
3	**trois**	trwah
4	**quatre**	katr
5	**cinq**	sañk
6	**six**	sees
7	**sept**	set
8	**huit**	weet
9	**neuf**	nerf
10	**dix**	dees
11	**onze**	oñz
12	**douze**	dooz
13	**treize**	trehz
14	**quatorze**	ka**torz**
15	**quinze**	kañz
16	**seize**	sehz
17	**dix-sept**	dees-**set**
18	**dix-huit**	dees-**weet**
19	**dix-neuf**	dees-**nerf**
20	**vingt**	vañ
30	**trente**	tront
40	**quarante**	karoñt
50	**cinquante**	sañkoñt
60	**soixante**	swasoñt
70	**soixante-dix**	swasoñt-**dees**
80	**quatre-vingts**	katr-**vañ**
90	**quatre-vingts-dix**	katr-vañ-**dees**
100	**cent**	soñ
1,000	**mille**	meel

Time

one minute	**une minute**	oon mee-**noot**
one hour	**une heure**	oon urr
half an hour	**une demi-heure**	oon **duh-mee** urr
Monday	**lundi**	luñ-**dee**
Tuesday	**mardi**	mar-**dee**
Wednesday	**mercredi**	mehrkruh-**dee**
Thursday	**jeudi**	zhuh-**dee**
Friday	**vendredi**	voñdruh-**dee**
Saturday	**samedi**	sam-**dee**
Sunday	**dimanche**	dee-**moñsh**

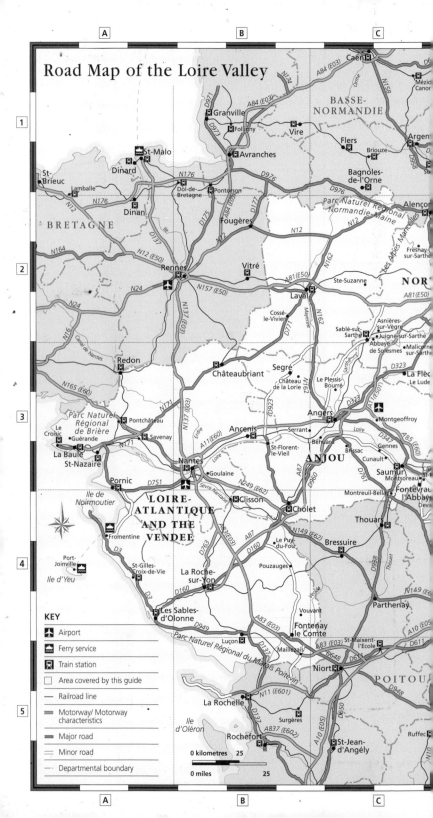